The Business Value of Virtual Service Oriented Grids

Strategic Insights for
Enterprise Decision Makers

Enrique Castro-Leon
Jackson He
Mark Chang
Parviz Peiravi

Copyright © 2008 Intel Corporation. All rights reserved.
ISBN 978-1-934053-10-2
No part of this publication may be reproduced, stored in a retrieval system or transmitted in any form or by any means, electronic, mechanical, photocopying, recording, scanning or otherwise, except as permitted under Sections 107 or 108 of the 1976 United States Copyright Act, without either the prior written permission of the Publisher, or authorization through payment of the appropriate per-copy fee to the Copyright Clearance Center, 222 Rosewood Drive, Danvers, MA 01923, (978) 750-8400, fax (978) 750-4744. Requests to the Publisher for permission should be addressed to the Publisher, Intel Press, Intel Corporation, 2111 NE 25th Avenue, JF3-330, Hillsboro, OR 97124-5961. E-Mail: intelpress@intel.com.

This publication is designed to provide accurate and authoritative information in regard to the subject matter covered. It is sold with the understanding that the publisher is not engaged in professional services. If professional advice or other expert assistance is required, the services of a competent professional person should be sought.

Intel Corporation may have patents or pending patent applications, trademarks, copyrights, or other intellectual property rights that relate to the presented subject matter. The furnishing of documents and other materials and information does not provide any license, express or implied, by estoppel or otherwise, to any such patents, trademarks, copyrights, or other intellectual property rights.

Intel may make changes to specifications, product descriptions, and plans at any time, without notice.

Fictitious names of companies, products, people, characters, and/or data mentioned herein are not intended to represent any real individual, company, product, or event.

Intel products are not intended for use in medical, life saving, life sustaining, critical control or safety systems, or in nuclear facility applications.

Intel, the Intel logo, Intel vPro, and Pentium 4 are trademarks or registered trademarks of Intel Corporation or its subsidiaries in the United States and other countries.

† Other names and brands may be claimed as the property of others.

This book is printed on acid-free paper. ∞

Publisher: Richard Bowles
Editor: David J. Clark
Content Architect: Bruce Bartlett
Text Design & Composition: STI Certified
Graphic Art: STI Certified (illustrations), Ron Bohart (cover)

Library of Congress Cataloging in Publication Data:

Printed in China

10 9 8 7 6 5 4 3 2 1

First printing, Version 1.0 October 2008

IMPORTANT

You can access the companion Web site for this book on the Internet at:

www.intel.com/intelpress/grid

Use the serial number located in the upper-right hand corner of the last page in the book to register your book and access additional material, including the Digital Edition of the book.

I would like to acknowledge the tireless support of my wife Kitty during the many virtually nonexistent weekends that it took to get the project accomplished. To her, this book is dedicated.

—E.C.

We dedicate this book to the contributors, reviewers, and Intel Press team who supported us through the development and completion of the project.

—J.H., M. C, and P.P.

Contents

Foreword xiii

Preface xvii

    A Bit of History   xviii

    An Industry Example   xxv

    What's in Store in This Book   xxvii

Acknowledgements xxix

Chapter 1   **The Emergence of Virtual Service Oriented Grids**   1

    Other People's Money versus Other People's Systems   4

    Virtualization, Service Orientation, and Grids   6

        About Grids   7

        Grids: A Physical Description   11

        Virtualization   14

        Service Orientation   15

        Virtualization + Service orientation + Grids = Virtual Service Oriented Grids   20

        Laptop Loss Management Service Revisited   22
        Structure of Virtual Service Oriented Grids   24
    End Points for Virtual Service Oriented Grids   29

Chapter 2 Virtual Service Oriented Grid Convergence   31

    Capability, Process, and Maturity in Business Transformation   32
        A Rhetorical Question   33
        The Internet Age   35
        About X-Engineering   36
    From Silos to Networks   41
        On the Need for Solution Stacks   41
        The Merging of Silos and Rise of Collaboration   43
    The Economics of Service Orientation   54
    Scalability of Service Oriented Architecture   58
        The Initial Siloed State   59
        Inside-out or Conventional SOA   61
        Outside-in SOA: SOA for Small and Medium Businesses   62
        Key Hurdles for Outside-in SOA   67
        Example: An Outside-in Managed Services Provider   69

Chapter 3 Virtual Service Oriented Grid Environment and Architecture   73

    Technology Development in a Federated Environment   75
        A Historical Perspective of Federated Technology Development   75
        Federated Technology Development Today   83
        Governance in a Federated Environment   85
    Composite Usage Models   87
        A Layered Framework for Usage Models   89
        Applying the Composite Usage Model to Virtual Service Oriented Grids   96
        Grid Usage Attributes   101
    The Virtualization Continuum in Virtual Service Oriented Grids   103

Balanced Grid Architecture: Architecting Computers for Performance   109
Architectural Balance   120

Chapter 4   Building Blocks for Virtual Service Oriented Grids   123

Virtualization   125
    Virtualization Usage Models   129
Service Orientation   134
    Service Oriented Architectural Tenets   136
    Services Needed for Virtual Service Oriented Grids   141
Grid Computing   146
    Types of Grids   149
    Challenges   150
The Commoditization of the Data Center   150
The Next Generation of Enterprise Computing   155
Building the Road to Virtual Service Oriented Grids   159

Chapter 5   Industry Standards and Consortia   161

Evolution of Standardization   162
Standard Consortia Landscape   164
Domains of Standards and Their Relationships   168
Trends and Challenges for the Development of Standards   174

Chapter 6   Technology Integration Under Virtual Service Oriented Grids   175

Selecting the Units of Integration   176
Integration of Information Technology Solutions   177
Integration in the Virtual Service Oriented Grid Ecosystem   179
    Demand from Web 2.0: Customer "Pull"   180
    Demand from Ecosystem Partners: Partner "Push"   182
Virtualization in the Utility Computing Infrastructure   183
From Virtual Servers to a Virtual Infrastructure   185

Service Orientation in the Computing Infrastructure   191
  The SOI Framework   191
  Hardware as a Service (HaaS)   194
  Technical Roadblocks for SOI   196
From Centralized to Decentralized Virtual Data Centers   198
Scalability of Service Orientation   202
Delayed Binding: a Useful Paradigm   202
Delayed Binding Optimizes Deployment Flexibility   204
Virtual Infrastructure Example   208
Technology Integration Patterns   210

Chapter 7 Case Studies for Deploying Virtual Service Oriented Grids   213

Delivering IT Services to the Home   213
  Federated Business Services   216
  Application and Data Services   221
  Virtual Infrastructure Services   224
Information Technology Architecture of an Electric Power System   230
  Brief History of Electric Power Systems   232
  Application of Virtual Service Oriented Grids to the Power Industry   234
  Grid Computing Example: Smart Electric Meters   241
Implementation of the Laptop Loss Management Service   248
  Methodology for Addressing the Stolen Laptop Problem   250
Storage in an Virtual Service Oriented Grid Environment   252
Democratization of Computing with Virtual Service Oriented Grids   254
Virtual Service Oriented Grids and Energy Usage   258
Business Opportunities for Virtual Service Oriented Grids   262

Chapter 8   Virtual Service Oriented Grid Strategies: Steps Toward the Future   263

Toward a Virtual Service Oriented Grid National Strategy   264
  A Maturity Model for the Adoption of Virtual Service Oriented Grids   267
  A Prescription for Virtual Service Oriented Grid Adoption   270
  A Dose of Realism   276
Building a Virtual Service Oriented Grid Corporate Strategy   277
Virtual Service Oriented Grid Strategy for Small Businesses   281
  A Maturity Model for Managed Services Providers   282
  Adoption of Virtual Service Oriented Grids in SMB Space   284

Epilog   293

Virtual Service Oriented Grids Today   294
The Future of Virtual Service Oriented Grids   299

Glossary of Acronyms   301

Index   307

Foreword

It is often the case that technology revolutions that have high business impact do not come from up and coming, emerging technology but from the apparent serendipitous confluence of different technology trends long in the making.

The vast majority of emerging technologies fail to be adopted as fast as their proponents and creators would like, no matter how hard they try to hurry things along. As the authors point out, for the automotive industry it took nearly fifty years of development in fits and starts until the adoption of assembly line methods marked the ascendance of Detroit and the US economy in the early twentieth century.

Even if an emerging technology takes off, it may have to go through a cycle of boom and bust until the long lasting benefits to society are finally realized. It happened with the Internet and the e-Commerce era in the 1990s as it happened with the railroad and the telegraph industry more than a century before.

During the emerging phase, potential beneficiaries of a technology cannot quite figure out how to benefit from it even when they think they know. It is not always obvious where the greatest benefits lie or the uses for the new capabilities. This lack of perspective led to conclusions such as the now infamous remarks (whether apocryphal or not) by Thomas J. Watson about the number of computers needed in the world or by Kenneth Olsen on the evolution of the PC market, even though they represent the brightest business minds of their era. Their remarks make absolute sense given the information they had at the time.

Usage models for evolving technologies do change over time. It is during one of these transitions that a technology becomes a shining star and its economic value rises by several orders of magnitude. Such is the case for three technologies that form the core of the book, namely, virtualization, service oriented architecture and grid computing.

Upon analysis of the apparent accidental rise of these technologies, it becomes clear that a number of factors catalyzed the transformation. This transformation is relevant for decision makers in industries that depend on information technology for their success. It is relevant because of upsets in the cost structure. It brings new business capabilities and because competitors will be very busy figuring out how to capitalize on these new developments. Standing still is not an option.

Taking virtualization as an example, it started as a technology to increase the utilization of the very expensive mainframes of half a century ago and to help applications overcome some of the physical limitations. More recently it has been pervasively adopted for commodity servers installed in data centers. The catalyzing factors have been Moore's Law, energy considerations, and the adoption of industry wide standards.

On Moore's Law, CPU performance has been advancing so fast that it's been outstripping the capability of applications to take advantage of this power. As a result, typical utilization factors for nonvirtualized servers are in the single percentage digits to low teens. If the performance of the CPU is doubled, in practice work does not get done twice as fast. The result is that if the work is done by a server with a utilization factor of 10 percent, this utilization is halved with the newer processor. Virtualization provides the opportunity to run concurrently multiple applications or multiple instances of an application in their own operating environment thereby increasing the utilization factor of servers overall. Because the cost of powering and cooling servers has become a significant percentage of the lifetime cost of the equipment, operating servers at 10 percent utilization represents a monumental waste. On a positive note, emerging standards at multiple levels has been making possible to mix and match resources to build best of breed solutions. Realizing this advantage is not automatic; it requires a carefully charted strategy.

On the software front, the generalized adoption of Service Oriented Architectures will bring essentially assembly line methods to software development and it will be even more revolutionary than assembly line methods for the automotive industry. It will involve not just single countries, but participants across the world working together and taking advantage of previous development at an increasing rate in a virtuous cycle. Opportunities will be open to participants in emerging and advanced economies alike along this exciting journey.

The authors' goal is to document and chart this journey in practical yet insightful ways and in plain language. This book will help the reader understand the dynamics behind developments in information technology at the strategic level, and based on this understanding, provide useful pointers on how to build an information technology strategy specific to your company, government or organization based on ongoing developments in virtualization, SOA and grid computing.

Dr. Wei-jen Lee
University of Texas - Arlington
Professor and Director Energy Systems Research Center
May 2008

Preface

A new era of opportunity is dawning for Enterprise IT. Recent developments in the IT industry point to the exact antithesis of the perfect storm condition that led to the dot-com crash in the late 1990s. In the speculative environment of that era countless new players entered the marketplace. However, in most cases there was nearly total divergence between the technologies proposed by these new players and the ROI, or even business value to the intended audience—if an audience was defined at all.

On the business side there has been considerable consolidation and soul searching after the dot-com crash where the marketplace has essentially weeded out most nonviable ideas.

It is not easy as saying that the brick and mortar companies "won" because they had more "substance." The economic landscape at the beginning of the third millennium is quite different than the climate at the start of the dot-com revolution, with new players, and old players gone or greatly diminished.

What strategies can be applied to optimize business outcomes in this business climate? In the next few chapters we will take a look at the confluence of the three technologies in the title of the book, namely, virtualization, service orientation, and computing grids.

A Bit of History

It would be wonderful news if we could claim that virtualization, service orientation, and grids represent the latest and greatest in terms of emerging capabilities. Alas, we can't lay that claim. The best we can claim is that the trio is old wine in new bottles. For instance, let's look at virtualization. The first efforts at virtualization can be traced back at least five decades to virtual memory and machine virtualization research done at IBM in the early 1960s for the IBM 360/67[1], the demand paging research for the Atlas computer at the University of Manchester[2], and the segmented memory design of the Burroughs B5000[3], to list just a few of many examples. If we include assemblers and compilers as a form of virtualization, we can push the clock back by at least another decade.

Compilers relieved computer programmers from the drudgery of using wire patches or writing programs using ones and zeros. A compiler presents an idealized or should we say *virtualized*, logical view of a computer. For instance, real-life computers have architectural oddities imposed by limitations in the hardware design, such as memory regions that cannot be used, or registers that can be used for only certain purposes. A compiler presents a uniform view of memory to the programmer. The programmer does not need to worry about details of computer architecture such as whether the machine is stack or register oriented, details that may be irrelevant to the application under development.

Likewise, service orientation has a similar vintage. The origins of service orientation can be traced at least to the early 1960s with the development of the Simula language at the Norwegian Computing Center in Oslo. Simula started as a simulation programming language, but also brought to light concepts that proved useful for general programming: it facilitated interoperability and re-use, reducing the cost and time to completion of software projects. Simula and derivatives found an application in VLSI design at Intel Corporation, California Institute of Technology, and Stanford University, became the development platform for the influential Smalltalk language at

---

[1] http://en.wikipedia.org/wiki/IBM_CP-40

[2] J. Fotheringham, *Dynamic Storage Allocation in the Atlas Computer*, Communications of the ACM Vol. 4, No. 10 (Oct. 1961), pp. 435-436.

[3] http://en.wikipedia.org/wiki/Burroughs_large_systems

Xerox Palo Alto Research Center (PARC) in the 1970s, and key concepts were incorporated in the C++ language still in use today.

Finally, opinions about the origins of grid computing vary widely. It is possible to argue that grids started in the late 1960s with the first efforts at networked computing, or in the early 1970s with the standardization of networking around Ethernet. Grid research as a method for collaborative, federated computing picked up steam in the late 1980s and early 1990s with projects on algorithmic sharing aimed at cycle harvesting such as Condor in the University of Wisconsin and Zilla at NeXT Computer. A number of integration efforts ensued, such as the NASA Information Power Grid (IPG). Grid computing acquired a distinct identity thanks to the effort of the team led by Ian Foster at the University of Chicago.

The technologies for virtualization, service orientation, and grid computing have been amply documented in books and the research and trade literature. We do not attempt to go deeper or duplicate the excellent work that other authors have done.

Instead, we explore how the interplay between virtualization, service orientation, and grids are fundamentally changing the value economics of how information technology is delivered, and in the process, how organizations that depend on information technology to carry their day-to-day business are affected in turn. The authors believe we are witnessing a true inflection point.

Without an attempt to be exhaustive, Figure 0.1 summarizes the historical relationship between key technologies that eventually led to the concept of virtual service oriented grids.

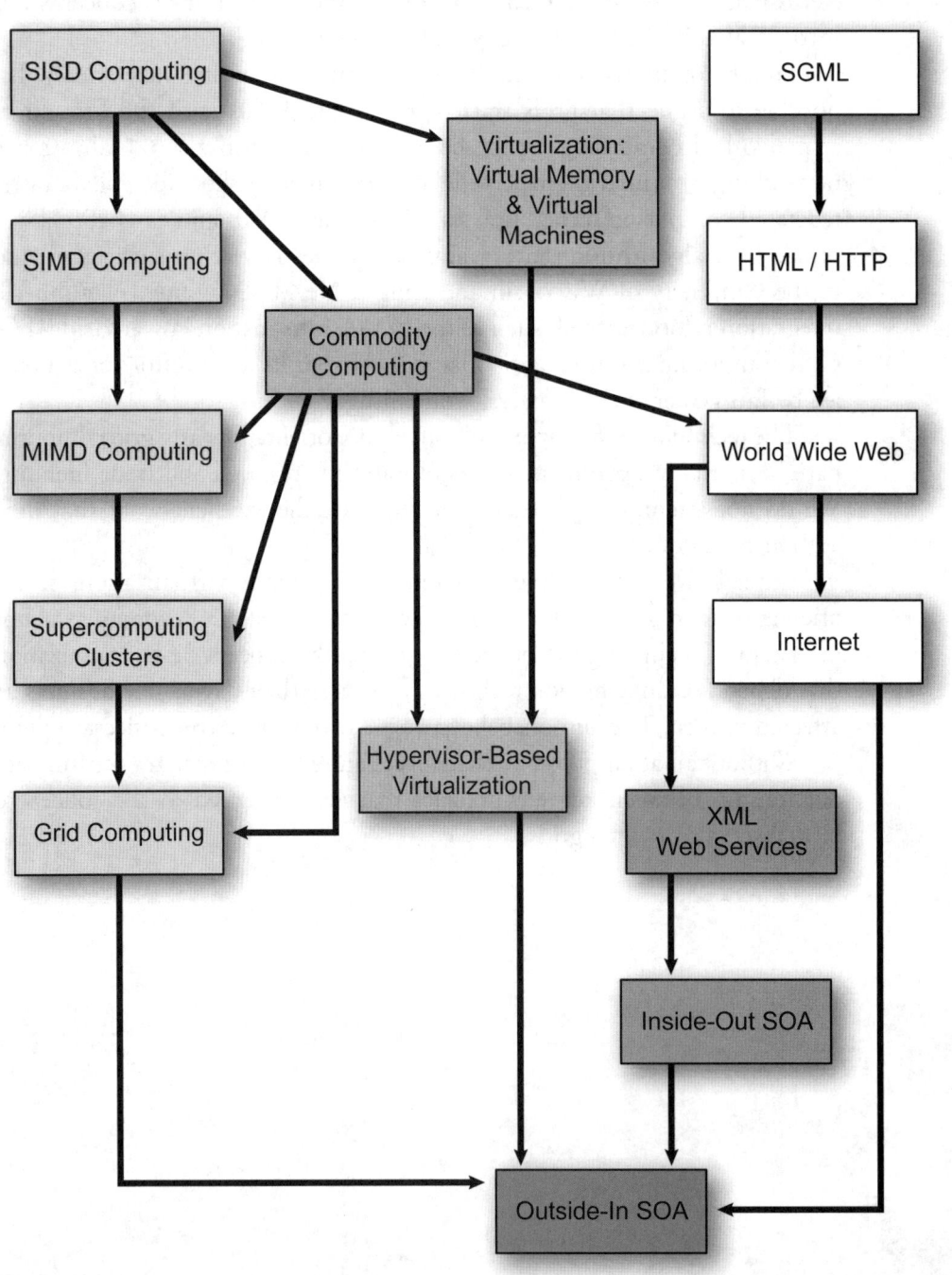

Figure 0.1 Technology Pedigrees for Virtualization, Service Orientation and Grids

The upper blocks start with the archetype Standard Generalized Markup Language (SGML) developed in the 1960s by Charles Goldfarb, Edward Mosher and Raymond Lone at IBM. The Hypertext Markup Language (HTML), a derivative of SGML, became the language of the Web and the Internet. The World Wide Web was initially used as a presentation interface for humans and certain aspects of it evolved into XML Web services for interoperable machine to machine communication. This machine to machine interface enabled modular composite service oriented architecture (SOA) applications, first within large enterprises (the inside-out model) and across enterprises small and large (the outside-in model). Chapter 2 covers these inside-out and outside-in models.

The middle blocks track the evolution of virtualization, initially applied to mainframes and eventually to computers based on commodity processors with hypervisors running as an intermediate layer between the hardware and the operating system.

The bottom blocks track the evolution of computer hardware, first with the single-instruction, single-data (SISD) style of computation initiated by mainframes in the 1950s. To improve throughput, certain computers were architected to apply a program to multiple data streams (single-instruction, multiple-data or SIMD.) These computers required data with a highly regular structure to take advantage of the extra power, and hence their applicability was limited. These restrictions were relaxed with SIMD computers, which allowed the constituent computers to operate on different data. Initially nodes in SIMD computers were linked together using proprietary high-speed interconnects forming supercomputing clusters all located in a single room. This setup was cost prohibitive for most applications except those requiring the highest performance. These restrictions were relaxed for grid computing where nodes can be geographically distributed, sometimes connected through the Internet.

The use of virtual service oriented grids is not yet pervasive in the industry. However, in this book we find quite a few examples, more often than not under different names. Organizations that use virtual service oriented grids will have a competitive advantage over those that don't and will likely have an economic influence disproportionate to their size.

This analysis would be of little practical value if it were not actionable. Hence, after we have established the dynamics of the interplay between the three undercurrents, we describe strategies and approaches that others have found useful. Using this insight, we attempt to discover and document approaches that will likely be successful in this new environment.

We assume that the reader is familiar with the fundamental elements of virtualization, service orientation, and grids and has been asked to evaluate and even forge strategies for adoption in his or her organization or is seeking enough insight into the processes to be able to issue meaningful directives to staffers to have these strategies adopted in an organization.

Resources deployed under this new old environment are said to be deployed in a *virtual service oriented grid* or VSG. While these resources are best characterized by the qualities brought by each technology, the resources have evolved and they are not quite identical to their ancestor technologies.

- These resources are inherently distributed, federated and replicated as in grids seen in high performance computing applications, yet they feature more general capabilities.

- The service oriented nature of these resources makes them highly interoperable and logically they are closely aligned with business entities.

- The virtualization capabilities at play allow these resources to be logically "detached" from the physical hosts on which they run. This detachment can be seen in multiple ways: A powerful host may be capable of supporting multiple instances of a logical entity, and such a logical entity may be bound to its host only temporarily. The entity may migrate to other hosts for reasons of fault tolerance, disaster recovery or performance.

The presence of virtual service oriented grids does not bring fundamentally different capabilities. After all they run on the same computers, networks, and data centers as the more traditional information technology architectures.

Borrowing the term from requirements engineering, what virtual service oriented grids bring into the equation are *nonfunctional* capabilities. To contrast *functional* capabilities with nonfunctional capabilities, a change in functional capabilities changes the system behavior or function. This is not to say that changes brought up by virtual service oriented grids are not significant:

- A virtual service oriented grid environment will still be useful for processing home loans or performing credit card transactions.
- The performance of these systems will be infinitely scalable for practical purposes: if the workload slows the system, there will be a way of adding more resources to bring response times back in line without hitting a wall.
- New services can be put together by composing more primitive services using compatible protocols. If these primitive services are already available, the new services can be assembled almost automatically and in near real time.
- The component services can be *in*sourced or *out*sourced. The size or *granularity* of the component services is much smaller than a traditional outsourced application such as payroll. The negotiation or handshaking to bring an outsourced component is automatic and machine driven as opposed to the months of negotiation that would take a large company to contract for a payroll service.
- The component services and the composite applications built from them are mutually *interoperable*.

In a virtual service oriented grid environment, the service components mentioned above may not be designed to behave as full fledged applications, but intended to be used as building blocks for applications. We will use the term *servicelet* or *microservice* to specifically denote service building blocks.

To bring another example, the outsourcing of software projects usually requires the same painstaking and lengthy process for both the service requester and the service provider.

In the 1990s the Internet unlocked trillions of dollars in value through *disintermediation*, essentially directly connecting producers and consumers and removing the middleman.

Ironically, service orientation has the potential of becoming even more momentous. It swings the pendulum in the opposite direction in a process of *reintermediation*. Only this time the middlemen will not be humans, but machines talking to each other through the service abstraction.

In this environment, it becomes possible to monetize a service that was initially custom built for use at a particular organization. Services become an encapsulation of intellectual property, a unit of value, discoverable and interoperable through standard interfaces.

As the market for services evolves and matures it is not far-fetched to see these services traded as commodities and sophisticated instruments developing, such as futures markets.

In this brave new environment the upfront cost of building a service component in the first place can be amortized over multiple instantiations. This reuse lowers the per instance cost of a service, which in turn lowers the implementation cost of the business application where the service is used. For service consumers, this is how the traditional cost benefit of SOA based applications is realized. By placing a service in the marketplace that perhaps initially was intended for in-house use, service purveyors have the option of generating additional revenue streams to offset development costs. Hence service components are no longer items in the cost side of the ledger. They can become revenue generators.

Compound applications built through servicelets will also become self-optimizing through metrics implicitly or explicitly defined in a service's service level agreement (SLA).

The consideration to SLAs in compound applications in both internal and external interfaces will naturally enable factoring in other nonfunctional requirements, such as regulatory compliance or quality and performance standards.

Consequently, in parallel with the disintermediation and reintermediation there will be a process of *disaggregation* and *reaggregation* of applications and services. As mentioned above, the granularity of the constituent components of an application will become far smaller than what is seen today. For instance, a payroll application is usually a single logical function outsourced to a service provider such as EDS. A virtual service oriented environment will allow an organization to mix and match a combination of business logic software, the data, the storage on which the data is hosted, the database used to access the data, and the servers on which the application runs.

Developing applications in a service oriented ecosystem will require a marketplace where a broad range of servicelets is available providing application architects and engineers with a broad palette to choose from to fit specific goals. For instance, it is possible to select servicelets encapsulating storage and server hosts in distributed locations for the purposes of disaster preparedness.

The servers used to build this application may actually be virtualized instances, not physical servers. The service consumer does not care or may not even be aware of whether the server instances are physical or virtual as long as the provider meets pre-agreed SLAs for performance and security. Universal interoperability will foster a market for commodities and futures for certain popular service components.

Conversely, servicelets need not be pure software entities; some functions can interact with the physical world: when a student at some university uses a course registration application, the registration process invokes a servicelet to purchase the corresponding textbook through a book supplier such as Amazon.com. The invocation of the Amazon.com Web service interface triggers a chain of events whose end result is a book mailed to the student's address.

The event chain may be extremely complex. For instance, the actual seller of the book may not be Amazon.com but one of the associated resellers. Throughout this chain information flows as needed to make sure the cost settlement is appropriate for each party according to the agreements in place and that the book is eventually mailed to the right address.

An Industry Example

Because of the expense associated with negotiation and teardown of business applications, these applications today tend to have a long life. Teardown may be a complex process involving the removal of on the premises applications and equipment and negotiating a new contract with an alternative provider. A virtualized service environment will make dynamic behaviors more practical. Decision makers will be able to gather supporting data in a fraction of the time considered possible today. An application could more easily be built to address a specific question or support a short duration campaign providing increased business agility.

Let's take the example of a food industry marketing analyst interested in performing a study on purchase patterns of a certain line of products using business intelligence (BI) methods.

The analyst licenses a customer loyalty database from a grocery chain company. The grocery chain is willing to grant such licenses to third parties as part of a strategy to create additional revenue streams from intellectual property generated from business operations.

In looking at the grocery chain, virtualization and service orientation will lower the barriers for mature industries with a vision to rediscover jewels of intellectual property they had all along in the form of data and processes, and find out that they can enhance their revenue in the services marketplace.

Conversely, service consumers may find it more economical to integrate servicelets from these companies rather than spending years in developing and honing the processes and knowledge internally.

The analyst rents a one-use instance of the customer loyalty database and goes to an application service provider (ASP) who orchestrates the following actions:

- Pulls out one encrypted copy of the customer loyalty database
- Purchases storage from a storage services provider in China to house the database
- Purchases a one-week use license from the services organization of a database independent software vendor (ISV). The database ISV turns around and rents two servers from a data center service provider for a week to host this run.
- Purchases a one-week license from the services organization of a BI ISV.
- Sends a single bill to the analyst's department.

The analyst issues queries from her desk and completes the week long research project. The ASP, as orchestrator, destroys all copies of the database in a provable manner and to the satisfaction of the data owner when the project is complete and the transaction is closed.

Here are some observations for this scenario:

- All data travels encrypted and compressed until it gets decrypted in memory. The only way to snoop would be to attach a digital analyzer to the processor bus. Hence service provider hosts are not even aware nor are they allowed to snoop on what their customers run in their data centers.

    The servers are tamper-resistant certified by third parties taking advantage of the pre-existing trust chain. An independent security services provider monitors and certifies data centers for a number of customers around the world.

If an attempt is made to open a cabinet during a sensitive run, the server is automatically shut down. Too many of these incidents may lead to the data center owner losing its license to run external jobs. This environment allows deployment of applications from resources available worldwide.

- All communication is encrypted requiring mutual authentication, respecting the requirements of each participant in a compound application. Interaction between mutually suspicious partners is always assumed.

The philosophy for these security measures won't be much different from communication taking place today in a potentially hostile Internet. The level of privacy and security is important for a reliable bill-back and cost settlement function.

The mechanisms also support tamper resistant system management actions that can travel across different organizations: when the infrastructure for this experiment is decommissioned, the database owner gets a proof that all copies of the database have been destroyed.

- Each player gets a view of a managed resource appropriate to their function: The host owner gets a view of the physical resources. Most requesting customers get a view of virtualized resources. In practice, differences between physical and virtual resources will be blurred.

This is a scenario for a highly dynamic, real-time, pay-as-you-go infrastructure. For companies highly variable seasonal usage it may be cheaper to rent than to host servers that are near idle all the time. ∎

What's in Store in This Book

The chapters in the book are structured as follows.

Chapter 1 covers basic definitions, and specifically the components of the virtualization, service orientation, and grid computing triumvirate and their synergistic relationship.

Chapter 2 describes the business environment that is fueling the demand for virtual service oriented grids that is at the same time making them economically feasible. Paradoxically, we see increasingly automated technology that presents an increasingly responsive, agile and personalized face to the customer. This evolution is driven by IT managers' quest for value, in terms of cost, scalability, agility, reliability and a slew of other abilities while improving service.

Chapter 3 provides insight into the architecture of virtual service oriented grid systems: how they are built, what they are good for, what are their limitations.

Chapter 4 covers the technology building blocks that make the architecture described in Chapter 3 possible.

Virtual service oriented grids are enabled not only through advanced technology. A necessary element is the upfront and tireless work done by standards committees to ensure service to service interoperability, covered in Chapter 5.

Chapter 6 covers strategic considerations for deploying a virtual service oriented grid infrastructure in its different manifestations as well as integration issues that arise in combining the building blocks described in Chapter 4 to build the technology vision described in Chapter 3.

In Chapter 7, we examine a number of case studies on virtual service oriented grids and understand the dynamics behind their industry adoption—or failure—and trace their evolution in the past, present, and future.

In a shift from an expository discourse in the previous chapters to a prescriptive style, Chapter 8 puts the limelight on the reader, using the foundation laid out in the prior chapters to help the reader build a grid strategy aligned with her or his particular business needs and conditions. Examples and case studies are provided with this chapter.

Finally, in Chapter 9 we button up in a succinct manner the concepts developed throughout the book.

Acknowledgements

Integration, collaboration, and synthesis are essential to SOA, and the content presented in this book reflects this spirit. The content reflects the experience and the creativity of many people and industry giants, perhaps under a new light. This book would not have been possible without their contributions through their written work, technical discussions, and even casual conversations and business meetings.

The authors have calibrated these insights with the experience from professionals at Intel IT through numerous joint projects spanning many years. The authors acknowledge their openness and willingness to share that experience, the duress of extreme work and budgetary issues typical of the industry notwithstanding. Some of the fundamental ideas in the book came from a strategic collaboration between Intel Solution Services and the Enterprise Architecture efforts led by the Intel Chief Architect and Vice President at the time, Prasad Rampalli. Today Prasad is the Vice President of the Digital Enterprise Group and Director of End-User Platform Integration for Intel Corporation.

The contribution of Stephen S. Pawlowski, Intel Senior Fellow and CTO for Intel Digital Enterprise Group is also acknowledged as the sponsor and initiator of this book project. The support of Intel Press Publisher Richard Bowles throughout the project has been greatly appreciated.

Keith Uebele went through most every chapter in the book. As a technology strategist at Intel, Keith is eminently qualified to review the material in this book. He was responsible for the corporate-level initial assessment of Web services strategy when the technology was first adopted by the industry and was on the upswing. He was also played an important role in the planning and strategy of the Enterprise Architecture practice for Intel Solution Services, an IT consulting organization at Intel Corporation. This book is much improved through the generous contribution of his time and Keith's unconditional willingness to share his experience and the breadth of his assessment, from the deeply conceptual to misplaced commas.

The support from Rick Echevarria, Vice President for Intel Sales Marketing Group and General Manager for Enterprise Solution Sales is also acknowledged.

Jason Devoys, Qui Hoang, Jim Hobbs, John Morton and John Baudrexl provided very helpful technical and business evaluations of the book content.

The authors acknowledge the contributions of the external reviewers, Dr. Jun-Jang Jeng, IBM TJ Watson Research Center, Dr. Wei-Jen Lee, Director of the Energy Systems Research Center at University of Texas, Arlington, Dr. Gerald Sheblé, Maseeh Professor of Electrical and Computer Engineering, Portland State University, and Dr. Shimon Y. Nof, Director, PRISM Center, Purdue University. Other reviewers include Jim Richmann, James P. Hobbs, and Tarasov Artem.

Special thanks to project manager Bruce Bartlett and editor David Clark who kept the project on track and the authors motivated through the gentlest but persistent nudges. The production team took the raw material and made a great looking book from it. I especially appreciate the work of, Ron Bohart, the artist who created the intriguing cover art.

Kathleen Masterson, Kevin E. Patterson, and Shelley L. Rowe performed a pivotal role in getting the word out about the book through their marketing efforts.

For anyone I may have missed, please accept my deepest apologies.

Enrique Castro-Leon
August 2008

Chapter 1

The Emergence of Virtual Service Oriented Grids

Computing is not about computers any more. It is about living.
—Nicholas Negroponte

Imagine the all too common scenario nowadays of a laptop from a large organization disappearing and carrying with it personal information of thousands or even millions of people and exposing them to identity theft. This amount of information would fit in a small portion of a modern hard drive, or even one of those ubiquitous USB portable storage devices.

In one of the most serious recorded incidents, the disappearance of a US Department of Veterans Affairs laptop containing the records of 26.5 million veteran and active duty personnel was taken from an employee's home in May 2006. In November 2007 in another incident, two disks containing personal information from 25 million British individuals and 7 million families were sent between two government departments through internal mail. The disks never made it to the destination, leaving the victims exposed to potential identity theft incidents.

Although it is impossible to prevent future similar incidents with complete certainty, the material discussed in this book will help in looking at this problem in a new light. This insight will provide not only hints about approaches to solving this problem, but also about who to approach to address the problem and to figure out how much it will cost to solve it. Beyond that, from a business strategy perspective, knowing about the cost is not sufficient; we want to optimize the cost over a desired planning period.

Grid computing can be rarefied stuff from academia of interest only to postdoctoral researchers. Grids can be complex, but can also help us solve complex and interesting business problems. The study of grids provides insight into the behaviors of complex systems and how to address knotty computational problems. Furthermore, if a business problem can be expressed as a computational problem, even if it is computationally complex, we get a shot at solving it. This thought is especially applicable as we move to an environment where computer cycles are essentially free, but human time is limited and expensive.

We will use grids in this book as the end point of an elaborate thought experiment in an attempt to elucidate the evolution of distributed computing as far as we can see. This thought experiment is relevant to the extent that it elucidates business planning decisions and technology strategies that need to be in place today.

A grid approach or grid-thinking is relevant even to organizations that do not have grids deployed and do not plan to deploy them in the immediate future. Grid-thinking helps discover relationships between otherwise disparate components in the physical, software, and business infrastructure of IT in a holistic approach. We will see these principles illustrated throughout many examples in the book. Of particular note is the home IT example in Chapter 8, where we extract principles observed in enterprise IT and apply them in a different setting, namely, in the small and medium business (SMB) and consumer space. We purposely attempt to transcend the gadgetry and describe an economic ecosystem that would deliver a capability to deploy and support IT services scaled down to be useful to SMBs and household consumers.

The principles described in this book will be useful in many other contexts. We expect these principles to be relevant for technology planning and strategy in emerging economies. Expecting emerging economies to follow the same development path as in more advanced economies is generally not an optimal choice. It can be argued that in the United States, for instance, the existence of an extensive landline communications infrastructure has created a technology and regulatory environment that actually *arrested* the adoption of newer technologies that deliver more advanced capabilities: micropayments by cell phone are available in China, Korea, and Japan but not the US. USA Today[1] reports that the average Internet download speed in the US is less than 2 megabits per second, a pitiful fraction of the 61 megabits per second available in Japan, and 45 in South Korea. Other countries that surpass the US are France (17 megabits per second) and Canada (7 megabits per second.) We incorporate business and usage models in our analyses in an effort to peer into the crystal ball and anticipate some of these roadblocks.

The main principle behind grids is that in the long run it becomes more feasible to solve a computational problem by connecting existing computing resources than to try building a single powerful computer. Because the computing resources cannot always be placed in a single box, or cabinet or room or even a city, these resources need to be connected with a network. The architecture of the network is highly relevant in determining the performance of the distributed computing system.

In the long run is an important qualification. If an application is not running fast enough, running the application in a faster computer may shorten the time to solution, but only to the point that the computer is faster. On the other hand, intuitively we can see that applying two computers to one problem can potentially halve the time to solution, and if we apply four computers, the time to solution is halved again. This is the principle behind multi-core CPUs. However, the transformation is not trivial. Applications need to be redesigned to take advantage of multiple cores. Otherwise they will be happy to continue running in one core no matter how many cores are available. It takes time for the software vendors to evolve applications to take advantage of the more powerful environment and hence the caveat.

Applications designed to run in a distributed environment will run faster in a distributed environment. The application of distributed computing principles provides a powerful thinking tool to address apparently intractable problems, such as the challenge of recovering data from stolen laptops. We will revisit this problem and analyze it from a grid perspective later in this chapter.

The common notion of a grid is that of a system encompassing thousands of computers and costing millions. In actuality, grid computing is not about trying to lift every rock under the budget universe in an attempt to find the tens of millions of dollars needed to deploy a multi-thousand node system.

---

1   http://www.usatoday.com/tech/news/techpolicy/2007-06-25-net-speeds_N.htm

This approach leads into solution space way too soon, before the pertinent questions have been asked, such as what are going to be the usage models, and even before the obligatory ROI question is asked, whether investment in such a grand scale is really necessary.

The treatment of grid computing in this book deemphasizes the solution of the grand challenge type of problems, such as the human genome, which as a matter of fact, was solved recently. The focus will be on enterprise and commercial settings, much more mundane problems found in enterprise computing, such as very large databases and engineering and financial calculations found in certain industry segments.

In this context, grid computing still entails solving problems in a grand scale, but through the use and reuse of existing resources. These resources can come in the form of currently underutilized servers in existing data centers, workstations in employees' desks or through outsourcing, which brings the next subject.

Other People's Money versus Other People's Systems

Scaling a business often involves OPM (other people's money), through partnerships or issuing of stock through IPOs (initial public offerings). These relationships are carried out within a legal framework that took hundreds of years to develop.

In the real world, scaling a computing system follows a similar approach, in the form of resource outsourcing, such as using other people's systems or *OPS*. The use of OPS has a strong economic incentive: it does not make sense to spend millions of dollars in a large system for occasional use only.

Even large scale projects that require significant amounts of computing power usually start with small trial or development runs, with large runs far and few between. Because of the data gathering cycle, some projects reserve the largest and most spectacular runs for the end. A large system that lies idle during development would be a waste of capital.

The use of OPS is facilitated by the other two technologies covered in this book: virtualization and service orientation. Virtualization makes the sharing of a physical resource practical, whereas the application of service oriented principles facilitates the reuse of these resources.

The sharing of idle workstations that motivated research projects such as Condor[2] at the University of Wisconsin in the early 1990s constitutes an early experiment in OPS.

On a macroeconomic scale there is a powerful economic motivation of OPS. A large grid system represents an investment of not tens of millions of dollars but hundreds of millions once the physical and staffing infrastructure are added. The hurdle is not as high as it might seem at first glance. Investment in resources this large are usually pooled, much in the same way an airline system, a shipping line, or even a skyscraper use shared or pooled resources. Hence change does not happen until industry momentum is behind it. A powerful motivator arises when entrepreneurs realize that a viable business is behind the technology.

Within an economic ecosystem, a group of people with skills in this area may decide to form a company that provides a grid service much more efficiently than it is possible at a departmental grid where staff tending it may have other jobs, lowering the cost overall to society for providing grid services.

Unfortunately, the full fledged use of OPS, where computing resources are traded like commodities in a vibrant and dynamic ecosystem, is not a reality today. Such infrastructure requires a sophisticated technical and legal infrastructure not yet available. This infrastructure is needed to handle service level agreements (SLAs), privacy, ensuring that intellectual property (IP) and trade secrets do not leak from the system, as well as user, system, and performance management, billing, and other administrative procedures.

The state of the grid today is quite primitive, similar to the state of commercial practices in the Europe of the seventeenth century, compared to the sophisticated trading markets and financial instruments that exist today. After all, grid technology is less than 20 years old as a distinct discipline. The good news is that progress is happening a lot faster. The authors estimate that grids will come of age in less than 20 years. At that point grids will be interwoven with the fabric of society to the point that they may actually lose the distinct identity they carry today.

Fortunately, there is no need to wait 20 years. There will be a continuum of progress with an increasing portfolio of applications as the infrastructure

---

2 Douglas Thain, Todd Tannenbaum, and Miron Livny, *Condor and the Grid*, in Fran Berman, Anthony J.G. Hey, Geoffrey Fox, editors, *Grid Computing: Making The Global Infrastructure a Reality,* John Wiley, 2003. ISBN: 0-470-85319-0

evolves. Some industries will adopt grids faster than others. Eventually society as a whole will benefit.

As an example, storage in data company-hosted data centers may become quaintly anachronistic. Storage will become a commodity, purchased by the terabyte, petabyte, or exabyte, depending of the most popular unit of the time with quality of service (QoS) defined by SLA. Storage brokers may also be storage providers holding data on their premises. For large accounts they could be pure play brokers, placing their data through a combination of storage providers according to complex statistical allocations that minimize their cost yet meet SLAs promised to customers. This is analogous to the reinsurance systems in use today by large insurance companies to manage risks and redistribute liabilities. Later in this chapter we will describe an example of a pooled storage system in a manner of existence proof.

The information this book provides is actionable in the sense that it is intended to help decision makers and strategists in charting a path that maximizes the value of grid computing to their organizations over a relatively long planning period spanning five to ten years. The reader will not find recipes for building specific solutions. The treatment of specific solutions is left for books dealing with aspects of grid technical architecture.

One basic assumption in the material presented is the notion of gradual adoption of grid technology within enterprise computing. This convergence will create excellent opportunities to generate stockholder value. Planning and charting a strategic path will allow organizations realize the benefits of this value.

Virtualization, Service Orientation, and Grids

One reason behind the increasing adoption of grids in the enterprise is the synergy with two powerful technology trends, namely, virtualization and service orientation. Let's explore each of these technologies and how they relate to each other.

About Grids

The origin of the term *grid* as in *grid* computing is shrouded in mystery and ambiguity. Because of the association of grids with utility computing and the analogy of utility computing with electrical power systems, it is likely that the term grid was coined to capture the concept of an electrical power grid, but applied to computer systems.

An electrical power system consists of a number of transmission lines ending up in bus bars. Bus bars may have generators, that is, power sources attached to them, or they may carry electrical loads. The generic name for a bus bar is a *node*. The aggregation of transmission lines and nodes forms a network or *mesh*, albeit a very irregular and sparse mesh. The set of reference lines in a map is also called a grid.

An electric power distribution system within a city is similar in structure to a transmission system that spans a state or even a country. The difference is that the system is much more interconnected because links run for every street, as opposed to being used as intercity ties.

Following on this analogy, a grid computing system consists of a set of computers in a network as illustrated in Figure 1.1. The computers in a grid are complete, functioning computers capable of working standalone. The network is understood to be a standards-based network, such as an Ethernet-based network or the public Internet.

A cluster is a specialized kind of grid where the nodes are usually identical and co-located in the same room or building. The network may be a low-latency, high-bandwidth proprietary network.

This definition of grid is recursive. For instance a cluster within a grid may be represented as a single node.

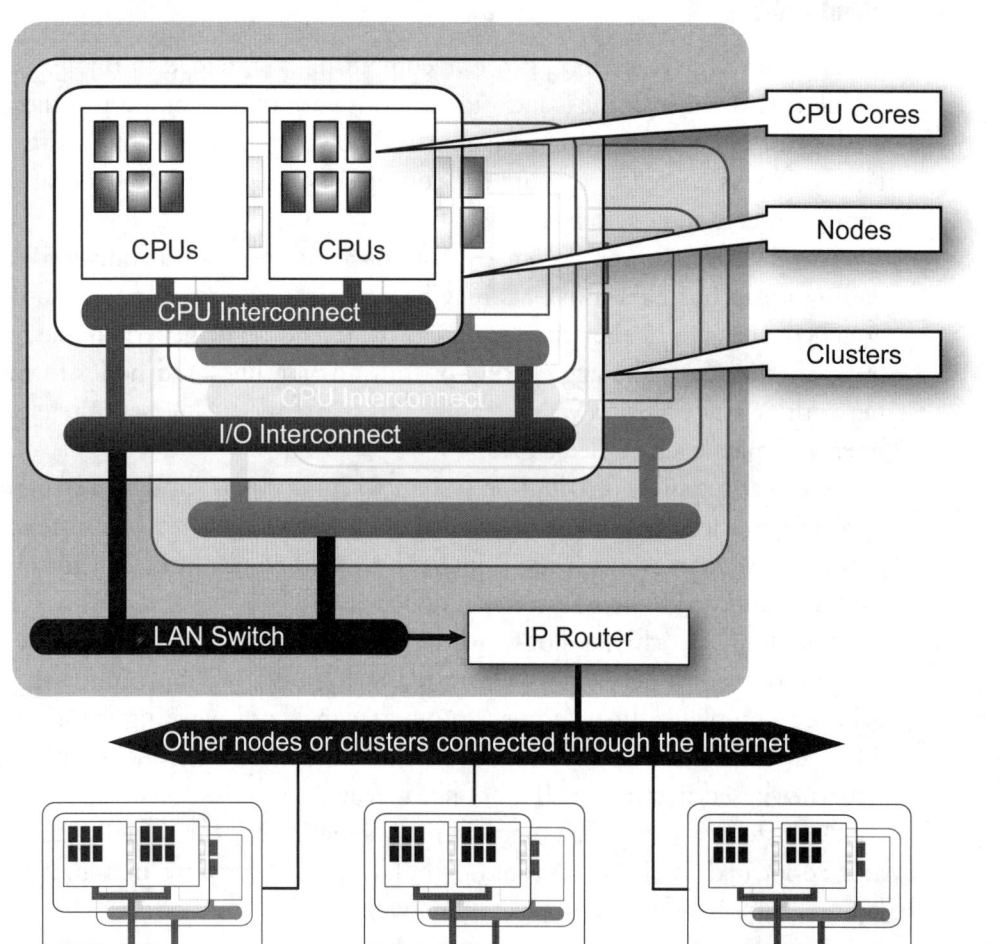

Figure 1.1   Structure of a Computing Grid

The development of grid technology started in the early 1990s as an alternative to running high performance applications on specialized supercomputers costing millions of dollars. Instead, grids allowed the use of less expensive workstations costing in the order of tens of thousands of dollars. As commodity PCs became more powerful, PCs gradually replaced workstations as preferred grid nodes.

High performance computing applications are run in parallel: multiple nodes or computers are applied to the solution of one problem with the goal of reducing the time to solution as much as possible. The computational complexity and the size of data sets are so large that even if they were solvable in one node, that run might take days, if not weeks or more.

We will refer to grids in a fairly generic way. Some writers refer to the subject as the GRID for GRID computing, which is not quite correct because the word *grid* is not an acronym. Likewise, some authors refer to grids as the Grid as if it were a single all-knowing, all-powerful Grid in the world in the Orwellian Big Brother sense. Actually the situation is exactly the opposite: grid computing deals with the challenge of managing distributed and federated resources, which is not too different from the proverbial task of herding cats. The rewards of successfully executing a grid strategy are many in terms of efficient use of capital and attaining business agility. A useful first step toward these goals is to demystify the concepts and the technology behind them.

Grids impose restrictions on the type of problems that can be solved. The nodes in a supercomputer can exchange information very fast and at high data rates: they have communication channels that exhibit low latency and high data bandwidth. A computer node running a parallel program requires intermediate results from other nodes in varying amounts depending on the type of application. If communication across nodes does not happen fast enough, the progress of the computation overall is impaired. The delay increases as more nodes are thrown into the computation. There is a point of diminishing returns on the number of the nodes that can be used effectively for a certain computation. This maximum number of nodes defines the limit for scalability for a specific system architecture. The scalability limits for grids are smaller than for specialized supercomputers. For certain applications, these supercomputers may be able to support efficient runs employing hundreds of nodes where scalability may hit a wall after just a few nodes.

A computing grid, reduced to its barest essentials, is a set of computing resources connected by a network. The computing resources comprise processing and storage capabilities. Networks are necessary because the computing resources are assumed to be distributed, within a room, across buildings, or even across cities and continents. The networks allow data to move across processing elements and between processing elements and storage.

Distribution introduces complexity. A single computer in one room would be easier to program and use than 1,000 smaller computers collectively possessing the same processing and storage capability, but scattered across seven continents. Obviously, distribution is not accidental; there must be powerful reasons for it to manifest itself or otherwise it would not happen. The reasons are economic, which ultimately reflect physical limitations of how powerful a single node can be.

When it comes to pushing the envelope for performance, building a single, powerful computer becomes more expensive than a group of smaller computer whose collective performance equals the performance of the single computer. Pushing technology to the limits to increase the performance of a single processor eventually leads to a cost wall requiring expensive tricks for small performance gains.

Under these conditions it becomes cheaper to attain additional performance through the use of replication. This dynamic takes place in multiple contexts. For instance, in 2004 Intel found that a successor to the Pentium® 4 processor, codenamed Prescott would have hit a "thermal wall." Because of the increase in the number of transistors in the chip and the need to operate the single processor at a higher frequency, the successor chip would have run too hot and consumed too much power at a time when power consumption was becoming an important factor for consumer acceptance. This realization led to the first generation of dual-core processors in 2006 carrying two CPUs in a chip. Each CPU possesses a little less processing capability, but the combined performance of the two cores is larger than the prior generation processor, and the power consumption is also smaller.

Similar economic considerations favor building processors with increasing number of cores as well as computers with multiple processors.

Replication allows overcoming the physical limitations of single processing elements. For instance, if it takes a single core 16 minutes to update 100,000 records, a server with two quad-core CPUs can theoretically do the job in 2 minutes. Four servers applied to the same job could reduce the job to a mere 30 seconds. The eight cores in a server and the four servers are said to be working the problem in *parallel*.

Unfortunately, parallelism comes with overhead. Even with the four servers the total processing time may end up at 1 minute, not the expected 30 seconds. Why? It's the computer version of too many cooks in the kitchen.

The database may not have a capability to lock records individually during the update. If two or more records are locked during a transaction, access to these records is serialized, and the update of the other records needs to wait until the CPU handling the first record is done. Furthermore, it takes time to move data across distributed computing system, and delays invariably ensue.

Another motivation for replication is to enhance availability. For instance, a grid with 10,000 storage data nodes has potentially 10,000-fold redundancy. The probability of losing data in this environment is practically zero. A 10,000-fold redundancy is likely overkill. In practice some of the replicated resources are used to enhance availability using relatively unreliable nodes and communication networks and some for scalability. Hence the 10,000 node data grid may end up with the storage capacity of 2,500 nodes with quad redundancy, still significantly larger than the storage capacity of a single node but still highly available.

What has taken grids beyond their high performance computing roots is synergy with two other emerging technology trends: service orientation and virtualization. In the next few chapters we will be documenting this process from a number of different angles.

Grids: A Physical Description

In the previous section we spoke about grid attributes and defined grids as computing nodes connected by a network. In this section we describe how grids are constructed. It may be useful to revisit Figure 1.1 as we go through the different elements in this section.

There is nothing special about nodes in a grid other than their being connected to a network with the purpose of working collaboratively in some common application. The connecting network needs to use open protocols such as TCP/IP; otherwise connectivity may be difficult to achieve. Here are some node examples:

- ■ *A laptop or desktop PC.* Any networked PC can become a member of a grid. A classic example of a grid application using networked PCs is the SETI@home program. It is also an example of *cycle scavenging*, where the application ran as a screensaver application when the PC's owner was not working at the machine. In a more formal environment, cycle scavenging is performed using high-end workstations, sometimes in global teams, where users in one country use otherwise unused resources in another country several time zones away.

- *A server in a data center.* A drawback of cycle scavenging is that the time to solution may be unpredictable because the target resource may be busy or unavailable when it's needed the most. In this environment it makes sense to deploy grid nodes as nodes fully dedicated to support grid applications. Furthermore, the nodes need not be departmental. They can be part of a company-wide resource pool. Beyond that, it is not far fetched to think about a grid service provider business model not unlike Web hosting where the service provider does business with multiple corporate clients.

- *Clusters and parallel nodes.* The makeup of the nodes in a grid has no architectural restrictions. A single node can be powerful indeed, consisting of a multi-CPU or a computer with multiple core computers or even a cluster. We distinguish a grid from a cluster in that the computers in a cluster (also called nodes) are generally co-located in the same building. The nodes in a cluster may be joined by a specialized network with higher bandwidth and lower latency than most grid nodes. The tradeoff is that these specialized networks may be proprietary or single-sourced. The use of a proprietary protocol in a cluster is not an issue as long as the communication in and out of the cluster is through a standard protocol.

- *Embedded nodes.* At the other end of the spectrum, the nodes in a grid can be simple, dedicated computers. These nodes are said to be *embedded* in an application. Examples of this case are the computers used in networking routers, in wireless access points, and even microprocessor-driven, intelligent electric meters, or as a matter of fact, any utility meter: gas meters, water meters, or cable company customer premises equipment. Another example would be the swarm of networked surveillance and traffic cameras and environmental sensors deployed in a city.

On the network side, the physical medium varies with distance, from Infini-Band or Ethernet in a LAN if the nodes are close by to a Metropolitan Area Network (MAN), a citywide network that connects buildings or a Wide Area Network (WAN) if the nodes span continents or oceans. The communication protocol is almost always TCP/IP.

There is some ambiguity about what constitutes a grid application. Not every distributed application is a grid application. On the other hand, if the application is currently constrained in some way, a grid approach may provide could provide a strong guidance about how the application should evolve. For instance, a compute intensive application such as a finance derivative risk calculation or the solution of heat transfer equations in a data center thermal model might require hours to solve.

Because of performance and software vendor licensing requirements, a common solution environment is to run the application in a single, fast server through a queuing system. As the sophistication of the customer base and the popularity of the application increases, the user community tends to grow and the jobs submitted also grow in complexity and hence take longer to get processed.

If it takes a day or so to get the results of a run, the time to solution is not one day. More often than not there are clerical or technical errors in the run that force a re-submittal. Often a user needs to submit a whole series of parametric runs, each with slight variations in the data, and perhaps these variations are dependent on the results that came back from the prior run.

If it becomes possible to reduce the cycle time for getting results back from 24 hours to one hour the development time can be shortened considerably. Conversely, cycle times longer than what the user community deems reasonable can make users impatient.

A common recourse to shorten cycle times is for the software vendor to provide a multithreaded version of the application that can take advantage of a multi-core CPU or even multiple CPUs in a server.

If the workload overtakes the capability of the most powerful server the next step up is to run the application in a cluster. This can get expensive and the cost hard to justify if the workload is uneven or seasonal. At this point a grid based solution may be the most efficient way to proceed where workloads are offloaded to servers elsewhere in the company, or perhaps even to servers outside the company. This is not an easy feat because the original application might need extensive retooling to run in a grid environment.

Virtualization

Virtualization uses the power inherent in a computer to emulate features beyond the computer's initial set of capabilities, including emulating complete machines, including machines of a different architecture.

This is mathematically possible because all computers are in essence automatons, to be precise, a special class of automatons called *finite state machines*: A machine in a specific operating condition or state that executes one instruction will always yield the same result for that instruction. Automatons are deterministic in their behavior: the same stimulus under the same conditions will always elicit the same behavior. A virtualized version of a machine requires billions of state changes and a significant amount of scoreboarding, that is, the host machine simulating a virtualized machine needs to remember the state of the virtualized machine at every step of the simulation. Fortunately, this scoreboarding is maintained by the host computer, and modern computers are good at this task.

Simulating the motions, that is, state changes of the virtualized computer in the host computer, takes more work on the part of the host computer. It takes more cycles in the host computer to simulate one cycle in the virtualized computer plus the overhead of scoreboarding. This overhead can range from 5 percent in the most efficient virtualized environment to orders of magnitude of slowdown. 5 to 15 percent is typical of virtualized server environments where the virtualized and host machines are of the same architecture. If through virtualization a machine that originally had a load factor of 15 percent running one application is now able to host four applications at a load factor of 60 percent, this means that the productivity with virtualization is now four times the original productivity, and hence even 15 percent of overhead is a fair tradeoff for the value generated.

Virtualization is also justifiable in environments where the cost of the hardware is a small fraction of the delivered cost of the application or in data centers or when power or space limitations impose limitations on the number of physical servers that can be deployed in the data center.

One of the first applications of virtualization was virtual memory from research done in the early 1960s as we saw in the preface. Virtualization allowed machines with limited physical memory to emulate a much larger virtual memory space. This is accomplished by storing data in virtual memory space in some other form of storage, such as a hard drive. Data is swapped in and out of physical memory as it is used. One down side of virtual memory is that it is significantly slower than an equivalent physical memory scheme.

On the other hand, in spite of the slowdown, virtualization presents some undeniable operating advantages. The nodes in a grid are easier to manage if they are all identical. They need to be *virtually* identical, not *physically* identical.

Virtualization is playing a role in the current trend toward the separation of data, the applications that manipulate this data and the computers that host the application.

Service Orientation

The notion of service orientation comes from the business world. Any business community or ecosystem is structured as a set of services. For instance, an automobile repair shop service in turn uses services from power utility companies, telecommunications services, accounting and legal services, and so on. A client submitting a work request for an automobile repair uses a highly stylized process (interface) that is very similar to the system by other service providers: any automobile repair shop accepts phone appointments, has a reception desk, and has a billing desk. On the other hand, activities not directly related to the business at hand such as processes for tax payments, need not be exposed.

Services are *composable;* businesses providing a service use services provided by other business to build theirs through a process of *integration* or *aggregation,* as illustrated in Figure 1.2.

Services can be *recursively composable:* Intel purchases laptops from original equipment manufacturers that in turn use Intel microprocessors. Intel benefits from the manufacturers' capability to integrate microprocessors into their products. Recursion is depicted in Figure 1.2, with S_4 supporting S_1, but also making use of S_1.

The largest and most complex organizations devised by humankind such as federal governments and multibillion global companies rely on thousands upon thousands of services across the globe for their functioning, and providers of these services can be global organizations on their own right.

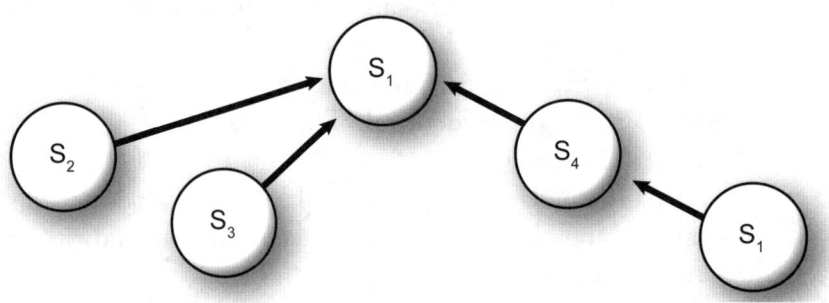

Figure 1.2 Composite Service S1 with Supporting Services S2, S3, S4 and S1 (through Recursion)

It would be difficult to imagine the largest automobile manufacturing companies if these companies had to also build core expertise in iron ore mining for building vehicles and drilling for oil.

Relationships in an economic ecosystem tend to be loosely coupled, sometimes very loosely coupled: once a car is sold, the manufacturer does not handle the refueling of the vehicle. The purchaser relies on a network of providers of energy services. However the energy services need to be there or the cars would not sell. This circumstance is what makes the bar for introducing alternative energy vehicles so high. The market for hydrogen-fueled fuel cell vehicles is very small today not necessarily because of the inherent complexities of the technology. It is also because the network of services that would support this emerging technology is not there yet.

Likewise, it could be argued that the market for pure electric or plug-in hybrid vehicles has not developed because of the range limitations of the available battery technology, making electric powered vehicles "too expensive," where too expensive means anything above USD 25,000. Yet traditional internal combustion engine vehicles in the range of USD 30,000 to USD 60,000 are not considered extravagant. This is not to say that electric vehicles are held to a different standard. This suggests that pricing may not be the real issue standing in the way of adoption. It is because the foundation services that would support a large market for electric vehicles are not developed: if every parking lot slot had a shock-proof inductive charging station, the relatively small range of these vehicles would be less of a concern.

IT applications and infrastructure expressly designed to function and support this service business world are said to be *service oriented*. A service oriented *architecture*, or SOA is any structured combination of services and technologies designed to support the service oriented model. There is no specific date or person associated with this technology trend. Rather, service orientation represents an evolution of preexisting trends, and it's certainly a product of its times. The adoption of service orientation accelerated considerably after the dot-com crash at the start of the twenty-first century, triggering an existential crisis for IT departments. One of the outcomes was a renewed effort to align IT with business need to underscore the value of technology in supporting business and possibly stave off reductions in force.

Service orientation is a transformative force today to the extent that the largest of the IT shops are retooling their operations behind SOA. The motivation behind this retooling is a significant reduction in operating cost.

Consensus in the industry has been building to align utility computing at least with business applications with the notion of service. A service in the generic sense is an abstraction for a business service. A service is defined by an interface. From an interface perspective, it can be as simple as a credit card purchase authorization that takes an account number and a purchase amount and returns an authorization approval. Or it can be as complex as the processing of a mortgage loan or almost any other business transaction, all the way up in complexity to a corporate merger or transnational agreement.

Services may be available from more than one entity and are discoverable (mechanisms exist to find them). Services are also fungible (an alternate provider can be substituted) and interoperable: If an alternate provider is chosen, the service must work.

Services also provide a binding mechanism or contract that can be sorted out right up to the moment the service is invoked. This binding mechanism can include functional specifications (the specific items exchanged during an invocation or transaction) or nonfunctional specifications, usually items related to quality of service (QoS) or service-level agreements (SLAs).

There are certain similarities between services and the notion of methods, procedures, or subroutines in programming languages. The difference is that services transcend programming languages and apply to business processes or, as a matter of fact, almost any human activity.

The need for the capabilities brought up by the notion of services was voiced by software engineers and language designers as far as the early 1970s. It is only today, during the first years of the twenty-first century, that the state of the art has advanced to allow this dream to be realized. The first incarnation of the notion of services has been attained through Web services as the mechanism for conveying information and the use of XML as a universally understood data format.

In a services environment, a fundamental assumption is that IT systems and processes are aligned and designed to support the notion of services. IT entities that conform to this notion are understood to be service oriented. Finally, IT entities that are put together (architected) to conform to service orientation are understood to follow an SOA.

In theory, every service could be built uniquely from the ground up. This strategy would be horrendously expensive because certain basic and common functions would need to be replicated. One common example would be the employee roster for a company, where one copy of this information would be maintained by human resources to keep track benefits, another by IT telecommunications for the phone directory, with several subsets scattered all over the enterprise. Most information systems started as local efforts and grew into more or less isolated silos. Service-oriented silos would bring no advantages over traditional silos. In fact, we can claim that SOAs bring no extra capabilities that could not be attained through traditional means. The advantage of SOA is mainly economic.

Because services are fungible, they also become reusable: Each time a service is reused, we have an instance of a service that does not need to be re-implemented. Because IT services are designed aligned with business, there will be less of a semantic gap in adapting them to existing and new business uses In a mature SOA environment, very few services will be built from the ground up. Most services will be built out of pre-existing services by composing or compounding already available services.

Applications built this way are said to be *compound* applications. There is no limit to how deeply this composition process can be implemented within applications, except for possible performance or organizational barriers.

A service in general can essentially be any human activity. IT practitioners deal with a more restricted notion of service. Although a service can trigger a physical activity, such as requesting the visit of a residential appraiser as part of home mortgage filing, a service in the sense of information technology needs to have a computerized front end that allows the service to be invoked or summoned by other services. The most commonly used technology to invoke a service is Web services. In this context, and elaborating on the initial discussion in the preface, we call the embodiment or realization of a service a *servicelet* or *microservice*.

In other words, a servicelet becomes the building unit for a compound application. It is usually implemented as a self-contained unit of hardware and software. Servicelets are designed to be combined with other servicelets into a compound application using Web services technology. A servicelet may be a service, but not all services can be used as servicelets unless they have the appropriate front end.

SOA is not free. Functionality cannot be deferred to other services ad infinitum. The buck needs to stop somewhere with an application that does the actual work, and this functional piece needs to be implemented at least once. Systems in an SOA environment need to be designed for reuse at additional effort and expense. For instance, making a service discoverable by other organizations usually means maintaining a service repository. This repository could be very informal, in the form of word of mouth or e-mail queries when architects and implementers know each other. Or it could be a formal universal discovery, description, and integration (UDDI) repository accompanied by Web services definition language (WSDL) mechanisms for describing services end points.

Instituting an SOA environment involves trading off extra costs upfront that will impact a project against a long-term common benefit. This is invariably a tough call, and a transformation toward an SOA environment will not happen without a deliberate top-down plan in place.

On the other hand, the strategic benefits SOA brings change the rules of the game. They are associated with organizations at the most advanced stage of the Gartner Infrastructure Maturity Model, where a policy-based environment is the norm, or in the last stage of enterprise architecture as documented by studies at the Massachusetts Institute of Technology (MIT)

Sloan Center for Information Systems Research (CISR), which shows that business modularity becomes ingrained in the organization's culture.

In this environment, IT resources can be repositioned swiftly to support almost any strategic and tactical need. An example of a tactical request would be a sales and marketing campaign in response to specific market conditions.

These goals become achievable not necessarily because the data center's physical plant can be grown at will, although an increased capability will become available, but because SOA allows rearranging and reusing existing resources in response to these needs.

IT becomes an instrument for business growth instead of a limiting factor. Discussions about IT budgets center on value—about how much IT will contribute to the business—instead of on a certain request can't be fulfilled because it would cost too much.

Service orientation first became known at the application level, and hence when we hear *SOA* we usually think of business applications. Actually, the effects are profound at every level of abstraction in a business.

Virtualization + Service orientation + Grids = Virtual Service Oriented Grids

Virtual service oriented grids have developed as a distinct subspecies from the original grids targeted to run high performance computing applications. This evolution broadens the market appeal of the original HPC grids. The original HPC grids continue evolving with emphasis on performance.

There are two distinct flavors of enterprise grids depending on where the hosting hardware is placed, namely data center grids and PC grids. PC grids are the contemporary descendants of the original workstation grids and may still be used as hosts for cycle scavenging. Nodes in PC grids are assigned to specific individuals in an organization. Figure 1.3 depicts the relationships just described.

Data center grids use server-based, anonymous nodes in the sense that the nodes are not assigned to specific users or even applications. Cycle scavenging in a data center setting is possible but rarely practical. Placing cycle scavenging under a separate administrative structure to sweep up computer cycles not used by the primary application would be a lot of hard work for little return for increasing server utilization. This scheme would be subject to significant political hurdles because of the opposition of the main application owners. It makes more sense to assign workloads to servers in a consistent and comprehensive fashion with all loads sharing an allocation of prioritized server resources instead of making a distinction between a primary workload and a cycle scavenging workload.

It could be argued that because there is a distinct owner for a laptop client, the scavenging model still makes sense. However, because the distinction between client and a server will blur, as will the distinction between "fat" and "thin" clients, the scavenging model for PC clients will also become obsolete. What we are left with is a set of service based applications to be run and a set of pooled hardware hosts to run them. The decision on where to run the services will eventually be made by the operating environment subject to the appropriate policies.

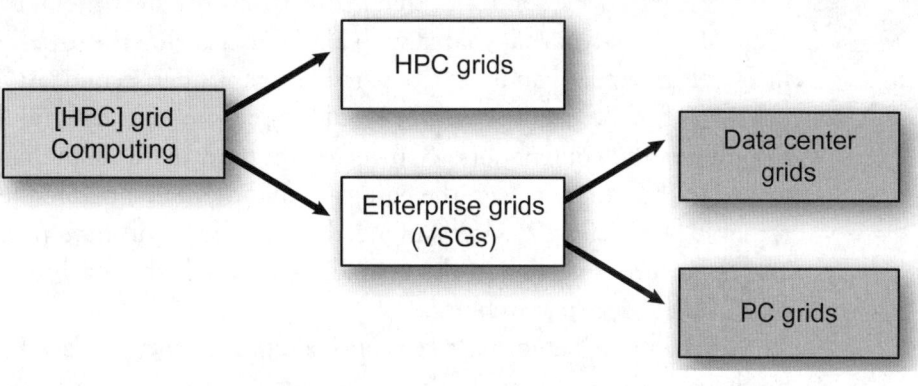

Figure 1.3 Grid Genealogy Showing the Evolution the Initial HPC Requirements for Low-cost, Scalable Computing to Grid Computing Today

This book is about the convergence of virtualization, service orientation and grids the analysis of this trend suggests looking at data in a different way. Somehow this convergence is leading to the dissociation of data, the applications that manipulate this data and the computer hosts that run the applications.

In a virtualized grid environment data is no longer bound to a machine, and hence protecting a machine from theft makes no sense. Data becomes disembodied; it is just present when it's needed and where it's needed and in a form appropriate to the device used to access it. Data might look to programs and users as a single entity, for instance as a single file. In actuality the system will store, replicate, and migrate the data to multiple devices, yet keeping the illusion of a single logical entity.

Laptop Loss Management Service Revisited

One would think that connecting a laptop to an always-on grid would provide a communication link to determine its location and to recover the asset or at least recover the data in the laptop's storage devices. Unfortunately we are not done yet. Some additional considerations are necessary.

Assume for the moment that it was possible to establish a WiMAX wireless link to an AWOL laptop. How much would it take to retrieve the contents of the hard drive? A WiMAX channel has a theoretical bandwidth of 75 megabits per second. But that is the bandwidth of the total traffic into a tower. This bandwidth is shared with all the users using the tower. A user will likely see an actual bandwidth of 2 to 4 megabits per second. At 4 megabits per second, if we do the math, it would take close to seven and a half days to pull out the contents of a 320-megabyte hard drive. If the hard drive is locked in the trunk of a car, the battery would drain first before the data were retrieved. Even if the device is plugged in, the thief will have plenty of time and opportunity to disrupt the upload, especially if the machine turns itself on and the lights start to blink.

Furthermore, being able to establish a link with the misplaced laptop does not help at all in addressing the UK incident because the misplaced storage devices did not have a laptop attached to them.

From a virtual service oriented grid perspective, the laptop represents just a terminal node in a connected computing grid. If the laptop as a device is combined with a data presence service, the laptop and the user's data can be treated independently. The hard drive in the laptop becomes just a caching device for the user's data. The control and ownership of the data is a separate problem and an excellent discussion topic. Suffice to say at this moment that the user decides how much is cached locally. The user may have concerns about uploading certain data to a storage provider. However if certain data is bound to the laptop, it will be lost with the device.

This issue aside, with a data presence service, the only data that needs to be recovered may be the last few files modified that might not have been uploaded, and the system state data that would allow the laptop to be replicated should the original machine not be recovered.

Once cached data has been uploaded, which might take a few seconds instead of a week, a system administrator can send a command to disable the laptop.

The administrative actions would be implemented through a hardware infrastructure such as the Intel® vPro™ technology and the specific data recovery actions would take place under control of a trusted platform module or TPM supported by the Intel® Trusted Execution Technology.

In the considerations for building a laptop loss management service so far it is important to note that a solution cannot be devised without taking into account associated business processes and usage models. The process consideration is what allowed the data recovery to be performed in seconds instead of a week.

Because data exists in disembodied form in the grid, supported by a storage servicelet, the UK government incident would not have happened in the first place. All it would take to do the interdepartmental transfer would be to send instructions electronically on how to link, retrieve, and decrypt the information for data that exists in the computing cloud.

What we have done so far in this section is analyze the problem at three logical levels:

- *Physical requirements*, including the compute engine (laptop), and the network (WiMAX links)

- *Application requirements*: running an application with good user experience may be latency sensitive and hence require large amounts of data cached in the laptop. On the other hand, if the user runs a Web-based client no local storage at all may be needed for mailboxes.

- *Data business requirements*: local laws, company rules, and personal preferences may dictate data that stays in the laptop even though, from a technical perspective it is operationally easier to migrate it to a storage provider. If the laptop is misplaced, it will take longer to recover the data if certain data is bound to the laptop.

For instance, in Chapter 3 we will see a manifestation of the same pattern in when we describe the *physical grid, the visible grid,* and *the business grid.*

Structure of Virtual Service Oriented Grids

Instantiations of virtual service oriented grids come under multiple guises, in what is known as Cloud Computing, the Service Oriented Enterprise, Enterprise 2.0, Web 2.0, the Predictive Enterprise and other concepts that combine distributed computing with a high level of integration between business and IT.

The implementation of these environments can also be understood in terms of three layers as illustrated in Figure 1.4:

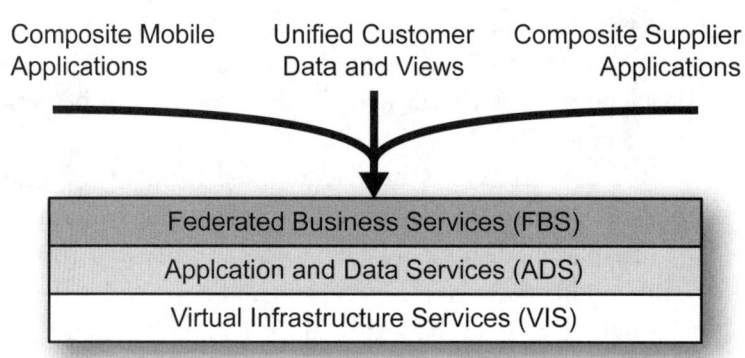

Figure 1.4 Abstract Three-Layer Structure for Virtual Service Oriented Grids

Any of these environments will support composite supplier applications and integrated supply chains. It will also support unified customer data and views. For instance, a customer booking a travel itinerary using a Web interface provided by American Express may be presented with information from a number of reservation systems, which may include Sabre, Galileo, Amadeus, or Worldspan. The American Express application integrates and provides a single, unified view to the end user from diverse resources. The American Express travel reservation application is an example of a *federated* or *compound* application.

Likewise, mobile applications, such as the e-mail service provided through a PDA, are constructed in a similar way.

The highest logical layer we consider for virtual service oriented grids is that of *federated business services* (FBS) built out of servicelets or microservices.

For the American Express example, the supporting reservation systems named above are the constituent federated services from which this application is built.

The next layer down comprises the *application and [technical] data services* (ADS). We use ADS as a generic term for similar terms developed in other disciplines and contexts. The ADS layer is made up by a collection of servicelets. Other authors use SOA to denote this layer or even Web services, given that Web services is the technology of choice for binding servicelets together.

At the bottom layer there exists a collection of physical resources from which the servicelets in the ADS are implemented. These resources are not accessed directly; they are made accessible through virtualization technology.

The resources above collectively denote the *virtual infrastructure services* (VIS) layer. Similar concepts have appeared in other contexts under the terms of service oriented infrastructure (SOI), utility computing, virtual infrastructure, infrastructure services, and the virtual data center. Using a mechanical analogy, the physical infrastructure acts like the engine that powers IT, and virtualization acts like a gearbox to make sure the engine's power is allocated efficiently among the wheels in the vehicle. Ideally, in this virtualized engine environment, each wheel would "feel" as if it had the engine to itself, enough for it to spin, but not so much that it causes handling problems for the vehicle.

This moniker FBS is relative, because any federated business service may have a software layer to export its capabilities and make them usable to other applications, in which case the FBS is also an ADS. Terms associated with federated business services are the *Semantic Web*, the *dark* or *deep* Web, Web 2.0 or Web 3.0, and composite applications.

Collectively, any set of federated business services is said to implement a computing cloud, a service oriented enterprise (SOE), or the notion of the Predictive Enterprise (Intel) or Enterprise 2.0.

Figure 1.5 exposes the next level of detail of the virtual service oriented grid decomposition shown in Figure 1.4. From a logical perspective, outsourced services, shown as the little clouds on the on the side of Figure 1.5, are seamlessly integrated with peer internal offerings and treated the same. The end user may not notice much functional difference. There may be differences in the cost to provide the service and in the QoS experience.

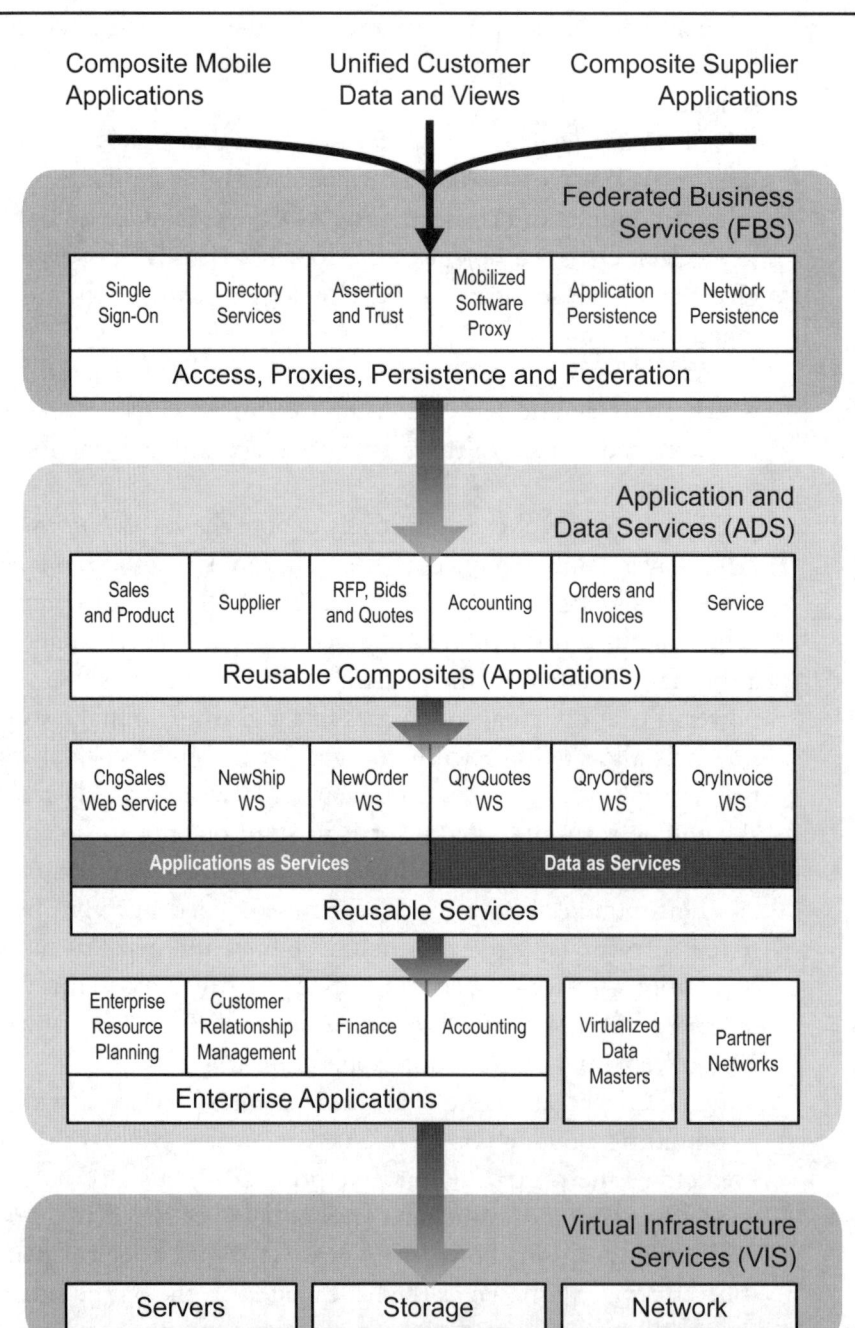

Figure 1.5 Detailed Logical Structure of Virtual Service Oriented Grids

The application and data services layer encompass the two "slabs" on top of the virtual infrastructure services slab, comprising traditional, single-vendor enterprise applications. Data at this level, identified as "virtual data masters" may be in a proprietary format. As technology evolves, the traditional applications are retrofitted to work in an SOA environment through the addition of middleware, essentially software "shims" that enable these applications to provide exportable and inter-operable interfaces under Web services technology. Doing so opens up applications and data to be used as servicelets or service components from which to build applications. This slab is represented by the reusable services slab in Figure 1.5.

The addition of software shims to pre-existing applications represents the better known *inside-out* model for SOA adoption, covered in detail in Chapter 2 and shown in Figure 1.6, whereby in-house applications are exposed as servicelets to be coupled through the use of Web services technology. In this layer the proprietary data of the layer below is exposed by transforming this data into XML format using a schema appropriate for the data context.

The availability of inside-out servicelets radically lowers the cost to deliver applications under new modes and models, such as mobile applications using cell phones, PDAs, ultra mobile PCs (UMPCs), mobile internet devices (MIDs), radio frequency identification (RFID) supply chain applications, and cloud computing mashups. These applications are delivered at the federated business services layer. The integration of federated business services provided by third parties leads to the *outside-out* model of SOA adoption, also covered in Chapter 2.

28 ■ The Business Value of Virtual Service Oriented Grids

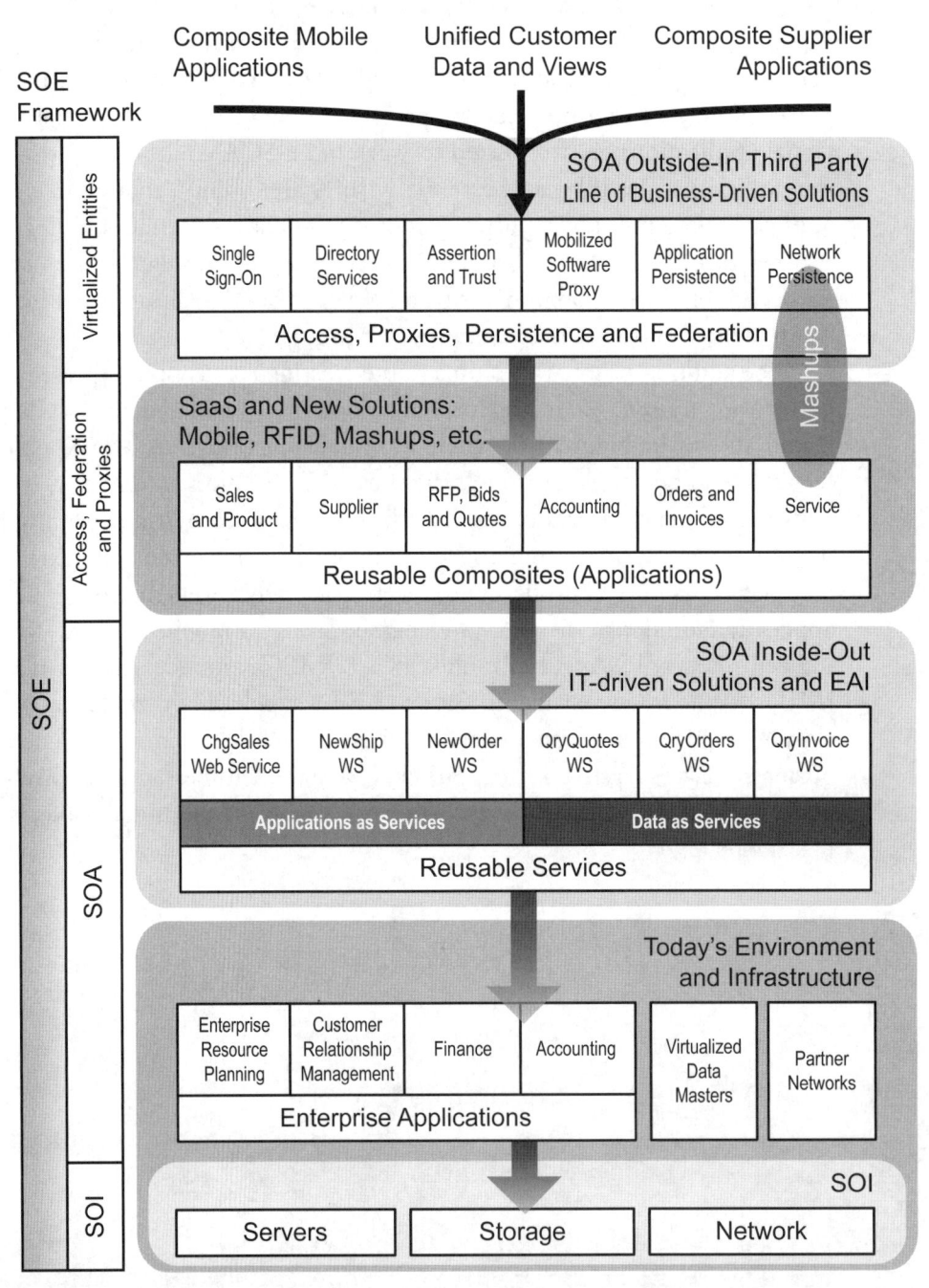

Figure 1.6 Technology Trend Analysis for the SOE Framework

We will revisit the laptop loss management service once more and architect one possible solution within the SOE framework described in this section after we have had the opportunity to look at business and architectural trends, the evolution of technology, standards, and integration issues in the intervening chapters.

End Points for Virtual Service Oriented Grids

The traditional notion of grids is normally associated with entities at the virtual infrastructure services level. The ideal VIS is one that can harness distributed, federated resources to attain a desired time-to-solution. The ideal VIS is infinitely scalable, with no serial bottlenecks allowing architects to select an acceptable technical solution within the cost versus time to solution continuum.

The same holds true for a virtual service oriented grid solution, with a broader scope. A virtual service oriented grid solution encompasses most any *business* problem addressed by IT, not just a technical problem. Furthermore the solutions actually represent a continuum, not the single points of more traditional approaches, allowing leeway for trading off cost versus implementation time.

If we look at grids as the physical underpinnings of virtual service oriented grids, skeptics often claim that grids are not ready for prime time. If anything, the opposite is true. Grids represent an advanced technical architecture that has been around for at least ten years. The main holdup for adoption of grids has been application integration. Our three-layer model comprising virtual infrastructure services at the bottom, application and data services in the middle, and federated business services at the top illustrates this dynamic starkly. A lot of work has been done on the engineering part. Much work remains at the application and business levels in figuring out how to integrate virtual infrastructure entities into smoothly functioning applications, and even more so in coming up with killer business capabilities.

A single CPU today is more powerful than a cabinet full of computers fifteen or twenty years ago. Does this mean that a computer today can solve a problem in a hundredth of the time it took to solve it that many years ago? Only under the right conditions.

Leaving this trend unchecked without making system and business level architectural improvements the time to solution becomes only marginally faster. Faster CPUs mean that the CPUs will spend more idle time without much improvement to the time to solution. Bringing up multi-core technology will make the problem even worse if no action is taken.

This pattern has been well documented in data centers as administrators have observed server utilization rates trending down over time. The trend cannot be ignored. It not only negates the investment made in improving processor technology. It has an impact on the bottom line in the form of capital expenses to acquire more servers and in the cost to administer and maintain the servers at a time when data centers have space limitations and are limited in power draw by the electric utility. This trajectory is not sustainable. In advanced economies, data centers already consume anywhere between one and two percent of the country's electrical energy production.

To summarize our discussion in this chapter, in the preface we made a very brief pass at the foundation technologies for this book, namely virtualization, service orientation, and grids. In this chapter we made a second, more detailed tour, mainly from the perspective of looking at the architectural underpinnings and the pain points that each technology addresses. In Chapter 8 we will make yet one more pass, this time with more emphasis on IT deployment considerations.

Chapter 2

Virtual Service Oriented Grid Convergence

The competitive difference is not in deciding what to do, but in how to do it... Process....is paramount.

—Lawrence A. Bossidy, Chairman of Honeywell Inc.

In the first chapter we discovered that although the concepts of virtualization, service orientation, and computing grids arose at different times and even in separate industries, it is becoming increasingly difficult to treat them as separate entities: in the current state of the computer industry the developments in these three areas have been overlapping and feeding upon each other, such as in the case of the concept of virtualization for enabling resource pooling in grids. These developments will transform how business is done in very essential ways, not because of the availability of new technologies as such, but because of a fundamental remake of the underlying value economics

This is not to say that new technology developments brewing as we speak are not intrinsically useful. From a business transformation and re-engineering perspective, some industrial trends beg for introduction into the foundation of a company's business operations to radically increase competitiveness. This chapter describes these trends and their relationship to this virtual service oriented grid, and then its economical benefits in the long run.

Capability, Process, and Maturity in Business Transformation

In this section we will see that technology adoption always takes place within a social and economic context. If a community is not ready for an invention, it will not take root no matter how wonderful it might be. On a smaller scale, the adoption of a new technology is a time-dependent phenomenon, which leads to the idea that its adoption is a function of organizational maturity and requires that the right processes be in place.

The converse is also true: As organizations and nations evolve and mature, they reach points in which change becomes almost obligatory. These transition opportunities can manifest themselves in one of multiple ways. Often it comes in the form of a crisis where a fundamental contradiction needs to be addressed. At other times, a moment of opportunity just arises, waiting to be discovered and plucked. A classic example is the development of the Apple† iPod†. The success of the product after its launch in 2001 did not depend on any single breakthrough technology. The genius of the idea was to combine a number of technologies that had been developed during the Second Internet along with a content distribution system. This distribution system was less than perfect but was something that content owners and consumers could live with.

The Second Internet itself illustrates the technology adoption dynamic. The First Internet was the research network financed by DARPA starting in the late 1960s. The transition to the Second Internet took place when the US government stepped out of funding the Internet and the continued development transitioned to the private industry[1]. This led to the dot-com and e-commerce bubble and subsequent bust in the 2000 to 2002 timeframe, where we had the case of technology racing ahead of society's capacity to absorb it. In the Third Internet we are witnessing a number of sustainable commercial successes (finally) for the Internet technologies developed in the 1990s.

With the iPod, Apple has captured the *zeitgeist* or spirit of the times for the Third Internet just perfectly and has enjoyed a spectacular commercial success because of it.

---

1   The milestone for this transition is the publication of the report *Realizing the Information Future, The Internet and Beyond*, ISBN 0-309-05044-8 by the NRENAISSANCE Committee in 1994 describing the role of the future NII or National Information Infrastructure replacing the NREN or National Research and Education Network.

A Rhetorical Question

Let's start our discussion with two rhetorical questions and a thought exercise: if a person in the early nineteenth century had been given an automobile would it have enabled that person to travel from one city to another in half the time that it would have taken to do the same on horseback? Second, if one of the armies in the Thirty Years' War[2] in seventeenth century Europe had been given automatic rifles, would it have changed the outcome of the war?

The answer is likely negative in both cases. A key observation is that both an automobile and an automatic weapon are *system* products that have meaning only in the social and economic context in which they were built.

Looking at an automobile, the hapless nineteenth century traveler would have no clue about the purpose of an automobile; that is, there would be no applicable usage models. Even if by some miracle that person learned how to operate the vehicle, it would be impossible to refuel it because the technology to manufacture highly refined gasoline [petrol] did not exist then and most existing roads would have been all but impassable. The support system that exists in the twenty-first century that includes manufacturing, a supply chain, a supplier network, and the road network simply was not available at that time.

Likewise, with the automatic rifles, assuming the soldiers did not accidentally kill themselves, the amount of damage would be limited by the ignorance of tactics for fighting with automatic weapons. Without a military-industrial complex behind the soldiers, it would not be possible to resupply and refurbish the weapons. Once the initial allotment of ammunition was spent, the weapons would be as good as clubs. Another problem would be that the system of interchangeable parts would not be invented for another three hundred years, and hence the notion of putting bullets in a metal casing and expecting them to work in any weapon would have been an alien concept.

Most of the systems mentioned in this book are complex. We will introduce a number of paradigms that we can use as tools to derive insight into the behaviors of complex systems. As in the application of the scientific method, capturing every nuance would be beyond the reach of the human brain. Instead we build models that reflect some essential characteristics of

---

2 The Thirty Years' War lasted between 1618 and 1648, ending with the Treaty of Münster. It was fought mostly in what is Germany today. Combatants included Sweden, Bohemia, Denmark-Norway, the Dutch Republic, France, Scotland, England, Saxony, the Holy Roman Empire, Spain, Austria, and Bavaria.

the system under study. The model is successful if the relationships it reveals have a predictive capability. The model is not necessarily reality nor unique. It provides a framework for humans to understand relationships of the subject system.

One such framework is *logical layering*. A complex system gets sliced into two or more levels in a divide-and-conquer approach. The assumption is that explaining a system's intricacies is simpler one layer at a time where each layer has a narrower scope than the entire system.

One example of logical layering can be applied to the automotive industry, shown in Table 1.1.

Table 1.1 Logical Layering for the Automotive Industry

Logical Layer	Description
Business Proces	Entities at this layer include transportation policies, regulation, and taxation as well as energy policies.
Network	Highway system, vehicle distribution system
Infrastructure	Energy supply system, vehicle factories, manufacturing and supplier system
Application	Mass transit, school transportation, personal transportation. A transportation "application" can be constructed out of one or more services; for instance, a mass transit application may have transit centers with feeders from taxis and parking for private vehicles.
Service	Vehicle-related services: Bus, shuttle bus, taxi, self-service, privately driven passenger vehicle, shared car pooling.
	Auxiliary services: leasing, towing, repair, insurance, dealers
Platform	A vehicle is usually one member of a "platform" sharing some mechanical subsystems and manufacturing processes. For instance, the second generation Toyota Avalon belonged to the same platform as the Camry, Sienna, Lexus RX300, Lexus ES, and the Toyota Highlander. The vehicle instances of a platform can be quite different: the Camry and Avalon are sedans, the Sienna is a minivan and the Lexus RX300 is an SUV.

This table implies that any new technology would require complementary processes, applications, services, and infrastructure at each layer to make technology really useful and realize its real potential.

Later in this book we will learn that logical layering is not sufficient to explain the processes we'd like to cover, especially to explain Web 2.0 phenomena. We introduce complementary paradigms as we get deeper into the material.

A quintessential example of logical layering is the seven-layer Internet ISO/OSI[3] model and associated TCP/IP stack. Chapter 3 covers the layered Internet architecture.

The Internet Age

The power of the Internet as a technology has been ranked as important as the inventions of electricity, the internal combustion engine, and the computer itself. Its ubiquitous access of information not only affects how people access the information but also fundamentally impacts how business organizations operate. Here are just some examples:

- FedEx encourages its customers to keep track of the package through its Web site. Why? It costs USD 2.14 to track a package if customer calls its customer center, whereas it only costs USD 0.04 when tracked by customers using the Internet. It saves FedEx 600,000 queries a day.
- The healthcare provider Humana Inc. spent USD 128 for each individual job application and resume that it processed manually. Through online job application, it only costs USD 0.06.
- GE is saving about USD 600 million a year just making one third of company procurement online.
- IBM also dropped its purchasing costs by USD 6.5 billion in two years after putting the procurement process online. Better yet, its contract cycle time has declined from one year down to 30 days.

Just like the automobile and rifle examples described before, the Internet is not a standalone technology that can make all these benefits happen immediately. The impact of the initial research on computer networks done at DARPA in the late 1960s and early 1970s remained limited for two decades. The acceleration of the growth of the Internet would not start until the invention of the World Wide Web at CERN in the early 1990s. It took more than 20 years for the Internet technology to propagate around the world and establish the current form of a global network. The Internet is much more than the technology itself, such as the e-mail system, browser applications, the HTML language, and the World Wide Web information repository.

---

3   International Standards Organization Open Systems Interconnection model.

Yet this is just the beginning of the Internet future. As powerful a tool as the Internet has proven to be, only a minute portion of its potential value has been realized. Getting a shot at fully realizing the benefits of the internet involves reengineering business operations, realigning resources, and putting together a collaboration network with external business partners and customers that benefits all concerned.

Danny Hillis, the legendary cofounder of Thinking Machine Corporation, pointed out a common problem of adopting the Internet at a speech at the Santa Fe Institute:

"All companies think of e-commerce as an add-on to their existing business. I call this the drive-in window mistake. When cars first came along, many businesses just assumed that they would add a drive-in window but that the rest of their business would essentially remain the same. The real impact of cars was to move shopping traffic from downtown to the shopping malls. Suddenly, realize it or not, everyone was in the shopping-by-car economy. In the same way, all business is becoming e-commerce. Adding a Web portal to your existing business is like adding a drive-in window to a downtown department store. Instead, information drives the entire process from discovering products to select them, transporting them, servicing them, and managing the relationship with the customers. Managers must rethink their entire business."

The history of the Internet is still being written, and by definition, the definitive outcomes will not be evident until we have them in the rear view mirror. However the fact that the specific outcomes are not known does not mean that planning and strategizing becomes a fruitless exercise and that this planning is starting from zero knowledge. Totally to the contrary: an awareness of the Internet as an agent of change suggests a fundamental rethinking of business processes. One example is the concept of X-engineering to be discussed in the next section on the classic marketing dichotomy between pull (demand creation) and push (direct selling).

About X-Engineering

"Incremental change is fruitless when it comes to embracing a technology that by definition creates radical business change." James Champy, Perot System Chairman of consulting practices and the coauthor of the bestselling book *Reengineering the Corporation*[4] said in his book *X-Engineering the Corporation*[5]. X-engineering requires that you rethink your whole business and all its relationships, not just with customers but also with suppliers, partners, employees, and competitors alike. The success of Solectron is a good example.

Solectron is a quietly brilliant leader in the little-known field of electronics manufacturing services (EMS). Solectron manufactures circuit boards, computers, routers, and communication equipment sold by well-known companies like Cisco, Dell, and Intel. Solectron not only competes with its EMS industry players but also needs to provide better quality with lower cost for its customers. Toward this objective, Solectron reengineered its entire business operations and manufacturing processes to promote seamless collaboration through the Internet with partners and customers. In the EMS industry, raw material constitutes a large portion of cost. Forcing suppliers to cut on material costs merely passes the problem to someone else and in the long term it is not a sustainable strategy, if it can be considered a strategy at all. Solectron instead focused on streamlining operations to reduce unnecessary costs and improve profit margins, both to Solectron and its suppliers. The manufacturer opened its internal ERP information system to its material providers, who in turn monitored the inventory of certain materials and supplied them in time to reduce the inventory cost. On the client side, Solectron elected to get deeply involved in the customers' product design. This level of interest opened a window for customers like Dell and IBM into Solectron's manufacturing processes in a confidence building exercise about Solectron's ability to manufacture superior products. Solectron also integrated its design and manufacturing teams with the customer's product design team. Sharing information and processes enables timely and correct decisions, which translates into a quality product delivered on time. Solectron is a two-time winner of Malcolm Baldrige National Quality Award for manufacturing.

Traditionally, business processes have been viewed as proprietary, kept secret to create competitive advantage. But X-engineering is transforming the processes to include not only the employees inside of company, but also the

---

4   Michael Hammer and James Champy, *Reengineering the Corporation: A Manifesto for Business Revolution*, Collins Business Essentials (2003), ISBN 0-0605-5953-5.

5   James Champy, *X-Engineering the Corporation: Reinventing Your Business in the Digital Age*, Business Plus (2003), ISBN 1-4466-7897-X

customers and ecosystem suppliers outside the company. The emphasis is the collaboration among all the participants to create larger value. The company secrets still remain under its control, but encapsulated in the technology made accessible to other stakeholders.

Technology deployment must go beyond automation of existing processes. It involves the rethinking of how a company's IT is implemented. It must go beyond the typical perception if IT as a cost center to the company. In this context, IT becomes the critical foundation for the success of such business reengineering within the broader scope of X-engineering processes. Going back to the FedEx example earlier in this chapter, the Web tracking system provided by IT becomes a tool for customer satisfaction and an essential part of business.

In his book *X-engineering Transformation,* James Champy highlighted two crucial characteristics of the new business processes, the pull of customers and the push of processes, and three key principles of implementation, *openness*, *mutuality*, and *interoperability*.

The notion that companies should be *customer driven* has been heavily promoted, but it is also ranked near the top of any list of most-ignored management dicta. Over the last decade with the Internet boom, heeding the cliché that *customer comes first* has actually been conferring a competitive advantage to companies that have followed the practice and started to change behaviors accordingly. The arrival of e-commerce provides consumers new powers to provide product feedback and selections with just a few mouse clicks. Consumers have much more variety of choices to select from and, better yet, they can compare the features and price side-by-side a task that was not practical prior to the ascent of the Internet. Does this visibility mean a challenge to manufacturing and service companies? No, the new order also creates an incentive for companies to look into their business processes seriously to discover new ways to compete and thrive. This incentive may prompt companies to improve coordination with their suppliers to control the inventory, perfect designs to fulfill customers' needs, shorten decision-making processes to improve time-to-market and so on. In other words, this customer *pull* or demand has demanded the company to develop a cross-organizational *push*.

Dell is one of the pioneers of such a vision. Michael Dell has often said "The Internet has allowed us to bring our customers and our suppliers inside our business to achieve shared efficiencies and greater loyalty." Some 90 percent of Dell's suppliers are now connected with the company's production line via the Web. The result is that Dell has reduced its inventory from 13 days' supply in 1997 down to 5 days' supply today, saving more than $50 million a year. Its state-of-the-art OptiPlex plant in Round Rock, Texas, can produce 20,000 computers a day with fully automated manufacturing processes for electronic order, computer assembly, computer customization, and shipping, but surprisingly the plant is managed by only half a dozen people.

Champy describes three implementation principles of X-engineering. These principles provide a profound insight into how to travel through this journey.

- *Openness*: There is always a risk to make company information too broadly available both for internal employees and outside partners or customers. This risk must be balanced against the benefits of a new market opportunity and streamlining company operations. This openness not only allows people to improve the transaction outcomes between vendors and clients to mutual benefit, with easier access of information; it also allows participants, that is, vendors and clients, to make better decisions with the right information.

- *Mutuality*: It creates a mutual commitment among the company, its partners, and its customers. Partners and customers demand the predictability, consistency, and reliability of the services. In turn, companies can understand their internal processes better: which processes are common but don't add much value and which are the company's core differentiators. With this information the company can then improve the quality of these services to ensure the service availability.

- *Interoperability*: This involves the company in defining the information interfaces and standard processes that allows partners to work with the company to exchange the information automatically and efficiently.

Interestingly, these X-engineering implementation principles are very much aligned with the principles of virtualization, service orientation, and computing grids.

Service orientation and its implementation in terms of Service Oriented Architecture (SOA) actually have been available for quite some time. But with the latest development of XML technology, SOA emerges again as the methodology to architect and implement company-wide and partner-to-partner collaborative architecture. The philosophy of SOA is to break up large, monolithic applications into small, reusable components, to align them with the business flow, both internally and externally, and then aggregate them into reliable services.

Accomplishing this goal involves a full examination of a company business strategy, its dependencies on business partners, and the needs of customers. The next step in this exercise is establishing a collaboration matrix and defining interfaces to ensure the availability and reliability of services. The exercise eventually leads to the creation of an interdependent business model that is both cost effective and efficient and competitive. This is exactly the spirit of three principles described by X-engineering.

In building a service oriented foundation, resource grids and virtualization are useful technologies for implementation with the same consistent set of design principles. Grid and virtualization technologies also break up the boundaries of infrastructure resources inside and outside the company into more flexible utility-like resources that can be deployed on demand.

Amazon.com has been a rising star since the inception of E-commerce and Web-based applications. Its major business has been online shopping, which started off with bookselling and then extended over to electronics, furniture, clothing, food, toys, in an increasingly broader line of businesses.

However, Amazon.com's strategy has also evolved in the last few years into becoming a business service provider to Amazon.com's ecosystem as well as the entire industry. Amazon.com wants to use its state-of-the-art USD 10 billion online store facility to assist in running other companies' businesses, initially small startup companies but eventually other medium and even large enterprises.

During the Internet boom period, Amazon.com spent billions of dollars perfecting their online operations, inventory system, and merchant distribution network. Now, Amazon.com wants other companies to reuse the infrastructure that they built, improving the efficiency and economies of scale of these business customers in the process.

Amazon.com's offering includes the Simple Storage Service, or S3, for which Amazon charges USD 0.15 per gigabyte per month to store data and programs on its vast array of disk drives. It also charges other merchants about USD 0.45 per square foot per month for real space in its warehouse.

Amazon.com also sells the Elastic Compute Cloud service, or EC2, renting computing power starting at USD 0.10 an hour for a basic server. Linden Labs, the well-known Second Life service provider, is an Amazon.com customer using this service to handle the fast growing demand of computing resources from its popular online virtual world.

From Silos to Networks

At this point we have a good understanding of the industry trends toward a more collaborative environment, how this collaboration is reshaping business processes, and how virtualized service oriented grid technologies are supporting this transformation. A collaborative environment represents the end state of a maturation process from an initial differentiated state. We will explore the transformation process in the following subsections.

On the Need for Solution Stacks

Historically engineering solutions to business problems have been built as logical stacks. An example of a stack is depicted in the automotive example in Table 1.1. The common term of industry *vertical* is easy to understand in this context and so well accepted that it is never put into question.

The development of a new technology usually occurs in a sparse environment: for multiple reasons there are few entrants at the beginning. There may be formidable technical barriers that prevent additional players from entering the arena, and the few participants may be fiercely competitive and secretive.

Industry verticals tend to develop in a particular environment. In a particular vertical segment, solutions tend to be developed in relative isolation within a niche. Developers in emerging fields usually have their hands full creating something that works to the point that they rarely look sideways to other industries, and the integration process for building a solution eventually acquires the shape of a stack. Traditionally there has been little functional sharing across industry vertical or even within instances in an industry vertical where players are in competition. Figure 2.1 illustrates the outcome of this process.

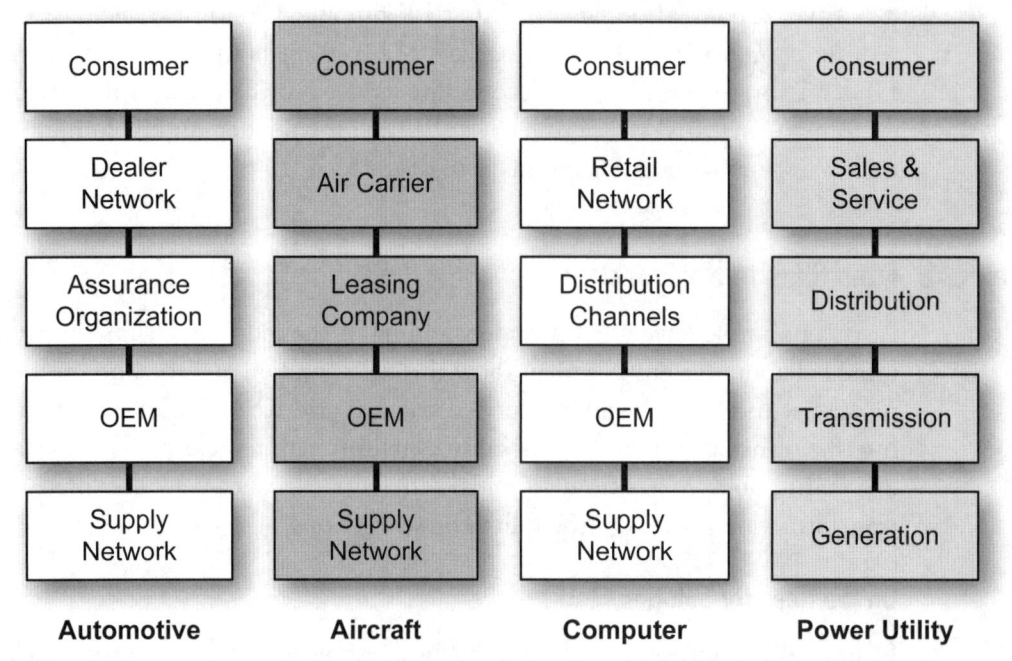

Figure 2.1 Silos in Industry.

Left unchecked, this pattern is also pervasive in large organizations, where the word *silo* comes to mind. For instance, a trademark of low-maturity IT organizations is the prevalence largely independent or autonomous IT at the group or even at the departmental level. In the absence of helper processes and technologies, silos require less inter-organizational coordination and hence are easier to build. However, the pain comes later in the form of duplication of resources, loss of critical mass in purchasing power and the extra cost involved in data reconciliation.

As a matter of fact, silos can develop at any level of a logical hierarchy. An industry can be "siloed" at one level but not at another. For instance, in the computer industry the infrastructure level used to be highly siloed, where even keyboards and monitors came from the same manufacturer until the PC revolution of the mid 1980s when it became possible to build computers from modular components assembled from a diversity of suppliers.

The components of a silo represent fully dedicated resources. This fact is not a major consideration in an emerging field: the demands imposed on a solution or system may not be high to begin with, and the capability to build a silo may be an accomplishment unto itself especially if the player is a first mover and time is of essence to have a solution ready before the competition.

As the emerging field matures and evolves, the basic capability brought up by the system becomes less of a differentiating factor and new considerations come into play, such as cost of delivery, reliability, availability and speed of provisioning and deployment.

At this point the original silo architecture is no longer optimal and its structure becomes a liability. A silo, being built out of dedicated resources may exhibit excellent quality of service once it's built. However, in the larger scheme, this approach is not cost effective.

The Merging of Silos and Rise of Collaboration

Cross-silo conflicts can trigger titanic corporate battles behind the scenes. More often than not these battles do not reach the public eye. On some rare occasion they surface in rather spectacular ways. One stark example is the debate over the "white spaces," on the comments solicited by the US Federal Communications Commission (FCC) regarding the use of the portion of the electromagnetic spectrum vacated in the transition from analog to digital TV. One group of companies, including Microsoft Corporation, Intel Corporation, and Samsung Micro-Electronics began lobbying the FCC to open this spectrum to mobile Internet services. A while later Samsung Electro-Mechanics' parent company, Samsung Electronics countered with another lobbying push *against* allocating the space to mobile Internet services. It turns out that Samsung Electro-Mechanics builds the company's components and chips, an activity that would benefit from allocating the spectrum to mobile Internet services whereas Samsung Electronics, responsible for building digital TVs and other consumer products, was concerned about possible interference with TV reception.

More often than not, for actors within the system it is difficult to identify or even acknowledge the contradictions that are playing out and when the system is about to hit a wall. The usual symptoms for these contradictions are an unbridgeable stalemate, runaway costs and an endemic inability of organizations to deliver a technical capability that business demands, including recurring missed schedules. Unfortunately, these symptoms are nonspecific: cost overruns occur all the time and it's essential to differentiate when an event has happened due to a structural change rather than to short term fluctuations in business.

The temptation is to continue refining the current path to manage risk. However the status quo may actually be riskier because it presents openings for new players to enter the field aiming for an upset victory. These are periods where staff morale may be on the decline because the runaway costs may be managed through mandated cuts.

The breaking of a silo can open economic opportunities for potential participants in a broad industry segment, leading to a period of spectacular growth. During this period newly founded companies like Dell in the earlier example became market leaders, whereas the stars of former leaders like Digital Equipment Corporation dimmed. This company was eventually acquired by Compaq.

What are the phenomena associated with silo breaking? Silo breaking is a discontinuous phenomenon triggered by a gradual reduction of integration costs for a complex system. This gradual cost reduction is facilitated by technology evolution and can simmer unnoticed for a long time until a tipping point is reached.

While costs of integration remain high, the most economical and viable method for building a system or solution is by growing a stack vertically. When the tipping point is reached, the economics of the silo no longer hold true. However the transformation that takes place after the tipping point occurs is not painless. More frequently than not, the incumbents who build the initial stacks have an economic interest vested in the current methods and will actively or passively resist the changes because of the short-term setback of business condition, or even attack new players who have come to realize the opportunities that are opening up.

Land's End in Dodgeville, Wisconsin is a good example for such transition. When its chairman, David Dyer, took his company online, it was a simple extension of its profitable mail-order business. "We did it because it perfectly leveraged our infrastructure and is a more profitable model long term."

But when Mr. Dyer made the move and cut its catalog circulation by 18 percent to reduce costs, the result was a disaster. Catalog sales of clothing for adults, its core business, dropped 9 percent, and its stock plummeted from USD 80 to USD 36.

Eventually Land's End started to evaluate the online design and created a new model for customers to interact with. One of the features is to allow two friends to shop together, each using his/her own computer. Another is to show the shopper how to select a swimsuit by entering the information of body shape and advising certain styles to avoid the "anxiety zones." At the same time, 400 phone operators were trained in how to guide the customers through the Web site and answer the phone or even use instant messaging.

All these changes were new to Land's End when they designed the online services. By analyzing the new business model and implementing new business processes, the company eventually turned around.

The year after the new changes went into effect, Land's End doubled online sales that accounted for 11 percent of total revenue, and experienced 20 percent growth of new customers, who were younger than its existing 35–54 year-old customer base.

Emerging technologies are making it easier to share resources across silos and even share stack components across silos. Companies find it easier to outsource what they consider non-core business functions such as payroll processing or even customer support. The main driver for these actions is cost arbitrage. Also note that the unit of sharing is far smaller than what each of the blocks in Figure 2.1 represents. Establishing these relationships in the first place require concerted and elaborate negotiations that might take several months to close.

In a virtualized service oriented grid environment, technology allows the service "atoms" to become far smaller. These atoms could be a terabyte of storage priced on a per month basis, or a single server instance. The server may be a virtualized server instance, with specifications defined by a service level agreement (SLA). Other examples are single seats for a specific application or an electronic mail service mailbox.

The units of service become so small that negotiations by humans are no longer practical. This is where standards for service discovery and description play a significant role.

Another essential characteristic of a virtualized service oriented grid environment is that the atoms become commoditized and fungible, that is, interchangeable. The user of a service can choose from among many providers of similar services.

Technically, the silos have not disappeared. Looking at a single company, it is still possible to build a logically layered diagram similar to the one depicted in Table 1.1. This approach is still useful for the analysis of a single organization.

However, when we look at multiple silos at once, we can see that the constituent atoms are functioning as layers in a stack and that some atoms are shared across stacks. This view is depicted in Figure 2.2. With technology maturity economies of scale introduce a strong incentive for reusing and sharing the atoms across stacks even when doing so introduces complexity and reduces architectural flexibility. Complexity is managed through open standards. The presence of standards is another indicator of technology maturity.

An automotive instance of Figure 2.2 is cars from a common platform marketed by two different manufacturers, such as the Chevrolet Prizm and the Toyota Corolla and the Pontiac Vibe and the Toyota Voltz based on the Toyota Matrix. These cars were manufactured at the New United Motor Manufacturing Inc. (NUMMI) plant in California for General Motors and Toyota.

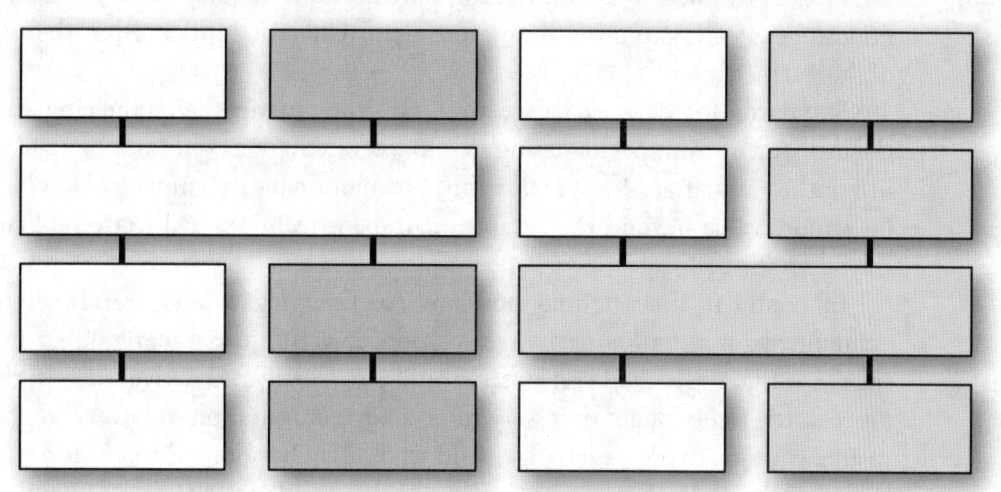

Figure 2.2 Integration through Outsourcing and Offshoring Breaks Silos and Leads to Shared Stack Components

This collaborative transformation is currently occurring in the industry under the rubric of service orientation. And true to prior revolutions, the implications of this change are hard to fathom at this early stage. However, the potential business and economic implications of this transformation are profound and go well beyond simple service substitution.

One example brought up by Andy Mulholland[6] is the comparison between the approaches used by eBay and more traditional electronic commerce (EC) hubs popular during the dot-com boom. The EC hubs were considered revolutionary in the 1990s, enabling economies of scale among trading partners.

A decade later, the jury has returned with its verdict: Most EC hubs failed to fulfill their promise and have been scaled back or dismantled altogether, whereas the rise of eBay has been nothing less than meteoric. Why? It turned out that the EC hubs were less than revolutionary, essentially a remake of the traditional IT siloed approach in a monolithic implementation that the partners deemed too inflexible.

---

6 Andy Mulholland, *From Big to Small: Moving from Monolithic Applications to Granular Services*, in *The Emergence of Grid and Service-Oriented IT*, Tabor Communications, ISBN 1-4276-0025-2.

Frequently there was one trading partner more "equal" than the others imposing its will, garnering little more than reluctant support from the rest of the partners.

Standards for data exchange were far from mature, guaranteeing that the investment from participating in a market exchange could not be re-used in another exchange. In actuality this "revolutionary" technology provided little more value beyond the extant, incumbent technology, Electronic Data Interchange or EDI.

In contrast, eBay figured out how to disaggregate and rearrange the components of a market exchange solution, lowering the integration cost to the point that individual consumers could participate and derive value in the process. It was no longer necessary to be a large corporation to be able to play in an electronic market exchange. And what eBay has done is to create a new business paradigm that generates the customer pulls for the real demand in real time and also creates a real-time push for the merchandise providers.

On this note, and at the time of writing, one problem that no one has figured out is how to deliver IT services to individual consumers. Today IT services are seen as a drag on business. Large corporations have the heft to shoulder the cost and provide these services to their employees. Small and medium businesses (SMBs) squeak by through a combination of bare bones in-house services and hiring managed services providers (MSPs).

An entrepreneurial organization that manages to turn this challenge upside down looking at IT (and customer services) as a business opportunity rather than a drag to the bottom line will become the next eBay.

Complexity and inscrutable technology represents an endless source of complaints from end users. Using computational resources, eBay has managed to hide enormous complexity behind a simple and intuitive interface. The authors believe, at least at the application level, that service oriented IT will be an essential ingredient for cracking this nut. Other authors have analyzed this problem from a business process perspective[7].

Another classic example is the dynamic behind the adoption of the automobile. It followed the emerging technology paradigm of siloed early development: in the late nineteenth century, every automobile was painstakingly built by hand down to the engine parts. At that point the automobile was very much an instrument for early adopters with significant disposable income.

---

7   James P. Womack and Daniel T. Jones, *Lean Consumption*, Harvard Business Review, March 2005.

Deployment thinking did not go much beyond simple stack substitution where the incumbent propulsion mechanism (the horse) was replaced by an internal combustion engine (or steam engine, or an electric motor). The term *horseless carriage* reveals the thinking behind the early usage models. Controls were unique for each vehicle make with little standardization.

The genius of Henry Ford was to apply systems thinking. He had an early platform (the Ford Model T) and established the personal transportation service model. His innovation went well beyond that, including the concept of assembly line at the infrastructure level, and he even worked at the business process level by paying factory workers more than the prevailing wages to stimulate demand for Ford Motor products. Although more vertically integrated by today's standards, for instance by owning a rubber plantation in Brazil, Ford Motor became one of the first large-scale system integrators developing a fairly sophisticated supplier network[8].

Organizations that can avail themselves of the appropriate emerging technologies and understand the underlying dynamics of this transformation process have an excellent opportunity to create new and sustainable competitive advantages and new business models, unlocking value that will foster long term growth.

A similar model can be built to analyze the aircraft industry. For instance, the Boeing 737 series can be construed as an aircraft "platform" with multiple model instantiations: the 737-100, -200, -200C, -300, -400, -500, -600, -700, -800, -900, and -900ER. It is not too difficult to continue building this model at the application, infrastructure, network, and business process levels.

These examples may seem far fetched, but examples exist closer to home. We can look at the history of computation at Thomas J. Watson's putative 1943 statement[9] "I think there is a world market for maybe five computers" actually made sense for the computer usage models of the time, such as calculating ballistic tables for the U.S. Army and Air Force.

The number of computers has been expanding as the audience has been expanding, from a few thousand by the mid 1950s as the first commercial applications took hold all up to several hundred million today counting PCs and portable devices.

---

8   Howard P. Segal. Recasting the Machine Age: Henry Ford's Village Industries. Amherst: University of Massachusetts Press, 2005. xvi + 244 pp., ISBN 978-1-55849-481-7.

9   Extensive research of T. J. Watson's writings and speeches has not yielded evidence that he ever made it.

The bottom line is that as the original stacks as illustrated on the left hand of Figure 2.3 start sharing more and more components as shown in Figure 2.2, the stack paradigm becomes less and less useful. At some point there are so many touch points between stacks that a graph, shown on the right hand side of Figure 2.3 becomes a more understandable representation. It is easier to think of applications as being built out of shared service components. Applications built this way are known in the industry as *compound* applications.

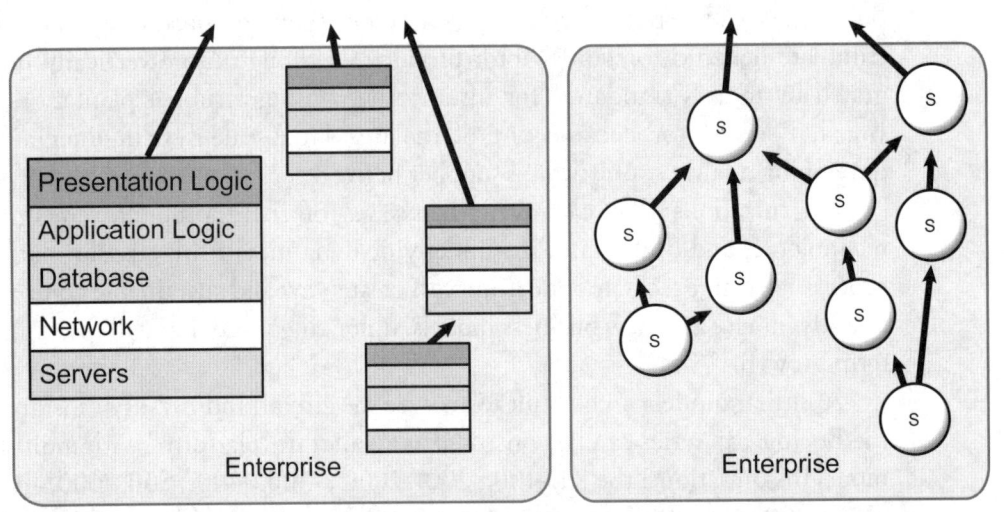

Figure 2.3   From Silos to a Network of Services. Cross Feeds across Silos Become Pervasive.

In this new environment, computing grids, or more specifically, virtual service oriented grids provide a convenient way of abstracting useful capabilities of collaborating collections of computers. As in the technologies that preceded it, the concept of grids started in a restricted context: high performance computing as a way of harnessing the computational power of networked workstations that otherwise lay idle. The scope of applicability has been expanding to selected industries: the financial services industry and oil exploration analysis. The circle of applicability for grids keeps expanding to this date.

One research study done in 2005 by Dr. Robert Cohen, an economist and fellow of the Economic Strategy Institute, indicated that the increased availability and ease of use of computation resources will encourage people to use those resources more often and this will in turn eventually stimulate demand for more computation resources. This demand will not be driven for demand's sake but because service consumers become aware of the benefits of the technology and invent more ways to apply it.

Here is an example of demand fueled by the agility that the new technology affords: if a financial risk analysis can be done within two hours instead of two days, with the pain of waiting lessened, the analyst will be encouraged to run the analysis more often than they do now for deeper insight into the processes under study. In other words, the newly acquired convenience starts to change people's behavior. The PC revolution is another good example compared to old mainframe computer usage. Since the computation power on a PC is much more capable than before, people can run different financial scenarios on a spreadsheet to analyze the best portfolio investment in a very short time. In turn, this creates demand for a more powerful PC. Computing grid technology tracks that trajectory exactly. With the flexible computing resources on demand, it will enable companies to analyze different scenarios effectively to address market changes.

The transition to a pervasive service network environment as depicted in Figure 2.3 lays the foundation for establishing an industry-wide scalable infrastructure for delivering future applications. Figure 2.4 depicts this new environment. An enterprise combines services from different *Service Oriented Providers*, or SOPs, perhaps combined with some homegrown services as a secret sauce. This leads to a flexible IT infrastructure capable of supporting end-to-end business processes both internally and across partners. The compound applications supporting these processes can be built and torn down in a snap by recombining constituent components.

Each enterprise will have a business-specific view of the data and components, essentially the focus of their business and differentiating factor. This *weltanschauung* or worldview, to borrow the term from philosophy, is very powerful. It is consistent with the computer science principles of separation of concerns and abstraction. This means that an entrepreneur with an idea can realize it very quickly by recombining services that are available in the market without having to build an IT infrastructure from the ground up. The Web 2.0 family of technologies is another manifestation of this principle.

This pattern is actually very old. A locomotive designer in the nineteenth century would not have been able to build an engine within a lifetime if the tasks started with prospecting, mining, and transporting the iron ore and coal. Had it not been for a mature steel industry delivering a range of grades of steel with known properties and even standardized sizes for nuts and bolts, the design task would have been impossible to carry out.

Our subject enterprise in Figure 2.4 may decide to export some of their services, effectively becoming another SOP delivering services to other service consumers. Amazon.com is an example of an industry leader. The chain ultimately ends with the consumer. The consumer may be blissfully ignorant of the fact that the whole world behind the product she or he has just purchased, or at least the IT world has changed. The only difference is in performance: packages arrive a bit faster, there are fewer quality problems, and when problems do occur, they get resolved quickly.

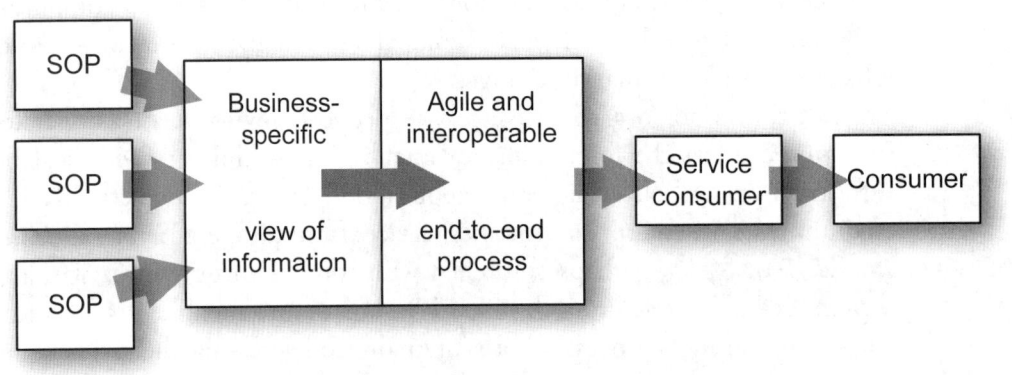

Figure 2.4   Services Architecture and Scalable Infrastructure

Most discussions today on virtualization, grids, and even service orientation emphasize technical and technological aspects and are essentially static. The inclusion of business and economic considerations allows building a more dynamic picture to draw educated guesses of the evolution of these technologies during the next five to ten years and discovering some of the opportunities that change will bring.

There are some observations that are not obvious from a first look at Figure 2.4.

- *Dynamism increases.* A case in point: the initial siloed environment on the left of Figure 2.2 does not preclude outsourcing: a company may outsource payroll, expensing, and e-mail options. These negotiations are performed by humans and may take months to complete. Significant disaggregation occurs as we move to the right in Figure 2.3. The number of service components grows to the extent that human intervention is greatly diminished. The integration is accomplished by architects and implementers using automated tools, or may become totally real time and automatic through the use of standardized discovery and interface description mechanisms.

- *Application development and integration cycles are radically shortened.* Under the traditional development model, the bulk of the time was dedicated to a phase characterized by design/ compile/ run cycles until the software was ready for a release, at which point work shifted to an assemble/ configure/ monitor phase, typically taking a fraction of the time spent in the first phase. A service oriented development model still calls for a development phase, but typically the cost of development is paid only once up front and is often borne by the independent software vendor (ISV) supplying the software. The solution assembly phase does not take more than in the old times and often a lot less due to the greater degree of tool sophistication today.

- *Rapid virtual service oriented grid deployments are enabled by standards.* The adaptive business networks just defined work because a high degree of interoperability is a given. A maturing industry provides the impetus for players, in spite of their competitive concerns, to gather together and do the work up front to ensure that offerings from different vendors work together. The dynamic playing here is that the synergy of the greater good brings much more value than the price to be paid for conforming to standards.

The Economics of Service Orientation

Virtualization and grid computing bring costs down by enabling the reuse and sharing of a physical resource, leading to a more efficient and higher degree of utilization for that particular resource, whether a computer or a network.

In this section we will explore structural economic changes brought up by service orientation. Most IT organizations today are under enormous pressure to keep their budgets in check. Their costs are going up, but their budgets are flat to decreasing as illustrated in Figure 2.5. The restructuring brought about by the concept of services and the reuse at the service level promises long lasting relief from the cost treadmill.

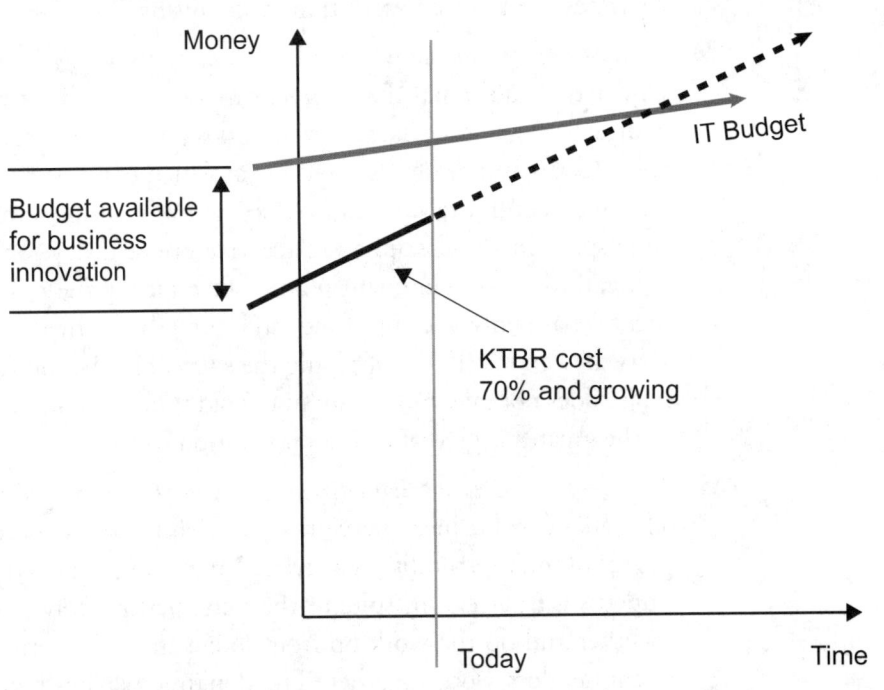

Figure 2.5 The Overwhelming Cost of Legacy.

In a certain sense, service orientation does not really bring new capabilities. Yet it has the potential to bring about profound changes because of the economics involved. Service orientation radically reduces the cost to bring in certain capabilities. We illustrate some of the cost dynamics in the four diagrams. Conceptually, a portion of IT budgets is used to maintain existing projects. This portion is important because is the part that "keeps the business running" (KTBR). In most IT organizations, the KTBR portion takes the lion's share of the budget. The downside is that the KTBR is backward looking, and it's only the leftover portion that can be applied to grow the business. There is another problem: the KTBR portion left unchecked tends to grow faster than IT budgets overall, and the situation is obviously not sustainable.

A number of strategies have been used in IT organizations to keep the KTBR growth in check. Let's take outsourcing for instance as shown in Figure 2.6. When outsourcing (and perhaps off-shoring) is brought in, costs actually go up a notch as reorganizations take place and contracts are negotiated. Once the outsourcing plans are implemented costs may go down, but still have the problem of sustainability. Another issue is that costs are growing faster in countries providing services, so in a few years these countries will reach parity.

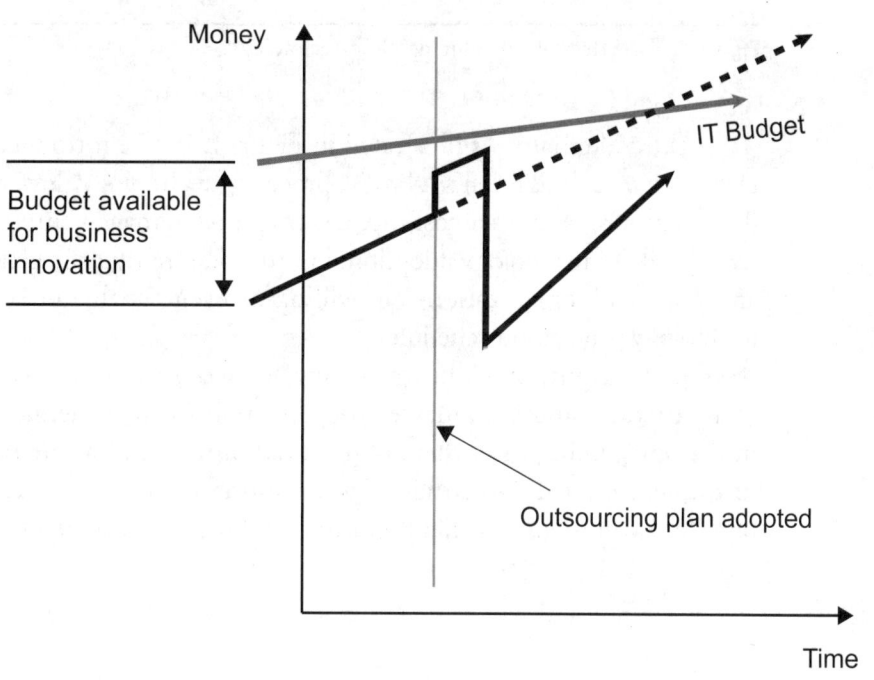

Figure 2.6 Effect of Outsourcing.

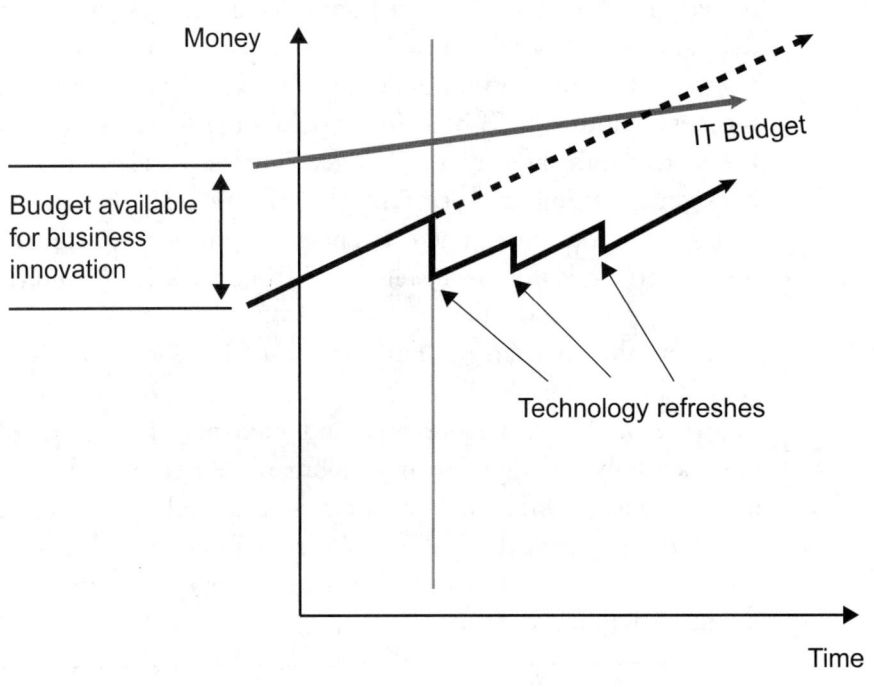

Figure 2.7   Effect of Introducing New Technology.

A third alternative is illustrated in Figure 2.7: The introduction of a new technology, such as Intel® vPro™ processor technology, lowers the cost of doing business, seen as a cost dip. Costs can be managed through aggressive "treadmill" of technology adoption, but this does not fix the general uptrend, and not many organizations are willing or even capable of sustaining this technology innovation schedule.

Finally, Figure 2.8 illustrates how service orientation eventually leads to a structural and sustainable cost reduction to the synergies of reuse. As in the outsourcing case, there is an initial bump in cost due to the upfront investment needed. Note that this transformation may take years to accomplish and will require difficult cultural and organizational adjustments.

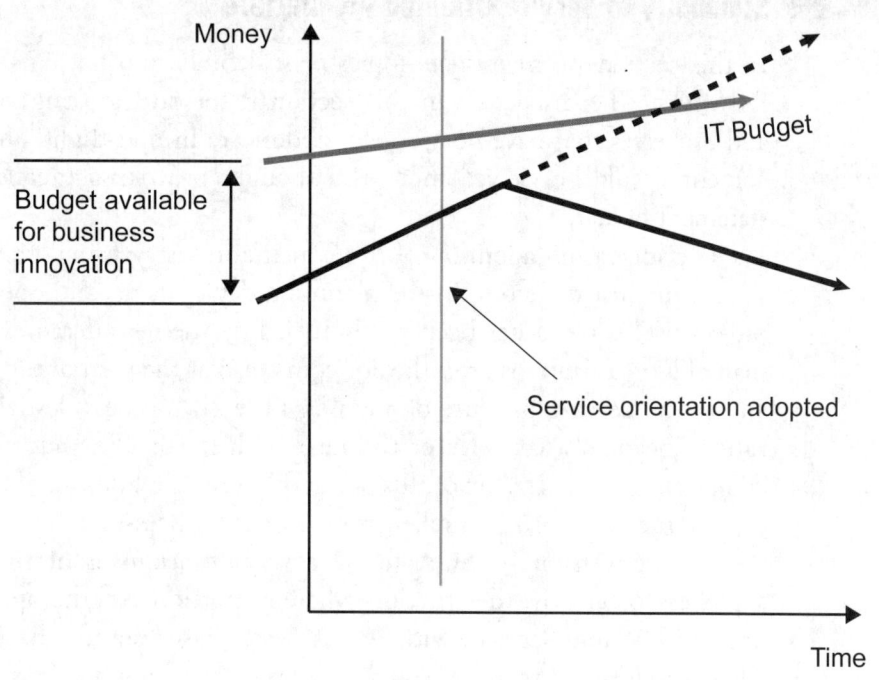

Figure 2.8 Structural Cost Reduction Attained through the Adoption of Service Orientation.

Service orientation brings a discipline of modularity that has been well known in the software engineering community for more than 30 years, but had been little applied in corporate-wide IT projects. As previously mentioned, the goal of service orientation is to attain a structural cost reduction in the delivery of IT services through reuse and standardization. There may be more upfront costs for architecture and planning as well as consideration for interoperability and security. However the benefits of modularity and interoperability will pay back as more and more services are developed and reused to attain the same results as we have seen in software engineering today.

In the end, aligning IT with business at a reasonable and predictable cost is a challenging problem. The best solution is attained through an integrated strategy that includes business process improvement (in the form of service orientation), technology, and an appropriate business strategy.

Scalability of Service Oriented Architecture

In this section we investigate topics of scalability and patterns of adoption for SOAs. The discussion in this section is forward looking, about events and processes that have not yet occurred or are in mid-flight, and hence the content should be viewed more as a thought provoking exercise than as a statement of fact.

The increasing adoption of SOA in the industry brings the promise of significant cost reduction in the planning, deployment, and operation of IT projects. This trend has been partly fueled by the near-death experiences of many IT organizations after the dot-com crash at the turn of the millennium and the increasing pressure of aligning IT with business, lest these organizations become a casualty of the next budget cut. The added regulatory compliance characteristic of this period has brought additional incentives to explore means to bring in relief from regulatory pressures.

The conversion to SOA for legacy applications is attained through a process of creative destruction whereby portions of the application are decomposed into services with Web services based standardized interfaces. These services can then be reused to support other applications. Conversely, new applications can be built by composing these services through their standardized interfaces.

The adoption of SOA in business computing environments is growing due to the promise of significant cost reduction in the planning, deployment, and operation of IT projects through reuse. However, the organic transformation from legacy enterprise applications to SOA applications has occurred mostly in large enterprises. Small businesses have largely been left out of the SOA transformation. We will see that an SOA approach is equally applicable to small and medium businesses (SMBs).

We describe a new pattern for the adoption of SOA and service delivery beyond the better known role of SOA in large enterprise transformation.

Through business-oriented services developed and delivered by independent service providers outside of corporate firewalls, small business can pick and choose the services they deem valuable. They can "mash up" these services to best serve their business needs following the SOA service integration concepts much in the same way it's done at large enterprises. Hence, for small businesses, SOA will no longer be an abstract concept and the exclusive game of large enterprises anymore. This is the *outside-in* pattern for adoption for SOA in contrast to the better known, conventional *inside-out* pattern seen at large enterprises.

To summarize, under the conventional inside-out approach services are built by composing simpler services from within the organization, whereas the outside-in approach assumes that smaller organizations will be able to build services from service components available in the ecosystem and offered by service integrators. Service integrators in turn may choose to build their offerings by using service components from other vendors. There is a potential for a rich and diverse ecosystem to develop.

The impact on SMBs is noteworthy due to the large potential audience: according to the US Small Business Administration, in the United States small businesses represent 99.7 percent of all employer firms and employ half of all private sector employees (http://www.sba.gov/advo/stats/sbfaq.txt).

This outside-in view of business-oriented service could become the guidepost for pervasive SOA adoption and transform how small businesses use computer technology.

We also realize that the outside-in SOA model may take a while to develop. Several significant technical barriers must be overcome requiring a concerted effort from industry players. The technical challenges are small compared to changes to business processes and social behaviors of people involved in business transactions of small business operations.

However, just as we witnessed in the adoption of the Internet and Web 2.0 for the consumer market, as long as we can deliver compelling benefits and lower barriers of entry, such an adoption can and will happen.

An awareness of this dynamic will help players identify opportunities for value added, service consumers and suppliers alike.

The Initial Siloed State

Following the familiar evolutionary pattern described earlier in the chapter, corporate applications have been deployed as stovepipes, as illustrated in Figure 2.9, one application per server or server tier hosting a complete solution stack. This state is essentially the state defined on the left side of Figure 2.3 Ironically, this trend was facilitated by the availability of low-cost Intel-based servers fifteen years ago that encouraged using the physical server as the unit of deployment.

Under this system physical servers are procured, in a process that takes anywhere from two weeks to six months. When the servers become available, they are provisioned with an operating system, database software, middleware, and the application. Multiple pipes are actually needed to support a running business. Some IT organizations use as many as 15 staging stovepipes to phase in an upgrade for the Enterprise Resource Planning (ERP) SAP application.

A first step toward an SOA transformation is to break some of the silos into smaller logical components and add Web services front ends to make these components available to other present and future applications. At this stage redundant components are identified and retired. The world that started looking like Figure 2.1 now is starting to resemble Figure 2.2.

Hence, with SOA, monolithic applications are broken into standardized services. Installing Web services front ends represent an extra development cost whose payoff is not immediate. In the beginning implementation teams may find the extra work to enable future re-use under an SOA discipline disruptive. Cultural and behavioral aspects need to be addressed to ensure the extra work for the greater good of the organization gets done even though it is not directly aligned with the immediate goals of the project. A significant amount of evangelizing and awareness campaigns will be necessary, and even then, the cultural shift will be slow and arduous.

Eventually a breakeven point is reached where the extra implementation cost of a given project is balanced by the global savings from reusing past projects. The end goal is to attain a positive balance sheet. This is not the time to give up on evangelizing, because the savings may not be visible to individual organizations, only to organizations that can observe multiple projects.

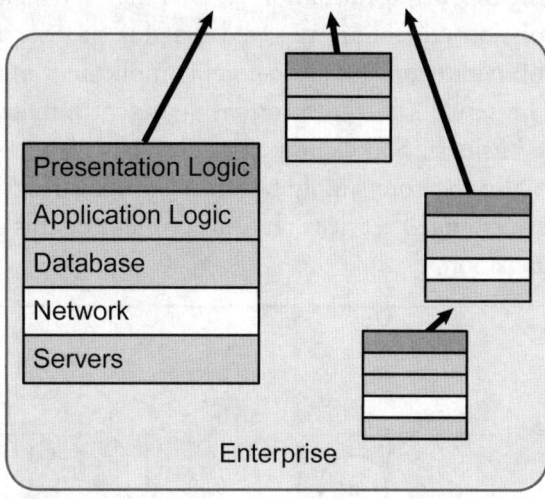

Figure 2.9   Traditional Application Stovepipes

Inside-out or Conventional SOA

Figure 2.10 illustrates the transition to SOA for a large organization. Stack layers have been replaced by service components and there is so much reuse that the stacks have all but disappeared.

Enterprise architects may find that some of the functions are generic and can be replaced by offerings from third party vendors. Note, however, that the consideration of "generic" is a function of the state of technology and the ecosystem. For some organizations it might be HR applications; for others it could be mailbox services or even a whole ERP implementation.

Even if the transformation is executed flawlessly from a technical perspective it may still cause disruption and pain: the original portfolio of internal services shrinks into a smaller and smaller core. If internal services are replaced with outsourced services at a lower cost, costs overall will go down. The smaller core will almost certainly lead to staff reductions and skills rebalancing. There will be less application development in house and a need for people with business and technical skills managing service vendor relationships.

The SOA transformation process may start small where services that are not mission critical are targeted first for substitution, while the IT internal development teams focus on core, complicated, mission critical services.

The services in the core may represent intellectual property (IP) critical to the business. Some companies may have few restrictions in this area, and eventually the core simply becomes so small that it's indistinguishable from other outsourced services. The attainment of this state completes the inside-out transition.

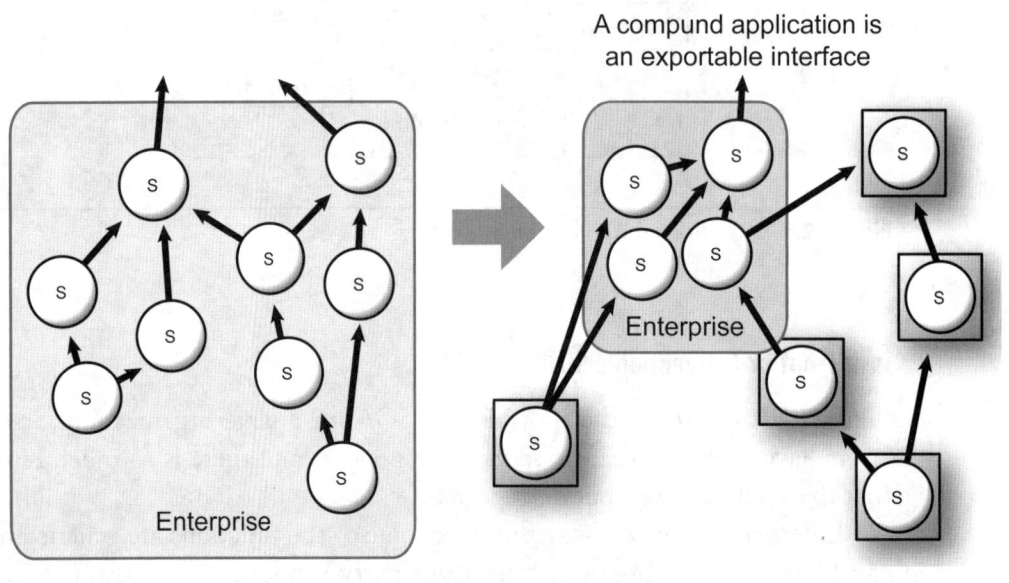

Figure 2.10 SOA in the Large Organization

Outside-in SOA: SOA for Small and Medium Businesses

In the previous section, we witnessed the transformation from inside-out to outside-in in large companies. In this section we will see that the same evolutionary process can be naturally extended to small and medium businesses (SMBs.) The difference is that the processes take place on whole ecosystems instead of a single large company.

By their very nature, SMBs do not usually have the luxury of a large IT budget, or a large IT department. Many of these companies have only a few IT literate employees acting as part time IT support. They would not be able to afford the "internal-only" SOA adoption model. Hence SMBs do not have the critical mass to establish the internal services portfolio for the inside-out process.

However, if we assume that large enterprises become first adopters for SOA, and in so doing a market for services gets created, SMBs can leapfrog the whole inside-out process. SMBs can start purchasing services from the outset. In fact once the ecosystem matures the inside-out model will become as obsolete as it is building in-house applications from the ground up today.

In a mature SOA environment, SOA compound applications will be built out of predominantly outsourced services. Figure 2.11 illustrates the concept. A well defined business process (such as purchase order creation and processing or a bank transaction) is represented by a set of SOA services instantiated by different users and integrated into a user solution supporting and driven by business need. In essence, the process of picking and choosing the right pieces for their businesses by SMB owners would look very much like a mash-up in the Web 2.0 world today.

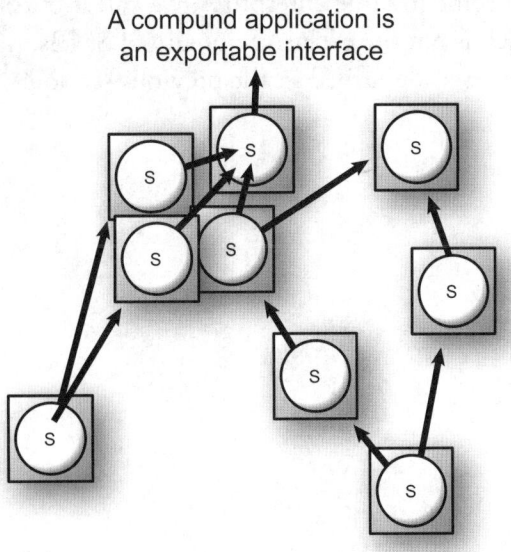

Figure 2.11 For the SMB Environment, the Enterprise Core Becomes Arbitrarily Small to the Extent that It Is No Longer Distinguishable.

Such an approach to adopt SOA could lead to a surprising result: the experience from the efforts in building strategies for instituting SOA in large organizations suggests that at some point in the maturation of the SOA market, large organizations will not be a precondition for SOA adoption. SOA can flourish in a small organization environment as well. This conclusion is also aligned with the very concept of openness and standardization of Web services. The processes are architecturally sound and technically feasible, even though there are technical and social behavior hurdles to overcome.

The adoption of SOA in SMB space will take place under a different dynamic: instead of reuse from within, or across organizations in a large enterprise, considered a necessary condition for critical mass, we will see the same critical mass, but with reuse now happening across whole economic ecosystems.

In other words, we are proposing a model for SOA deployment that depends on multiple ecosystem players providing composite applications that are used to build more complex SOA-style composite applications. Under this environment we can expect a degree of specialization where the individual services are provided by smaller players with the appropriate expertise. This situation is illustrated in Figure 2.12. To distinguish this approach from the traditional "internal only" or "inside-out" approach to SOA specific to large enterprises, we call it outside-in SOA. The outside-in approach is not the exclusive domain of SMBs; it can also take place in large enterprises as described in the previous section.

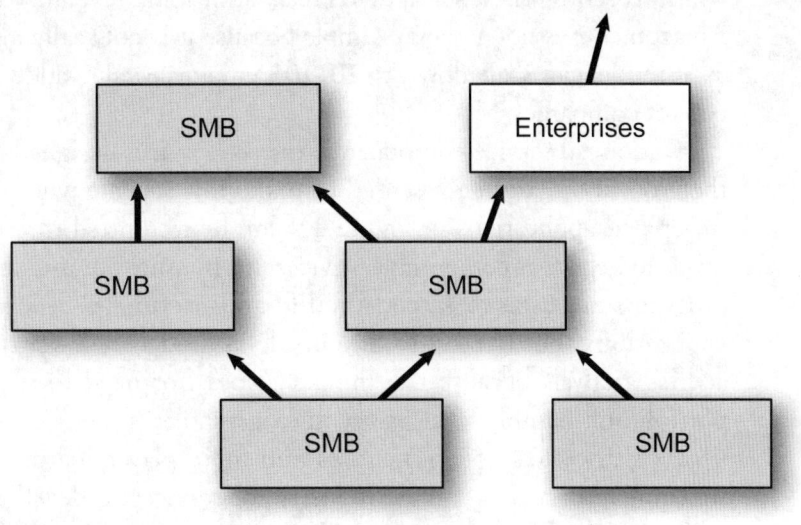

Figure 2.12 The End State Is a Rich, Diverse Economic Ecosystem with an Excellent Impedance Match between Technology and Business Needs

Who has a vested interest in making the transformation to outside-in SOA take place? It is a truism in an economic ecosystem that the cost equation for some players translates into an identical revenue consideration for another player. The whole ecosystem benefits when the value received greatly exceeds the cost expended for purchasers, and when sellers realize additional demand for products and services because of this value.

Consumers of services stand to gain because of the lower cost overall for procuring application capabilities via compound applications through compound services. Software tools vendors will benefit through offerings that target an outside-in SOA environment, and likewise vendors of technology building blocks. These building blocks must have SOI capabilities as documented in Chapter 6 that support automated provisioning and the concept of virtualized appliances.

Relationships among services providers will grow in fairly complex ways. Services providers will become both providers and consumers of services. Even companies that are not traditionally services providers like Amazon.com are beginning to develop a surplus service capability. These companies will start selling these services to create additional revenue streams. Actually Amazon.com is not a good example because it is not really a small company. This model can scale down to 10–100 employee value-added reseller (VAR) type of companies.

Canonical service components, that is, services designed as services from the ground up, are not essential to make this scheme work. The traditional stovepiped applications in Figure 2.9 can be retrofitted through middleware shims to behave as composable services in a manner not unlike screen scraping programs are used to extend the life and usefulness of legacy mainframe applications. The barriers to the outside-in model are lower than they appear at first analysis because the industry does not need to wait until a large portfolio of reusable services becomes available.

As service technology matures and more players partake of the market we can expect a rich cottage industry for services to develop with offerings available to build most any application imaginable. This market will be highly diversified across geographic regions driven by local needs and regulations. In this environment it will be cheaper simply to build specific functionality by contracting out constituent components in the marketplace rather than building the same functionality wholly in house.

The paradigm of the automobile or the aircraft industry, with a huge supply network, will also apply to software applications.

The outside-in approach differs from traditional outsourced arrangements: the negotiation of an outsourced payroll function may involve months and real people at the table. On the other hand, outside-in transactions will be eminently automated and highly dynamic through automated registries and discovery services and using open standards. One such transaction might take from a fraction of a second to no more than a few seconds.

Key Hurdles for Outside-in SOA

There are a number of challenges that will need to be addressed before outside-in SOA becomes pervasive in the industry.

Security and Privacy

- Security and trust is fundamental to outside-in SOA, as resources and services are in cyberspace and may even cross national boundaries. Service consumers need trustworthy means for securely validating the origination and quality of a service offering before it can be used. Service providers need to know their services are used by legitimate consumers and that they will be compensated.

- Conformance with government regulations and export controls is essential as is the need to be auditable with non-repudiation tracking.

- The security mechanisms need to be tamper-resistant and available through neutral parties. A combination of hardware, software, and biometrics will be needed to offer trustworthy and convenient protection to service consumers and service providers alike.

Performance and Quality of Service

- User expectations of response time must be met despite the fact that services are broadly distributed over the Internet. Web based protocol optimization and acceleration will be needed.

- A performance penalty is inherent in the distributed nature of outside-in solutions and needs to be factored in the solution design.

- A services consumer may not be able to find the exact desired profile in a single service offering. On the other hand a specific functionality and QoS may be attainable through service composition.

Bill-backs & cost settlement

- A trusted way must be established to track service usages and bill back to the services consumers.

- A non-repudiation capability is a must.

Data encryption and transformation
- Data needs to be striped, replicated, compressed, encrypted, and relocated to meet target quality criteria.
- Service registry and publication/discovery must be instituted.
- Service registries must be created to publish, discover, subscribe, validate, and invoke services.
- The service and directory infrastructure needs to be trusted and secure. The fact that they are not available today constitutes a strong deterrent for both service providers and service consumers to publish and use services.

Business process standardization & validation
- Business processes and its components need to be standardized to the point that independent services providers can focus on constructing services, less on interface issues.
- Standardized business processes will facilitate services interoperability.

Functional testing
- Once services from different service providers are integrated into a complete solution for a service consumer, they need to be verifiable through simulation or other means without impacting already running services.
- Innovative techniques will be necessary for functional testing with live systems, for instance those involving money transfers. As an example, this is done all the time with the PayPal service through small test transfers.

Cultural and behavioral changes
- Business owners (especially SMB owners) need to see the benefit of adopting well tested business processes and widely used services while minimizing risks. Service providers will need to make an effort to ensure their services are trustworthy, secure, with a tangible business value.

- Government and regulatory agencies also need to encourage and nurture a culture of leveraging shared services to build business solutions, very much like the support behind e-business and e-government. It will help to build a strong ecosystem for outside-in SOA adoption.

Let's look at an example illustrating the concept of composition of services. In the spirit of this section, the example forward looking illustrating service orientation technology can lead the way to new business models, where the same benefits brought by service orientation within a company can actually be realized across entire economic ecosystems.

Example: An Outside-in Managed Services Provider

In this section we describe a hypothetical scenario involving a relatively small MSP (Managed Service Provider) enabled by an outside-in environment. Today this scenario is possible but it accessible only to very few companies with deep pockets that can afford the internal investment under the monolithic scenario described in Figure 2.9.

This MSP is horizontally specialized and does not directly own any data centers or even any hosted servers. In fact this MSP may be renting the software in a pay-as-you go SaaS (Software as a Service) model. This MSP operates under a narrow horizontal model, making a business out of specific domain expertise and the cost differential between the value of services provided and the cost of the constituent services. The barriers to entry into new businesses will be small because capital costs are minimal compared to a company that extends ownership down to brick and mortar, enabling the MSPs to be extremely nimble.

The trend toward distributed, multi-tier data center designs has been taking place for the past fifteen years. A parallel trend in software is the gradual separation of computing engines from the applications and from the data being operated upon. Until very recently, an enterprise application was tightly bound to a physical server (compute engine) and used direct-attach storage, that is, data was kept in hard drives inside the same server boxes. This arrangement was reasonable from the standpoint that the data in a hard drive was tightly bound to the application that created it.

The first boundary to be breached is the divide between compute engines and applications: advances in software engineering made it possible to run an application in a multiplicity of platforms. The emergence of storage area networks (SANs) and network attached storage (NAS) took the data out of the boxes. These technologies increased data availability and disaster recovery readiness. In the past five years the adoption of XML Web services interfaces accelerated this trend through increasing interoperability and by making data usable by most any application.

What has not changed in this process is the prevalence of vertically integrated solution stacks. Compute engines, applications and data can be mixed and matched. However, except for very specific exceptions involving outsourcing, the common notion is that these three elements do not cross corporate boundaries. These boundaries will be breached as well under an outside-in SOA environment and as part of the technology maturation process. The reasons will be simple economics: outsourcing storage will lower cost and yield higher operational efficiencies than an equivalent in-house solution.

Enterprise application services will be procured through a hierarchical, multi-layered ecosystem. Technology maturation makes specialization possible with opportunities to add value at each layer.

As illustrated in Figure 2.13, starting from the bottom right, the hypothetic ecosystem postulates the existence of wholesale storage providers. These storage providers rent storage by the terabyte per month at specific QoS parameters: latency, bandwidth, locality and uptime. Above the storage wholesalers are the storage aggregators who "blend" the offerings from the storage wholesalers and combine the wholesalers "single malt" offerings into products to meet specific SLA (service level agreements). Value added features at this level may include encryption, striping, and data migration and replication services.

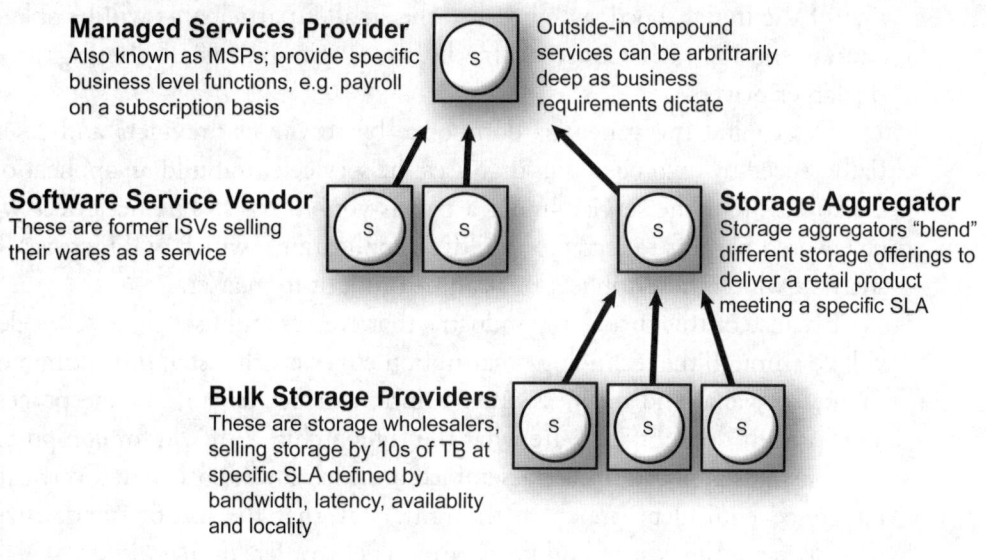

Figure 2.13 A Multi-tiered Application Services Provider

Striping allows data to be partitioned across multiple providers, making it very difficult to reassemble except by the originators. At the top of this pyramid, an MSP can combine offerings from several ISVs, including database, vertical applications and presentation services vendors into a specific "retail" offering. These offerings can run the whole gamut of outsourced applications available today, from e-mail sold by the mailbox (in quantities from one to several hundred thousand), to services like payroll, healthcare settlement services, CRM (Customer Relationship Management) and ERP.

Even though qualitatively the service offered by the small MSP might not be much different from the offering by a large company, with the number of players in the market both in the numbers of MSPs and servicelet providers, the combined economic impact represented by these providers will likely be several orders of magnitude larger as compared with the current conditions today. Outside-in SOA leads to diversity of offerings and competition, allowing the economies brought in by SOA to be spread across entire ecosystems, including small businesses and individual consumers.

The diversity of services offered will likely be much larger compared to that of the initial siloed state because the smaller participants will be able to address specific niches unreachable by the single-size-fits-all offerings from the larger players.

The capital investment is done once by servicelet providers and essentially reused by each customer that uses the servicelet to build an application. Customers rent the service under a pay-as-you-go basis. The net effect will be lowered barriers to entry for building applications, which will increase the speed at which these applications can be brought to market.

Because of this speed, any industry that creates and uses these servicelets will go through the technology maturation curve much faster, unlocking new sources of value and business opportunities for participants in the process. This process does for software what the Intel architecture did for computers: new business applications are assembled at much lower cost than a vertically integrated equivalent, much in the same way that the use of standardized parts lowered the cost of building computers by orders of magnitude.

Chapter 3

Virtual Service Oriented Grid Environment and Architecture

What is design? It's where you stand with a foot in two worlds —the world of technology and the world of people and human purposes —and you try to bring the two together.
—Mitch Kapor, Founder of Lotus Development Corporation

There exist three essential properties that define the character of virtual service oriented grids: federation, a multi-layered structure, and scalability. At first blush, grid systems look complex and indeed they are. However, it is possible to gain a fundamental insight about their behaviors and capability by looking at them as collections of federated resources, decomposing them into logical layers and understanding that one of the main goals for grids is to build a highly capable system out of a potentially unlimited number of components with limited capability.

Federation properties are apparent in most grid deployments and have been amply documented. What is less obvious is that the concept of federation applies to processes for the technology development and the management of the grids themselves. This chapter focuses precisely on the less documented aspects of federation in technology strategy and development.

Virtual service oriented grids are inherently complex if only due to the sheer size and number of components involved. However, complexity does not imply total chaos. A careful analysis reveals certain consistent patterns that are helpful in strategic decision making even when certain technical aspects are less than evident. These patterns become evident once we recognize that multiple levels of abstraction are at work at any time. We use a divide-and-conquer approach, the *composite usage model,* to define logical layers within a grid system and analyze each layer separately. The approach allows us to answer fundamental questions such as where and how virtual service oriented grids can be deployed. We can even make inferences about the organizational impact of virtual service oriented grid deployments.

Virtualization as commonly understood refers to a number of technologies whose goal is to map multiple logical entities, represented by a virtual machine, to one physical server or node. That is, the traditional notion of virtualization defines a many-to-one relationship with the hardware. A virtual service oriented grid environment extends the relationship from many-to-one to many-to-many.

In other words, as virtual machines become disembodied from their physical hosts, each resource can be managed independently to meet a specific policy, service level or quality of service criteria. The flexibility and convenience of this capability cannot be understated.

In this new environment, the traditional virtualization paradigm still holds: if a hardware host is underutilized, it will be easy enough to throw in additional virtual workloads to increase the utilization to a predetermined level. The new capability allows extending this paradigm on the hardware side: if an application needs to be throttled up to increase throughput, under a virtual service oriented grid environment it should be easy enough to add processing or storage resources to meet a desired performance goal.

In other words, virtual service oriented grids define replicated pools of fungible, distributed resources. Traditionally a great disparity has existed between the capability of a compute engine and the workload it runs. If the workload is too small, utilization factors are also small. CPUs are idle most of the time, which is indicative of underutilized infrastructure. If workloads are too large, tasks take a long time to execute. If workloads are variable, it becomes difficult to size up the most appropriate computing engine. The usual recourse is to design the system for peak loads, which is expensive and leads to poor utilization.

In a grid environment it becomes possible to throttle the resources applied to a task to have it completed on time as per business requirements.

It is possible to apply fewer resources when cost is an issue or more when performance is the main goal. This replication is attained through the coordination of distributed resources. We will see that performing calculations in the presence of physical separation brings quite a few challenges, a challenge we can't avoid because building a computer with unlimited performance that is also co-located is not physically or economically feasible.

Technology Development in a Federated Environment

Federated technology development is really a universal concept applicable to any large scale technological endeavor, but it is especially applicable to grids because of grids' federated nature. We will see that the patterns that govern grid technology evolution were already present sixty years ago at the dawn of the computer era. Very fittingly, we start this section with a historical perspective of the early manifestations of these patterns to build an insight on how these patterns can be used to advantage to build business and technology strategies related to grids.

A Historical Perspective of Federated Technology Development

How should technology development projects involving virtual service oriented grids be managed? Traditional projects tend to be managed in a more or less serialized fashion. Each step in the series essentially forms a pipeline. As an example, let's consider a simplified series of steps needed to create a microprocessor based computer.

The pipeline starts with basic research on properties of semiconductor materials, which form the basis for designing the fabrication processes. The next step is to carry out the logic design based on the properties of the fabricated devices. The output of this work is finished microprocessors. Microprocessors aren't very useful as self-standing devices. They need the support of a cadre of chips, collectively known as the *chipset*. Microprocessors and chipsets are integrated into baseboards. Baseboards are mated to enclosures, power supplies, and peripherals to make finished computers. This process can be represented by a pipeline illustrated in Figure 3.1

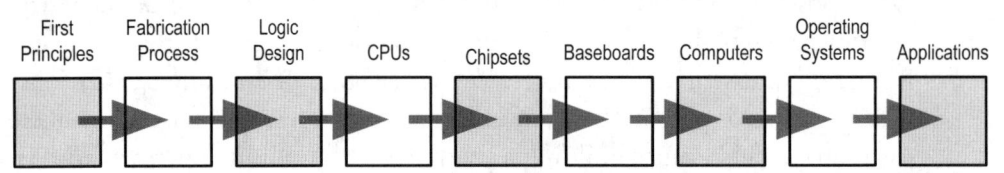

Figure 3.1   A Serial Technology Development Pipeline

Until the early 1960s, building a computer system meant re-creating the complete pipeline from beginning to end. Every new computer model represented years of effort from the manufacturer.

For the end user the process of selecting a machine was also grueling and often a no-win endeavor: if an enterprise customer outgrew a machine configuration, the attainable range of upgrades was limited by the limitations of the model design. Bringing in a larger machine meant a complete infrastructure remake including rewriting the application software.

On the other hand, purchasing a large machine with room to grow required a large investment upfront to pay for the unused capacity.

The IBM System/360 (S/360) was revolutionary in that it was conceived as a system that separated architecture from implementation. The initial announcement in 1964 included an unprecedented range of models: 20, 30, 40, 50, 60, 62, and 70.

The following generation, System/370 introduced in 1970, incorporated a number of advances in the hardware technology and the programming environment, such as support for virtual memory, yet it was capable of running the System/360 software unchanged. The effect of this strategy is shown in Figure 3.2.

Chapter 3: Virtual Service Oriented Grid Environment and Architecture ■ 77

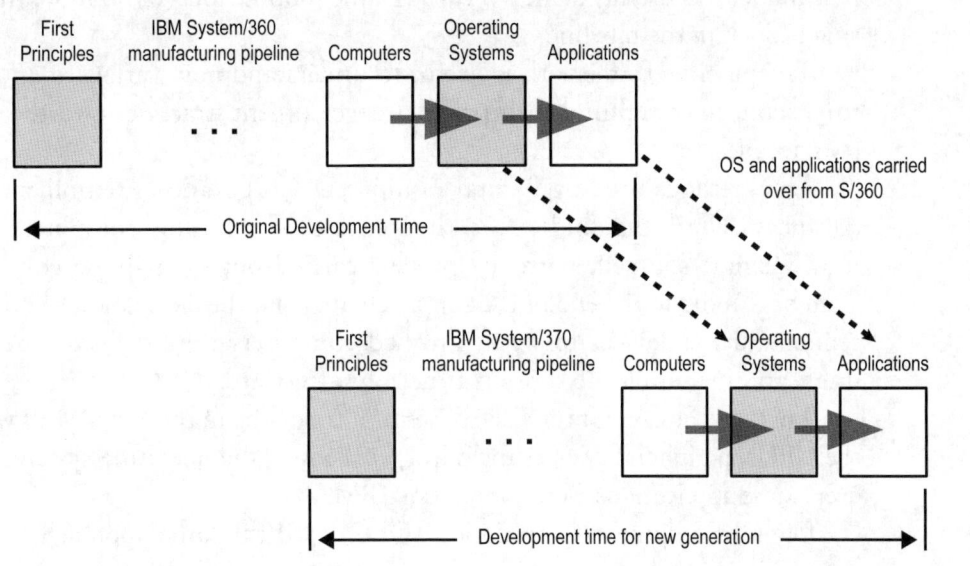

Figure 3.2 Development Time for Newer Generation Is Compressed by Carrying the OS and Applications from the Previous Generation.

While the development of System/360 represented a multiyear effort by IBM, newer models could be introduced at a minimal level of disruption to existing customers, and customers did not have to throw away their prior multiyear investment in software as the price for entry into the new generation.

Even members of the successor architecture System/370 machines could run the prior generation operating system and applications unmodified, albeit in emulation mode with some overhead. The travails of engineering and building an operating system have been amply documented in Frederick Brooks' book[1].

This approach to building computers shortened development cycles and gave IBM a time-to-market capability and advantage that put IBM as a technology leader for decades.

Moreover, the different models within the initial S/360 series allowed fine tuning the offerings to encompass a broad range of applicability without the need to rebuild the complete pipeline each time. In fact, the introduction of a

---

1 Frederick P. Brooks, T*he Mythical Man-Month: Essays on Software Engineering*, 20th Anniversary Edition, Addison Wesley (1995), ISBN 0201835959

new model was usually achieved through the modification of no more than a single block in the pipeline.

The pipeline framework is useful to understand how various manufacturers continued refining their product development strategies over the next two decades.

The methods used by Digital Equipment Corporation exemplify these advances. Until the mid-1970s the process of building computers was mostly single sourced, with the process carried out by a single company from beginning to the end of the supply chain, from the fabrication of critical semiconductor devices to when finished computers were delivered to end users, and including the support functions afterwards.

This was the case for the IBM System/360 starting in the early 1960s when the CPUs, peripheral devices including keyboards, the operating system, and even some applications were sourced by IBM.

Digital Equipment Corporation (DEC) used the same approach of distinguishing architecture from implementation that made IBM so successful. This time, the company applied the approach to a landmark line of minicomputers, the PDP-11.

The range of models within the PDP-11 line offered by Digital was even broader than that of the IBM S/360 spanning two decades and a number of manufacturing technologies in the implementation, as shown in Figure 3.3.

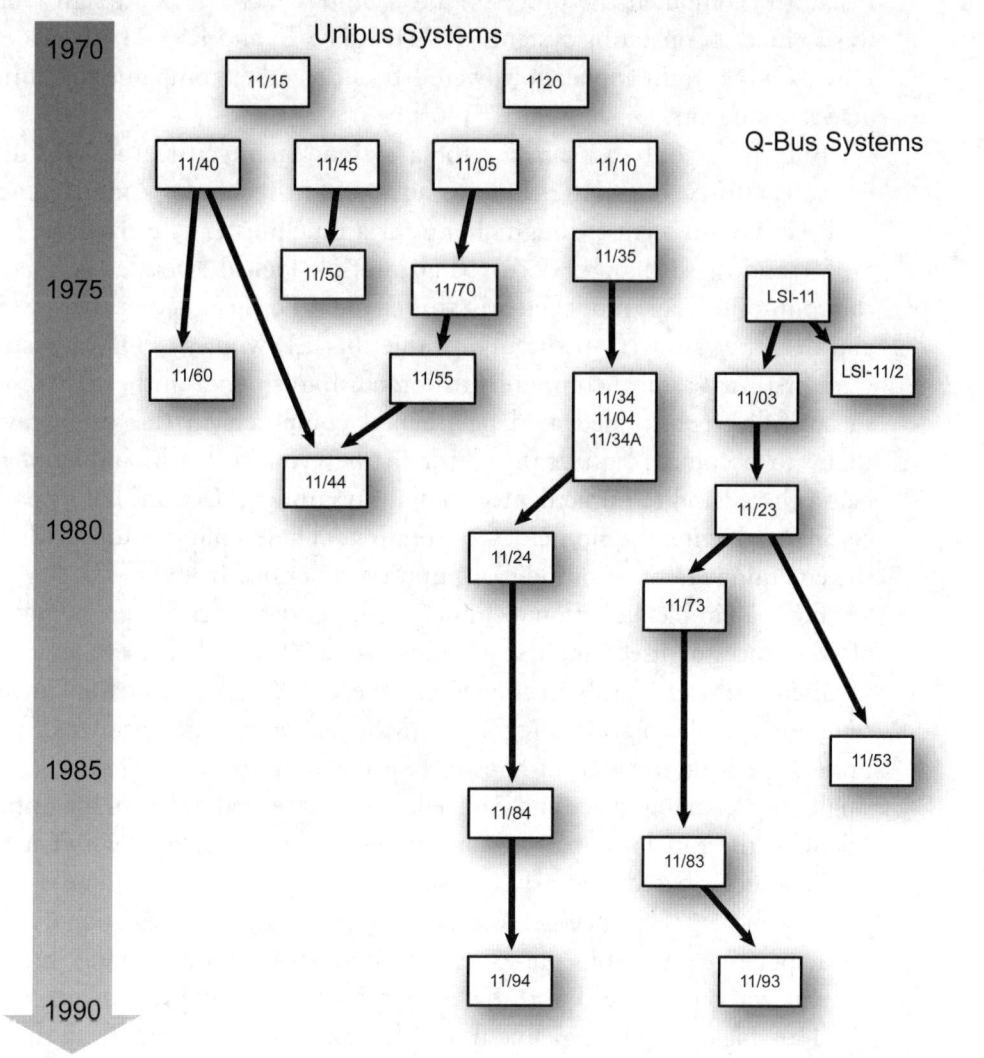

Figure 3.3   Evolution of the PDP-11 and Implementation Technology.[2]

A PDP-11 installation in the mid-1970s might have consisted of a PDP-11/45 computer, a VT100 combined keyboard and CRT display, a DECtape tape drive, an RX11 floppy disk drive and a DECwriter II LA36 printer terminal.

---

2   Adapted from http://hampage.hu.

Inside the computer, the processor bus, Unibus was a DEC design. There was a choice of operating systems, RT-11, RSTS/E, and RSX-11, all made by DEC. Only certain applications were left out to other companies or hungry graduate students.

But this is only a snapshot for a system architecture that it still in use today, forty years later. Due to advances in technology management, PDP-11 systems went through change at a much faster rate than the IBM S/360, and these changes occurred at multiple logical levels, as defined by the composite usage model later in this chapter. For instance the IBM S/360 and derivatives stayed in the mainframe market, whereas PDP-11 systems were first used as minicomputers for processing lab data in the 1970s, were successfully repositioned as departmental computers in the 1980s, eventually to become a significant player in the growing OEM industry, and being cloned and re-implemented, not always under the control of its parent company, Digital Equipment Corporation. These changes foreshadowed the emerging era of commodity computers described below.

From an implementation technology perspective, initial implementations of the processor used small scale integration (SSI) and discrete logic that required multiple boards to implement the CPU. Subsequent implementations used medium scale integration (MSI) to reduce the number of parts until large scale integration allowed the machine to be implemented in a single chip, enabling space and cost reductions of several orders of magnitude. Likewise, the initial core-based memory was eventually replaced with CMOS, semiconductor based memory.

As radical as these changes seem, they were actually very evolutionary, each one happening on top of a pre-existing technology base. Each change brought benefits without the need to throw away prior technology investments.

The single supplier pipeline model for computer manufacturing did not last forever. IBM unwittingly started the next revolution. An IBM design team working in Boca Raton on the upcoming model 5150 decided to make heavy use of outsourced technologies, including operating system software from a then obscure company called Microsoft. The IBM PC was introduced in 1981.

The primary driver for this work was time to market. To speed up the design and integration process, IBM had to be fairly open in disclosing the specifications of the various subsystems making up a personal computer.

IBM also took on a new role that took prominence at the beginning of the third millennium: that of a systems integrator. We now realize that this role is seen in many industries old and new: companies like Boeing and General Motors represent only the tip of an iceberg. If we look at the size of the 787 project, the dollar amount associated with the supplier economic activity of suppliers related to the 787 project is many times over the economic activity by Boeing. It is not the case that Boeing is trying very hard at becoming a smaller company. This process is disruptive for Boeing and places enormous cost pressure on the members of the supply chain. The transformation is taking place because the third party development paradigm minimizes the cost per aircraft delivered.

The relative openness of the PC provided opportunities for emerging, fast-moving companies to step in and become suppliers, first to IBM, and later within the industry segments that arose.

What IBM did not realize at that time were the emerging supply dynamics characterizing the behaviors of the different elements in the pipeline. The most consequential change probably went unnoticed at the time: a turning point was taking place in the economics driving the pipeline. The single supplier development pipeline made sense when the computer industry was nascent and there was little in the way of collective knowledge.

Even while the company was outsourcing portions of the technology, it was not clear that IBM was aware of the changes taking place and the forces being unleashed as evidenced by the company's ultimately futile attempts to control the product development process. In spite of the efforts by IBM, the development of the PC developed its own momentum beyond it, or in fact, any single company or organization to control.

There were a number of significant events along the way, any one of which could have been considered pivotal:

- IBM published the specifications for the expansion bus for the new machine. The side effect of this action was to fire up the market for third-party add-on cards. The initial, basic machine had very limited capability, initially configured with 16 kilobytes of memory up to a maximum of 64 kilobytes. This was no different than the PDP-11 of ten years before.
- The machine was not very useful with very limited line graphics in the display, and the I/O capability went little beyond the keyboard,

display, and a cassette tape. However, the expandability of the machine captured the imagination of the technical community, and the availability of third party expansion cards began to make the machine really useful. The variety and functionality of third party cards went beyond what IBM could have built single handedly.

- IBM tried to put the genie back in the bottle with the successor of the first system bus, the ISA, or Industry Standard Architecture bus. IBM designed the successor of the ISA bus, the Micro Channel Architecture or MCA bus and promptly proceeded to tightly control its specification and licensing. It did not work. Industry consortia developed alternatives, first the EISA bus, an extended version of the original ISA bus, followed by the PCI bus a few years later. The Microchannel bus was never widely adopted by the industry and was essentially bypassed.

- PCs have a firmware program that runs first when the machine is powered on that allows the machine to recognize certain hardware devices such as hard drives and the video card in preparation to the installation of the operating system. This program is known as the Basic Input/Output System, or simply by its acronym, the BIOS. IBM required a license for the manufacturers to use the BIOS. In the early 1980's companies such as Computer Data Products and Compaq reverse-engineered the BIOS, opening the path to the manufacture of PC-compatible machines that were built without the intervention of IBM.

- It might be possible to argue that Microsoft's 1990 decision to bail out of the joint development of OS/2 was done for purely selfish reasons. It is also a demonstration of players attempting to maximize the economic outcomes. Had OS/2 continued to develop with Microsoft, but under IBM's direction, it is very likely that the capitalization of Microsoft would be a fraction of what it is today. Independent third parties developing technology pipeline elements maximized positive economic outcomes overall. It must be noted that as in any economic playfield, everybody doesn't always win. While the dynamics of the game are not zero sum because of the significant growth involved, the process still generates winners and losers.

Federated Technology Development Today

The business environment at the beginning of the twenty-first century is considerably more complex and challenging, but at the same time richer and rife with opportunities than the environment documented in the previous section. We witnessed how IBM was able to compress a long development pipeline through abstraction and reuse. This approach to development was inward-looking, geared at optimizing the steps and components to build and develop the finished product, whether a mainframe or a minicomputer. The end product was a single product or line of products marketed globally. The main difference in today's economy is the added geographical and cultural dimensions for both product development and delivery.

It is not uncommon to have design teams in the United States, India, China, and Israel collaborating in the development of a line of products. The scope of the activities may include software and hardware development, manufacturing processes, or even IT and business processes.

The scope of the development is no longer inward-looking in the coordination of the design elements. It has also become outward-looking in that the goal of having one product line that fits all global markets no longer exists. The expectation is that the revenue potential will not be realized unless the products are tailored to fit local needs throughout the globe.

One mechanism for managing the daunting complexity of this process has been to serialize the development process across geographies. If one geography has developed skills for Phase A, say product design, and another for Phase B, manufacturing, a "natural" approach is to let Phase A finish before a handoff to Phase B. The boundary between Phases A and B are so distinct that there is no duplication in this process. Unfortunately this approach brings the worst of both delays associated with a sequential approach with the potential for disconnects associated with geographically distributed development teams.

A somewhat counterintuitive observation is that, in the long run managing these processes in a distributed fashion leads to improved business outcomes. In the management of distributed teams, there is always a tradeoff between the cost communication and the cost of development. In some case the cost to communicate and coordinate is higher than the cost to develop, a fact that suggests that allowing duplication of effort under some circumstances may actually yield a product that satisfies the needs of multiple markets at lower cost. For instance a project that has the engineering done in the United States before a handoff to marketing teams around the globe may result in a product that is a poor fit in geographic regions outside the US, increasing global marketing costs yet with poorer sales.

Under these circumstances, it might make more sense to break the pipeline earlier to do part of the engineering work across multiple geographies. Figure 3.4 illustrates the distributed development process.

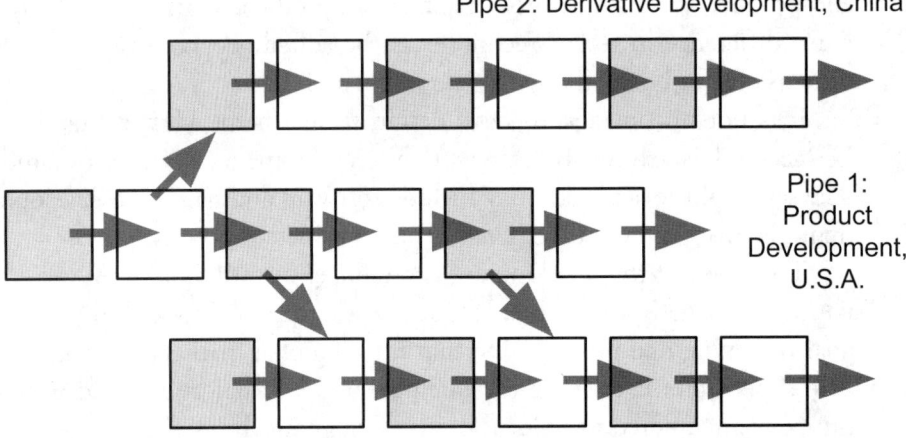

Figure 3.4 Distributed Development Pipeline

This paradigm is seen often in distributed computations. As explained in the section on balanced grid architectures later in this chapter, when a processor needs intermediate results that are normally computed by another processor further away, the software engineer or algorithm designer estimates the tradeoff between the cost of carting off data that's available somewhere else versus the cost of recreating the same data locally. If the transmission delay idles a processor while the data arrives, there is nothing wrong in recomputing the same data locally if doing so speeds up the computation overall.

The approach we are recommending is forking the development pipeline early on in the development process. However, the forking points need to be established through a careful strategic analysis. While forking brings a business benefit from improved time-to-market, it also brings a cost in terms of geographically duplicated efforts, divergence of similar processes in different regions and loss of volume economics.

While parallel development may not improve the time to first product shipment, products intended for international distribution can be brought to market much earlier, perhaps even before they ship in the home country, as business conditions dictate.

In sum, an FTD analysis ensures that local requirements are applied locally, not globally where they would bring over-specification, that is, requirements and constraints that serve no business purpose. These requirements add unnecessary drag to the processes. This approach is especially applicable to companies deploying distributed, regional design centers.

An FTD approach encourages an open discussion of these tradeoffs, enabling an organization to explicitly decide the level of autonomy most beneficial for current and anticipated business conditions, how constituent regional organizations should collaborate, and to discuss desired global business outcomes.

At some level, blocks are treated as single, atomic logical entities. This does not prevent FTD from being applied recursively or hierarchically. At the top level pipes may represent workflows between international subsidiaries or different companies altogether, whereas blocks in a pipe represent business groups. Drilling down into a single block may reveal relationships across departments within a business group.

Single blocks can be monolithic as well. When this happens, under the FTD framework it may be a worthwhile exercise to determine whether further decomposition would lead to improved business outcomes.

Governance in a Federated Environment

From an intuitive perspective, FTD represents a business outcome optimization exercise along a single dimension as depicted in Figure 3.5. At one end of the spectrum, a local organization enjoys total freedom to make decisions. This is the equivalent of no coordination at all, and hence, synergies due to the coordinated action of multiple organizations are never realized.

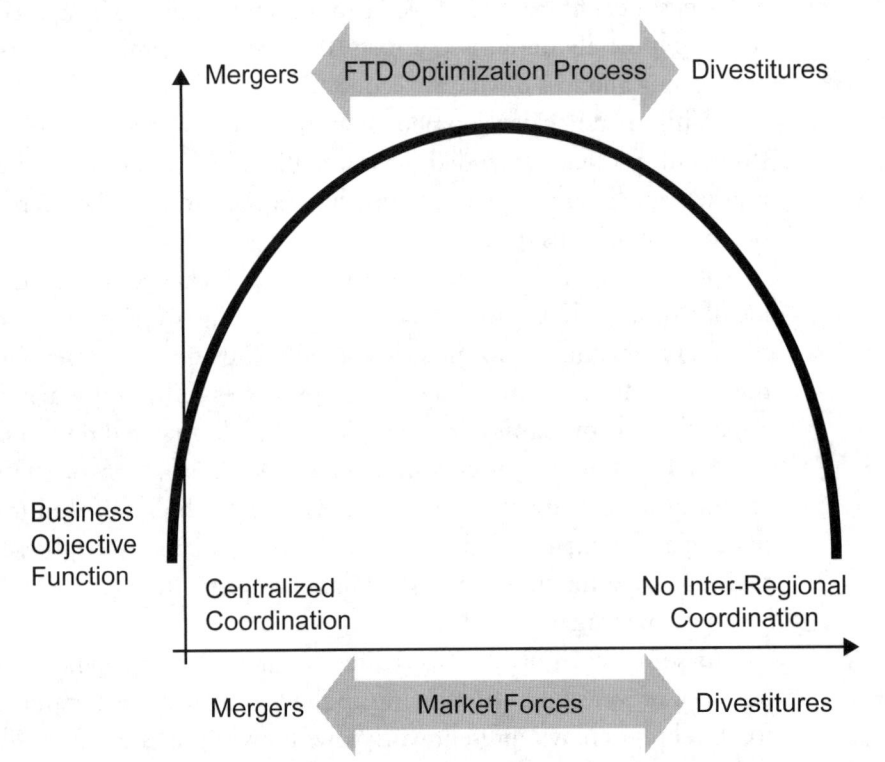

Figure 3.5   Business Optimization in a Federated Environment

At the other end of the spectrum is a centralized organization where every subsidiary operates under uniform mandates and processes. This situation is less than optimal as well because it may lead to over-specification or red tape: processes that have no tangible business results carried out only because they have meaning in some other locality.

Companies go through mergers or divestitures in attempts to optimize these outcomes. FTD is useful in providing insight into the underlying dynamics.

Because most companies started small and because of complexities in managing large organizations, there is a tendency to view regional variances as departures from the norm and hence most organizations exhibit a bias toward centralized approaches.

For instance, corporate budgets might be managed from headquarters, in an environment where regional offices must secure approval from headquarters for any major program spending and headcount authorization.

Data centers in an outsourcing arrangement constitute an example where forcing identical processes would lead to suboptimal results. Because of higher cost of labor in the US pipeline, data centers are designed to minimize this component with greater consideration to lights out operation, whereas the cost of equipment in India is relatively higher, and hence asset management is probably a first consideration. It makes little sense to apply the same rules across the two geographies as long as the parties in an outsourcing arrangement abide by the contractual rules. In fact, an outsourcer implementing FTD would likely have a competitive advantage through lower capital and operational expenditures.

The concept of federated technology development captures organizational dynamics involved in the development of some form of technology, whether a product or a service. The understanding of these dynamics increases agility in large organizations by facilitating the discovery of task parallelism and local decision making where global decision making would introduce drag.

A federated approach allows variance in the processes used by an organization, and rather than treating it as an anomaly to be minimized. Engineering and business process need not be identical across regions, but they need to be interoperable. This relaxation may lead to cost reduction overall.

Composite Usage Models

Consider the following hypothetical but not unlikely scenario: an industry analyst doing research on virtual service oriented grids is attending the annual party of a small, fast growing and technically savvy company and well-known early adopter of virtual service oriented grids. As part of her research on virtual service oriented grids, she asks the same question to a number of people attending the party: what is the value that virtual service oriented grids brings to their fast growing organization?

The answer from the CEO: "Virtual service oriented grids bring extraordinary freedom in balancing in-house and outsourced resources to achieve the goals I have set for this company ahead of the competition." To which the CFO adds: "The aspect of virtual service oriented grids I value the most is the infinite flexibility of the technology in allowing me to pick the optimal balance between capital and operational expenses."

The reply from the CIO could not be any more different: "The virtual service oriented grid technology allows me the flexibility of deploying hardware in any data center in the globe and still be able to meet the aggressive cost constraints given to me for this year."

The CTO came with yet a different remark: "Virtual service oriented grids promise unlimited scalability in running the applications that are vital for the operation of this company."

When the analyst asked the IT Director for Global Facilities, he declared "The hardware interoperability virtual service oriented grids has allowed me to acquire and retire hardware at a pace commensurate with the ability of my data centers to host the hardware, and stay within budget. Compatibility across nodes is no longer an issue: my relationship with my customer is governed by pay-for-performance service level agreements."

Finally, a software engineer comments to the analyst: "Before the adoption of the virtual service oriented grid environment software development was done on a departmental cluster, which was overcommitted most of the day to the point that engineers had to run the most time-consuming test during evenings. The new virtual service oriented grid environment allows engineers to utilize resources across the globe and these bottlenecks have become a thing of the past."

The reader may have inferred at this point that all the answers to the initial question are technically correct. The responders each thought they were talking about grids, but they were looking at different logical aspects of the same subject. The next section describes one such logical model that puts all the views in perspective. This model is useful because it brings insight into the processes defining observed grid behaviors and because this insight also brings a predictive capability: this knowledge will enable the reader to make reasonable predictions and to build corresponding technology strategies to optimize target business outcomes.

A Layered Framework for Usage Models

In the dialog in the previous section it was clear that the CEO was associating the question about grids with business processes, the CIO was looking at IT processes, the CTO was looking at the computer architecture, yet they *were all talking about the same subject.*

Since each of the respondents was successful in their jobs, it is reasonable to assume that all the responses were correct. The conceptualizations in question were distinctly different, yet they are related somehow. We will attempt to uncover some of these relationships in this section.

In our discussion of federated technology development we found that technology does not develop at random. Developers have a strong incentive to minimize cost. We also found that the most common pattern to reduce cost is through reuse. The level of reuse is a function of technology maturity. The focus of early developers and users is in making the emerging technology work. With the excitement of pioneering work, reuse is usually far from the minds of the players. Reuse as a pattern is not obvious in the beginning even when a protagonist is actually practicing it, as we witnessed with the IBM case study. However, companies that figured this out early on, sometimes in spite of themselves, were rewarded handsomely in the marketplace.

Not surprisingly, our research indicates that the simplest way to arrange the conceptualizations is a vertical stack. This structure is reminiscent of the silos we discussed in Chapter 2, but with a twist: the primordial silos are inflexible and tightly bound together while the components of a grid stack are loosely coupled. But we are getting ahead of our story.

We will explain the concept of logical stacking first in an abstract sense and apply it to a specific example, finally coming back to the grid, or virtual service oriented grid example.

Complex systems created by humans as well as naturally occurring systems can be analyzed in a layered fashion. This is a divide-and-conquer approach that enables the human brain to grasp the behaviors of systems of otherwise intractable complexity one step at a time. Even then, enough complexity remains so that each layer can become a distinct discipline unto itself.

Let's start with an example: a layering in the Life Sciences would start with Ecology as a discipline that spans whole environments. The disciplines of Zoology and Phytology, Entomology, Physiology, Biology and Molecular Biology would reside in successive steps of greater and greater detail.

The quintessential example in computer architecture is the ISO OSI model for computer networking consisting of seven layers, namely physical, data-link, transport, network, session, presentation, application. This model is useful in explaining the workings of the Internet, illustrated in Figure 3.6.

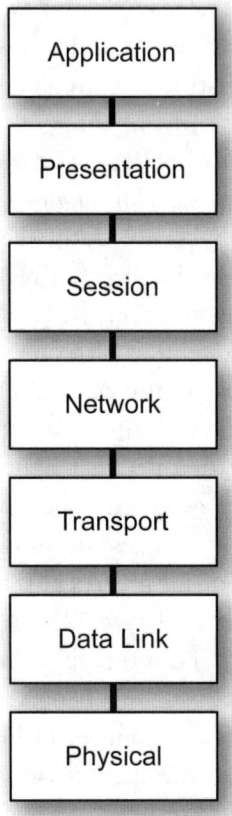

Figure 3.6   The ISO OSI Model

The ISO OSI model is conceptual and abstract, because it does not refer to any particular network. The Internet happens to be a particular instantiation of the ISO OSI model where any layer in turn can have multiple implementations and can be replaced at will to produce different "flavors." For instance, the Internet can function over wired networks using copper cables but also can function in a wireless medium. The only difference is the replacement of the physical layers, perhaps Ethernet Category 6 cables in the wired case and Wi-Fi in the wireless case.

The generalization of this concept is depicted in Figure 3.7.

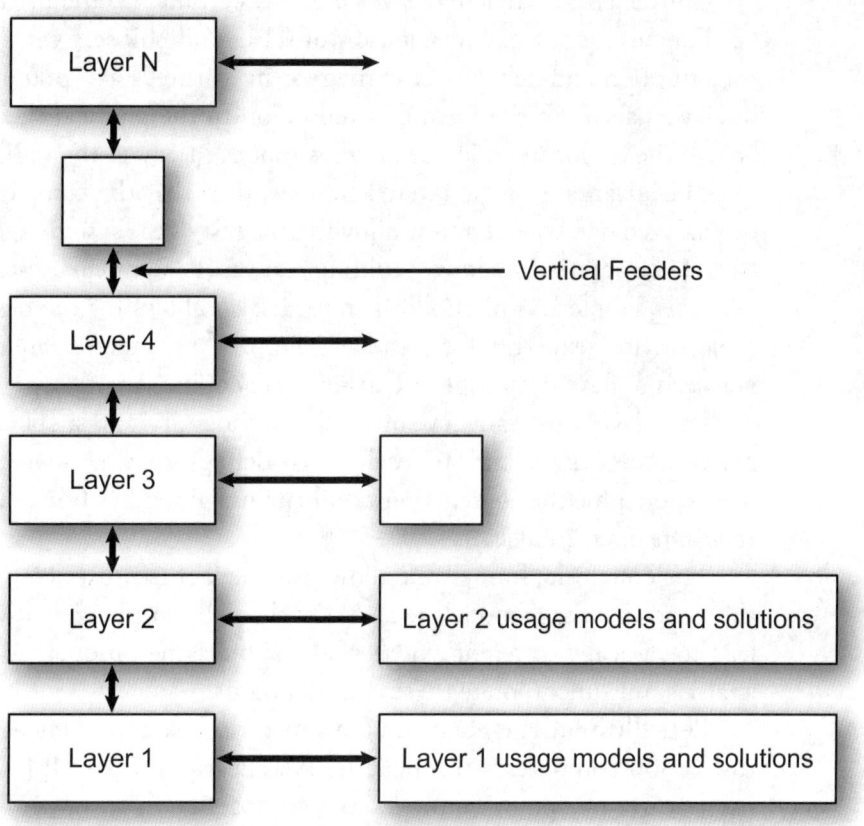

Figure 3.7 A Hierarchical Usage Model Framework

This model is a framework. It is not a usage model but a template from which specific layered usage models can be instantiated. The layer selection is not unique. There is no right or wrong layering choice. A selection is chosen to yield the best insight into the system behaviors. The up and down arrows are called *vertical feeders*.

A particular layer imposes *requirements* to the next layer down. For instance, as we will see shortly, a *cluster* is made of interconnected individual *nodes* or computers. If the cluster "layer" is to deliver a certain level of performance, this requirement imposes a minimum performance level for the constituent nodes, members of the "node" layer.

Conversely, a particular layer exposes certain *features* to the next layer up. For instance, a new generation of CPU and chipsets with lower power consumption and new power management features has a potential effect on the layers above in the form of a reduction in the physical size of the baseboard, the enclosure, and the power supplies in which the CPU resides.

The advantage of the layered framework is that the complex system can be analyzed one layer at a time allowing the rest of the system to be abstracted out. This approach allows building extremely complex systems through relatively simple and methodical steps. It also allows for the development of subject matter expertise for each layer. For instance, a hardware designer does not need to have deep expertise in software engineering.

Each layer also can develop a distinct identity and a subculture for its practitioners. In particular, each layer defines specific *usage models*. The meta-model for the aggregation of all the usage models brings the notion of *composite* usage models.

The composite framework allows for the fact that user communities and the associated usage models for each level can be surprisingly diverse and can lead to radically different experiences for the same product. A usage model analysis must incorporate these considerations.

Let's illustrate this concept with a historical example. The Apple[†] Macintosh[†] 8500 computer introduced in 1995 featured the well known ease-of-use features of Apple computers in a compact chassis, shown in Figure 3.8. However, this compact form factor was a source of mischief for technicians: adding memory modules required disassembling the chassis, removing the internal expansion cards and loosening the baseboard. See Figure 3.9. This process was extremely time consuming and required utmost skill to avoid damaging system components inside the case. This issue was addressed with the Power Macintosh[†] G4 introduced in 1999. This time the chassis opened in a clamshell fashion without the need of tools, conveniently exposing the innards for servicing as shown in Figure 3.10. This model was heavier and bulkier than the old 8500, perhaps a little less convenient for the user, but much more serviceable.

In this example we are dealing with two levels: the node level, where the user is the consumer end-user, and the baseboard level, where the user is a computer technician, as shown in Figure 3.11. For the consumer end-user the two models were quite similar, a view certainly not shared with the technician repairing or upgrading the systems.

Figure 3.8   The Apple Macintosh 8500.

One corollary from this example is that for a requirement for a system or product to be successful, it needs to be satisfactory to the constituencies at each layer.

Figure 3.9   The Apple Macintosh 8500 with the Case Removed.

Chapter 3: Virtual Service Oriented Grid Environment and Architecture ■ 95

Figure 3.10 The Apple Power Macintosh G4 with the Case Swung Open.

The usage model analysis for this example is shown in Table 3.1

Table 3.1 Usage model analysis for the Apple Macintosh 8500 and G4 machines.

Logical Level	User Community	Usage Models
Operating System	Consumer end user	Desktop usage
System Box	IT repair staff	System maintenance & repair

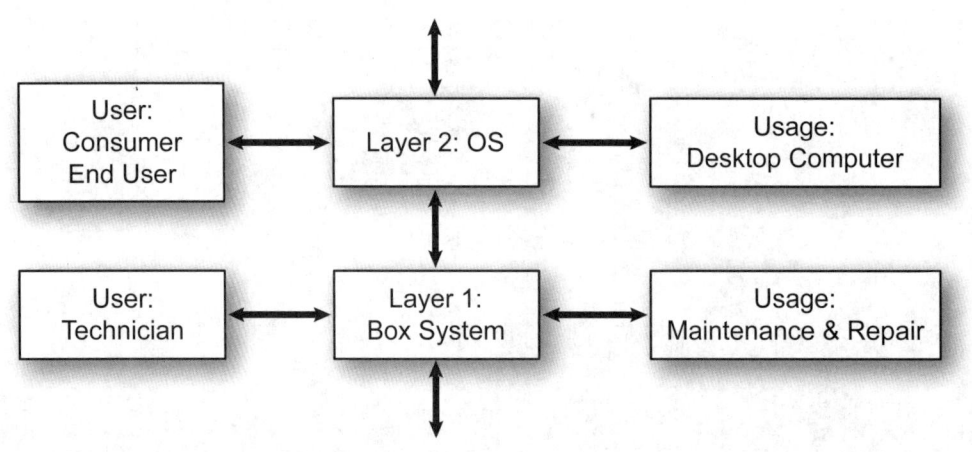

Figure 3.11 Graphical Depiction of the Usage Model Example

Usage model analysis constitutes a tool to provide economic justification for capital purchases. We go through this process in our personal lives before we select a home. Usage patterns provide insight into the type of home we want to buy: its distance from work; whether we need an apartment, penthouse, condo, a hotel room, or a house; whether we want to rent or buy; even the layout of the dwelling itself is considered. These are single layer purchases. Strategists with the hospitality industry need to look at multiple layers. Likewise, the task of assimilating an emerging technology into an organization usually requires analysis at multiple layers.

This analysis brings two benefits: inferences about usage models for the whole system (derived from the layer-by-layer analysis) and system attributes or features that have been optimized holistically up and down the composite chain, not piecemeal. Doing so increases the appeal of the product or system to the broadest audience increasing the likelihood of market success.

Applying the Composite Usage Model to Virtual Service Oriented Grids

At this point we have the analytical tools to apply the Composite Usage Model to virtual service oriented grids, easily one of the most complex systems devised by humans. Earlier in this chapter we hinted at some of the layers in the grid structure. In this section we discuss a possible layering system consistent with the composite usage model.

A number of roadblocks exist today preventing the broad adoption of virtual service oriented grids. An application of the composite usage model helps explain some of the underlying dynamics for the roadblocks: traditionally grids have been promoted as technical solutions to attain a high level of computational performance. It might be true that there is enormous unrealized technical potential. However, proponents of grids as a technical solution have not documented the associated business impact, that is, *business* usage models. Without this crucial piece it is difficult to justify the budget to build a grid infrastructure.

In fact, we have two constituencies, one technically oriented, the other business oriented. The business oriented constituency is the one eventually asked to justify the purchase decision. In organizations where these two constituencies have not communicated well, the usual result is gridlock with little progress toward the adoption of virtual service oriented grids. In the process an organization may miss opportunities to realize value for the company.

These observations suggest that we start with two major areas, namely, areas related to business usage models and those related to technical usage models. For lack of a better name, we call these areas the *business* grid and the *visible* grid. The moniker "visible" stems from the fact that this area comprehends the most traditionally documented portions of the grid, namely, grids as collections of interconnected computing nodes and associated applications.

Since grids eventually run on physical nodes and networks, we have added a third major layer down below, the *physical* grid, to encompass the structure of the hardware elements.

The visible grid encompasses nodes linked via an interconnect or LAN/WAN technology designed to move data across nodes as fast as possible. Nodes in a room are organized as a cluster and usually owned by a single departmental entity.

In describing virtual service oriented grids in terms of the Composite Usage Model, it's useful to make a couple of observations. First, there is nothing fundamentally exotic about grids. Most grids are built with run-of-the-mill computing and networking components. Higher performing components are applied for specific needs and when the budget allows. In some cases, grids are actually built by composing *lower* performing components. A class of grids, which we will call embedded grids, is built from low-performance, embedded processors optimized for low power consumption. What distinguishes a grid is the structure or architecture, whether intentional or accidental, that links together otherwise ordinary computing components. Second, the structure of the business grid is defined by the organizations around them, not by which hardware components are used.

The business, visible, and physical grid represents one possible layering system for a virtual service oriented grid. This layering, illustrated in Figure 3.12, is useful for analyzing the overall behaviors of a grid system. The boundaries between the three bands are somewhat fuzzy and overlap each other. These layers roughly coincide with the three main architectural layers for business applications covered in Chapter 1, namely the Virtual Infrastructure Services, Application and Data Services, and Federated Business Services, from the bottom up.

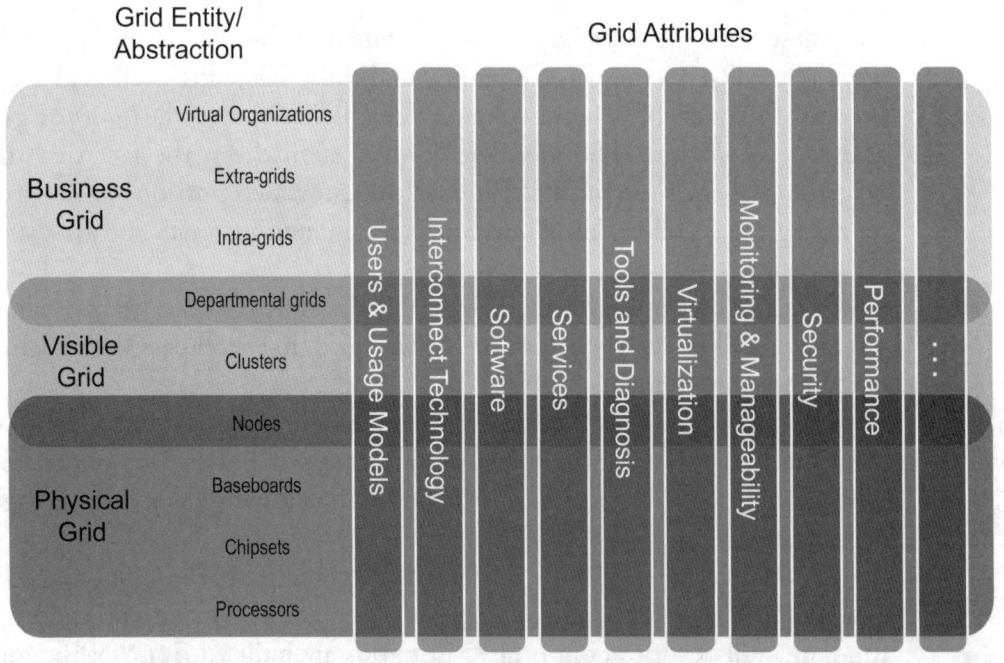

Figure 3.12 The Layered Usage Model Framework Instantiated for Grids

When we look at the physical grid alone, we see the computer nodes that make up that grid and perhaps the network that link these nodes together. We don't see the operating systems and the applications that run on the nodes. Hence when we investigate usage models for the physical grid we are essentially thinking about uses for the grid hardware. In this context, a usage model is representative if a node is part of a data center–based grid or workstation cycle scavenging grid or an embedded grid.

Under the Composite Usage Model, the physical grid needs to be responsive to requirements coming from the next layer up, that is, requirements imposed by the visible grid. The requirements may include minimums for interconnect latency and bandwidth as well as memory latency and bandwidth, which are actually properties of the CPU and chipset architecture in layers below. Physical grid features usable by the visible grid layer above might include the number of cores and CPUs in a node and the specific interconnect architecture offered.

Usage models applicable to the visible grid might include interactive or batched modes and usage models specific to the industry vertical to which a departmental grid is applied. Requirements imposed by the business grid into the visible grid might include a resource identification, access and authorization for the nodes in a cluster. Features might include interconnect performance, defined by the underlying interconnect performance of the cluster and the cross-sectional bandwidth.

Usage models at the business grid level might include in-sourced and out-sourced usage models. Requirements imposed by the business grid may include protocol interoperability that allows the integration of grid resources across extended geographical regions or specific requirements needed to meet government regulations on business practices or the transfer or diffusion of intellectual property.

As implied above, the model for each of the usage bands is not monolithic. A more detailed understanding of the system requires a corresponding refinement in the layers.

The maximum exponent for the physical grid is a node or individual computers. The components inside a computer represent a successive refinement. In other words, nodes are made up of circuit baseboards; baseboards provide physical and electrical support for chipsets, and chipsets in turn provide logical support for the CPU that powers a node.

Likewise, nodes in the visible grid are organized into clusters and departmental grids.

Going up the chain for the business grid, if a number of departmental grids in a company are physically and locally joined, they form an *intra-grid*. For business reasons a grid may be constructed from a combination of in-sourced and outsourced grid resources defining an *extra-grid*. At the highest level, we define *virtual organizations* and their associated (interconnected) computer resources. The term virtual organization is attributed to Ian Foster[3].

As hinted above with the problem of the two constituencies, there is no consensus yet in the industry about generally accepted usage models for the Business Grid. These usage models are very much work in progress. Coming up with these usage models constitutes an essential step in monetizing grid technology. The most passionate exponents of grid technology come from the technical community working at most at the level of the Visible Grid.

Without precedents and known best practices, decision makers working at the Business Grid level are unwilling to take the next step and invest in grids. What we effectively see here is a *business gap* for grid adoption where technical advocates can't come up with a convincing business value proposition for the technology and business decision makers can't justify the risk of investing in a technology perceived as unproven.

A virtual service oriented grid approach may help to bridge that gap by enabling a very incremental, pay-as-you-go strategy. One of the hurdles is the perception of need of a high level of capital investment, which is really a non-issue for applications assembled from servicelets.

Once the perception of high capital cost has been overcome, it will become easier to incorporate grids into strategic technology adoption plans. In fact, "instant" grids are already possible through leasing servers from hosting data centers to be used as nodes. Organizations with a tradition for being first adopters will likely test the waters first and will start harvesting the value from the emerging virtual service oriented grid environment. The lower barrier to entry not only will make it easier to try the first play, but also to experiment and discover new value chains.

---

3   Ian Foster et al., *"The Anatomy of the Grid: Enabling Scalable Virtual Organizations,"* International Journal of High Performance Computing Applications, Volume 15, Issue 3 (August 2001)

Because of the niche opportunities, demand for grid services in a virtual service oriented grid environment may spur demand for a diverse community of specialized small grid services providers.

Grid Usage Attributes

Running vertically across bands are *usage attributes*. Attributes are logically consistent across the vertical spectrum but have unique manifestations at each layer. For instance, if we look at the software attribute, the software running at the CPU level is microcode. The software running in a bare metal node is the firmware. Applications run at the cluster level. There is even "software" running in the business grid in the form of IT processes, such as the rules for the procurement resources. At the virtual organization level the software comes in the form of business processes as shown in Figure 3.13. The illustration also shows the economic impact of an entity for each of the layers.

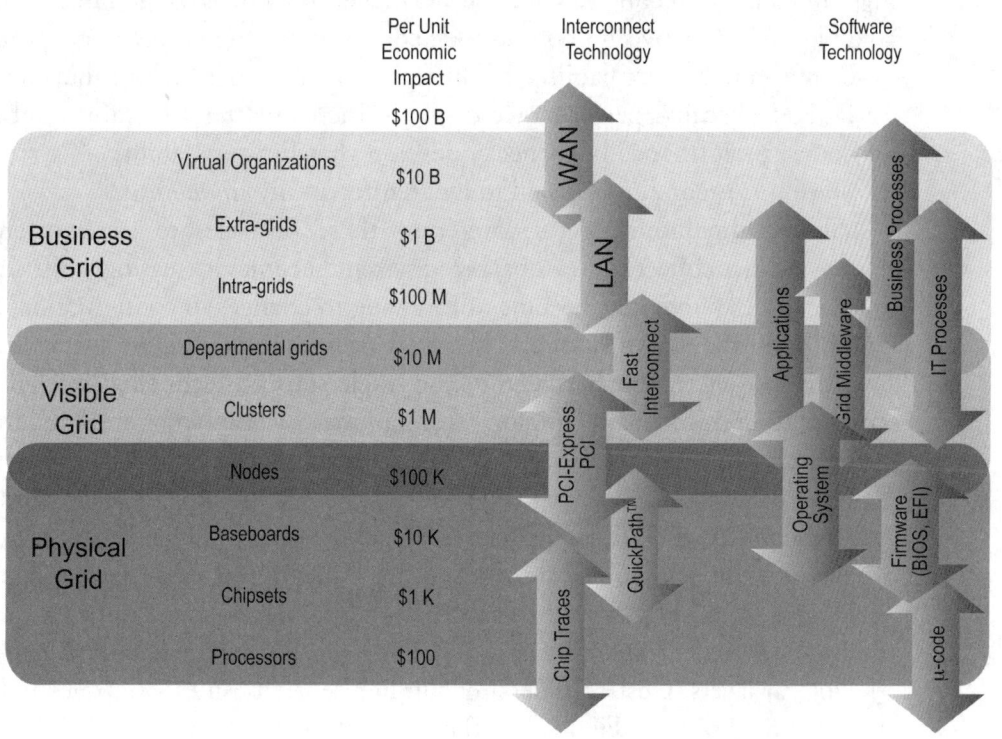

Figure 3.13 Composite Usage Model Showing Interconnect Technology and Software Technology Attributes Instantiated across Multiple Layers

For a given attribute, a grid implementation may be missing the attribute at certain levels, or attributes at adjacent layers may not be coordinated. This is a telltale sign of architectural incompleteness and an indication of a possible problem. For instance, the node management software, used to keep track of temperatures and the physical integrity of a node may not communicate with the software used to manage clusters. This gap will inconvenience users: the user might be interested in using nodes that are not overheating, or nodes with specific characteristics. For example, if a quad core node is allocated to a job, an application that is not multithreaded will use only one core, leaving the other three cores idling.

Another example is the interconnect architecture illustrated in Figure 3.13. Until InfiniBand[†] technology became available, building clusters with a fast interconnect at the application level was an expensive proposition using single-sourced technologies. It was impossible to obtain a minimum level of interconnect performance for most applications. The alternatives were to use the interconnect technology for the next level up. The large gap in latency and bandwidth between node-to-node communication and memory speeds severely limited the scalability of clusters. Clusters can't be built beyond a certain size because performance does not increase after a certain number of nodes; performance bottlenecks develop that limit scalability. A system exhibiting this condition is said to be architecturally *unbalanced*.

Skilled programming can overcome these obstacles to some extent. However, an architecturally unbalanced system becomes increasingly difficult to tune. The system may become unforgiving to changes in configuration, at which point the cost of labor also becomes an important cost consideration.

Another alternative has been to use single sourced technologies at great cost, or to customize a technology from a lower level in what amounted to a research project. An example of this approach is the Sandia Red Storm system built on a variant of the HyperTransport technology. In other words, the availability of InfiniBand closes an architectural gap and opens the opportunity of bringing cluster computing into the enterprise mainstream.

Figure 3.13 also shows roughly the range of economic significance for each unit at every level. The cost per unit increases exponentially going up the logical layers. Cost considerations influence the business strategies to be used for deployment. Figures for the physical grid are low enough to treat these assets as commodity components. Outright acquisition for entities at the business grid level, which may encompass whole economic ecosystems, may not make sense. USD 10 Million may represent a significant chunk of change for a department and a significant roadblock to deployment especially if the technology is unproven. Instead, strategies should be geared toward resource sharing, perhaps through consortia. With maturing standards, a service provider network will eventually develop that will deliver grid resources on a pay-as-you-go basis.

The composite usage model is also applicable to other contexts, such as the deployment of a PC system with manageability features (managed clients). The instantiated model will not be as complex as the one used for a grid system. Usually three to four layers will do the job. The benefits will be the same: a rapid identification of stakeholders for each layer, the usage patterns for each layer providing checks and balances against other methods already in use.

The Virtualization Continuum in Virtual Service Oriented Grids

One common notion in everyday life is the notion of a motive *force* and its relationship to a *workload*. This paradigm is evident in multiple domains. An extension of the paradigm is that the force and the workload must be balanced according to the rules of the particular domain.

In the labor marketplace, any job needs to be matched with a worker with the right level of skills. If the worker possesses skills that are way beyond the necessary for the position, the employer ends up overpaying for the tasks in the particular position, and the employee may find the position boring.

If the worker is under-qualified, the job does not get done, which can be costly to the employer, and the worker may grow frustrated.

Tools such as retraining or recruiting methods for identifying people with matching skills are needed to ensure a match.

An analogy can be drawn in the automotive world. An automobile engine has two essential properties: rotational speed, which is how fast it spins, and torque, or twisting force. The product of speed times torque determines how much *power* the engine can deliver. Power defines the amount of work an engine can potentially carry out, for instance how fast it can accelerate.

The most common type of engine today is the internal combustion engine or ICE. ICE engines are not matched at all with the workload of turning the wheels of an automobile. An ICE engine runs way too fast, in the range of 700 to 4,000 revolutions per minute and with too little torque to be useful in turning the wheels of an automobile. If an engine were to be connected to the wheels directly, it would stall because the torque the engine could deliver could not overcome the inertia and the rolling resistance of the vehicle; the car would just lurch and stall. Little of the power output of the engine would actually be delivered to the wheels.

To ensure efficient power transfer, a device called a *gearbox* or *transmission* is interposed between the engine and the wheels. The output axle of a gearbox connected to the wheels spins slower, but the torque is proportionally higher, so the speed-torque product, the power, remains the same, minus a small percentage due to transfer losses. In fact, the gearbox is adjustable, offering anywhere from four gears in automobiles to over a dozen in large trucks. If the gearing is too high, the engine struggles to keep speed and possibly stalls. If the gearing is too low, the gearbox allows the engine to spin very fast, but the actual speed will be slow. Because of the mismatch, the speed-torque product will be less than the power that the engine can deliver.

A similar concept exists in audio electronics under the notion of *impedance match*. In this case, the voltage and current replace the notion of rotational speed and torque, respectively.

In audio electronics the engine is represented by an audio amplifier, and the workload is embodied by the speakers to which an amplifier is connected. The goal for this system is to make the power delivered to the speakers as large as possible because power is what eventually gets converted into audible acoustic energy.

Both the speakers and the amplifier have inherent impedance. Impedance is the opposition a device exerts against current going through the device. The level of opposition is measured by the voltage that develops across the terminals of the speaker. Power is defined by the voltage-current product.

If the speaker impedance is too low, the current limit of the amplifier is reached before there is any significant voltage, and the delivered power is small. If the impedance is too high, the voltage limit for the amplifier will be reached with a small current, and again the delivered power will be small. Although less common today with solid state amplifiers, a transformer can be used to match the impedance of the amplifier with that of the speakers in use.

A similar dynamic takes place in the assignment of application workloads to servers. Server performance has grown ahead of application needs.

Because of the actual workload demand or due to bottlenecks elsewhere in the system, a typical server running a single application may be doing useful work running the application code between 2 and 20 percent of the time. This number is called the *utilization factor*. The rest of the time gets spent running an idle loop waiting for work or running housekeeping tasks such as virus scanning.

What happens when a server running at a 20 percent utilization factor gets replaced by another server that runs twice as fast? If the performance of the application is limited by network performance or I/O performance, the system responsiveness will stay relatively unchanged. Because the work the server gets done in half the time, this means the utilization factor goes down from 20 percent to 10 percent.

On the other hand, keeping a server online represents a sunk cost. In the past few years the cost of the electricity to run servers has become a significant cost component of a server total cost of ownership (TCO) for a server, and as a matter of fact, of the cost to operate data centers housing these servers, much higher than anticipated when the data center was first built.

We will cover the issue of I/O and network bottlenecks later in this chapter. Meanwhile, it is a fair question to ask about what can be done to capture the 80 to 98 percent of the processor cycles not utilized to run application code.

One possible measure is to request the software manufacturer to optimize the application. This can be done to some extent, but it is a slow and painful process subject to product development and upgrade cycles that can take years. This is not practical for an end user seeking relief in a matter of weeks. Furthermore, in many cases the integration needs to be specific to the host machine or the data center configuration on which the application runs. In this case application optimization is too blunt a tool to be of immediate use. Integration considerations also bring another roadblock: enterprise applications do not usually stand alone, but are made of a combination of multiple applications to fulfill a service or a business function. Optimizing a single application in this group does not necessarily increase the server utilization for the service overall.

If an application cannot be sped up to take additional processor cycles, a remedy would be to run *multiple* applications at once. These applications could be run within the confines of a single operating system instance using the *process* abstraction. In many cases this is not a practical idea for technical and administrative reasons.

Certain operating system resources such as a file or a certain database record are unique. This means that if a process gets hold of one of the unique resources, all other users needing the resource have to wait, even if there are multiple processors available to carry out the work.

Likewise, running multiple applications within an OS instance usually requires a retuning of the constituent applications, more likely than not an impractical alternative because of the expertise needed and the expense involved.

Two alternatives are left that transcend the confines of a traditional operating system: *consolidation* and *virtualization*.

Consolidation consists of running two to as many as two dozen instances of operating systems and associated application stacks on one physical machine through the intervention of software layer called the *hypervisor*.

Consolidation is usually a fairly static exercise involving the analysis of historical performance traces of the target applications and apportioning the applications to physical servers to increase utilization levels but not to the point they become overloaded. There are complications to this process:

- *Workloads are peaky.* Workloads exhibit daily, weekly, monthly, or even seasonal variations reflecting business activities in addition to random variations.
- *Workload mix changes over time.* A balanced workload apportioning may cease to be over time. This requires a regular re-apportioning, bringing new servers on line as needed or re-consolidating loads.

Virtualization is an evolutionary development of consolidation requiring incremental capabilities in the hypervisor layer as well as more advanced IT processes. Under a virtualization environment, the matching of workloads to physical servers is no longer a process of static physical mapping. The application environment is viewed as a pooled set of instances of application stacks that gets mapped into another pool of physical hosts in a highly dynamic environment. Application instances get assigned dynamically to the least loaded servers in the host pool. If a server becomes overloaded, some of the virtualized application instances running in the server can be migrated to a less loaded server.

Virtualization can be seen as the most advanced exponent of an application to host mapping continuum. In a traditional system where there is one application per physical server, launching an application instance requires provisioning and landing a new server. In a consolidation environment launching an application instance means binding a server image to a target server based on historic performance. This is a software-only action, unless a server for a new group of applications is being readied. The allocation is initiated manually. In a virtualized environment the goal is to map the application to target host automatically based on specific metrics or service level agreements (SLAs). Even after an application has been bound to a host, the application may be moved to another host to maintain the committed SLAs.

Two trends are evident as we look at the evolution from physical application mapping to server consolidation to server virtualization:

- *Move toward late binding.* In a physical mapping environment an application image may be able to run only on a specific server configuration, say a dual-socket server. In a consolidation environment the application is tailored to run in a configuration determined by the virtualization hypervisor. As long as this configuration is present, it does not matter which physical host is actually assigned. In a virtualized environment an application is literally "disembodied" and can move from host to host.

- *More dynamic behaviors.* The move toward late binding enables more dynamic behaviors. In a physical mapping environment the speed at which an application can be launched is determined by the landing speed of the physical host. If the allocation requires going through a procurement process the time necessary can range from weeks to months. A consolidation environment requires manual reconfiguration, but no physical allocation in most cases. The reconfiguration can be performed in matter of hours, certainly no more than a few days. In a virtualized environment this period gets compressed to a few minutes or even seconds.

When a capability is introduced that compresses a task that used to take months to mere seconds, this is a game changing capability. An important exercise at this point is to figure out what processes and business models will be affected by this capability. For instance, the enhanced dynamic capability may lessen the need to deploy servers in house and to spend the associated capital upfront. The servers could be acquired through a data center hosting provider delivering servers on demand. The servers delivered would be virtual servers. Whether the server resource is physical or virtual, for the customer it does not matter as long as the contracted service level agreement is met.

So far we have studied one side of the coin of the virtualization continuum: the assumption has been that a physical host is capable of running multiple application instances. Up to this point the focus of our effort in matching workloads to computers has been to pack as many instances as possible to a host to increase server utilization.

The introduction of grid concepts greatly expands this horizon of possibilities:

- *Resource pooling.* The virtualization component of virtual service oriented grids enables partitioning most any physical resource into a set of pooled resources. While virtual, these resources are very marketable, and because the resources are disembodied they can be deployed and managed with the utmost agility.

- *Virtual service oriented grids extend the virtualization continuum.* Conventional wisdom looks at the concept of virtualization as a means for increasing the efficiency of a physical computing resource by enabling the physical entity to host several virtualized entities. Virtual service oriented grids extend the continuum from one physical entity to many virtual entities to the reciprocal, that is, one virtual entity may actually encompass more than one physical entity. The continuum gets extended from one to many to many to one.

Why does extending the virtualization continuum represent a useful proposition? Because no matter the speeds of execution attained with the fastest processors, there are always classes of problems whose time to solution is of interest.

It is true that problems that used to run in the fastest supercomputers can now be run in laptops. Curiously enough, the execution vehicle has changed, but the time to solution has not: one of the authors (Enrique) has been running a Computational Fluid Dynamics (CFD) simulation to model the thermal behaviors of servers deployed in data centers. A similar program would have taken a few hours to run in a supercomputer fifteen years ago. Today it runs in a laptop as fast and with as much memory, but a run still takes 2–3 hours to complete. An application architected to run and take advantage of multiple resources in a virtual service oriented grid environment and divide up the work across multiple processors in a grid. The run can be finished in minutes instead of hours.

Imagine a large database containing billions of records and terabytes of data. Furthermore, picture the database being accessed by a population of end users in the millions. If the database is implemented with access through a single server, all requests for access get queued up behind that single server. This is a performance-robbing, artificial constraint. A database is an inherently parallel entity: it can be accessed and updated by a large population of users without errors as long as users don't attempt to access the same record at the same time. Records are locked to prevent inconsistencies when two users try to use the same record. For this reason, databases lend themselves to a virtual service oriented grid treatment very well: the larger the database, the larger the number of processors that can be dedicated to access it without too many collisions. An application that allows resources to be increased with size to manage time to solution is said to be *scalable*.

Balanced Grid Architecture: Architecting Computers for Performance

The ENIAC machine in 1943, an acronym for Electronic Numerical Integrator and Computer, was arguably the first large-scale electronic computer using electronic vacuum tube technology. It weighed about 30 tons, occupied close to 700 square feet and consumed about 150 kilowatts of electric power.

Today, a microprocessor-based computer is a fingernail-sized device inside a laptop computer weighing less than 5 pounds and is much more powerful than the original ENIAC in spite of the reduction by 5 orders of magnitude in weight and mass.

Does a larger device automatically mean a faster computer? To some extent and only if the devices are built out of the same generation of technology. A similar situation occurs with automobile engines: in principle an 8-cylinder engine tends to be more powerful than a 4-cylinder engine with the same displacement per cylinder. The 8-cylinder engine is heavier than a 4-cylinder engine. Using a different technology, say turbine technology, it is possible to build an engine lighter than the 4-cylinder engine, yet more powerful than the 8-cylinder engine.

The pattern that we are beginning to see is that for any device, a larger version of the same device can be designed to deliver more power at the expense of some tradeoff, such as weight or complexity.

Let's examine some of the tradeoffs required for building computers. In its barest essence a computer consists of a central processing unit or CPU, which with today's technology is housed in a single computer chip. This is shown in Figure 3.14.

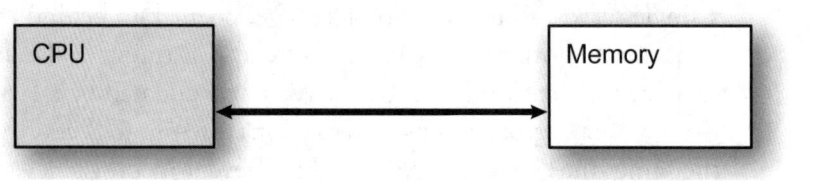

Figure 3.14 Canonical Computer

Unfortunately, this canonical architecture is impractical. First, any information stored in memory disappears and gets lost as soon as the computer is turned off. Most memory today exhibits this behavior. It is said to be *volatile*. Second, storage in memory is relatively expensive. The memory in most computers can hold only a few programs at a time, not the hundred or thousands that come with most any contemporary computer.

Provisioning the computer with a hard drive circumvents this problem, as shown in Figure 3.15.

Chapter 3: Virtual Service Oriented Grid Environment and Architecture ■ 111

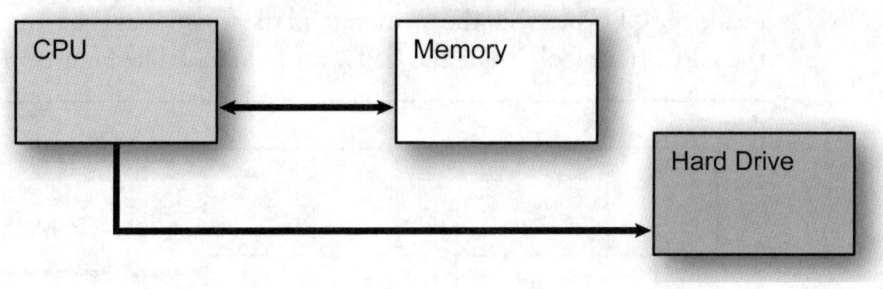

Figure 3.15 Adding a Hard Drive

If we abstract out the CPU and memory into a computer or *node*, we end up with a graph that has identical structure to that of Figure 3.14, as shown in Figure 3.16.

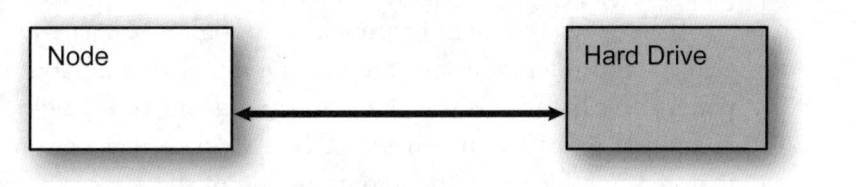

Figure 3.16 A Computer Node and Associated Storage

There is yet one more problem. Going back to Figure 3.14, present day system memory is much slower than the CPU. Because of the physical distance between the CPU and memory, when the CPU requests a datum from memory, it will take a while for the electrons from this request to reach memory and the datum to reach the CPU plus the processing time at the CPU's memory controller. In fact, memory is so slow that a modern microprocessor can execute hundreds of instructions before the round trip is completed. The computer still runs, but it would spend most of the time waiting for the response from memory, and it would run at only at a small fraction of the potential speed.

To address this problem, a very small amount of very fast storage is added inside the CPU between the memory and the functional logic units comprising the CPU. If we look inside the CPU, it would look like Figure 3.17.

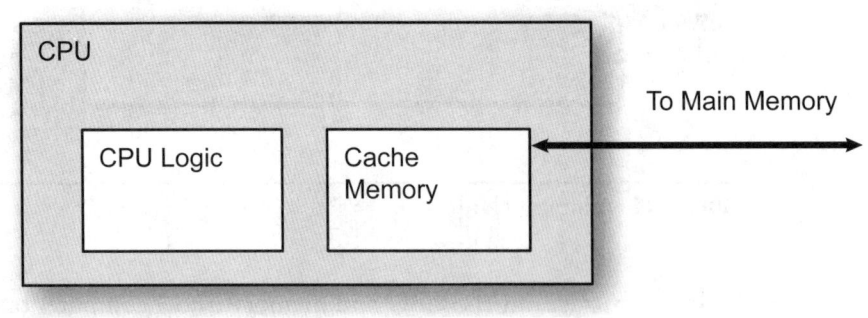

Figure 3.17 Adding a CPU Cache

What we have seen in Figures 3.14 through 3.17 is a pattern of a computer element and a storage element repeated multiple times. Table 3.2 captures this pattern. We have added two more rows or elements: for a group of computers connected to a local area network (LAN), data that does not fit in a node is stored in a file server, in a continuation of the same pattern. The top row represents the same nodes, but as entities connected to the Internet through a wide area network (WAN).

Table 3.2 Computer-storage hierarchy

Level	Computer Element	Connecting Technology	Storage Element
5	Collection of nodes in the Internet	Wide area network (WAN), fiber optic cables or satellite wireless links	Storage Service
4	Collection of nodes in a LAN	Local area network (LAN), Ethernet copper or optical cables	File server
3	Node	I/O interconnect, hard drive cables or ribbons	Hard drive
2	CPU	CPU bus/interconnect, baseboard circuit traces	Main memory
1	CPU logic	In-chip circuit traces	Cache memory

Table 3.2 also captures the *connecting technology* used to link a computer element to the respective storage element for each level. We have also added a column capturing the numbered *logical level* for reference in this discussion.

Nodes are connected to a file server using local area network (LAN) technology, usually some form of Ethernet, an industry standard, which comes in the form of 10 Mb/s (10 megabits per second or legacy), 100 Mb/s ("Fast"), 1 Gb/s (1 gigabit/s or 1000 Mb/s) and 10 Gb/s, informally "10 Gigabit." The most common physical medium for conveying data for Ethernet is UTP (unshielded, twisted pair) cables or optical fiber for some forms of 10 Gigabit Ethernet. Servers in a network are shared by multiple nodes through Ethernet switching devices.

A number of industry standards define connectivity from a node to the hard drives in that node, the most common being ATA, also known as IDE and SCSI. ATA stands for Advanced Technology bus Attachment; IDE stands for Integrated Drive Electronics, and SCSI stands for Small Computer System Interface. These interfaces were initially parallel interfaces, meaning one wire was assigned to carry each bit. More recent serial versions of these interfaces are being adopted, known as SATA, serial-ATA and SAS, serial-attached SCSI, respectively. Physically they come in the form of bundles of cables or cable ribbons that run from a socket in the baseboard to the respective I/O devices. High performance computers may use InfiniBand or storage area network (SAN) technology as an overlay technology for I/O.

The connection from a CPU to memory is usually implemented as traces in a circuit board that run from the socket housing the CPU to memory modules. This connection historically has been in the form of a bused bundle of traces or "bus" shared by multiple chips in a baseboard with a specification particular to a processor generation. More recently the bused interconnects have been replaced by point-to-point serial interconnects. An example is represented by the Intel® QuickPath technology.

The connection between the CPU logic and the cache memory is usually in the form of circuit traces inside the microprocessor. Some computer designs have cache memory outside the CPU chip, but these designs are less common today for commodity computers.

Ideally all of a computer's memory should be as fast as cache memory. In reality the chip has room for only a few megabytes of cache memory. Likewise, the baseboard has room for only a few gigabytes of memory. Anything that does not fit in the main memory needs to go to the hard drive as a file or as part of the virtual memory mechanism.

Remarkably, a well-tuned application can run almost as fast as if the application were run from cache. How is this accomplished? A program running a loop tends to stay within the loop for a long time. If the loop is stored in cache, it will run at the cache speed. This behavior is known as the *locality of reference* for a program. There is a small delay while the cache is loaded with a program fragment, but once the cache is loaded, the program will run very fast. If it fits, the portion of code stored in the cache is known as the *working set* for the program. A well tuned application behaves like an exquisitely choreographed trapeze act where the cache is loaded with a working set, the application runs for a while until the working set is exhausted and flushed, and the cache is reloaded with the next working set over and over again until the execution of the application completes.

Choreographing this behavior is no small feat. The data in the cache is loaded from memory. The data in memory is loaded from the hard drive. Essentially, each storage element behaves like a cache for the next level up in the hierarchy. As we go up in the hierarchy, the size of the working set grows commensurately with the size of the storage element.

In fact, in most cases the real performance is significantly lower than the potential performance. All it takes is a small misstep for the whole choreography to seize up, requiring a restart. These missteps occur for are many reasons, internal and external. An internal reason could be a working set that is too large for the cache. Under this circumstance, reuse is insufficient to hide the overhead of loading and flushing the cache. Sometimes it is not obvious which portion needs to be loaded in the cache next. If the system makes a wrong guess, the cache needs to be reloaded, which takes extra time. A portion of the cache may be flushed too soon, again forcing a reload. There is an intrinsic penalty in the delay caused by a reload. The penalty for loss of synchronization can be much greater because recovery may involve the higher layers (I/O or networking), which react much more slowly. An external reason could be delays caused by another program in a multi-programmed environment.

What we have described up to this point is a *scale-up* architecture where the abstractions describing the behavior of a computer are stacked on top of each other as depicted in Table 3.2.

A *scale-out* architecture is also possible through the *replication* of a computer element at any level. Scale out occurs at level 1 in the form of multi-core microprocessor technology. It occurs at level 2 in the form of computers with dual or quad or higher socket count. Scale-out at level 3 through the use of InfiniBand or some proprietary technology to link nodes together. Scale-out at level 4 is essentially LAN networking, so commonplace that we rarely think of it as a form of scale-out.

Note that the definition of scale out in this book is a bit different from definitions seen in the industry, which are usually application defined. For instance, scale-out is usually associated with multiple front-end Web servers in a network and scale-up is associated with 4- or 8-way servers running a database application. For the purposes of this discussion, we consistently refer to scale-out only when replication is involved. To avoid confusion, we will refer to the industry understanding of scale-out in a multi-socket server simply as "level 2 scale-out". We will refer to the multiple front-end Web servers as a form of level 4 scale-out.

Not all computer architectures are created equal from a performance standpoint. The intrinsic processor performance constitutes a necessary but not sufficient condition in a virtual service oriented grid environment. If the system is incapable of delivering the data on time to a CPU for processing, it is irrelevant how fast the CPU can crunch on the data. As we saw, if the delays of the higher levels are exposed to the CPU, the delivered performance may fall into single percentage digits relative to the total capability of the CPU. Hence it is crucial to take a holistic approach where all the elements in the system are brought into consideration.

Storage element size matters. A larger cache allows running programs with fewer cache reloads and reduces the likelihood of working set size mismatches. A larger main memory reduces the likelihood of virtual memory thrashing where a portion of program data is brought in from the hard drive, used once, and then pushed out. Under this circumstance the computer spends most of the time doing I/O with little real work accomplished.

In a virtual service oriented grid environment the quality of the interconnect technology gates the overall potential performance. Two essential parameters define the performance of an interconnect technology: *latency* and *bandwidth*.

Latency is the delay between the time a computer element requests a piece of data and the time the first byte of the requested datum arrives. In a scale-out environment, communication between peer computer elements is possible. Latency applies equally as well for communication between peer computer elements. We can apply this concept to everyday life. For instance, the latency for postal mail is anywhere between 1 and 7 days, which is the time it takes a letter to arrive to its destination.

Bandwidth measures how fast data can be transferred from a storage element to a computer element or between computer elements. This speed is measured in bytes per second.

Table 3.3 captures representative latency and bandwidth figures for each level with present day technologies:

Table 3.3 Representative latencies and bandwidths

Level	Computer Element	Latency	Bandwidth
5	Collection of nodes in the Internet	0.1–10s	0.0001 – 10 GB/s
4	Collection of nodes in a LAN	0.1–1 ms	0.001 – 10 GB/s
3	Node	1–100 µs	0.1 – 10 GB/s
2	CPU	50–500 ns	10 – 100 GB/s
1	CPU logic	1–10 ns	10 – 1000 GB/s

Note: GB/s denotes gigabytes per second; Gb/s or Gbps denotes gigabits per second

Low latency and high bandwidth at each level are obvious figures of merit to characterize performance in a system. In a virtual service oriented grid environment the performance of the interconnect is no less important in defining the performance of the system overall.

How do interconnect performance metrics define the overall system performance? One way to see this mechanism at work is to look at the mission of the interconnect not just as a high speed data pipe. Its mission is really to refill the storage element at the next level down as fast as possible. This refilling operation needs to get accomplished *before* the actual data is needed as the penalty for exposing latencies to the next level down are high. An architecture that makes this refill operation easy to accomplish is said to be *balanced*. An unbalanced architecture develops *bottlenecks*, meaning portions of the system get starved, unable to move forward with unfulfilled data requests.

Perhaps it is meaningful at this point to realize that the considerations for operating a computer tend to mimic real life. For instance, a busy person in a physician's waiting room will instinctively try to reach for the PDA and catch up with email or attempt to read a book or leaf through a magazine. This is an exercise in *latency hiding*: it is possible for a computer system to do useful work while waiting for data by scheduling another task during the presumed idle period. The task need not be directly related to the task at hand. It can be any other task, perhaps a lower priority task. The only requirement is that the task be ready to run to fill the waiting void.

One obvious pattern from Table 3.3 is that latency gets larger and bandwidth gets smaller toward the higher levels. This is to be expected because the larger physical distances involved toward the higher levels, from millimeters at level 1 to possibly across continents at level 5. Hiding latency at level 1 may include the scheduling of a few hundred instructions, whereas hiding latency at level 5 may include the redesign of the locking strategy of a database to increase the level of transaction concurrency. As the "bump" of latency between one level to the next becomes larger it also becomes increasingly harder to hide the latency. Desktop and laptop processors offer two levels of cache and high end server processors feature up to three levels of cache. Defining an intermediate level is one architectural mechanism to reduce the dissonance from one level to the next.

Another critical juncture takes place at the node level: the latency of hard drives can be as much as five orders of magnitude larger than the latency of main memory. Hybrid hard drives, which carry a large nonvolatile memory buffer, essentially a cache, in the order of gigabytes were designed to reduce the latency from positioning the drive head over the platter. In fact, the buffer is so large that the disk platter does not need to spin continuously anymore. Most of the data traffic takes place in the buffer at near memory speed with an occasional spin-up when a cache reloading or flushing is needed.

For scale-out computers, given the current state of technology, peer-to-peer communication at level 4 represents a challenge for similar reasons. Peer-to-peer communication involves moving data that resides in the memory of one node to the memory of another node. The cheapest medium for carrying this exchange is using the LAN. Unfortunately, if we allow for the delays in network processing, latencies in the order of 100 to 200 microseconds are not uncommon. On the other side, a CPU deals with memory speeds with latencies in the order of 100 to 200 *nanoseconds* or three orders of magnitude smaller. This is because most computer systems today are not normally provisioned with a level 3 interconnect for peer-to-peer data exchange such as InfiniBand because of the expense involved. Level 3 interconnects are normally installed for I/O.

This gap is very difficult to bridge, and it limits severely the classes of applications that can be run on the system in scale-out mode. For high performance systems, this gap used to be addressed through custom, expensive high speed networks. To keep costs down, InfiniBand technology has been increasingly taking on this role.

We have made the argument that the discontinuity in latency from one architectural level to the next must not be too large. A similar argument can be made for the discontinuity in bandwidth. How large can this discontinuity be? It depends on the requirements of the particular application running in the system. Some applications are not latency sensitive or require very little in terms of intermediate results computed by other nodes. Others exhibit poor performance in a scale-out environment. From practical experience, and as a rule of thumb, for most applications, the bump in latency and bandwidth from any level to the next should not degrade by more than a factor of 10. To the degree that any of the gaps is larger than 10, the system becomes *unbalanced*, that is, it easily develops bottlenecks that no amount of software tuning can circumvent. We call this architectural rule of thumb the *Rule of 10*. Simply stated, the Rule of 10 says that *the degradation in latency and bandwidth between any two consecutive architectural levels in a computer system should be no worse than a factor of 10.*

There are no absolutes; it's all matter of degrees and balance: fewer levels are better, smaller gaps between levels are also better, but attaining these two goals makes the system overall more expensive. Single-application systems are easier to architect and build, and some applications will run well even in purportedly "unbalanced" systems.

Table 3.4 captures a latency worksheet for a typical server. Each storage element in a server exhibits an intrinsic delay. For instance, when the CPU requests a datum from memory, the table indicates that for this particular server, it takes 100 nanoseconds to get the first byte from memory. Of interest in this table are the Rule of 10 latency ratios obtained by dividing the latency in a given row over the latency in the row immediately above.

An architecturally balanced server would have all the ratios at 10 or below. This means the server can operate at register speeds yet handle data sets as large as the largest storage element under consideration.

Servers today do not possess the ideal ratios. The 80,000 ratio between hard drive and memory latency indicates an immediate trouble spot, representative of the I/O bottlenecks that modern servers experience. One way of addressing the large latency gap is through the introduction of additional storage rungs; for instance, through the use of solid state drives or hybrid drives with very large solid state caches.

Table 3.4 Calculation of Rule of 10 Latency Ratios in a Server

Storage Element	Latency	Latency Ratio over row above
Registers	0.3 ns	n/a
L1 Cache	0.6 ns	2
L2 Cache	3 ns	5
L3 Cache	18 ns	6
Main Memory	100 ns	5
7.2 K RPM Hard Drive	8 ms	80,000
NAS	100 ms	12
Outsourced storage provider	1s	10

An example of latency and bandwidth tolerant application are Monte Carlo simulations used as the basis for many financial services industry (FSI) applications. Systems running this one application are essentially massive random number generators. The network is needed to load the data at the beginning of a computation and collect the results at the end with little communication in between; in which case a high performance level 3 interconnect is not necessary. This behavior makes Monte Carlo simulation a good application match for most grid systems today. A virtual service oriented grid environment needs to support a broader range of applications and will probably require a stronger level 3 interconnect.

Two useful metrics can be derived from the latency and bandwidth figures in an interconnect. The first is the bandwidth-latency product M. If B represents bandwidth and L represents latency, then

M = LB

M is measured in bytes, and can be thought of as the *characteristic message size*. For instance, a level 3 InfiniBand link that can transmit data at 1,000 MB/s (megabytes per second) with a latency of 1 μs (microsecond) will have a characteristic message size of 1,000 bytes. This is the amount of data that needs to be sent across the link ahead of time to hide the latency of the link. Smaller is better. Compare this number with the characteristic message size for an IDE hard drive yielding 100 MB/s and running at 7,200 RPM, which is 0.83 MB or over 800 times larger. This means that the optimal size for disk reads is in chunks of 0.83 MB. It is possible to issue reads of smaller size, but this means that the second read is issued before the data from the fist read has returned.

The second figure of merit is the ratio of bandwidth over latency:

A = B / L

This ratio is the *bandwidth acceleration*, measured in terabytes per second squared (TB/s2). We mentioned that a small characteristic message size is generally better. However, this could be because the interconnect link is really slow. Computing the bandwidth acceleration metric disambiguates the reason for a small characteristic message size. For instance, a DSL broadband link may offer a bandwidth of 8 Mb/s (megabit per second), that is, 1 MB/s at a 1 ms (millisecond) latency. The characteristic message size of this link is the same as the InfiniBand link above. However, the bandwidth acceleration number for the InfiniBand link is A = (1 GB/s)/(1 μs) = 1,000 TB/s2. The bandwidth acceleration number for the broadband link is only A = (1 MB/s) / 1 ms = 1 GB/s2. Hence the bandwidth acceleration for the broadband link is worse than the same number for InfiniBand by a factor of one million.

Architectural Balance

If there is one fundamental notion in this chapter about architecture is that of balance. Any solution imaginable is invariably a compromise between conflicting requirements. This holds true for both technical and business considerations.

For instance, we saw that parallel computation is a mechanism to overcome the performance limitations of single CPUs either through CPUs containing multiple cores or by ganging computers together.

Deploying parallel processing brings complexity. More often than not legacy applications can't take advantage of parallel resources. In order to quantify the problem and make it tractable we introduced multi-layered frameworks that allow a divide-and-conquer approach to perform a quantitative performance analysis.

The business equivalent for distributed computing in a virtual service grid environment is the problem of federated technology development: it is possible to develop a world product at a single design center. It is difficult for a centralized development organization to factor in requirements from multiple geographic regions. More likely than not, the resulting product will not be a good fit for most global markets. Hence, for global companies product development needs to be spread out across multiple countries. Doing so requires more complex technology management processes.

The bottom line is that for most strategic technology planning exercises there is no right or wrong answer. Every alternative needs to be qualified with pros and cons. Hard decisions may be required as in most cases there is no clear winner. Without an attempt to be comprehensive, after all, strategy is by definition an open ended exercise. In this chapter the authors have covered a number of approaches applicable to technology planning, which they hope will be useful to the reader. The approaches are both qualitative, providing a sense of direction in the planning process, and quantitative with examples on how to quantify architectural balance at multiples level of abstraction.

Chapter 4

Building Blocks for Virtual Service Oriented Grids

Good order is the foundation of all good things.
—Edmund Burke, *Reflection on the Revolution of France*, 1790

Nothing is particularly hard if you divide it into smaller jobs.
—Henry Ford, US automobile industrialist (1863–1947)

As in other computing paradigms before, virtual service oriented grids represent the synthesis of a number of different technologies that evolved over many years. Perhaps what is different this time around is that virtual service oriented grids acknowledge business needs as one of the primary engines for this evolution. On the architecture side, the concept of reuse figures as one of the fundamental principles in terms of building blocks defining the new environment as well as in the reuse of legacy systems.

Legacy systems in many cases represent a substantial investment and the fruits of many years of refinement. To the extent that legacy applications bring business value with relatively little cost in operations and maintenance there is no reason to replace them. The adoption of virtual service oriented grids does not imply a wholesale replacement of legacy systems by any means. Newer virtual service oriented applications will coexist with legacy for the foreseeable future. If anything, the adoption of a virtual service oriented environment will create opportunities for legacy integration with the new environment through the use of Web services based exportable interfaces. Additional value will be created for legacy through extended life cycles and new revenue streams through repurposing older applications.

To understand how the different components of virtual service oriented grids came to be, we have to look at the evolution of its three constituent technologies: namely virtualization, service orientation, and grids. We also need to examine how they get integrated and interact with each other to form the core of a virtual service oriented grid environment. This chapter also addresses the tools and overall architecture components that keep virtual service oriented functions as an integral business services that deliver ultimate value to businesses. Figure 4.1 depicts the abstract relationship between the three constituent technologies. Each item represents a complex technical domain of its own. In the following sections, we describe how key technology components in these domains define the foundation for a virtual service oriented grid environment, elements such as billing and metering tools, SLA management, as well as security, data integrity, and so on. In the end of the chapter, we discuss architecture considerations to put all these components together for tangible business solutions.

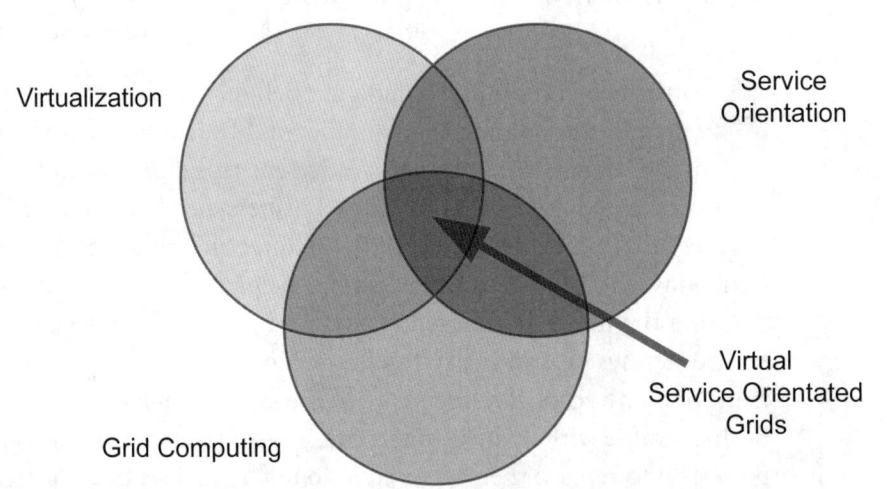

Figure 4.1   Virtual Service Oriented Grids Represent the Confluence of Three Key Technology Domains

Virtualization

Alan M. Turing in his seminal 1950 article for the British psychology journal *Mind*[1] proposed a test on whether machines were capable of thinking by having a machine and a human behind a curtain typing text messages to a human judge. A thinking machine would pass the test if the judge could not reliably determine whether answers from the judge's question came from the human or from the machine.

The emergence of virtualization technology poses a similar test, perhaps not as momentous as attempting to distinguish a human from a machine. Every computation result, such as a Web page retrieval, a weather report, a record pulled from a database or a spreadsheet result can be ultimately traced to a series of state changes. These state changes can be represented by monkeys typing at random at a keyboard, humans scribbling numbers on a notepad, or a computer running a program. One of the drawbacks of the monkey method is the time it takes to arrive at a solution[2]. The "human" or manual method is also too slow for most problems of practical size today involving millions or billions of records.

Only machines are capable of addressing the scale of complexity of most enterprise computational problems today. In fact, their performance has progressed to such an extent that, even with large computational tasks, they are idle most of the time. This is one of the reasons for the low utilization rates for servers in data centers today. Meanwhile, this infrastructure represents a sunk cost, whether fully utilized or not.

Modern microprocessor based computers have so much reserve capacity that they can be used to simulate other computers. This is the essence of virtualization: the use of computers to run programs that simulate computers of the same or even different architectures. In fact, machines today can be used to simulate many computers, anywhere between one and thirty for practical situations. If a certain machine shows a load factor of five percent when running a certain application, that machine can easily run ten virtualized instances of the same application.

---

1 A.M. Turing, Computing Machinery and Intelligence, Mind, Vol. 59 No. 236, October 1950

2 http://en.wikipedia.org/wiki/Infinite_monkey_theorem

Likewise, three machines of a three-tier e-commerce application can be run in a single physical machine, including a simulation of the network linking the three machines.

Virtual computers, when compared to "real" physical computers, can pass the Turing test much more easily than when humans are compared to a machine. There is essentially no difference between results of computations in a physical machine versus the computation in a virtual machine. It may take a little longer, but the results will be identical to the last bit. Whether running in a physical or a virtualized host, an application program goes through the same state transitions, and eventually presents the same results.

As we saw, *virtualization* is the creation of substitutes for real resources. These substitutes have the same functions and external interfaces as their counterparts, but differ in attributes, such as size, performance, and cost. These substitutes are called *virtual resources*. Because the computational results are identical, users are typically unaware of the substitution. As mentioned, with virtualization, we can make one physical resource look like multiple virtual resources; we can also make multiple physical resources into shared pools of virtual resources. Virtualization creates a layer of abstraction between the physical resources, such as computing, storage, and networking hardware, and the virtual resources required by applications. In many cases, virtual resources can have functions or features that are not available in their underlying physical resources.

In fact, the concept of virtualization has been around for a long time. Back in the mainframe days, we used to have virtual processes, virtual devices, and virtual memory. We use virtual memory in most operating systems today. With virtual memory, computer software gains access to more memory than is physically installed, via the background swapping of data to disk storage. Similarly, virtualization concepts can be applied to other IT infrastructure layers including networks, storage, laptop or server hardware, operating systems, and applications. Even the notion of process is essentially an abstraction for a virtual CPU running a single application.

Virtualization on x86 microprocessor based systems is a more recent development in the long history of virtualization. This entire sector owes its existence to a single company, VMware; and in particular, to founder Mendel Rosenblum, a professor of operating systems at Stanford University. Rosenblum devised an intricate series of software workarounds to overcome certain intrinsic limitations of the x86 instruction set architecture in the support of virtual machines. These workarounds became the basis for VMware's early products. Native support for virtualization hypervisors and virtual machines has been developed to improve the performance and stability of virtualization. A prime example is the Intel Virtualization Technology (VT) family. A side effect of hardware support for virtualization has been the reduction of barriers to new market entrants. As virtualization becomes a dominant trend for enterprise applications, more robust hardware support for virtualization will be available. Following VMware's success, more recent market entrants have brought in a number of alternatives. Many of these offerings—not only Xen and KVM but also Denali and OKL4—are available as open source software.

The availability of a free bare-metal x86 hypervisors represent a highly disruptive influence to incumbents, representing a thorn in the side of VMware, similar to the influence of Linux on Sun's Solaris business and JBoss to BEA's WebLogic. The opportunities for new entrants tend to lie in the low-end of the market, representing a strongly commoditizing influence for the hypervisor. In the end, the end user benefits through lower cost and a broad variety of offerings. This portends tight integration of the hypervisor with hardware platforms, very much like the way most operating systems are bundled with every instance of hardware platforms shipped by original equipment manufacturers today.

To look further into the impact of virtualization on a particular platform, Figure 4.2 illustrates a typical configuration of a single OS platform without virtual machines (VM) and a configuration of multiple virtual machines with virtualization. As indicated in the chart on the right, a new layer of abstraction is added, the virtual machine monitor (VMM), between physical resources and virtual resources. A VMM presents each VM on top its virtual resources and maps virtual machine operations to physical resources. VMMs can be designed to be tightly coupled with operating systems or can be agnostic to operating systems. The latter approach provides customers with the capability to implement an OS-neutral management infrastructure.

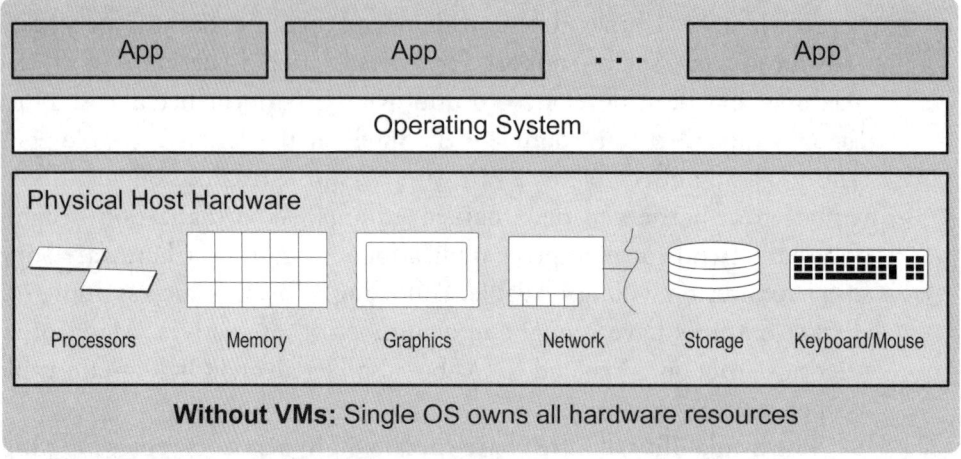
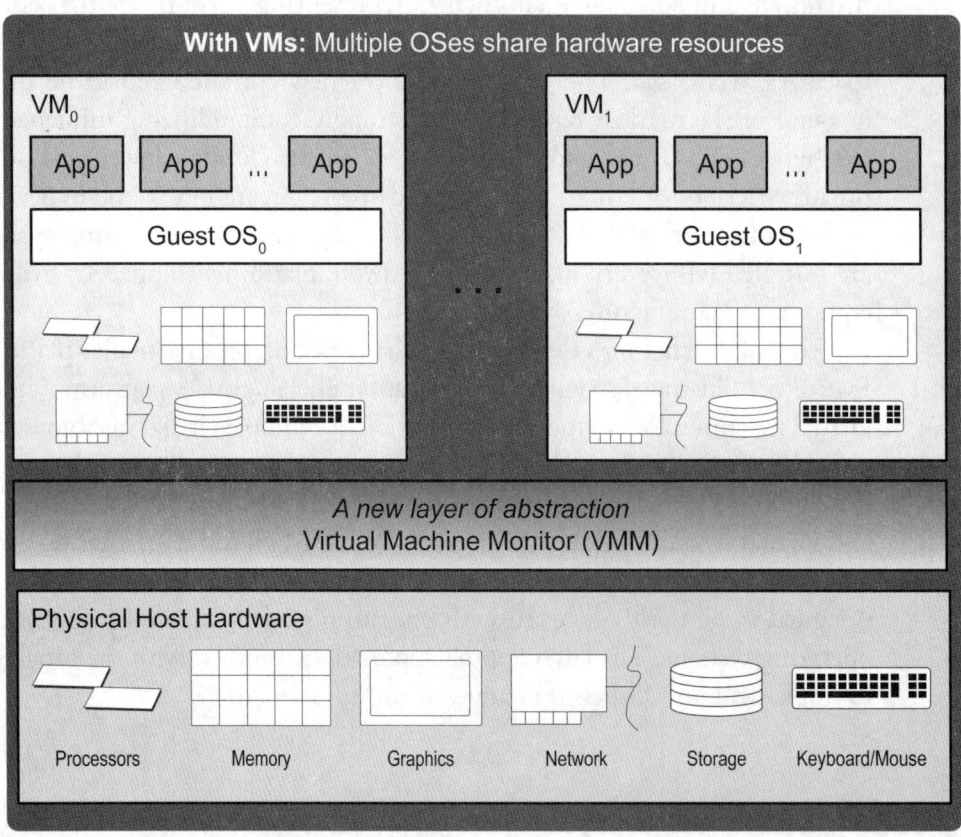

Figure 4.2   A Platform With and Without Virtualization

Virtualization Usage Models

Virtualization is not just about increasing load factors. It brings a new level of operational flexibility and convenience to the hardware that was previously associated with software only. Virtualization allows running instances of virtualized machines as if they were applications. Hence, programmers can run multiple VMs with different operating systems, and test code across all configurations simultaneously. Once systems administrators started running hypervisors in test labs, they found a treasure trove of valuable use cases. Multiple physical servers can be consolidated onto a single, more powerful machine. The big new box still draws less energy and is easier to manage on a per machine basis. This server consolidation model provides a good solution to "server sprawl." More and more usages start to emerge with the concept of virtualization. But there is much more. Typical virtualization usages are summarized in Figure 4.3.

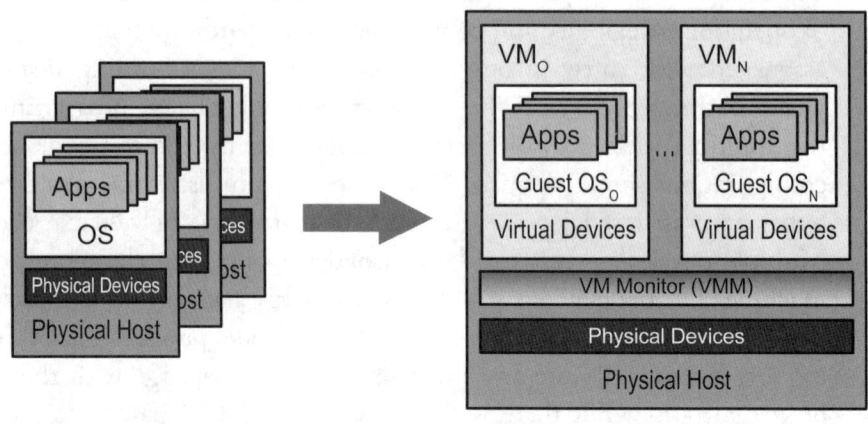

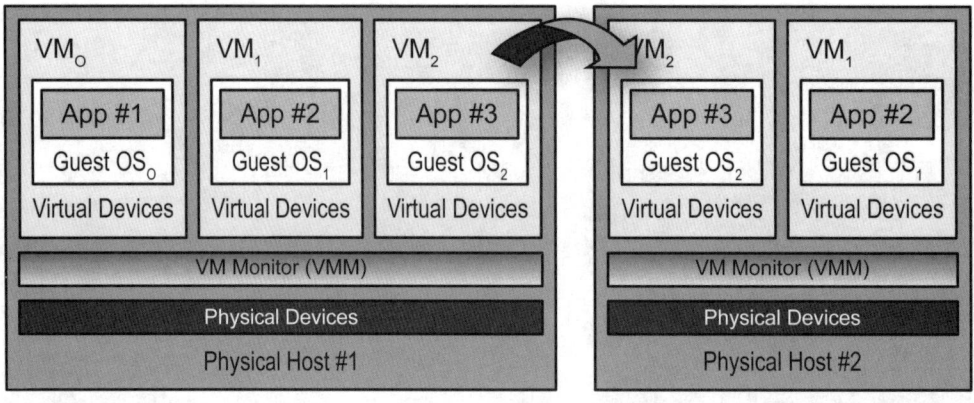

Figure 4.3a Typical Virtualization Usages

- Server Consolidation: Virtualization eases server sprawl via the deployment of applications running in virtual machines (VMs). It simplifies legacy system migration. Application instances can be run safely and moved transparently across pooled hardware. It provides a dial to regulate server utilization rates from 5–15 percent

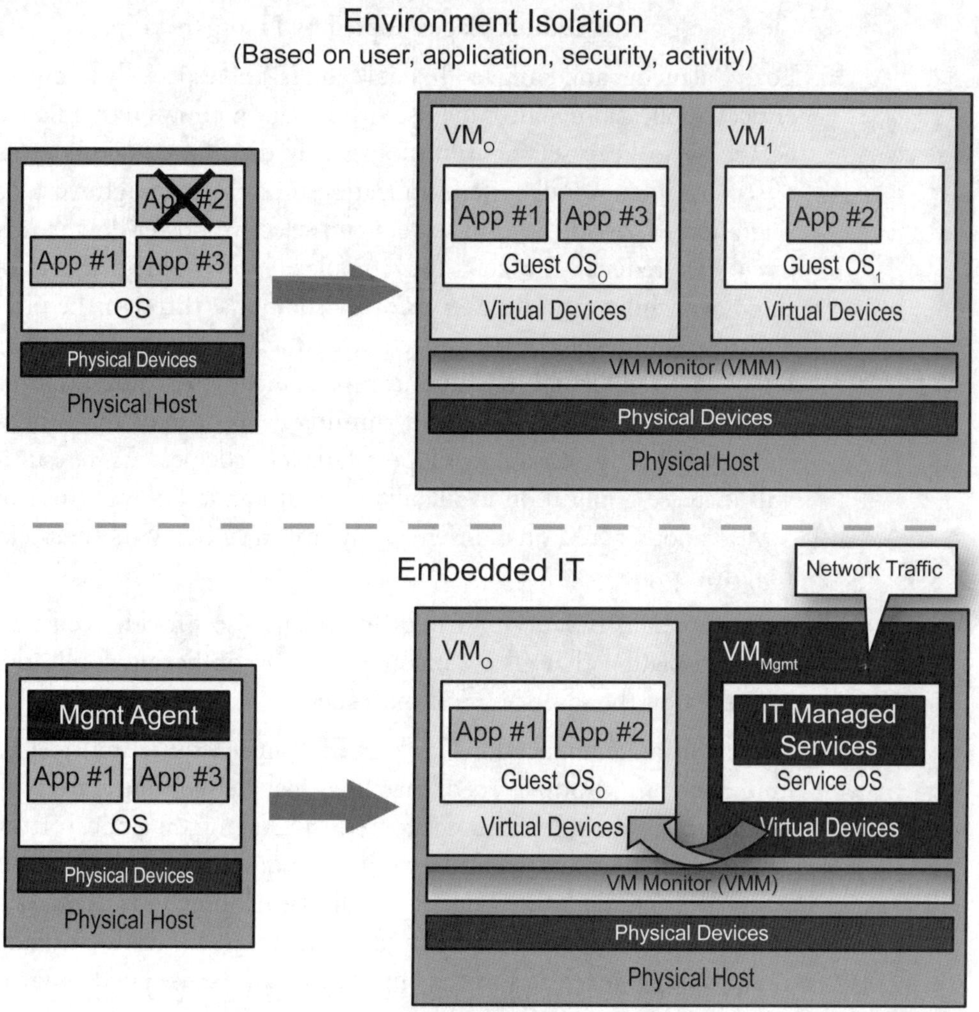

Figure 4.3b Typical Virtualization Usages (continued)

to 60–80 percent. This usage focuses on reducing the box count, that is, the number of servers in an existing data center infrastructure, allowing the retirement of older hardware or extending the life of legacy applications. Server consolidation benefits result from a reduction in the overall number of systems and related recurring costs (power, cooling, rack space, and so on). This is the most common and often the earliest virtualization usage adopted by IT organizations.

- Load Balancing and Failover: In data centers, and especially in mission critical application environments, virtualization allows dynamic load balancing to keep server utilization evenly distributed across a pool of servers. The overall system utilization increases through workload migration to low utilization servers and selective power-downs. This usage can reduces the cost and complexity of business continuity (high availability and disaster recovery solutions) through the use of dynamically allocated virtual machines. Allocation can be done on the fly because the virtual machines comprise mostly software resources. This is a lot less expensive than running a number of machines as standby running reserve to support failover schemes. As a result, it will increase application availability by automatic failover from one VM to another VM on a different physical machine without application disruption.

- Environmental Isolation: Virtualization can also provide secure and reliable isolation that allows incompatible or conflicting applications to coexist on the same physical machines.

Large corporate applications such as ERP may require multiple machines to run. Multiple sets of machines may be required for test and development work, for instance to perform staging on a new software release. Different sets would be needed for development, prototyping stress testing, and other tasks in the development process. This multiplicative effect can quickly become onerous. With virtualization, multiple machines in the application can be assigned to virtual machines in a single physical host. In practice, the same tasks can be handled by as few as a third as many servers.

Even the network setup may get simpler as portions of the network connecting virtual machines within get absorbed into the VMs in the host.

In addition, development VMs can be rapidly provisioned by reusing preconfigured systems, expediting the staging process.

- Embedded IT and virtual appliances: In the most sophisticated virtualization configurations, system management and security agents are typically installed in the application OS today. It is possible to allocate an extra VM to provide seamless platform management and security. This scheme would be highly tamper-resistant because of the logical isolation across VM instances. Because there is higher logical isolation across VM instances than across processes in an operating system, it will be more difficult for viruses and worms running on virtualized instances to disable management functions and security agents. Systems become more robust and resilient and less vulnerable to crashing after unintentional mistakes.

  With virtualization it becomes easier to tune special service appliances, such as VOIP, video streaming, video conferencing, and the like by running them as separate VMs, or actually, as virtual appliances (VAs), logically separated from application VMs with the mix of instances designed to work within the envelope of the physical host or SLA requirements.

Within the IT technology portfolio today, the most significant benefits from adopting virtualization are undoubtedly reducing total cost of ownership (TCO) and increasing IT agility. As side benefits, virtualization reduces application deployment cycles, the ongoing, recurring support and management costs, in addition to the one time, upfront capital costs.

These benefits, as outstanding as they are, represent only the beginning. There exist additional "helper" technologies complementing and amplifying the benefits brought up virtualization. For example, extended manageability technologies will be needed to track and manage the hundreds and thousands of virtual machines in the environment, especially when many of them are created and terminated dynamically in a data center or even across data centers. Grid computing technologies are needed to orchestrate disparate types of physical systems to become a pool of virtual resources across the global network. In this environment, standards based web services become the fabric of communicate among heterogeneous systems and applications coming from different manufacturers, in-sourced and out-sourced, legacy and new alike.

Service Orientation

Service orientation represents the natural evolution of current development and deployment models. As described earlier in the book, the movement started as a programming paradigm and evolved into an application and system integration methodology with many different standards behind it. The evolution of service orientation can be traced back to the object-oriented models in the 1980s and even earlier as discussed in the preface and the component-based development model in the 1990s. As the evolution continues, service orientation retains the benefits of component-based development (self-description, encapsulation, dynamic discovery and loading). Service orientation brings a shift in paradigm from remotely invoking methods on objects, to one of passing messages between services. In short, service orientation can be defined as a design paradigm that specifies the creation of automation logic in the form of services based on standard messaging schemas. Moreover, this logic tends to be usefully defined in terms of business entities rather than entities dictated by the technology of the day: As an example, in the electrical power industry partner to partner data exchanges are still in their infancy. Control and operational information, or metadata, is transmitted from remote terminal units (RTUs) on site through dedicated data links. RTUs are computers functioning as primitive information routers. RTUs from different manufacturers use proprietary and incompatible protocols. Because of these particularities, any information architecture for a power system today needs to mention RTUs explicitly, essentially hard binding the architecture to a specific technology and making innovation difficult.[3]

Messaging schemas describe not only the structure of messages, but also behavior and semantics of acceptable message exchange patterns and policies. Service orientation promotes interoperability among heterogeneous systems, and thus becomes the fabric for systems integration, as messages can be sent from one service to another without consideration of how the service handling those messages has been implemented.

Service orientation provides an evolutionary approach to building distributed systems that facilitate loosely coupled integration and resilience to change. With the arrival of Web Services and WS* standards, service-oriented

---

3   Effective Power System Communication Requirements for Deregulated Power Industry, A. Maun Than Oo, A. Kalam, A. Zayeg, The 2004 IEEE Asia-Pacific Conference on Circuits and Systems, December 6-9, 2004. ieeexplore.ieee.org/iel5/9700/30611/01412962.pdf?arnumber=1412962.

architectures (SOAs) has made service orientation a feasible paradigm for the development and integration of software and hardware services.

Unfortunately, the benefits offered by service orientation and SOA have been obscured by hype and confusion that increasingly surround the terms and capabilities. Some even wishfully promote service orientation and SOA as panaceas for all enterprise IT problems. However, service orientation does offer some specific benefits when combined judiciously with other information technologies.

- **Progressive and based on proven principles:** Service orientation is evolutionary (not revolutionary) and grounded in well-known information technology principles taking into account decades of experience in building real world distributed applications. Service orientation incorporates concepts such as self-describing applications, explicit encapsulation, and dynamic loading of functionality at runtime—principles first introduced in the 1980s and 1990s through object-oriented and component-based development. What is new for service orientation are the ways to achieve the benefits of these principles. Instead of method invocation on an object reference, service orientation shifts the discourse to that of message passing, a proven method for scalable distributed systems integration. Therefore, service orientation is naturally easy for developers and IT engineers to grasp and internalize. IT staff have been familiar with such information technology principles for years, so digesting and adopting them represents only an incremental step.

- **Product-independent and facilitating innovation:** Service orientation is a set of architectural principles supported by open industry standards independent of any particular product. It leaves plenty of room for software and hardware vendors of different sizes to innovate following these principles yet conform to common standards to achieve interoperable solutions. The emergence of Web 2.0 and Web 3.0 in recent years represents a good example of innovation based on the original service oriented principles. This explains the popularity of Web 2.0 and Web 3.0 as prime examples for distributed service and application integration. The monolithic application architecture of the past is slowly fading away. A new and innovative service-oriented application development or integration paradigm is emerging. Faster and more flexible time-to-market business models and technologies, such as SaaS (Software as a Service), PaaS (Platform as a Service), "mashups," and so on are built on top of the principles of service orientation.

- **Easy to adopt and non-disruptive:** Service orientation can and should be adopted through an incremental process. Because it follows some of the same information technology principles, service orientation is not disruptive to current IT infrastructures and can often be achieved through wrappers or adapter to legacy applications without completely redesign the applications. Therefore, service-oriented development can often be achieved using the skills and technologies customers already have today. As more service-oriented software and hardware are available, more complex solutions could be built over time. The fact that adoption strategies for service orientation can be charted to yield very visible benefits helps enormously in overcoming objections from skeptics and political hurdles.

- **Adapt to changes and improved business agility:** Service-orientation promotes a loosely coupled architecture. Each of the services that compose a business solution can be developed and evolved independently. As a result, the technology enables business processes to be loosely coupled bringing enormous flexibility to executive decision makers and systems architects alike in selecting vendors and making decisions on whether to use internal resources or outsource certain functions. Businesses can achieve better agility through services based on open standards by making changes to service components and service interfaces in a timely fashion without big impacts to the overall solutions. Compare this with the situation of monolithic applications, where it typically requires weeks to implement the smallest change due to the constraints and underline dependencies of closely coupled application architecture. Not surprisingly, business agility is often seen as one of the biggest business benefits of service orientation.

Service Oriented Architectural Tenets

The fundamental building block of service orientation is a *service*. A service is a program interacting through well-defined message exchange interfaces.

The interfaces are self-describing, are relatively stable over time and versioning resilient, and shield the service from implementation details. Services must be designed for both availability and stability. Services are built to last while service configurations and aggregations are built for change. Some basic architectural tenets must be followed for service orientation to accomplish a successful service design:

- **Designed for loose coupling:** Loose coupling is a primary enabler for reuse and integration. It is the key to making service oriented solutions resilient to change. Service oriented application architects need to spend extra effort to define clear boundaries of services and assure that services are autonomous (less dependencies), to ensure that each component in a business solution is loosely coupled and easy to compose (reuse).
  - *Encapsulation:* Functional encapsulation, the process of hiding the internal workings of a service to the outside world is a fundamental feature of service orientation. This is a concept that was highly promoted in the object oriented designs and continues to be a primary consideration in designing a service.
  - *Standard interfaces:* We need to force ubiquity at the edge of the services. Web Services provide a collection of standards such as SOAP, WSDL, and the WS-* specifications, which take anything not functionally encapsulated for conversion into reusable components. The goal of these standards is to provide consistent and predictable usages in the programming model at the edge of the service.

    Introducing a new service interface protocol that lives on the outside of the service without a capability to be discovered and reused means it can be used only once, forcing duplication across applications and a tight logical coupling between the intended consumer and actual producer. This is a key challenge for many of the WS-* standards today, as there are so many of them and interoperability is not guaranteed.
  - *Unified messaging model:* By definition, service orientation enables systems to be loosely bound for both the composition of services, as well as the integration of a set of services into a business solution. Standard messaging and interfaces should be used for both service

integration and composition. The use of a unified messaging model blurs the distinction between integration and composition.

- **Designed for connected virtual environments:** With advances in virtualization as discussed in the previous section, service orientation is not limited to a single physical execution environment, but rather can be applied using interconnected virtual machines (VMs). This virtual network of machines is usually referred to as a service grid. Although the original service orientation paradigm doesn't mandate full resource virtualization, the combination of service orientation and a grid of virtual resources hint at the enormous potential business benefits brought by the autonomic and on-demand compute models.

    - *Service registration and discovery:* As services are created, their interfaces and policies are registered and advertised using ubiquitous formats. As more and more services are created and registered, a shareable service network is created. These services, along with intermediaries, become discoverable by solution integrators and become the basic building blocks for creating and integrating solution in the rich ecosystem described in Chapter 2. To elaborate the example earlier in this chapter, we can envision information exchanges accompanying the power exchanges in the electric power industry evolving in this direction. This will finally allow the economies of scale envisioned by deregulation.

    - *Shared messaging service fabric:* In addition to networking the services, a secure and robust messaging service fabric is essential for service sharing and communication among the virtual resources. This allows value-added messaging services to facilitate communications service providers and service consumers, such as message transformation, content-based routing, load balancing, authentication, and many others. A solid messaging service fabric not only helps in the decoupling solution components, but also can be used to address basic messaging quality of services (QOS) concerns such as availability, security, and integrity.

    - *Resource orchestration and resolution:* Once a service is discovered, we need to have effective ways to allocate sufficient resources for the services to meet the service consumer's needs. This needs to happen dynamically and be resolved at runtime. Resource orchestration among a pool of virtual resources is required to start, stop, or migrate services appropriately to meet the consumer's needs. This means special attention is placed on discovering resources at runtime and using these resources in a way that they can be released and regained based on resource orchestration policies.

- **Designed for manageability:** The solutions and associated services should be built to be managed with sufficient interfaces to expose information for an independent management system, which by itself could be composed of a set of services, to ensure that the entire loosely bound system will work as designed. Due to the nature of service orientation, the service management has to be dynamic and accessible. It is vital to the combined quality of services of a system because the integrity of a loosely bound system is significantly more important in mature networks where services are shared and new versions of shared services are introduced independently.

- **Designed for scalability:** Services are meant to scale. They should facilitate any target number of different service consumers defined by the business. Architecturally, services should take advantage of the latest programming technologies for multithreading and have clear definition of service boundaries (functionalities and interfaces). In addition, management facilities have to be in place to measure the quality and health of services. Virtualized services can replicate themselves to efficiently use most any physical resource.

- **Designed for federated solutions:** Service orientation breaks application silos. It spans traditional enterprise computing boundaries, such as network administrative boundaries, organizational and operational boundaries, and the boundaries of time and space. Services will have the ability to cross corporate or transnational boundaries, requiring a high degree of built-in security, trust, and internal identity, so that they can negotiate and establish federated service relationships with other services following given policies administrated by the management system.

Obviously, cohesiveness across services based on standards in a network of service is essential for service federation.

In a federated environment, it is possible for technology to run ahead of legal and regulatory boundaries. For instance, although it might be possible to encrypt and package a data set for remote execution in another country to any desired level of tamper-proof strength, laws in the originating country may make it illegal to move the data. In this case any legal statutes trump technological options. Flexibility from service orientation still allows outsourcing to countries where these operations are allowed.

We have talked about the concept of service orientation and key architecture tenets. There are still a lot of myths and hype surrounding service orientation. Table 4.1 is a summary to demystify some common misunderstandings.

Table 4.1 Service Orientation Myths

Myth	Fact
Service orientation is a technology.	Service orientation is a design philosophy independent of any product, technology, or industry trend.
Service orientation requires Web Services.	Service orientation can be implemented using Web services, but using Web services will not necessarily result in a service oriented solutions.
Service orientation is new and revolutionary.	Service orientation is not new. EDI, CORBA, and DCOM were conceptual examples of service orientation.
Service orientation ensures the alignment of IT and business.	Service orientation cannot assure IT and business alignment. It may enable the alignment, if used wisely.
Service orientation reduces implementation risk.	Service orientation cannot in itself lower your implementation risk, but can help lower your risk if used properly.
Service orientation requires a complete technology and business-processes overhaul.	Service orientation should be incremental and built on your current investments.
Service orientation requires an army of consultants.	This may be true during the initial adoption of SOA until a SOA culture is established. Regardless, there needs to be a long term cost payoff.
We need to build a service-orientated solution.	Service orientation is a means, not an end.

Services Needed for Virtual Service Oriented Grids

To make virtual service oriented grids work as described in Chapter 3, a set of foundation services is essential. These services are the building blocks for a solution stack at different layers.

Fundamental services can be divided into the following categories similar to the OGSA (Open Grid Services Architecture) approach, as outlined in Figure 4.4. The items are provided for conceptual clarity without an attempt to provide an exhaustive list of all the services. We highlight some example services, along with a high-level description.

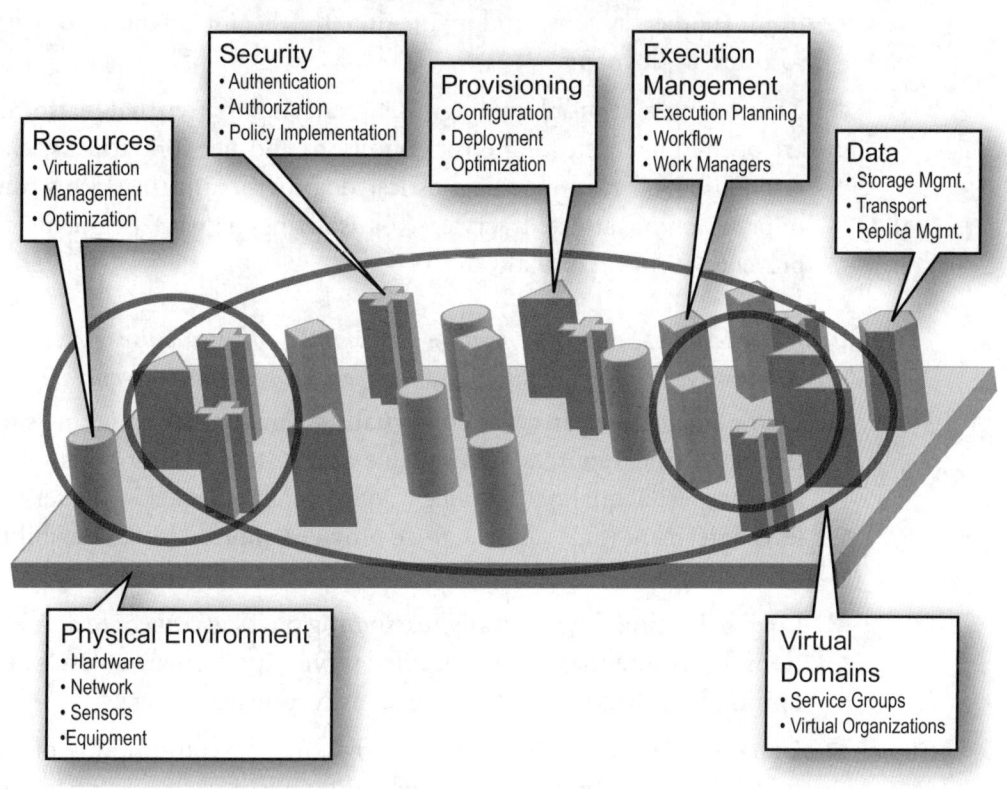

Figure 4.4 OGSA Service Model from OGSA Spec 1.5, July 2006

Resource management services: Management of the physical and virtual resources (computing, storage, and networking) in a grid environment

- **Asset discovery and management:** Maintaining an automatic inventory of all connected devices, always accurate and updated on a timely basis.
- **Provisioning:** Enabling bare metal provisioning, coordinating the configuration between server, network and storage in a synchronous manner, making sure software gets loaded on the right physical machines, taking platforms in and out of service as required for testing, maintenance, repair or capacity expansion; remote booting a system from another system, and managing the licenses associated with software deployment.
- **Monitoring and problem diagnosis:** Verifying that virtual platforms are operational, detecting error conditions and network attacks, and responding by running diagnostics, de-provisioning platforms and re-provisioning affected services, or isolating network segments to prevent the spread of malware.

Infrastructure services: Services to manage the common infrastructure of a virtual grid environment and offers the foundation for service orientation to operate

- **QoS management:** In a shared virtualized environment, making sure that sufficient resources are available and system utilization is managed at specific quality of service (QoS) level as outlined in the service level agreement (SLA). This service provides unprecedented flexibility in meeting SLA.
- **Load balancing:** Dynamically reassigning physical devices to applications to ensure adherence to specified service (performance) levels and optimized utilization of all resources as workloads change.
- **Capacity planning:** Measuring and tracking the consumption of virtual resources to be able to plan when to reserve resources for certain workloads or when new equipment needs to be brought on line.
- **Utilization Metering:** Tracking the use of particular resources as designated by management policy and SLA. The metering service could be used for chargeback and billing by higher level software

Execution management services: Execution management services are concerned with the problems of instantiating and managing to completion units of work or an application.

- **Business processes execution:** Setting up generic procedure as building blocks to standardize business processes and enabling the interoperability across heterogeneous system management products.
- **Workflow automation:** Managing a seamless flow of data as part of the business process to move from application to application. Tracking the completion of workflow and managing exceptions.
- **Execution resource allocation:** In a virtualized environment, selecting optimal resources for a particular application or task to execute.
- **Execution environment provisioning:** Once an execution environment is selected, dynamically provision the environment as required by the application, so that a new instance of the application can be created
- **Managing application lifecycle:** Initiate, track status of execution, and administer the end-of-life phase of a particular application and release virtual resources back to the resource pool.

Data services: Moving data as required, such as data replication and updates; managing metadata, queries, and federated data resources.

- **Remote access:** Access remote data resources across the grid environment. The services hide the communication mechanism from the service consumer. They can also hide the exact location of the remote data.
- **Staging:** When jobs are executed on a remote resource, the data services are often used to stage input data to that resource ready for the job to run, and then to move the result to an appropriate place.
- **Replication:** To improve availability and to reduce latency, the same data can be stored in multiple locations across a grid environment. Updates to data in one location may be propagated to the others according to a specified consistency policy.
- **Federation:** Data services can integrate data from multiple data sources that are created and maintained separately. Different data sources can

establish a federated trust relationship so that data can be served in an integrated interface and query structure, even though they are physically and logically separated. Service consumers may access data through secured interface seamlessly access data from the federated data sources without knowing the underlying federation details.

- **Derivation:** Data services should support the automatic generation of one data resource from another data source.
- **Metadata:** Some data service can be used to store descriptions of data held in other data services. For example, a replicated file system may choose to store descriptions of the files in a central catalogue.

Security services: facilitate the enforcement of the security-related policy within a grid environment.

- **Authentication:** Authentication is concerned with verifying proof of an asserted identity. This functionality is part of the credential validation and trust services in a grid environment
- **Identity mapping:** Provide the capability of transforming an identity that exists in one identity domain into an identity within another identity domain.
- **Authorization:** The authorization service is to resolve a policy-based access-control decision. The authorization service consumes as input a credential that embodies the identity of an authenticated service consumer and, for the resource that the service requestor requests, resolves, based on policy, whether or not the service requestor is authorized to access the resource.
- **Credential conversion:** Provide credential conversion from one type of credential to another type or form of credential. This may include such tasks as reconciling group membership, privileges, attributes, and assertions associated with entities (service consumers and service providers).
- **Audit and secure logging:** The audit service, similarly to the identity mapping and authorization services, is policy-driven. The audit service is responsible for producing records that track security-relevant events.

The resulting audit records may be reduced and examined so as to determine whether the desired security policy is being enforced.

- **Security policy enforcement:** Enforcing automatic device and software load authentication; tracing identity, access, and trust mechanisms within and across corporate boundaries to provide secure services across firewalls.

- **Logical isolation and privacy enforcement:** Ensuring that a fault in a virtual platform does not propagate to another platform in the same physical machine, and that there are no data leaks across virtual platforms which could belong to different accounts.

- **Network access control (NAC):** Restricting what a service can do until verification is obtained so that the service is compliant with the processes in the compound application it is to support.

Self-management services: Reduce the cost and complexity of owning and operating a grid environment autonomously.

- **Self-configuring:** A set of services adapt dynamically and autonomously to changes in a grid environment, using policies provided by the grid administrators. Such changes could trigger provisioning requests leading to, for example, the deployment of new components or the removal of existing ones, maybe due to a significant increase or decrease in the workload.

- **Self-healing:** Detect improper operations of and by the resources and services, and initiate policy-based corrective action without disrupting the grid environment.

- **Self-optimizing:** Tune different elements in a grid environment to the best efficiency to meet end user and business needs. The tuning actions could mean reallocating resources to improve overall utilization or optimization by enforcing an SLA.

Grid Computing

The most common description of grid computing includes an analogy to a power grid. When you plug an appliance or other object requiring electrical power into a receptacle, you expect that there is power of the correct voltage available, but the actual source of that power is not known. Your local utility company provides the interface into a complex network of generators and power sources and provides you with (in most cases) an acceptable quality of service for your energy demands. Rather than each house or neighborhood having to obtain and maintain its own generator of electricity, the power grid infrastructure provides a virtual generator. The generator is highly reliable and adapts to the power needs of the consumers based on their demand.

The vision of grid computing is similar. Once the proper grid computing infrastructure is in place, a user will have access to a "virtual computer" that is reliable and adaptable to the user's needs. This virtual computer will consist of many diverse computing resources. But these individual resources will not be visible to the user, just as the consumer of electric power is unaware of how their electricity is being generated. To reach this vision, there must be standards for grid computing that will allow a secure and robust infrastructure to be built. Standards such as the Open Grid Services Architecture (OGSA) and tools such as those provided by the Globus Toolkit provide the necessary framework. Initially, businesses will build their own infrastructures, but over time, these grids will become interconnected. This interconnection will be made possible by standards such as OGSA and the analogy of grid computing to the power grid will become real.

There are many definitions of grid computing and many different names created for similar concepts, such as autonomic computing, on-demand computing, adaptive datacenter, and the list goes on. By contrast, let's look at what grid computing is *not* about. It is not artificial intelligence, and it is not some kind of advanced networking technology. Neither is it a magic bullet to address every problem in the enterprise. Grid computing is a network of virtual computing resources, tools, and protocols for coordinated and automated resource sharing and problem solving among pooled physical devices. These devices can be distributed across the globe, heterogeneous, autonomous, and transient.

Combined with virtualization and service-oriented technologies, grid computing is emerging as a viable technology that businesses can use to increase ROI and bring more productivity out of IT resources.

Grids have been evolving over time as technology progresses. Different grids exist for different purposes. Some are dedicated to intensive computing for science research, while others focus on increasing resource utilization and business agility. Figure 4.5 is a brief summary of grid computing evolution.

As mentioned in the preface, the ancestry of grids is rooted in HPC (High Performance Computing) technologies, where resources are ganged together toward a single task to deliver the necessary power for intensive computing projects like weather forecast, oil exploration, nuclear reactor simulation, and so on. In addition to expensive HPC super computer centers, mostly government funded, an HPC grid emerged to link together these resources and increase utilization. In a concurrent development, grid technology was used to join not just supercomputers, but literally millions of workstations and PC computers across the globe.

As the technology to share resources and scavenge idle computing cycles progresses, people begin to apply these technologies to harvest idle cycles on PCs and servers to "steal" idle cycles for scientific computing uses, such as cancer research and space exploration, that are not time critical. However, this type of grid will not be able to support mission critical business applications required by an enterprise environment. Nevertheless, the value of sharing idle resources and increased utilization is very attractive to enterprise solutions. A key point here is that quality of service or QoS needs to be part of the matchmaking or negotiation when a resource is allocated to fulfill a business need.

In the enterprise environment, there are many servers in the data center that are underutilized. Building solutions on servers with particular provisioning requirements takes a long lead time. The opportunities of increasing server utilization and shortening solution development cycle drive the integration of virtualization and grid technologies. Since an enterprise often operates in a heterogeneous environment, the principle of service orientation to drive compatibility and integration is very a natural result of driving the grid computing concept to the enterprise. Virtual service oriented grids represent the result of this evolution process and become the foundation of the predictive enterprise vision outlined in the Chapter 2.

148 ■ The Business Value of Virtual Service Oriented Grids

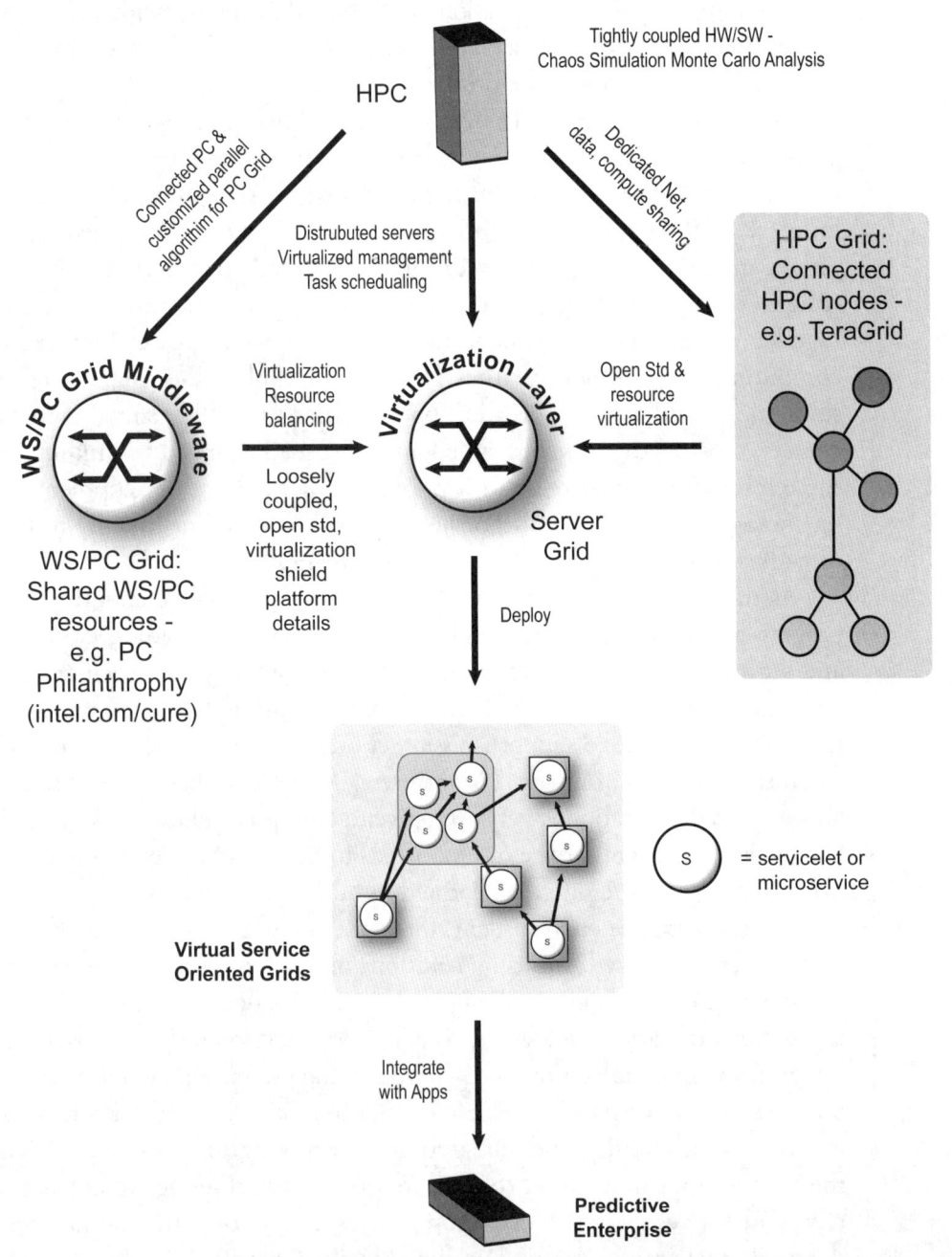

Figure 4.5 Evolution of Grid Computing

Types of Grids

Grid computing can be used in a variety of ways to address various kinds of application requirements. Often, grids are categorized by the type of solutions that they best address. The following primary types of grids are summarized below. Of course, there are no hard boundaries between these grid types and often grids may be a combination of two or more of these.

Compute grids: A computational grid is focused on setting aside resources specifically for computing power. In this type of grid, most of the machines are high-performance servers. Applications are typically scientific computing, engineering simulations, and so on. The HPC grid in Figure 4.5 is an example of this type of grid.

Scavenging grids: A scavenging grid is most commonly used with large numbers of desktop machines. Machines are scavenged for available CPU cycles and other resources. Owners of the desktop machines are usually given control over when their resources are available to participate in the grid. PC and workstation grids to spare idle cycles for special computing tasks are examples of this type of grid.

Data grids: A data grid is responsible for housing and providing access to data across multiple organizations. Users are not concerned with where this data is located as long as they have access to the data. For example, you may have two universities doing life science research, each with unique data. A data grid would allow them to share their data, manage the data, and manage security issues such as who has access to what data. A data grid can be used to implement a consumer data presence service where a consumer can place her data and the data stays "there" in the ether, always available regardless of location and the device used to access it. A data grid for a data presence service can be implemented with an architecture similar to the multitiered application services provider example in Chapter 2.

Enterprise grids: An enterprise grid is to leverage computing resources in an enterprise boundary to support mission critical enterprise applications by providing access of processing power and data services through virtualized infrastructure. Enterprise users are not concerned with where the computing power and data is located as long as they have access to them on-demand. VSG is aimed for this type of grid.

Challenges

Making applications work in a grid environment. Right now, most applications work in server or desktop environments. One set of processors does the work. On a grid, the work can be parceled out to as many systems as are needed to do the work, and each system contributes to the task. The results are then automatically assembled and sent back to the requesting system. A new breed of middleware to coordinate and orchestrate application jobs will be needed to deliver a seamless experience to the requesting customer.

Security: Security is definitely an enormous requirement—we don't want just anyone accessing grid resources. And those who add their systems to a grid will want to control who has access to use their resources, and when. It is an interesting paradox to manage; on one hand, by definition, grid computing requires sharing and flexible shifting of resources; on the other hand, we have to make sure that the grid environment is secure and applications and data are protected properly.

Reliability and performance: If the grid doesn't perform the job well and fast, the businesses case for it certainly diminishes.

Ease of use for end user: To make grid suitable for an enterprise environment, it has to be easy to use and transparent to end users. A complicated set up and modification to application may be tolerable for scientists who use HPC and HPC grids, but it is not going to work for the enterprise environment.

The Commoditization of the Data Center

Data centers play an important role in the virtual service oriented environment. Data centers provide a significant portion of the virtualized infrastructure services. The most convenient way to deploy a large number of dedicated grid compute nodes and storage resources is simply to house them in a data center. Resources in data centers can be scaled to fit the anticipated demand growth. By definition, resources mined from cycle scavenging are opportunistic and their growth is subject to the requirements of the primary purpose of the resources.

Data center virtual infrastructure services come in all shape and forms, from commodity servers, mainframe, and network resources to storage area networks. Ownership patterns for these resources run all over the map. The resources can be owned by the enterprise or outsourced; they can be centralized, one large data center delivering services to multiple business units, or they can be federated and pooled across the enterprise.

In the early 1990s, enterprises began adopting commodity servers instead of using mainframe and RISC-based hosts for enterprise applications. The cost of the hardware was much higher than it is today. When a mainframe ran out of capacity, it had to be replaced in a literal forklift upgrade costing millions of dollars. RISC-based upgrades were relatively inexpensive, costing a few hundred thousand dollars each.

Commodity servers had an attractive value proposition, with the option of additional capacity in increments of tens of thousands of dollars and often even less. What hindered the adoption of these servers at that time was the computing power and the fact that software vendors did not see these machines as viable vehicles for running mission-critical applications.

The capability of commodity servers grew at a much steeper rate than that of their mainframe or RISC counterparts. This trend accelerated during the dot-com boom of the late 1990s. Both fledgling companies and rising upstarts found they could deploy these servers very quickly without long procurement cycles. For commodity servers, conventional wisdom indicates that the norm was a *one application per server* provisioning approach. Actually, it was worse than that. Deployments with *many servers per application* were not uncommon at all, starting with the classic three-tier distributed architecture that splits storage, application logic, and presentation logic (Web server) onto different machines. Furthermore, an often-used mechanism for improving Web server performance was to split the front end into several servers with each server taking on requests on a round-robin basis.

This approach made sound economic sense at the time because it brought business agility that was unattainable with more traditional technologies. It also provided logical isolation to compensate for the perceived early brittleness of the Windows† operating systems. Unfortunately, this build-out proved to be unsustainable. After gradual change over the years, the cost equation is different today. Some factors at play are

- *Power density.* The number of transistors in a CPU has gone up by several orders of magnitude, from less than one million to several billion. Although the features are smaller, transistors are so densely packed that power consumption per CPU has actually increased. In a similar dynamic, the transition from pedestal to rack to denser blade form factors is pushing per-cabinet consumption to close to 20 kilowatts or even 30 kilowatts. Thermal management has become a serious issue in data centers.
- *More sophisticated servers.* Servers with increasing degrees of fault tolerance increase power consumption, mainly through increasing replication with redundant power supplies and RAID hard drives with their inherent redundancy. Power supplies have a baseline power consumption even at idle when they are not providing any power to the circuits they feed. Likewise, the built-in redundancy in RAID schemes reduces the effective areal data density in disk platters.
- *More sophisticated setups.* Mirrored, geographically distributed data centers mean that two servers in a failover configuration essentially double power consumption. In general, deploying architectures that avoid single points of failure means more devices powered on at any given time.
- *Hardware costs.* Hardware costs dramatically decreased and price/performance improved, with other cost components such as energy and labor growing in prominence. Today we want servers that are not so power hungry and are easy to provision and manage.
- *Cost of electricity.* The cost of electricity has gone up so much that with the extra current draw, electricity becomes a significant portion of the operating expenses and the server's total cost of ownership (TCO).

What are the issues? As previously mentioned, over the last 15 years, IT organizations have responded to the growing demand for IT services with a provisioning approach based on dedicated physical servers. At least initially, the hard binding between applications and physical servers made the infrastructure easier to manage and to establish lines of ownership. However, this approach has led to a condition affectionately called *server sprawl* because so many of them are deployed. Strategies to house these servers have resulted in a distributed computing architecture with multiple geographically dispersed data centers. As part of optimization strategies, data centers are often located near users housing applications that serve a particular region. However, these strategies are no longer workable. Some issues at the forefront are:

- *Inflexibility.* Widely distributed systems cannot react or be reconfigured as quickly co-located systems, making it harder for IT to respond rapidly to changing business needs. Also, many distributed systems are unable to share resources effectively.

- *Underutilization.* Without the ability to share resources, servers and storage systems must keep sufficient capacity in reserve to accommodate demand spikes. As a result, these systems rarely operate at their full potential. Adding resources when systems do approach their capacity requires an extensive IT effort. The magnitude of that effort can slow the response to change.

- *Over-provisioning.* This is the other side of the coin of under-utilization. As in network design, traditionally it has been difficult to address the issue of quality of service in networks. The usual strategy has been to throw bandwidth at the problem. A similar situation happens with servers in the data center where the machines need to be specified to accommodate peak loads. Without specific measures, load factors frequently end up in the single percentage digits. Energy efficiency, measured in MIPS/watt, becomes atrocious under these conditions, since servers still draw a significant portion of peak load current even when they are idling.

- *Complexity.* Distributed systems can be complex and hard to monitor and manage. Maintaining these complex systems requires staff with advanced skills coordinating tasks across multiple data centers. In some cases, the complexity of these systems also adversely affects availability of services.

- *High costs.* Monitoring and maintaining such complex infrastructures is labor-intensive and costly. High administration costs, coupled with low resource utilization, yield suboptimal return on IT investments.

As IT organizations develop plans to address these mounting challenges, enterprises are also placing additional requirements on IT. The move toward collaborative business models, where vendors, customers, and business partners all share real-time information using common applications is driving the demand for greater IT integration across and beyond the enterprise. IT departments need to accommodate that demand while also giving enterprises the agility to respond quickly to changing business conditions. The need to address ongoing challenges and new demands, all while improving return on investments, has placed tremendous pressure on IT departments. Most computer industry leaders feel that enterprises must adopt a new vision of the enterprise architecture for IT to once again serve as a key tool in driving the enterprise forward.

To overcome these challenges and work toward building the data center of the future, the computer industry is embracing a new approach to enterprise computing: a utility computing infrastructure incorporating the capabilities and requirements to run the emerging common application infrastructure. In a utility environment services are delivered when needed in a standardized fashion

The heterogeneity of present day physical computing resources such as servers, storage, and networks gets in the way of an ideal utility computing environment. To circumvent this problem we envision the application of virtualization techniques to consolidate into high-density data centers managed with virtualization software and automated provisioning tools.

By deploying a utility computing infrastructure, enterprises can

- Dramatically simplify IT management
- Improve resource utilization, increase the return on investment
- Enhance IT flexibility
- Set the groundwork for a collaborative business model
- Increase business agility

A strategic outcome is that enterprises can redirect resources previously reserved for keeping systems running can be redirected to innovation and strategies for capitalizing on market changes.

The utility computing approach makes it easier to track what Forrester analyst Andrew Bartels whimsically refers as MOOSE spending[4], that is, spending to maintain and operate the IT organization, systems and equipment as percentage of company revenues. In a climate of flat spending it is desirable to keep the MOOSE component also flat or make it smaller to free up budget to innovate.

The Next Generation of Enterprise Computing

The emerging vision for the enterprise architecture is a multilayered architecture where applications draw on shared services and computing resources. The utility computing infrastructure is the foundation for that architecture. By deploying the utility computing infrastructure today, enterprises can realize tangible, immediate benefits while taking an important step toward building the data center of the future.

The ideal of utility computing is harder to realize in the data center than it is with electricity. For one thing, electrons are very small and one electron looks like any other (they are fungible). Data center resources are more granular and less interchangeable. Servers are larger than electrons and two- and four-socket servers are not necessarily interchangeable or even interoperable. However, we can get closer to this ideal through architectural and operational measures. This is the vision for utility computing.

As an example, a virtualized environment can be set up to hide the diversity of hardware platforms through the support of a small library of virtual machine configurations that can run on a broad range of physical servers. However, it must be noted that without a deliberate strategy sprawl can take place in virtual space as well, leading to a runaway and unmanageable number of virtual machine configurations.

In any case, the goal is not to move to a perfect 100 percent fungible environment as most electrical utilities are today, but to optimize certain business outcomes. In fact, even in the electric power industry there is a movement in the *opposite* direction, at least to differentiate power by source as a consequence of the rise of environmental concerns: electricity coming from renewable resources like solar or wind is charged at a higher rate.

---

4   http://www.forrester.com/Research/Document/Excerpt/0,7211,40453,00.html

Hence, reaching an ideal utility computing environment is not really necessary to enjoy the benefits. Once electrons are mixed in a wire, they cannot be distinguished by source, so these electrons belong to different classes only through the magic of accounting.

The business drivers for the new vision of the data center are strategic cost reduction and agility. A corresponding development underway in the application infrastructure is highly synergistic with this vision.

An encouraging factor for this transformation is that strategies and plans can be set up so the benefits are accrued early on. This is an essential consideration to ensure the support of the community to support the investment needed. Of course, the full benefits of the transformation will not be attained until a more advanced stage is reached, but it is important to underscore the linkage between investment and the ensuing benefit from the earliest.

The movement toward the next generation in enterprise computing is epitomized by the adoption of service oriented architectures (SOA) in application space and the pervasive use of virtualization in the hardware platforms. We believe that the pervasive adoption of SOA can only happen if the physical infrastructure also supports a service oriented paradigm, in other words, the *physical infrastructure* itself becomes service oriented. For this purpose, we postulate the notion of a *service-oriented infrastructure* or SOI. The virtualization play tends to happen at the SOI layer.

Under SOI, we start observing some abstract service-oriented behaviors in the infrastructure similar to those seen at the software layers (for example, automatic discovery and interface description) that take us closer to autonomic configuration. An SOI capability radically reduces the time it takes to provision resources and simplifies the day-to-day operational drudgery. Unavoidable configuration mistakes can be rapidly addressed.

This transformation will certainly not take place in a single phase. Meanwhile, and consistent with a philosophy of reuse, it is possible to "service-enable" or retrofit existing resources to make them service oriented through the addition of a thin middleware service layer acting as a shim. In this sense, SOA is very evolutionary: Nothing that can be reused is thrown away. The shims will be gradually phased out as technology evolves and resources become service oriented from the ground up.

Note that with service orientation, we are at the threshold of business transformation, not unlike the transition from horse driven vehicles at the end of the nineteenth century.

The obvious change that came about when vehicles were fitted with internal combustion engines was that horse buggies became faster "horseless" carriages.

Not anticipated at the time was that automobiles would transform society itself, bringing in a new transportation infrastructure and redefining basic relationships in society, such as Henry Ford's moving assembly line concept.

The long-term effect of a service-oriented, utility computing concept in the data center is hard to predict, yet exciting. What we can say is that as in the automotive industry a hundred years ago, the transformation will go well beyond carrying existing processes more rapidly.

Likewise, it would be short-sighted and naïve to expect that under a utility computing environment the current processes for planning, deployment, operations, and data center infrastructure layout would be retained, with the only difference being the processes being carried out faster.

Changes will occur within each of the infrastructure, application, and business layers. Analyzing the infrastructure layer in isolation is clearly insufficient to assess future evolution. Analyzing each of these layers individually is a good start. But the analysis is not complete until we understand the interactions across layers.

For instance, consolidating data centers may actually increase the distance between data, the servers that operate on them, and the consumers of an application.

The increasing distance leads to a corresponding increase in latency among application components. The effect of increased latency is highly nonlinear, with some application components slowing down so much that they appear to hang. Application response times become unacceptable for the business function that the application supports. Even worse, the integrity of the application itself may get compromised. An application-mapping analysis is recommended to assess the effect of increased latencies before they affect the business.

Likewise, the manageability infrastructure could break if measures are not taken to make the system latency tolerant. Recent experience indicates that when some shops with management capabilities implemented with ad hoc shell scripts consolidate on a global basis, an alarm may take as long as four minutes to propagate, even though the endpoint-to-endpoint link latency is much shorter.

Finally, if we take as a given that in the advanced maturity stages data centers become policy-oriented and business drives IT, it will be hard to ignore business considerations at both the strategic and tactical levels.

We can speculate that the increased fungibility of resources, that is, where resources can be drawn from an undifferentiated pool under utility computing, will blur organizational boundaries. Once differentiation goes away, it may no longer be economically viable or justifiable to maintain departmental data centers; they may become divisional or company-wide. Beyond that, cross-company barriers may disappear as well. In other words, the trend toward outsourcing can be expected to accelerate. Outsourcing will not only encompass applications under the concept of software-as-a-service (SaaS), but will also likely include the physical plant. Because of advancing storage and server consolidation technology, we cannot expect that servers and data will end up under the same provider or same roof.

Data centers may become very large, with one provider taking on one function for several enterprises, or very small in the case of a specialty service provider.

A prerequisite under this new environment is that the architecture, processes, and analysis methods applied will need to be scalable beyond what is common practice today.

Systems in the data center of the future will be much more complex. At the same time, much of the power of these systems will be harnessed to hide and manage that complexity. The higher-level abstraction under SOA will make this apparent simplicity possible. For instance, the increasing fungibility of services will make it possible to switch to an alternate application provider according to a preset policy with only minor impact to the business. Data may not be affected at all if it is under a third provider or, as could very well be the case, under a federation of providers whose statistical behaviors have been carefully blended to deliver very precise SLA characteristics.

Building the Road to Virtual Service Oriented Grids

Adopting the building blocks described in this chapter does not mean the road to virtual service oriented grids will also be built. Issues with legacy, policy, and security will continue to exist. IT shops will continue dealing with uncooperative vendors, shortage of engineering talent, and the traditional cost pressures. Virtual service oriented grids have a better shot at these issues than traditional approaches, better visibility into the future through elevated abstraction levels, and agility with a capability to make faster corrections when events are not going the right direction.

It goes without saying that even if the transition toward virtual service oriented grids becomes a phenomenal success this milestone will only set the bar for the next revolution. This is actually a desirable outcome; it is representative of a nimble and lean IT organization in step with the business it supports and ready to take the company to the next step up in revenue.

Chapter 5

Industry Standards and Consortia

The nicest thing about standards is that there are so many of them to choose from.

—Ken Olsen, Founder of Digital Equipment Corporation, 1977

Standards are essential to interoperability. A virtual service oriented environment is by definition a large system of interoperating hardware and software components from a diverse cast of vendors, so large in fact that it would be impractical for any single vendor, even among the largest and most diversified, to offer a complete, vertical solution stack. And even in the hypothetical case that one vendor could have such an offering, end users would be wary of potential lock-in. For the same reason, it would be unacceptable to have one vendor dictate what a standard should be. Even when a group of partners accepts a standard based on one vendor's offering, there is usually a ratification process with broad participation. Therefore, in the world of grid and Web services standards, it is not unusual to see collaboration from all players in this space, even though some of them could be fierce competitors at the product level. This state of affairs is usually associated with the quaint term of "coopetition."

Consistent with Ken Olsen's tongue-in-cheek remark, there are many standards to chose from at all levels to serve the different purposes of innovative solutions. Many organizations and companies are working together to create yet another WS-* spec every year. The alphabet soup of standards is getting bigger and more complex every year. In other words, the existence of standards does not imply simplicity. There is such a thing as "too many standards." Standards from two different organizations may conflict or overlap. In some cases there are gaps or ambiguities that can make offerings from two vendors incompatible even though each vendor claims its offering conforms to standards. The Tower of Babel syndrome is more than a theoretical possibility. No matter how hard each individual works, the goal of building a complete and interoperable virtual service oriented grid stack is still not quite there yet, for the two reasons mentioned above: for lack of an appropriate standard or because even when two implementations are presumably standards-conforming, they are not necessarily interoperable. While there is still a long way to go to close the gaps of open standards, this is not the same as saying that virtual service oriented solutions are impractical. To the contrary, the fact that the technology is rapidly evolving may bring handsome return to first adopters because many opportunities have not been claimed.

Evolution of Standardization

In the early days when information systems were vertically integrated, single sourced solutions, these proprietary solutions became de facto standards. IBM's Systems Network Architecture (SNA) is a good example of an early network standard that was defined and developed by IBM and became a widely adopted standard before the Internet took off. Likewise, a de facto standard allowed Amdahl to build "plug-compatible" mainframes that ran IBM software.

The motivation and use of standards can be traced back centuries before the computer industry. The motivation for standardization is mostly for safety, quality, or the needs for mass production of certain products (steam boiler, telephone, nuts and bolts) that will fit and interoperate when installed. Standards are promulgated by a wide variety of organizations: industry consortia, government agencies, nationally accredited standards organizations (such as ANSI) or internationally accredited standards organizations (such as ISO).

With the emergence of the PC and distributed client/server computation model in the early 1980s, and through the feverish era of e-commerce in the 1990s, information systems have undergone rapid innovation. With the expansive and complex hardware, software, network, and storage solutions deployed during these years combined with the dynamic evolution of technology and business needs, monolithic solutions from single or a few vendors have given ways to multi-vendor distributed Web-based solutions. The needs for standards to ensure service quality and interoperability of information systems are more important than ever to support the ever increasing business needs. Many industry consortia were started to meet these needs.

Uncoordinated or even competing standards efforts are wasteful for the industry as a whole, and to some extent, self-defeating by creating more problems than they solve. For instance, whenever standards overlap as it is more likely with maturing technologies, incompatible solutions may arise, defeating the purpose of the standard in the first place. The span of technologies under virtual service oriented grids cannot be covered by a single company, or even a single standard. Collaboration on standards across the whole range of participants is absolutely necessary. The trend toward collaboration among the standard bodies and industry consortia has been encouraging; with efforts to develop strategic alliances to systematically address the issues around building more open and interoperable standards. Moreover, significant effort has been invested in eliminating complexity and overlap, simplifying complex standards where appropriate, and streamlining layers to support the real-time protocol handshakes associated with virtual service oriented grids.

Each standard consortium has bylaws dictating organizational structure, operational processes, IPR (Intellectual Property Rights) policies, membership rules, and standards ratification procedures. Each participating company needs to pay annual membership fees depending on the roles it plays.

The definition of IPR policies constitutes a critical piece of the bylaws. The IPR policies must clearly spell out how intellectual property is allowed into the standard and how it is to be shared amongst the constituent members.

Regarding XML, Web services, and grid computing, most of the standards are usually RF (royalty free). Most of these standards are not promulgated with the goal of generating royalty fees. The benefit to members accrues from the market growth facilitated by interoperability. The relative success of the Internet and the Web today can be traced to the wide adoption and proliferation of royalty-free open standards. The success of Web services and grid computing will depend at least as much on open standards, if not more.

Companies intending to join a particular standard consortium need to study the bylaws and IPR policies very carefully. The benefit of participating in a RF standard definition is to influence the direction and content of the standard, so that the products from the participating companies have the advantage to set direction and get the market mover advantages to accelerate standard adoption.

In the following sections, we dive into several specific Web services and grid computing standard consortia to highlight the specifics of each consortium and how to work with them.

Standard Consortia Landscape

A number of standards-making organizations contribute to the development of standards at different levels that affect how virtual service oriented grids are deployed. As mentioned before, no single standard organization exists that can do enough work and do it fast enough to keep up with the increasing needs for standards in this area. Moving forward, the contribution from leading standard organizations in and leading industry players working together will be essential to develop standards at all levels to make virtual service oriented grids work and succeed.

Table 5.1 lists a few major players driving the standardization of Web services and grid computing. Industry leaders tend to have a membership in more than one standards organization. Industry leaders, such as IBM, Microsoft, Intel, Sun, Oracle, SAP, among others are also the most visible supporters of standards organizations. Members also come from academia and first-line end user sectors (banking, manufacturing, governments, and so on) and make standard organizations a gathering place of many different interested parties to drive toward the common goal of achieving interoperable business solutions.

Table 5.1 Web Services and Grid Computing Standard Consortia Summary

Consortium Name	Description
W3C www.w3.org	The World Wide Web Consortium (W3C) is an international consortium, founded by Web inventor Tim Berners-Lee in 1994. W3C's mission is: To lead the World Wide Web to its full potential by developing protocols and guidelines that ensure long-term growth for the Web.
IETF www.ietf.org	The Internet Engineering Task Force (IETF) develops and promotes Internet standards, cooperating closely with the W3C and other standard bodies; and dealing in particular with standards of the TCP/IP and Internet protocol suite. It is an open, all-volunteer standards organization, with no formal membership requirements.
OASIS www.oasis-open.org	OASIS (Organization for the Advancement of Structured Information Standards) is an international consortium that drives the development, convergence, and adoption standards for security, e-business, and web services. Founded in 1993, OASIS has more than 5,000 participants representing over 600 organizations and individual members in 100 countries.
WS-I www.ws-i.org	WS-I (Web Services Interoperability) is an open industry organization chartered to promote Web services interoperability across platforms, operating systems and programming languages. Founded in 2001, WS-I has about 130 member companies.
DMTF www.dmtf.org	DMTF (Distributed Management Task Force) is the industry organization leading the development, adoption, and promotion of interoperable management initiatives and standards. DMTF currently has more than 3,500 active participants representing 39 countries and nearly 200 organizations.
OMA www.openmobilealliance.org/	OMA (Open Mobile Alliance) is the leading industry forum for developing market driven, interoperable mobile service enablers. Founded in 2002 by nearly 200 companies including the world's leading mobile operators, device and network suppliers, information technology companies and content and service providers.
OGF www.ogf.org	The Open Grid Forum (OGF) is a community of users, developers, and vendors leading the global standardization effort for grid computing. The OGF community consists of thousands of individuals in industry and research, representing over 400 organizations in more than 50 countries. The OGF is the "new" organization that resulted from the merger of the Global Grid Forum (GGF) and the Enterprise Grid Alliance (EGA).

Not all standard organizations are created equal. They started at different times for a variety of reasons motivated by diverse needs for integration and interoperability. Standards organizations tend to follow a life cycle, growing organically over time, tracking changes in technology and business. It is hard to draw clear boundaries between standards organizations supporting virtual service oriented grids. Figure 5.1 presents a rough depiction of the relationships amongst several key standard organizations.

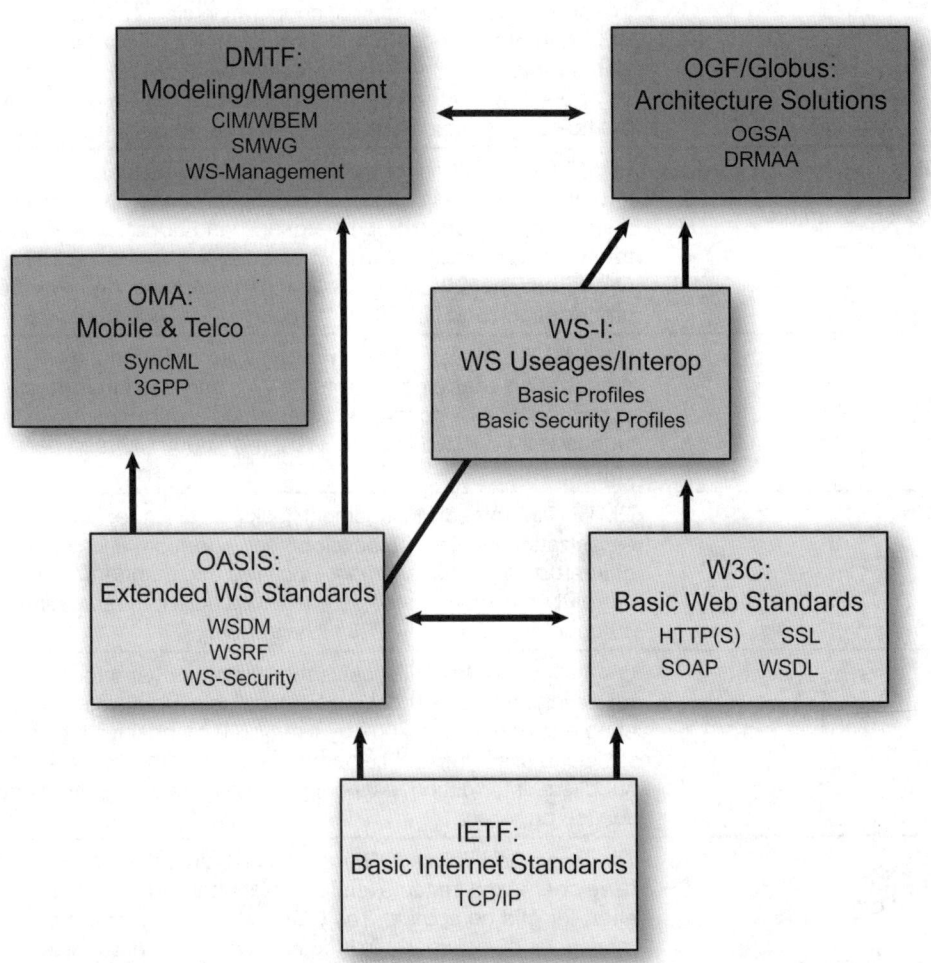

Figure 5.1   Standard Consortia Landscape and Their Relationships

The IETF defines TCP/IP and some of the most fundamental Internet standards addressing the basic transport protocols. It works very closely with W3C and other standard organizations. Some of the W3C standards are also ratified by IETF.

W3C is the home of many foundational Web standards. It defines the basic standards for Internet content such as HTTP, HTML, and so on. It also defines XML and Web services foundation protocols such as SOAP, UDDI, and WSDL. It is not an overstatement to assert that the W3C is the cornerstone standard organization for the entire Internet and Internet economy. The W3C is one of the most respected standards organizations in the industry.

With an initial focus on e-Business standards like ebXML and DocBook, OASIS has evolved into a primary standard organization for many key Web services standards (WS-Security, WS-Trust, WS-BPEL, and many more). OASIS has more flexible policies for working group operations that result in shorter standard definition cycles. As a result, OASIS attracts many web services standard proposals and has become a key player for Web services standards at all levels of the solutions stack.

WS-I is a relative new standard organization. Its focus is to drive common implementation profiles of Web services standards based on certain usage context and use cases. So far, WS-I has defined WS-Basic Profile and WS-Security Profile, standards that have greatly enhanced the interoperability of Web services solutions from different vendors. WS-I played a critical role in realizing the value of web services.

DMTF focuses on cross-platform management standards. It defined the common information model (CIM), an object model for platform description. Based on CIM, there are many variations of management profiles defined by DMTF for system component descriptions, and system diagnosis. DMTF is also home for many web services-based management protocols including WS-Management and WEBM (Web-based Enterprise Management).

OGF is a combination of GGF (Global Grid Forum) and EGA (Enterprise Grids Alliance) focusing on developing OGSA (Open Grid Service Architecture) for grid standards. The OGF works very closely with the Globus Alliance (http://www.globus.org), an open source community developing fundamental technologies behind grid services.

The OMA specializes in mobile device standardization. Traditionally, cell phones and PDAs have not been the same category of computing devices as PCs, laptops, and servers. Therefore, mobile standards were significantly different. With the convergence of computing and communication mobile devices, mobile standards are also moving toward Web services and supporting common foundations like SOAP and WSDL. Mobile devices will be increasingly important portal devices to access services provided by the virtual service oriented grids.

Domains of Standards and Their Relationships

As we stated in the previous sections, virtual service oriented grids solutions are complex. They are typically divided into the following major categories: business processes, overall grid service architectures, and underlying enabling infrastructures. Similarly, related standards could be laid out in such a way that the lower layers support and enable the upper layers. We can divide a very complex problem into several smaller, less complex, more manageable sub-problems to address the specifics of standardization in each layer. Another advantage of the layered architecture is to allow different standards organizations to work on different layers concurrently while remaining connected. This shortens the time needed to solve the overall problem.

Many similar attempts have been made in the past to create a layered view and complex business solutions. One of the most widely used attempts at classifying electronic business transaction standards is the ISO Open-EDI Reference Model (ISO/IEC 14662), illustrated in Figure 5.2. The ISO described a two-layer system, defining business transactions in terms of a Business Operational View (BOV), which focuses on the business aspects of business transactions; and a Functional Service View (FSV), which encompasses the information technology aspects of these transactions.

- Business Operational View (BOV)
  - The semantics of business data in business transactions and associated data interchanges
  - Rules for business transactions: operational conventions; agreements; mutual obligations

- Functional Service View (FSV):
  - Functional capabilities: capability of initiating, opening, responding and tracking the progress of transactions
  - Service interfaces: user application interface, transfer infrastructure interface, and so on.
  - Protocols: Security mechanism handling; protocols for inter working of information technology systems of different organizations; translation mechanism.

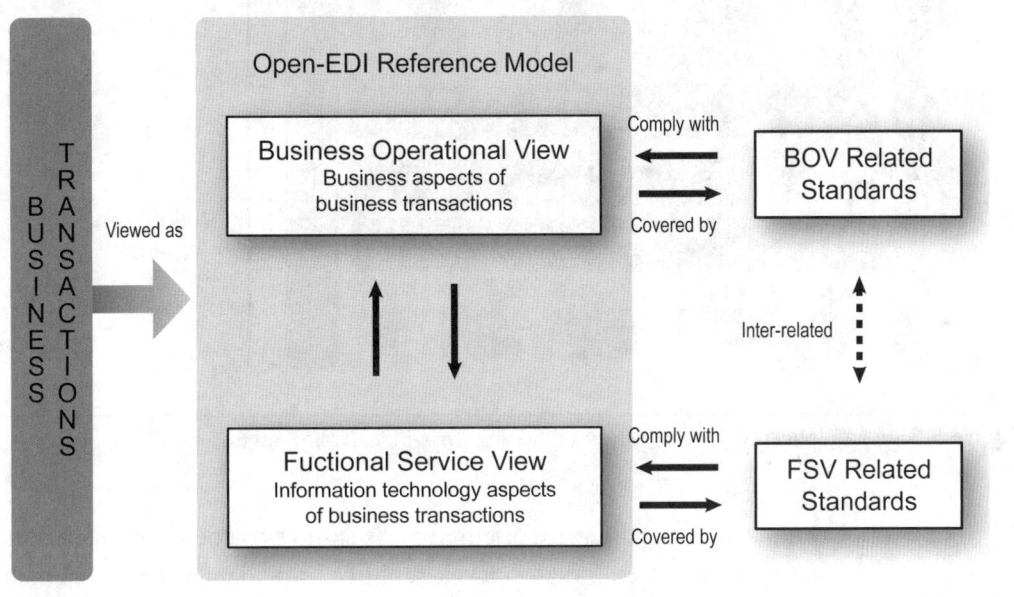

Figure 5.2 Open ISO-EDI Reference Model

Following a similar pattern, looking at the standards for virtual service oriented grids, we can come up with a similar layered view of the different types of standards and how they relate with one and another. Figure 5.3 illustrates such a view. This view takes into consideration the directions of each of the leading standards organizations and industry consortia we discussed in the previous section.

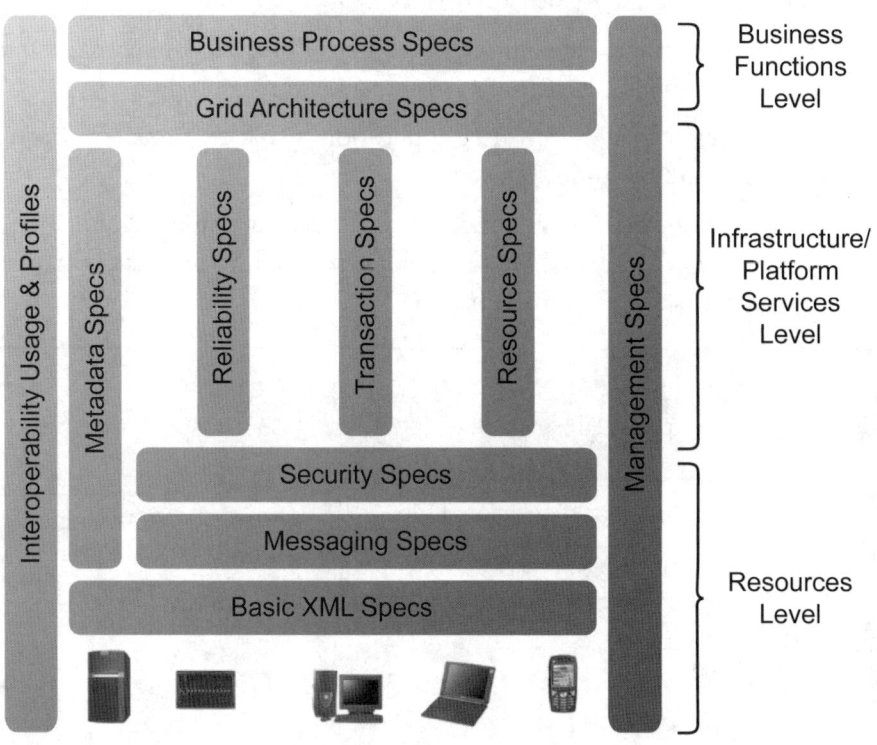

Figure 5.3 A Conceptual View of Virtual Service Oriented Grid Standards

Overall, the virtual service oriented grids standards could be divided into three general categories. The top level, roughly coincident with the elements of the Business Grid defined in Chapter 3, defines the standards for business processes that support business applications to accomplish business goals. This level is highly business oriented. It requires much customization and the decision making processes require direct human intervention. This is the most complex layer in terms of achieving common standards. In many cases, businesses are reluctant to discuss their business processes and are unwilling to allow them to be codified into industry standards because they view these processes as competitive advantage.

In the middle, roughly aligned with the Visible Grid described in Chapter 3, are standards to define the grid service architecture and associated services standards to support the grid architecture allowing computing resources to be manipulated through standard Web services to support discovery, access, and orchestration. This is the area in which the most work needs to be done in terms of standardization and automation. Business owners and IT managers want to get the benefit of agile and cost-effective computing infrastructure. They do not have the technical skills and patience to look inside the details of how infrastructure components are resourced and managed. This layer can potentially bring the most benefit from standardization and automation. Nonetheless, the standardization at this layer will not be possible without corresponding support of the resource management layer from the bottom.

At bottom, roughly in alignment with the Physical Grid described in Chapter 3, resources are managed directly through their native management interfaces from the hardware level to the operating system. Standards at this level involve monitoring (such as obtaining the state of the resource, which includes events), setup and control (such as setting the state of the resource), and resource discovery. These resources are managed by following the description given by an information model defining their properties, operations, events, and their relationships with each other. Standards at this level are useful at overcoming the diversity of hardware devices and operating systems involved in a grid computing environment. Without precise and interoperable cross-platform resources description and management standards, the entire grid computing infrastructure is simply not feasible.

Manageability and interoperability span multiple logical levels, each with particular challenges. Standards are needed to address these challenges through common protocols, payload formats, implementation profiles and reference designs, ensuring that different components and layers of virtual service oriented grids will work together. In a data center for a hosting provider, for instance, power consumption by physical hosts must be mapped to the virtual machines running on the hosts to assist in the fair billing of services. In turn, a SaaS provider leasing virtual machines from the hosting provider needs to roll up power consumption from the leased virtual machines into power consumption numbers that are meaningful to the purchaser of SaaS.

At the very bottom of the stack are hardware devices for which discovery of resources, provisioning, and monitoring are fundamental operations, if they are to support a virtual service oriented environment. This means that for the hardware devices at this level, standards-based processes are needed to represent computing resources, report events, and to provide interfaces for control. To make these hardware level services more accessible by other services and application upper layers, XML and Web services (SOAP and WSDL) are commonly used standards to attain interoperability across different hardware types and different vendors.

Components or servicelets in a composite application communicate via messages. Basic XML standards are the foundation of all service-oriented standards, defining document formats and for accessing the data within the documents. This syntax is used to express specifications in the layers above for defining the representation of services and processes. Examples of basic XML standards are XML DTD (Data Type Definitions), XSLT (Extensible Stylesheet Language), and XML Schema.

Messaging standards define message and envelope structure and layout definitions, consistent with the requirements of the application. This layer addresses the need to record session and communication settings for message transport in order to enable coordination between service sessions. This layer is the foundation of communications among all the layers. It provides the lower-level message exchange support for all the other layers above. The most popular messaging standard is SOAP (Simple Object Access Protocol). There were several other messaging standards in the past. However, they have mostly converged to SOAP. SOAP is defined by W3C

Services security standards define the security protocols needed to protect credentials of business entity, encryption/decryption of transaction sessions over the messaging layer, as well as key management through the life of business processes. Examples: WSS (WS-Security), WS-Trust, and SAML (Security Assertion Markup Language).

Metadata standards include the descriptions of service payload of business transactions, such as information model, configuration structure, data dictionary entries, and special business document formats. This layer specifies the structure and semantics for particular business processes. It is built on top of the basic XML standards with knowledge of particular business processes required for business transactions. Example of metadata specifications are DocBook and ebXML Registry Information Model from OASIS.

Reliability standards are used to establish reliable and verifiable connections between service providers and service consumers. In many business transactions, the messaging layer needs to be secure and reliable. In the case of business-to-business (B2B), non-repudiation auditing is required for all business transactions. It is essential to make sure that message exchanges among business entities are secure, reliable, and auditable. Reliability specifications are built on top of messaging and security standards. Examples of this category are specifications WS-RM (WS-ReliableMessaging), WS-MC (WS-MakeConnection) from OASIS.

Transaction standards are used to describe interactions among services and business processes. They describe allowable (legal) patterns and rules of business content exchanges following certain protocols among entities engaged in a transaction. Examples of this category are specifications from OASIS focusing on transactions, WS-Transaction TC (Technical Committee) with their WS-Coordination, and WS-Atomic Transaction.

Resource standards are used to describe different types of computing and communication resources in a virtual service oriented grids environment, as well as the methods to discover, monitor, and manipulate these resources. Protocols in this layer are built on top of DMTF CIM (Common Information Model), and use the basic XML format and messaging services for resource orchestration. An example from this layer is WSRF (WS Resource Framework) from OASIS.

Grid architecture standards are aimed at organizing diverse components in a unified architecture that make up a virtual service oriented grids computing environment as a single virtual system—even when provided by different vendors or operated by different organizations. A good example of grid architecture specification is OGA (Open Grid Architecture) from OGF, which addresses the need for standardization by defining a set of core capabilities and behaviors that address key concerns in Grid systems.

Business process standards support business process automation= based on Web services. In a virtual service oriented grids environment business process standards need to leverage the virtual resources provided by virtual service oriented grids and provide means to maximize output for a given business process. A good example of this category is WS-BPEL (WS Business Process Execution Language) from OASIS.

Trends and Challenges for the Development of Standards

One of the biggest challenges for virtual service oriented grids standards is to ensure interoperability. This may sound redundant. The purpose of developing standards is, after all, for scalability and interoperability.

The current panorama for virtual service oriented grids is today is much less than perfect. Interoperability in virtualization is not even a consideration today. An image file x from vendor A will not run in the hypervisor from vendor B. On the other hand, for SOA and grid computing there is an embarrassment of riches. These two technologies have attracted an enormous interest from industry practitioners and are evolving very quickly.

This level of interest has led to the formation of multiple standards-making organizations as described earlier in the chapter. It is not uncommon for the jurisdictions of these organizations to overlap. The differing views of the universe from each organization make it very likely that when the overlaps occur, their recommendations will be inconsistent with each other, if not in outright conflict.

Also, technology has not evolved to the point to guarantee that two products from different vendors will interoperate even when the vendors claim their offerings are standards compliant. Instances of incompatibility tend to decline as technology matures.

Standards organizations put together "plug fests" or "interoperability parties" to promote consistent implementation and interoperability of its standards. Some new consortia, like WS-I, were formed for the sole purpose of developing interoperable profiles for heterogeneous system implementations.

Eventually, in the interest of the greater good, perhaps organizations start coordinating activities if only because their participants are also members of two or more of the standards organizations involved. On occasion the best solution is to merge two otherwise separate standards or the organizations involved. Convergence and alignment of the many existing virtual service oriented grids standards is very critical to achieving the grand vision outlined by the predictive enterprise.

Chapter 6

Technology Integration Under Virtual Service Oriented Grids

Good plans shape good decisions. That's why good planning helps to make elusive dreams come true.
—Lester R. Bittel, *The Nine Master Keys of Management*

There is no question that IT now plays an essential role in enabling global enterprises to achieve their business and strategic goals. Over the past 15 years, IT departments have dramatically expanded their infrastructure to address an increasing number of enterprise objectives. For many organizations, this tremendous growth of IT resources has led to the creation of widely distributed infrastructures that are complex, costly to manage, underutilized, and difficult to scale.

At the same time, additional requirements are being placed on IT. The move toward collaborative business models—in which vendors, customers, and business partners share real-time information relying on a common application infrastructure under the emerging Service Oriented Architecture philosophy—is driving the demand for greater IT integration of processes not only within the enterprise but also across business partnerships. Integration cannot come at the expense of nimbleness; it comes with a requirement for agility to help the enterprise respond quickly to changing business conditions.

Selecting the Units of Integration

Complexity notwithstanding, the art of building an *application* or *solution* to solve a business problem is in essence very simple: it consists of selecting components or building blocks in such a way that, when joined together in some form in a *system*, the application of the system will address the business problem. The process of selecting and joining the components of a solution is called the *integration* process.

Building an information technology solution is fundamentally identical to the approach humans have used to build most any object for thousands of years.

Let's take a look for instance at the actions associated with building a piece of furniture, such as a bookcase or a table. The furniture maker starts by selecting the woods, fasteners, adhesives and finishes. Once the materials have been gathered, the furniture maker proceeds to build the desired product.

One fundamental question is to decide on the granularity of units of integration. The process for making furniture described above is not the only one possible. Today, this process would be considered fine grained, the process that a hobbyist or artisan would follow. The process yields a relatively small number of high value units. Each finished product is really one of a kind, even when multiple instances of the product are made from the same plans. This integration method may be too expensive for office applications and for most home furniture.

For most office and home applications a more practical solution will be to integrate the furniture on site from prefabricated components. The component maker delivers precisely machined components in kits to be assembled at the customer premises or at the store prior to delivery.

The tooling needed to fabricate these components is expensive, capable of machining pieces very precisely and in large volumes, but this investment is amortized over the large number of units placed in the target market. Once the machined parts are available, the final assembly can be done in minutes instead of the weeks it would take to fabricate a similarly functional unit from raw wood.

Integration of Information Technology Solutions

We have just seen that the level of abstraction of the components in a solution determines the solution's cost and practicality. The level of abstraction in turn is a function of the state of technology or determined by other factors than economic. Some customers may still have a need for a high-value, custom made piece of furniture, assembled from scratch, that is, from low-abstraction components, in which case a prefabricated kit will not fit the bill.

On the other hand, if low cost, large volume, and timely delivery are the primary concerns, components must be selected at the highest level of abstraction that the current state of the art allows. For IT applications, the highest level of abstraction today is represented by prefabricated service components, the servicelets or microservices introduced in Chapter 1. The servicelet abstraction is powerful, enabling the assembly of an application in minutes to days instead of years. A historical perspective will provide context.

Looking at the state of technology, when the United States Army needed the ENIAC in the 1940s to compile ballistic tables (see Chapter 3), the computer had to be built from vacuum tubes, resistors, inductors, capacitors, and other primitive components. In the 1950s "pre-made" computers became available, albeit expensive. Still, software applications had to be written in-house.

In the 1970s third party software applications became the accepted norm. However, building applications still required significant in-house coding. The use of packaged software became the norm through the 1990s. It required less custom coding than building an application from the ground up, at the same time raising the level of abstraction for the components of a business solution.

Custom coding brings extremely fine granular control over the behavior of an application in the same way a customer ordering a handmade piece of furniture can specify most any texture, shape, or finish. In spite of the fine control, the downside is high cost and complexity.

Business requirements today tend to tend more toward lower cost and timely predictable delivery than to customization capability. A pre-made software module may represent hundreds of thousands to millions of lines of code that do not need to be developed and debugged in house. In-house development today applies only to new technology or for customization for which there is no packaged commercial equivalent.

Doing unnecessary software development in house would extend a project by months or years. A software vendor might have done a similar investment, if not more. However, the software vendor has the luxury of amortizing this investment over the large number of copies licensed.

Hence, a software vendor can afford to invest to a degree that would not be possible in an in-house project. It's a win-win situation where the end customer gets to use a highly refined product and the software vendor can make a profit. It's a situation similar to the furniture example, where the consumer purchases very precisely machined, prefabricated components. The consumer would not be able to justify the cost of this machinery for a one time application.

The packaged software paradigm entered a period of crisis with the introduction of grid computing due to the highly dynamic behaviors required by the new environment. Under grid computing, resources for a program run, or a *job*, are allocated on the fly at runtime. The resources include computers, applications, and data.

Under the traditional packaged software business model, software licenses for applications and the operating environment are tightly bound to a physical machine. What happens in a grid environment where the application is run exactly once on possibly thousands of rented nodes, the results are extracted, and the resources are disbanded at the end of the run?

A traditional per node or per computer license would result in an exorbitant charge, which really makes no sense, because a traditional license covers an extended usage period, not a single run lasting from a fraction of a second to a few minutes.

Software vendors have been at a loss coming up with mutually acceptable licensing schemes from charging full bore to charging for a fractional processor use. These challenges provided an incentive for users in scientific and engineering communities to adopt open source software.

With the advent of virtualization, contradictions of the traditional licensing arrangements became more obvious and the audience affected grew significantly, putting pressure on solution vendors. With virtualization the linkage between applications and the physical CPU became even more tenuous and exposed a fundamental collision course between the packaged software model and the emerging virtual service oriented grids. The issues apparent to the scientific and technical community also became issues for the enterprise as a whole.

No amount of refinement will likely address the licensing problem as manifested today in a virtual service oriented environment. This is a fact evidenced by the ambiguous and inconsistent responses from software vendors when asked how their licensing contracts should apply to a virtualized environment.

An offshoot of these contradictions has been traditional software vendors having to deal with a crisis challenging the core of their revenue model and the increasing popularity of the service model in all their guises: software as a service (SaaS), platform as a service (PaaS), hardware as a service (HaaS), and other manifestations.

As previously mentioned, the lowest cost solution comes from integrating components at the highest level of abstraction possible allowed by present technology. Nobody would think of integrating a solution by building a computer from resistors, inductors, and logic components.

In this transition period between the prevailing deployments of packaged software to a service-based model we are starting to see hybrid solutions, consisting of physical resources running packaged software and service components, both in-sourced and out-sourced. We can expect an increasing prevalence of service components, not just software but also infrastructure services such as computers, storage and meta-services like service clearinghouses, security, and brokerage services. The motivation is not technology for technology's sake, but the relentless pressure toward cost efficiency.

Integration in the Virtual Service Oriented Grid Ecosystem

The key difference between the traditional IT infrastructure design and the approach used for virtual service oriented grids resides in the focus on the targeted audiences and how this focus drives the subsequent design.

The traditional IT infrastructure design approach is very much technology centered, with the goal being to find out how to optimize the IT infrastructure through the technologies, such as server virtualization, grid modularity, or application components.

The virtual service oriented grid approach starts with the target audience. The approach tackles a challenge head-on by acknowledging from the outset that the audiences for the applications, as well as the building blocks for the applications, are both internal and external to the company as explained in the section *Structure of Virtual Service Oriented Grids* in Chapter 1. Audiences include company customers, who may produce and consume with company information through the Internet. They may also include the company partners and supply chain members, who supply services, information, and raw materials to build or manufacture the company's products.

These relationships follow the principles of *openness*, *mutuality*, and *interoperability* espoused by James Champy and described in Chapter 2. For instance, under mutuality, a company is in a symmetrical relationship with its partners, with the company simultaneously joining partner networks and exchanging information with partners.

The virtual service oriented architecture factors in all the targeted audiences mentioned from the outset. Accomplishing the same with a traditional IT approach would be challenging at the least because the integration components are relatively low level and difficult to map to the business entities associated with the target audiences.

Demand from Web 2.0: Customer "Pull"

The use of servicelets does not bring an unqualified improvement in application deployment compared with traditional methods. In fact, architects and engineers will have to deal with loss of control, servicelets that do not quite fit the intended purpose, security, and QoS issues. What servicelets bring is a much higher level of abstraction, which lowers the amount of effort needed to bring a new application online.

Servicelets may be derivatives of already popular services that can bring "stickiness" to the target composite application. This stickiness or "customer pull" is highly desirable; it represents the set of circumstances that creates demand and stimulates business. Such is the case with the emergence of digital communities under a set of technologies collectively known as Web 2.0.

Web 2.0 technologies provide interoperable software components with a social context. The interoperable components and high level of abstraction allows carrying out new concepts to realization very fast, encouraging developers to try out new ideas at relatively low cost, quickly weeding out concepts that do not pan out. When the social component hits a resonant chord, tight communities can form around these applications with fiercely loyal followings. The Web 2.0 environment creates unique entry points for users in specific communities. For instance, *Facebook* has targeted the college student community; *LinkedIn* provides a social network for the professionals. The free or low cost operating model for users and consumers and access through the Internet can build a massive following.

Examples are the Google free search engine, map, and *Gmail* services, *Flickr* provides a free picture posting service, and the well known *YouTube* provides video posting services. Individuals and businesses can avail themselves of these community and free services, in the process creating a snowballing effect that attracts even more users into the community encouraging participation and the creation of even more content.

Digital Web 2.0 communities not only provide an environment to socialize with like minded members, but also provide an influential breeding ground that can determine the fate of certain products or services. An example is the recent series of protests in front of the French Carrefour supermarkets in China due to alleged support of Tibet independence cited in the Internet community; thousand of protesters gathered outside of Carrefour supermarkets for many days and caused Carrefour substantial daily losses in the order of USD 15 million.

Conversely, Internet Web 2.0 based communities have created a significant customer pull for certain kinds of products and services. Savvy businesses will know how to ride this wave to their financial advantage. Businesses ignore these trends at their peril, risking being undercut by nimbler and more visionary rivals.

There is another development taking place on the device side, at the virtual infrastructure service layer. Demand for mobile devices, including cell phones, portable digital assistants (PDAs), and Mobile Internet Devices (MIDs), has grown exponentially in the last 10–15 years. For cell phones alone, in 2005 Gartner predicted a figure exceeding one billion handsets by 2009. The number was nearly reached in 2006 with 991 million units sold; the estimate for 2007 is 1.15 billion. Estimates for the number of cell phone subscribers vary between 2.5 and 3 billion at the end of 2007. In particular, the UN telecommunications agency, the International Telecommunications Union estimates 2.68 billion cellular subscribers worldwide.[1]

Mobile devices, which started as communication devices eventually morphed into data access devices. The launch of Apple's iPhone in January of 2007 accelerated this trend. Users converted these communication devices into highly personalized data devices. The integration of Web 2.0 services plays right into this trend, creating communities and bringing flexibility to users, allowing users to acquire multiple persona presences depending on context, a feature that customers find valuable. These services are available twenty four hours a day, seven days a week, and 365 days a year.

For solution suppliers, their prime strategic motivation is satisfying user needs and making a business in the process. This is true whether the service customers are internal or external. IT organizations, VARs, and systems integrators are subject to the same dynamic. Web 2.0 business innovators, such as Apple, Google, Yahoo, eBay, and Amazon.com have understood and internalized this dynamic, building and remaking their infrastructure to provide the value-added content in the Web 2.0 communities.

A well-known example is Amazon's Elastic Computing Cloud (EC2) services that provide on-demand computing and storage services. It is also important to understand that these strategies do not for a minute constitute the exclusive domain of Internet companies. In Chapter 2 we highlighted Solectron as a revolutionary "traditional" company providing access to their CAD layouts to their partners to reduce the time-to-market and improve product quality.

Demand from Ecosystem Partners: Partner "Push"

Besides the customer "pull," it is also necessary to examine the other side of the coin, partner "push." This trend is more applicable to large companies attempting to optimize their supply chains and to minimize the cost for their supplier network overall. It is a tension of opposites: an environment where the deck is stacked in favor of some players at the expense of others is not sustainable in the long term. Success in similar exercises has been mixed. Some have been moderately successful, such as the adoption of EDI and RosettaNet

---

1   http://www.cellular-news.com/story/25833.php

technology, some less so, such as WalMart's effort to encourage the adoption of RFID technology or the Web-based trading exchanges of the 1990s.

Necessary conditions for successful partner push initiatives are Champy's principles of openness, mutuality, and interoperability. For instance, potential supplier participants in the Web-based exchange Covisint for the automotive industry in the late 1990s felt that openness was against their interest, reducing their margins at a time they were already squeezed by the major OEMs (automobile manufacturers); it was difficult for an environment of mutuality to thrive when relationships were adversarial, and with established one-to-one relationships, interoperability was not a formula to grow into new markets but to introduce additional risks.[2]

The promise of a virtual service oriented environment is that it brings a level playing field where participants have an opportunity to succeed based on skill, ideas, and vision. Standardization efforts must emphasize this goal toward a level playing field, and not to cement unfair competitive advantages. For instance, in order to provide timely information back to customers, the integration with company internal departments and/or external supply-chain partners becomes critical. There are a few initiatives in the industry trying to standardize the supply-chain vocabulary, business process framework, and interface methodologies. Value-Chain Operation Reference (VCOR) is one such example. This will help to build the foundation for partnerships while virtual service oriented technology gets adopted inside the partner companies.

Virtualization in the Utility Computing Infrastructure

For most enterprises, achieving a complete utility computing infrastructure, where new resources can be seamlessly added, removed, or modified without altering services or applications, will be a multiyear process. But enterprises can begin to deploy a utility computing infrastructure today. As noted above, the good news is that this transformation is not a case of "magic happens at the end." The economic benefits of virtualization are immediate and commensurate to the level of technology adoption and integration. Early successes do help in building momentum for further advances.

---

[2] http://outsourced-logistics.com/operations_strategy/outlog_story_7439/

Virtualization is a mechanism that allows overlaying a number of abstracted resources over a single physical resource. Depending on the particular view, virtualization allows the reuse of the physical resource by multiple virtualized entities, or constitutes a mechanism for increasing the utilization factor of the physical resource. A virtualization strategy takes advantage of the fact that virtualized resources can be allocated two or three orders of magnitude faster than physical resources.

Depending on the degree of adoption maturity, the pooling of virtualized resources can span geographical and organizational boundaries. A broader span increases economies of scale. Interestingly enough, the size of the organization is not an overriding factor as we have seen with the Outside-in SOA adoption model. In fact, this line of thought can be carried even further as the example of adoption at the consumer level illustrates in Chapter 7.

This process is no different to adoption processes in other industries: in many countries private ownership of automobiles is taken for granted, while fleet ownership in the form of rentals and leasing constitute a relatively small proportion of the units sold each year. Automobile rentals can be likened to a form of "virtualized" ownership. Rental companies strive to maximize the utilization rate of their fleet by renting and leasing to multiple customers.

The viability of virtualization has been made possible because today's servers have become so powerful that it is possible to run a traditional three-tier distributed application unmodified within a single box, and not just one instance, but anywhere between 5 and 30 instances complete with the connecting network.

Some enterprises might not need to run 30 instances of any given application within their wall. Hence, even a single server might be overkill. However, new business models soon become apparent. The 30 instances may be a boon to a hosting service provider because accommodating the needs of a new customer might be as simple as allocating a new virtual server without incremental investment.

Virtualization makes the utility computing infrastructure possible. Virtualization techniques enable IT departments to pool server, storage, and network resources and then quickly reallocate those resources as needs change.

Using virtualization, IT groups can reduce data center complexity by consolidating multiple applications onto fewer servers. For example, instead of using five distinct servers, each running a single application, an enterprise can use virtualization techniques to create five virtual machines for those applications on a single physical server.

Virtualized storage works in a similar way. A collection of disk drives can be pooled into a storage area network (SAN) with virtualized volumes and shared by applications on multiple servers. Through resource virtualization, IT departments can be much more responsive to changes in user demand.

From Virtual Servers to a Virtual Infrastructure

As we discussed in Chapter 4, virtualization can manifest itself across a broad range of usage models ranging from server consolidation to dynamic resource allocation to virtual appliances. Fast and effective IA86 virtualization lets companies consolidate servers and cut power consumption. It gives IT operators many more options for provisioning and configuring IT resources. As a result, the technology is enjoying rapid adoption.

However, adding a hypervisor to existing hardware platforms constitutes only a first step. A robust and manageable virtualization solution for the enterprise requires much more than deployment of hypervisors. Those 5 to 30 virtualized images per server mentioned earlier in the chapter represent an explosion in the number of managed entities relative to the number of hardware entities. Without careful planning, the outcome would be trading one problem for another.

A transition to a virtualized environment requires additional infrastructure to support thousands of virtual machines distributed over hundreds of physical systems at a data center, in some cases across multiple data centers. While the promises of virtualization to solve IT problems are very exciting, it also poses new IT infrastructure challenges to manage the sprawl of virtual machines. This is the next frontier of virtualization innovation that drives both hypervisor vendors and traditional systems management develop virtualization infrastructure products to cope with the rapid growth of virtualization deployment.

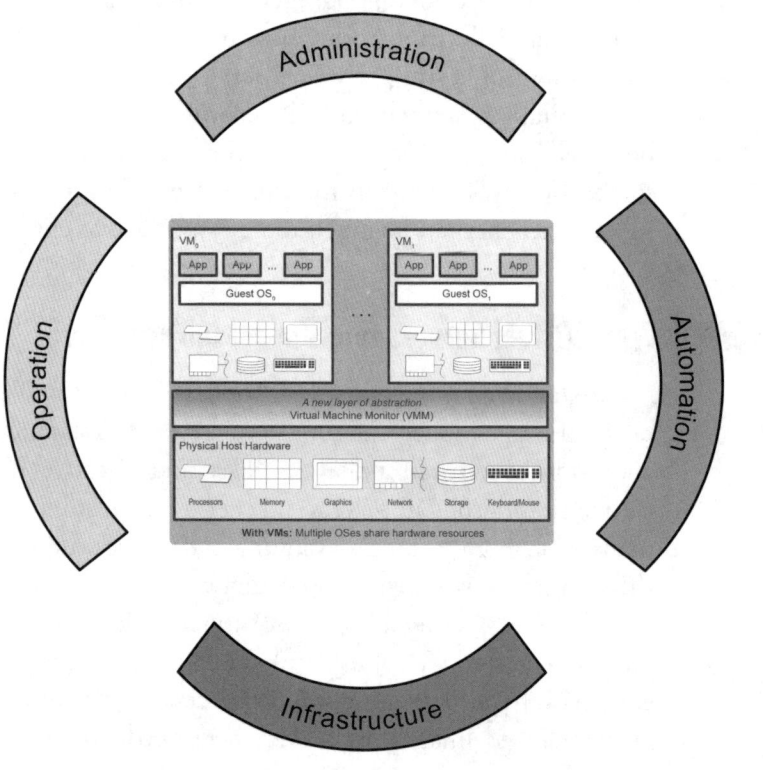

Figure 6.1   Virtualization Infrastructure: Managing VM Sprawl

As in most instances of technology adoption, virtualization is not a magic bullet. A broader view of the IT environment is necessary to accrue the benefits. Deploying hypervisors will not do it. Figure 6.1 highlights key components needed to build a robust virtualization environment that supports servers with hypervisors and multiple virtual machines running in a datacenter.

Picture a data center environment with a multiplicity of virtual machines running on every physical server with the application and system status for the virtual machines closely monitored by a central management console including, the virtualization management system itself.

The initial provisioning of hundreds of physical servers and allocation of thousands of VMs to applications need to be handled automatically by the virtualization management system, including bare metal provisioning.

In this environment, management policies trigger dynamic reallocation of compute resources to meet the changes of workload, power, temperature, system availability, or other events in the environment. Technologies like VMware VMotion† pick up a running VM and move it to a clone on another physical machine. The virtualization management system should decide when an event or a collection of events will trigger a dynamic resource allocation, what applications need to move and where to move, what resources are available for the migration.

In addition, a data center is likely shared by more than departments and even business owners. Under these circumstances, data centers will become easier to manage when the units of resource allocation are virtualized. Instead subscribing to physical servers to run their applications, stakeholders subscribe to VMs and services that manage the VMs. Administrative functions allow metering the usage of VMs and computing resources, either as the basis to share the datacenter costs or to come up with the actual billings in case of a co-located or outsourced facility.

In addition to the management of virtualized managed objects, data center security needs to take VM-level security into consideration, which bring a slew of new considerations to the already challenging management of security for physical entities.

Furthermore, data center capacity planning needs to incorporate virtualized compute resources, storage, network bandwidth, and so on, not to mention power, thermal and cooling. It is much more complicated than running a hypervisor on a server. The adoption of virtualization is not defined by the deployment of a few hypervisors. Results will be disappointing without a holistic approach.

A useful framework to plan a virtualization infrastructure is to think of the four subsystems surrounding virtualized servers, as indicated in Figure 6.1. The diagram is centered on a server farm (managed systems). There could be hundreds or thousands of physical machines. Assume that each server is running a hypervisor and multiple virtual machines. Each virtual machine has its own operating systems and applications. Behind the server farm sits some kind of storage infrastructure—a SAN, for example. As the number of servers increases, the problem of managing them and mapping their interdependencies becomes increasingly intractable.

The virtualization paradigm is applicable not only across multiple machines but within a machine as well. Virtualization will ease the administration of machines with 100 or more cores. On a dual CPU computer, each CPU with 128 hyperthreaded cores will contain 256 logical processors. Applications today, which will become the legacy applications of the future, will have trouble using that many CPUs efficiently, which will lead to abysmally low numbers for utilization rates and energy efficiency. Virtualization can enable a multitenant environment where CPUs are assigned to different applications or application instances, perhaps dynamically. The same can be said about network resources such as network interface controllers (NICs) where the available bandwidth is parceled out to fulfill the needs of different applications.

In general, management tools to play the following functions:

1. **Administration:** The management console provides centralized management for all hypervisors and their VM guests including provisioning, re-provisioning, monitoring, metering of virtual resources. This function also manages security and the center's overall system integrity:

    - *Basic housekeeping:* Provides wizards and templates to simplify the provisioning of new virtual machines. It may also include some rudimentary task automation and even monitor utilization of the physical server's CPU, memory and I/O performance, metering of virtual resource usage.

    - *Security management:* Security administration is an important part of the administrative tools. It works with security infrastructure to manage security between applications, VMs, and physical machines. It also inspects traffic on the virtual network for malware and mitigates risks when they happen.

2. **Automation:** This function enables system administrators to script complex processes to be triggered by specific events or to run at specified times. In addition, another important function of automation is to optimize the resource allocation mix to maximize compute capacity at the data center and in accordance to pre-established policies.

- *Event handling:* Specialized monitoring functions examine the performance not only for physical servers, but possibly as well for hypervisors, VMs, operating systems, and applications. Event handlers carry out the responses to system stimuli and contingencies, based on predefined policies.

- *Optimization:* Agents are deployed with automation tools, monitor hypervisors, application performance, and physical server utilization to help streamline datacenter resource utilization performance against SLA (service level agreement) and increase computational capacity yield as well as optimizing resource consumption at the data center.

3. **Operation**: This function covers many aspects related to the operation environment of virtualized servers, including VM security, data center level capacity planning, facility monitoring and controls.

    - *Capacity planning:* Includes an asset discovery and management function to find suitable landing targets for new and existing applications. It also tracks data center capability against given thresholds (compute capacity, power/UPS capacity, AC capacity, equipment aging and obsolescence) and recommends acquisition or replenishment of new capacity as needed.

    - *Facility monitoring and control:* Besides the monitoring of servers at the data center by the central management console, the physical datacenter facility needs to be monitored and managed as well. The power and cooling conditions, physical security surveillance, and other facility management aspects need to be constantly monitored and controlled. This is no different from managing physical entities in a data center today. However, the physical aspects of the facility will become less visible or relevant to data center stakeholders, if only because drawing resources from a pool makes users less vulnerable to the failure of any single physical resource.

    - *Infrastructure:* Server virtualization needs an infrastructure, the network, and the storage fabric. In addition, a security infrastructure need to be built into the virtualization environment, essentially providing a set of security primitives to the VMs and applications. Lastly, backup and high-availability (disaster recovery) needs to be built in as well into the infrastructure in order to attain reliable business computing.

- *Virtual fabric:* Virtual servers need to be connected with storage and the network. This requires I/O virtualization—the fabric that connects from the server to the SAN and LAN, which are also virtualized, with built-in redundancy, abstracted from physical details. Ultimately, through such a virtual fabric, all servers in a data center can be treated as bare-metal compute nodes that can be provisioned and re-provisioned according to need.

- *Security infrastructure:* Centralized credential validation, certificate management, access control, virus prevention/detection, and so on are all elements needed for a typical enterprise to operate securely. They will also be needed to build a virtualized server farm. These elements include security services needed at different levels from business transactions to physical servers.

- *Backup and high-availability:* Business continuity and contingency planning are a must for enterprise applications as part of the basic infrastructure services. Some virtualization technologies, such as VMware Consolidated Backup and VMware HA offer new perspectives to make backup and high availability easier to attain in virtualized datacenters.

In general, when it comes to virtual server deployment in an enterprise environment, it is not what comes with the box that matters, but what is around the box: the virtual infrastructure. This infrastructure is essential to successfully plan and build a virtualization strategy. Without the virtual infrastructure necessary to take advantage and support the virtual servers, any payoff from virtualization will remain in the future. There are no shortcuts to virtualization. It took IT shops many years to perfect their techniques for the physical data center. In this sense, the journey to build a virtual capability will take several years. The silver lining is that data center stakeholders will start reaping the benefits from virtualization at the outset, albeit gradually. The journey promises to be as exciting as getting there.

Service Orientation in the Computing Infrastructure

Service orientation concepts have become increasingly popular in enterprise application integration (EAI) to cope with the increasing complexity of enterprise computing. In a similar progression, recent developments in Web 2.0 and AJAX programming also cast a new light on service orientation applied to client computing that provides more flexibility and customization capability to address the enormous range of needs usually seen on the client side.

It is fair to say that service orientation will play a role in most any concept of enterprise computing. The evolution toward service orientation will inevitably change the way the underlying IT infrastructure is managed, as service oriented architecture (SOA) provides a more flexible and abstracted infrastructure layer to support the new computing paradigms.

One such paradigm is the concept of service oriented infrastructure (SOI) providing an abstraction layer for infrastructure orchestration and management services. The combination of SOA and SOI will help organizations attain the goal of the Service Oriented Enterprise or SOE.

This section focuses on the SOI framework definition and demonstrates how end-to-end infrastructure management solutions can be architected through the SOI framework. We will also highlight the value of services provided at bare-metal hardware level and the potential of hardware as a service (HaaS).

The SOI Framework

A service oriented infrastructure (SOI) is a very modular and flexible IT fabric based on standard building blocks which are highly configurable to meet today's very rapidly evolving requirements. It lies close to the bottom of the virtual services infrastructure described in Chapter 1.

Looking at the Service Oriented Enterprise as a multilayered structure, the SOI layer focuses on the orchestration and virtualization of compute, network, and storage resources.

The SOI ensures resources are made available in the amount and location required by the service oriented architecture (SOA) layers above it.

Within the SOI abstraction, the physical details of a device are hidden by software on the platform. The device can then be managed through a more abstract software interface also defined as a service.

SOI is optimized to handle the high volume XML traffic associated with Web services applications. Devices use XML to communicate across, making possible the interoperability of management and security services built into each of the component building blocks.

The SOI provides a way to manage computing resources in lockstep with application requirements both at initial deployment, and as the workload or requirements change, effectively enabling an integrated design, deployment, management lifecycle.

The standardized and loosely-coupled nature of SOI also reduces complexity and increases the potential for automation by enabling devices to do self-diagnosis and self-repair, with minimal involvement from higher levels.

More specifically, the SOI layer of a service oriented enterprise manages the following tasks:

- *Orchestration*: Managing hardware as a set of distributed and to some extent, fungible resources, shifting from a static, "one-application-per-box" paradigm to dynamic provisioning based on real time workloads and activities. This provides the ability to realign compute, network, and storage resources as needed.

- *Asset discovery and management:* Maintaining an automatic inventory of all connected devices, always accurate and updated on a timely basis.

- *Provisioning:* Enabling "bare metal" provisioning, coordinating the configuration between server, network, and storage in a synchronous manner, making sure software gets loaded on the right physical machines, taking platforms in and out of service as required for testing, maintenance, repair or capacity expansion; remote booting a system from another system, and managing the licenses associated with software deployment.

- *Virtualization:* It becomes possible to run multiple applications sharing one physical machine or storage device to increase utilization rates, or allocate multiple machines and storage devices to one application to increase performance. In other words, one-to-one dependencies between applications and platforms are removed. This capability provides unprecedented flexibility in meeting service-level agreements (SLAs).

- *Load balancing:* Dynamically re-assigning physical devices to applications to ensure adherence to specified service (performance) levels and optimal utilization of all resources as workloads change.

- *Capacity planning:* Measuring and tracking the consumption of virtual resources to be able to plan when to reserve resources for certain workloads or when new equipment needs to be brought on line.

- *Monitoring and problem diagnosis:* Verifying that virtual platforms are operational, detecting error conditions and network attacks, and responding by running diagnostics, de-provisioning platforms and re-provisioning affected services, or isolating network segments to prevent the spread of malware.

- *Security enforcement:* Enforcing automatic device and software load authentication; tracing identity, access and trust mechanisms within and across corporate boundaries to provide secure services across firewalls. Includes quarantine services to contain attacks and prevent the spread of viruses. Provides adequate provisions for insider attacks.

- *Logical isolation and privacy enforcement:* Ensuring that a fault in a virtual platform does not propagate to another platform in the same physical machine, and that there are no data leaks across virtual platforms which could belong to different accounts.

- *IT operations processes:* Setting up generic micro IT operations as building blocks to standardize IT processes and enabling the interoperability across heterogeneous system management products.

As illustrated in Figure 6.2, The SOI provides an abstraction service layer to SOA applications. The backend IT infrastructure management also needs to be service oriented in order to support and manage the applications and infrastructure. Service oriented management (SOM) is a part of the service oriented computing infrastructure that provides management services and interfaces to IT engineers.

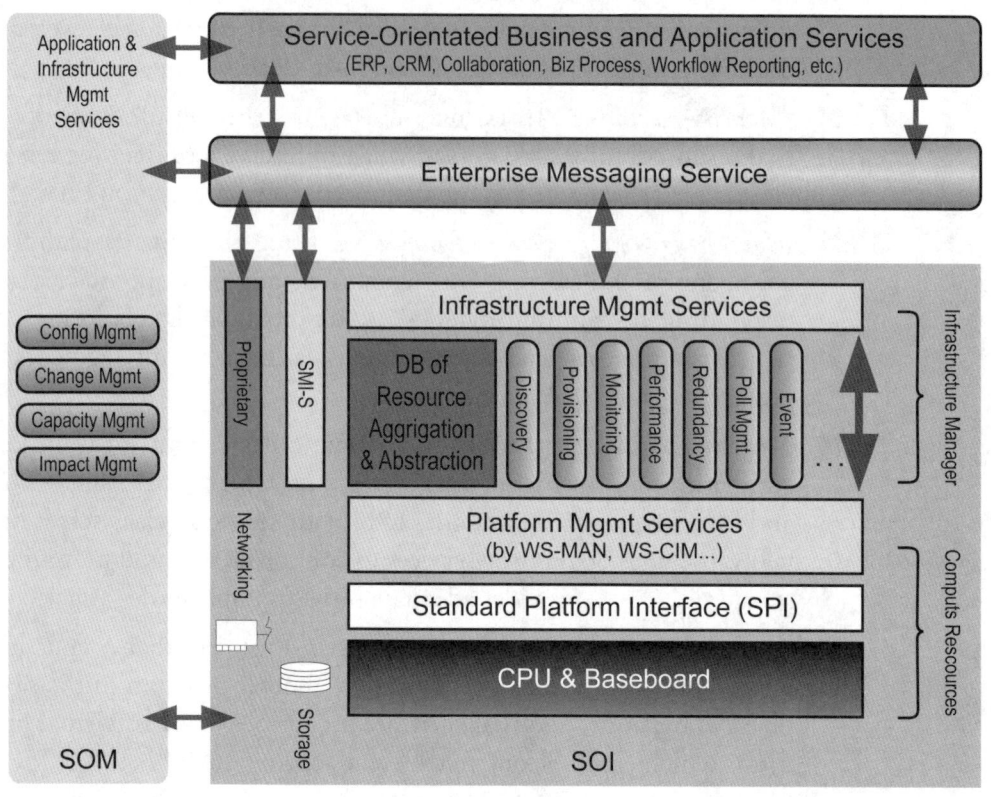

Figure 6.2 A Service Oriented Infrastructure Framework

Hardware as a Service (HaaS)

Along with the service orientation paradigm shift, software as a service (SaaS) and IT as a service have been discussed at different forms. To complete the story, we need to think about hardware as a service (HaaS) as well in such a way that hardware itself is designed with service orientation concepts from the very beginning with built-in service abstractions available at bare-metal level.

HaaS can be defined as hardware and firmware based autonomous devices that provide standard services to interact with other parties in a service oriented architecture. HaaS devices constitute basic building blocks for SOI and interact with other orchestration and management services from SOM as well as to provide seamless services to the SOA layer.

A HaaS device must have the following defining characteristics:

- *Service Abstractions:* Define "basic service units" and provide service abstractions, hiding hardware and firmware implementation details. This abstraction is essential in keeping the device autonomous and interoperable with other service providers / consumers. Examples of service abstraction could be: device status information, basic device controls (power on/off), provisioning, re-provisioning, and systems configurations.

- *Standard Interface:* In a service oriented environment, standard service interfaces are critical to interoperability and sharing of services across heterogeneous platforms. This is especially true to HaaS because many different SOA applications run on top of it and hardware should be designed for general IT infrastructures. It is not practical to expose HaaS services through proprietary interfaces, because this limits service adoption and defeats the purpose of service orientation. Therefore, HaaS has to support open service standards like Web services—the same standards that software and applications can understand. In this way, SOI, SOA, and SOM will interact with HaaS components the same way as they interact with software components.

- *Change tolerant:* The traditional thinking of hardware is that it is very efficient and reliable, but not very flexible and adaptive to change. With HaaS, the concept of hardware could change fundamentally. Hardware becomes flexible and programmable and provides basic services upon installation with or without software. It will interact and adapt to the environment it was applied and behave appropriately.

- *Policy Driven:* As part of an overall solution, a HaaS device has to understand the response to policies that dictate an IT environment. HaaS could have a built-in policy engine to interpret policies downloaded from the IT environment. At minimum it will be able to respond to instructions and directions from the upper layers of IT management services (such as orchestration, service level agreements, and quality of services).

HaaS will bring new opportunities and challenges for hardware designers and vendors. Provisioning hardware at higher levels of abstraction and enhanced security will require significant rethinking, especially when these functions are available at the bare metal state. Nonetheless, HaaS will beneficial overall in accelerating the adoption of SOA and increase the productivity of IT professionals facilitating business through building end-to-end solutions.

Technical Roadblocks for SOI

The service oriented computing infrastructure will not be realized without significant effort, including the engineering associated with product and platform design and development, all the way to solution integration. Beyond that, the engineering factors do not represent the whole picture as there are social and psychological hurdles to overcome.

Here are some of the challenges that need to be watched carefully:

- *Instituting a Service oriented Design Culture:* A firm service oriented design concept must be present during all phases of development, from product/platform design through solution integration. The hardware and software vendors involved will need to actively identify basic service components and semantic models to support the service information model. Software and hardware products should behave as services out of the box. System integrators will need to think service orientation as well and how the different components in the environment interact effectively as services. Of course, tool and service oriented engineering methodologies are needed to assist their work.

- *Building a HaaS Platform:* HaaS is a new concept and there will be significant challenges in building HaaS devices. It will take time and effort to make platforms service ready. Industry practices are not yet in place for the installed base to make the transition to a new service-based environment, let alone to address issues of interoperability with legacy and the management of stability and complexity.

- *Service Standards:* Web services standards are still evolving. Different implementations of the same standard do not yet work well together. Despite work done by standard bodies (OASIS, WS-I, W3C, and others), achieving full interoperability of heterogeneous Web services implementations is still not easy. Addressing the interoperability issues will require a concerted effort.

- *Information Modeling and Policy Description:* Common information modeling is essential to communicating service semantics and service orchestration. A policy language that is understandable by heterogeneous products is also very challenging. The goal here is to make the service oriented infrastructure truly plug and play, yet incremental relative to legacy. This might be accomplished by defining meta-layers between legacy and the new service oriented infrastructure, an approach not unlike the one used for SOA conversion projects.

- *Service publication and management:* Even though standards for Web services directories and registries exist (UDDI, WS-Management Catalog, and so on), they do not as yet have practical ways to publish, identify, and manage diverse services at different levels. For a typical service oriented IT infrastructure, not all the infrastructure services need to be visible at the application and business process layers. Appropriate abstraction and shielding of services are needed to reduce the complexity of service management. A combination of global service direction and local service catalog may be a way to strike the balance. Another interesting challenge is to validate that a published service is still valid before invoking it. When competing services are found, select the one that is most appropriate to the situation.

- *Unintended consequences:* Last, but not least, the service oriented infrastructure will be powerful and expressive. It will still not prevent operator errors. In fact, safeguards and checks and balances need to be in place to prevent unintended errors. For instance, imagine that an operator makes a mistake and requests 1,000,000 nodes for a job that was intended to run on 1,000 nodes. This is possible if there is a hidden *K* somewhere in the resource request. The system will happily allocate the million nodes and bill the department for that many nodes. The event can lead to an expensive mistake.

From Centralized to Decentralized Virtual Data Centers

We have already discussed how the tight binding between physical servers and applications that run on them leads to underutilized servers. The resulting armies of servers need to be housed in large, expensive, power hungry data centers. Consolidating data centers in an effort to optimize the physical plant through economies of scale helps to some extent, but results in even bigger data centers.

One reason this approach made sound economic sense for some time was because it brought business agility that was unattainable with more traditional technologies. At some point, the agility ran its course as well due to the challenges of managing server sprawl.

What are the issues with centralized data centers? Only the largest corporations with the deepest pockets can afford them. The cost of building a data center can exceed USD 2,000 per square foot. Hence a large 100,000 square foot facility might represent an investment of USD 200 million. Because of this high cost, smaller businesses cannot deploy them and the benefits of technology remain accessible only to the largest organizations.

Fortunately, this situation is changing even today. A number of market players are delivering applications on a subscription basis under the software as a service model (SaaS) as a new channel. Some players are well known, such as Salesforce.com, which provides a CRM (Customer Relationship Management) service and Google with Gmail and an office productivity suite that can be accessed through a Web browser. The software vendor Intuit offers both venues for the Quickbooks accounting product targeted to small and medium businesses (SMBs), where the customer can license the product under a traditional software purchase agreement or can subscribe to the Web version. In fact, the boundary between the two modes is blurry: A customer who elects to license the application can sign up for additional functionality as a subscription, for instance credit card, payroll processing, and selected banking services.

The mega–data center will not go away immediately given the economies of scale. These large facilities may become accessible not only to large corporations, but also to a large number of small businesses enabled by advances in virtualization and service orientation technology.

Companies in the Internet Portal Data Center (IPDC) market segment stand to gain from this trend. Players in this arena include Google, Microsoft

Office Live in the US, Korea Telecom in Korea, Tencent and Baidu in China, and Media Exchange in Japan.

One side effect of these trends will be the "horizontalization" of data center services. A fully owned large data center is very much a manifestation of a silo as discussed in Chapter 2, with fully owned physical infrastructure and a combination of licensed and in-house applications.

A company building such a large scale facility incurs in significant financial risk. The investment period and planning horizon can easily span 25 years, and many unforeseen events can happen within that span. Even with this long time horizon, risks need to be managed in a manner consistent with the company's risk profile. Data centers cannot be treated any differently from other assets from a risk perspective. Virtualization introduces flexibility in how these risks are managed.

The adoption of virtual service oriented grid technology will literally break the walls for the applications running in those mega–data centers. They will be free to "move" to any place that can run them more efficiently or cheaper depending on the optimization goals. If an application cannot be run locally, it can be run in a different site within or even outside the company. This is what concept of *cloud computing* is about: computing resources are fungible and available in virtualized form somewhere in the connected computing world.

The evolution of Web 2.0 and SaaS (Software as a Service) model, especially if data centers are built following the principles described in this book, will bring the benefits of the virtualized data centers to a broader audience, including small businesses and individual consumers, available today only to the large enterprises who can afford the millions of dollars to build a physical data center. Actually, virtualization is a trend that will truly lift all boats, small and large stakeholders alike, with benefits of lower TCO and increased agility. In fact, with virtualization, the fully owned data center may eventually become an expensive alternative applicable only to specific niches.

In a typical IT environment, and for practical purposes, key enterprise applications such as CRM (Customer Relationship Management), B2B (Business to Business), partner trading gateways, ERP (Enterprise Resource Planning), Payroll, and HR (Human Resource) Systems are hosted internally in a centralized enterprise data center model.

However, in the cloud computing model with decentralized virtual data center, IT departments will become horizontally specialized without necessarily owning or managing large data centers, with just a few CPE[3] servers providing synthesis and integration services as points of presence for service providers somewhere in the Internet cloud. In fact some of the applications may be renting in a pay-as-you go SaaS model.

Instead of building vertical expertise in house, the role of IT departments will shift to managing and integrating applications by a variety of service providers and to building a service portfolio to fulfill the organization's business needs. This transformation will occur gradually in the industry as it becomes relatively more expensive to build vertical expertise in house compared to outsourcing it. This is simply a continuation of the trend away from coding applications in house that took place over the last two decades.

Due to the nature of SOA, IT organizations will not be locked to a particular services provider. They will have choices and can easily switch as business needs change, affording businesses a level of agility unknown today.

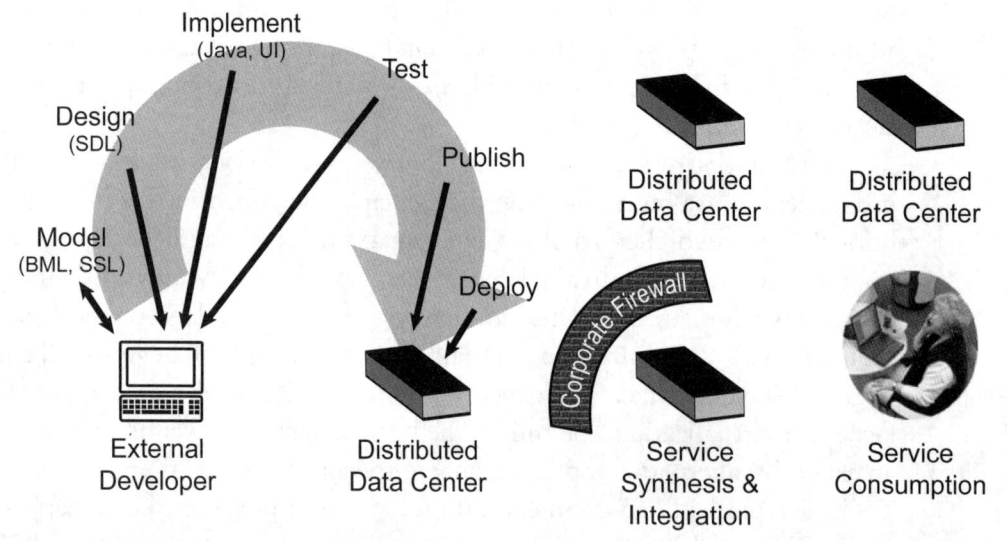

Figure 6.3 Creating and Sharing Typical Outside-In Services Using a Decentralized Model

---

3   Customer Premises Equipment

As illustrated in Figure 6.3, an independent service provider goes through the typical service development process from a modeling phase to a design to an implementation phase. Once a service is developed, a rigorous test process ensures service integrity and quality. The service then will be transferred to a data center for publishing and deployment. Since services are independently developed, they can be deployed at smaller data centers at geographically disperse locations. Services will not be monolithic; a service's implementation may invoke services from other service providers. The service provider becomes not only a vendor, but also a consumer of services. This dynamic will lead to a fertile economic ecosystem of fungible resources, where parameters that matter are codified in SLAs (service level agreements.)

Two evolution models are possible under the decentralized data center dynamic: Large Internet online service providers, like Google, Yahoo, and Microsoft Office Live will build mega–data centers and operate them in most cost-effective ways and achieve the economies of scale to offer services to the to large audiences. These services may include bulk e-mail services, measured in thousands of mail boxes or CRM services measured by the hundreds of seats.

Enterprises could pick and chose "pieces" of services based on their needs and integrate them together for their businesses. Alternatively, more specialized, possibly smaller niche players could take on these undifferentiated services to build services for specific vertical markets, such as a service provider delivering a complete IT package designed for construction companies. Franchise companies could build a customized IT package to be instantiated with every new franchisee.

The economics will be such that traditional centralized data centers will eventually lead to decentralized virtual data centers. This trend needs consideration as a guidepost for future deployment with a lot of thought given to finding out whether specific function blocks are available or will become available from service providers in the industry before following the traditional alternative of adding more servers into the mix and paying for them now and later.

Scalability of Service Orientation

Some experts argue that SOA in general (and the underlying SOI concepts in this chapter in particular) are applicable only to large enterprises with the critical mass to provide the reuse opportunities to justify service oriented design. This is correct under what we call the inside-out SOA paradigm that assumes an internal SOA effort serving the enterprise around it.

As we have seen in Chapter 2, in the small and medium business (SMB) space and in emerging markets, the outside-in paradigm where organization being served is actually a whole ecosystem, often larger than most any individual enterprise. In this environment the vehicle for delivering services is not an internal IT department but some services provider. Under this light an outside-in example is that of a Web hosting service using first generation (software-based) virtualization technology where a fractional server for a new customer is quickly allocated by launching a virtual server on some pre-existing physical machine. This process is completed in minutes instead of the weeks it would take to provision a physical machine.

Even for large enterprises, applications will be created using a mixture of internal and outsourced services, leading to a hybrid model.

Delayed Binding: a Useful Paradigm

A useful frame of mind to envision the capabilities of virtualized service oriented grids is to see them as the ultimate form of outsourcing in an environment where any business problem that requires computation can be assembled on the fly, on demand from distributed resources across the world. These resources can cross departmental, company, and even national boundaries. The units of outsourcing are no longer fairly large corporate functions such as payroll or customer relations management or large infrastructure entities such as complete data centers. These units can be as small as a virtual machine that runs in a server or even a single program run.

How these resources are marshaled and deployed is a function of the state of technology. As technology capabilities advance, the flexibility and the ease of deployment for the resources increases, and the granularity of the resources becomes smaller and smaller.

The integration process of putting resources together into a working solution is called the *binding* of the resources. We will cover the concept of binding with more detail in the next section. Once a solution has been bound together, by definition there is little room for change.

Flexibility comes from a capability to defer the solution binding to later and later phases in the integration process. A virtualized service oriented grid environment represents the end point of this deferred or delayed binding progression where the binding is postponed until the program for the solution is executed.

Systems designed under the early binding paradigm need to have all the references to other components resolved at design or implementation time to the extent that these references can actually be embedded in the programming code. For this reason, this architecture is said to be *tightly coupled*. [4]

As in the siloed environment described in Chapter 2, a tightly coupled architecture is relatively simple and easy to visualize. Tightly coupled systems are also efficient in the use of computer resources because there is no need to spend resources finding and matching the various components at run time. This environment carries less of a burden for standards compliance or the overhead of matching dynamic components at run time.

The down side for a tightly coupled architecture is relatively limited flexibility and scalability. This architecture is challenged when applied across departmental and company boundaries because in partner to partner communications, the case where critical components cannot be defined until run time is more the rule than the exception.

Updating and propagating changes in a tightly coupled system is a labor intensive process. Once a development project is launched, any unforeseen new requirements will likely gum up the works and lead to schedule slips and budget overruns. Project managers for these projects, aware of the potential disruption of new requirements can be, work very hard with stakeholders to ensure that all knowable factors have been voiced and incorporated in at the project start.

Systems that support delayed binding and allow discovery and matching of resources at run time are said to be *loosely coupled*. Loosely coupled systems rely heavily on predefined agreements, data formats and protocols, which,

---

4 Strictly speaking, early binding and tight coupling are not necessarily correlated, except that early binding provides more opportunities for tight coupling later, for instance through the cross referencing mentioned in the text or hard coded constants that makes code difficult to adapt.

if they are of interest to a broad industry segment, are sanctioned into some standard. In fact, delayed binding is possible only because this significant up front work. Fortunately, it needs to be done only once with only an occasional tweak thereafter.

The tradeoff for loosely coupled systems is in the heavy run time overhead needed to discover and assemble the component resources of a service oriented application. A significant number of cycles is needed for encrypting and decrypting, compressing and decompressing data streams across distributed resources; security protocols among mutually suspicious components need to be enforced and cost accounting needs to be maintained for the appropriate billing settlement of resources. This computing overhead seems an appropriate tradeoff in an environment where distributed computing cycles are abundant and getting cheaper and where human resources are finite and getting more expensive.

Delayed Binding Optimizes Deployment Flexibility

Binding in computer science jargon refers to the set of operations necessary to put together a number of software components in order to produce an executable entity; that is, a program that ultimately can be run.

An analogous process takes place during the production of a movie. Movies are built one scene at a time. Normally it is not practical to make a movie in one shooting from beginning to end. Some of the scenes may even be from documentaries whose producers might not have been aware that their scenes one day would be part of a larger movie.

The bigger picture, if the pun is allowed, begins appearing in the editing room where formerly disparate scenes are joined or *bound* together into a logical and meaningful sequence of scenes as dictated by the movie script.

The motivation for delayed binding is that to the extent it's possible to delay when parts of a system being built become fixed and bound to its intended function the more flexible the behaviors of the system can be elicited. Continuing with the movie analogy, it may make sense to shoot all the scenes and retakes in an expensive set one after the other even though they may appear in a different order or in separate scenes in the final cut or the director may be considering alternate sub-plots and endings. Once the shipping prints are made, changes become very difficult. That is, the binding process is complete once prints start to ship in the shipping print. Further changes become expensive at this point, short of recalling and reprinting the reels.

Software systems behave in similar ways to movie production due to their complexity. When the first compilers were put together in the mid-50s, it soon became clear that large programs had to be broken up into smaller pieces to manage complexity. The need for logical partitioning led to the notion of Fortran *subroutines* (Fortran was one of the first compiled languages), also called *functions* or *procedures* in other computer languages.

Software engineers realized that procedures did not have to reside in the same file: they could be compiled from separate files. Certain references to other programs could be left unresolved, such as variables that would have to be computed by procedures in other files. A second software tool, called a *linker* or *binder* was used after the compiler to resolve these references. It would take object files produced by separately compiling source files and string them together in single executable program.

Even though the original source program was built from separately produced pieces, typically all of the source files had to be compiled at once to produce an executable program. Systems were fairly brittle; very small changes in a source file could cause the program to fail.

In the next step in technology, software architects realized that the interface to certain functions would change very little from implementation to implementation. For instance, the sine function would always take one argument, an angle. These functions could be pre-compiled into a *library* once and reused over and over again by re-binding the library to new programs. As long as the interface would not change, that is, the type, syntax, and semantics of the arguments in a procedure call, it was not necessary to recompile the source code for the libraries involved. A modicum of forward compatibility was also attained: newer versions of a library could be "slid under" a running system just by re-linking it, without having to recompile the whole system. Stable interfaces led to the notion of APIs or *application programming interfaces*. Also, with well-known interfaces available, it became possible to link object files built produced by different computer languages.

Even with libraries, a change in a source or an object file requires a rebuild of the complete computing system. For most products in the market, this is impractical. Consumers do not have the capability to recompile and rebuild a software system that is usually provided by third parties. The update is usually accomplished through the normal product cycle. Typically it takes one or two years for software products to catch up with the new capabilities. Users keep using their old executables until they purchase newer versions of the software.

The ability to perform binding at runtime was attained in the mid-1980s and early 1990s with "componentized" objects, namely the System Object Model (SOM) from IBM, the Component Object Model (COM) from Microsoft and Common Object Request Broker Architecture (CORBA) in the Unix systems.

Client/server systems were built using these technologies. Binding considerations introduce system dependencies, which in turn have practical consequences in terms of maintenance costs. Client/server systems built with componentized objects do not need to stay in absolute lockstep. However, the software can't be usually out of step more than one or two revisions. The software manufacturer defines the range of compatibility between client and server components.

One last barrier remained: this binding could only occur within a single software "universe", that is, a computing system had to be all Microsoft using COM, or all Unix using CORBA. "Cross-universe" systems can be built, fairly expensively, using proprietary software connectors, each job being one-of-a-kind. These connectors are known as *middleware*.

In a tightly coupled client/server system the software components between the client and the server, and even the software components that reside within the client and the server are compatible by *exception*: two components cannot be assumed to work together unless *explicitly* designed by the manufacturer to be compatible. In a service oriented environment the converse is true: users expect compatible components and it's up to the manufacturer to demonstrate that it is so. Incompatibilities are considered defects. This level of compatibility is an absolute requirement for virtualized service oriented grids because the resources involved in a computation may have been marshaled from different organizations or even companies and requiring that the software versions of the components involved be in lockstep would be a practical impossibility.

How has deferred binding afforded flexibility? There has been a profound acceleration in time-to-market: At the dawn of the computer era every software system had to be built from the ground up. Every software system meant setting up a one-of-a-kind development project. Projects typically lasted 2 to 6 years. The introduction of libraries reduced this time somewhat, but every software system still had significant amount of custom code. The use of componentized objects has reduced the build time to a 3–12 month time frame because even though there may be application-specific code written, there is still a significant amount of "glue" code that needs to be written. The promise of a service oriented environment is that this connectivity will eventually be negotiated and established in real time. The overused notion of agile business will eventually become obsolete and give way to real time business.

This time-to-market acceleration has been accompanied with a corresponding reduction in integration costs. In the late 1950s it was possible to purchase shiny new IBM 7090 system for about USD 4 million (in 1958 dollars!) Made to order, custom built down to the keyboards and hard drives (drums in those times.) In the mid 1970s it was possible to buy a Digital Equipment Corporation† PDP 11/40 minicomputer for about USD 40,000. Assembly line techniques were used that allowed the reduction in cost by two orders of magnitude. Some components from different manufacturers were integrated in by Digital, but no other company sold the same design (reverse engineered Russian copies, and the not too successful effort to sell mail-order kits through Heathkit† notwithstanding.) Now a hobbyist can go to a computer store and purchase a retail motherboard, processor, memory, sound and video cards, hard drives, keyboard, mouse, monitor and a computer case, all from different manufacturers, and expect all to work together in a functioning computer, all for as little as a few hundred dollars.

This capability of cobbling together seemingly disparate hardware and software components that interoperate to make a perfectly working system is what is about to happen with Web services. The evolution is not about to stop. In about 10 years it's entirely conceivable that dozens and dozens of computers worth only a few dollars each will be embedded in home appliances, in sensors in the home itself, and even in garments.

All of them capable of communicating through Web services technologies that are just beginning to take hold. The interoperability of parts was made possible by extraordinary industry collaboration in establishing standards. Intel has a very strong history in taking a leadership role in the creation and adoption of standards. The same process is now taking hold of the software industry, primarily through the W3C consortium, and the results will be equally revolutionary, if not more.

Virtual Infrastructure Example

We are now ready to formulate the architecture or a business solution for the example in the preface with which we opened the book.

- As illustrated in Figure 6.4, a grid manager server rounds up the federated infrastructure services for the data mining analysis. A copy of the historical customer database for three grocery stores is stored at a storage service provider in China (SAN storage in Figure 6.4). Each database is contains nearly 20 gigabytes of data.

- The grid manager then allocates twelve virtual CPUs from a data center provider in India (virtualized server pool in Figure 6.4), each CPU with 4 gigabytes of memory and starts a data mining run. The number of CPUs and memory are chosen based on MIPS estimates provided by the independent software vendor, providing enough horsepower to finish a run within six hours. This provisioning should suffice for a couple of trial runs and one final run to be completed within the week specified for the project.

  Although the analyst is not explicitly aware of the actual physical configuration, the twelve virtual CPUs were allocated out of sixteen hyperthreaded CPUs in a two-socket server. The analyst does not really care; the SLA specified 1,000 MIPS per CPU and the specifications of the machine indicate an actual yield of 1,500 MIPS. To eliminate variances from the SLA, the service provider instructs the hypervisor to bind a core to a pair of hyperthreaded CPUs for the duration of the run.

- The analyst (represented by Data Miner Client in Figure 6.4) interacts with the ISV's business intelligence service using the ISV's application server as a point of presence. The analytical model is stored in the in a secure metadata management database from a business intelligence services provider.

- The separation and partitioning of data, applications and compute engines means that every actor in this analysis exercise gets only a fractured view of the activities taking place. This separation allows selecting a security scheme appropriate to the application, data travels and gets stored in encrypted form. If privacy or security requirements are high, data gets decrypted only in the memory of the machines running the data mining application, and at the source (analyst) and consumption points. The application and data get bound at the very last minute at the server hosting provider, making it difficult for the hosting provider to even tell what kind of application the hosting provider was contracted to deliver.

- When the data mining runs are complete, data consumers can access the results through a portal (gateway) provided by the ISV application service. Data consumers use a run-of-the-mill browser to access the results.

- Resource consumption is tallied and aggregated by each one of the actors. Eventually the Business Intelligence services provider comes up with a single bill that gets presented to the analyst, including an internal report to log infrastructure usage and costs to improve estimation capabilities and optimize the infrastructure. The view of the system is logical, appropriate to each user category. For instance, the report may tally total storage consumed without being specific on whether SATA, SAS, or solid state hard drives were used.

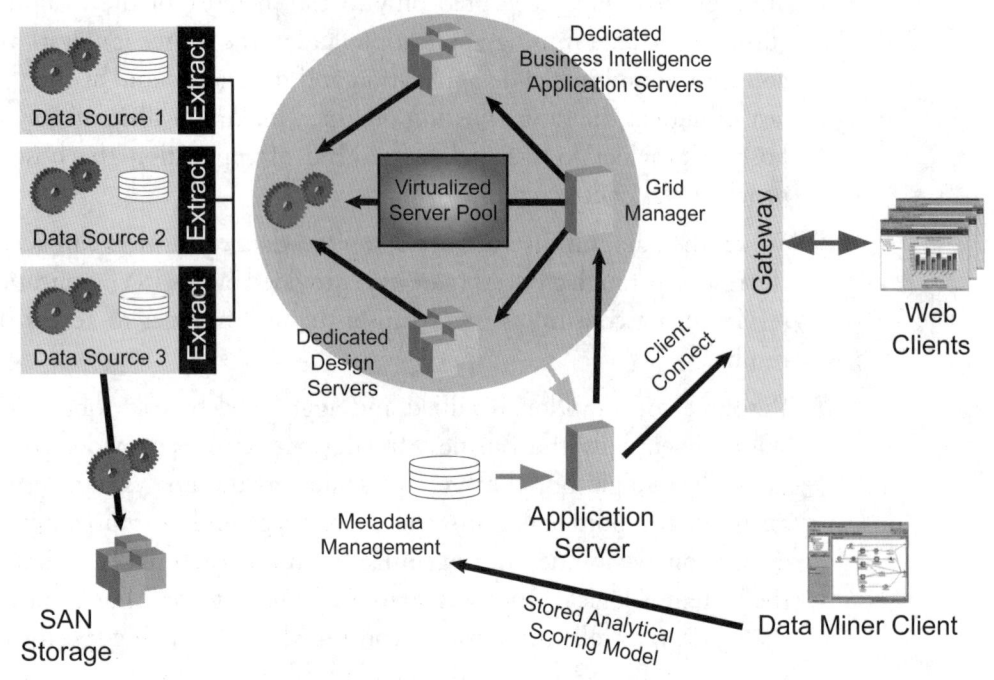

Figure 6.4 Business Intelligence Virtual Service Oriented Grid Example

Technology Integration Patterns

In this chapter we have discovered that integration patterns have not changed much since the beginning of the computer industry. In fact, similar patterns are evident in other industries that can be traced back centuries.

What do change are the specific units of integration. Units of integration become larger and more powerful in some measure allowing one to accomplish more at the same cost. To address the imperative of staying competitive, in the information industry, strategic decision makers need to be aware of the shifting winds that occur every few years. Indicators for the shift come in the form of a seemingly intractable challenge. We are in the middle of such a change in the present, from a prevailing model consisting of fixed solution stacks to a model where solution components are assembled on the fly.

Assembly on the fly will encourage a pay-as-you-go system likely to benefit consumers. An indicator of this change is the crisis with the traditional software licensing mechanism, which assumes that a software license is attached to a specific piece of hardware. This is no longer true with the increasing prevalence of delayed binding and on-the-fly resource allocation. Traditional licensing is becoming more and more cumbersome and gets in the way of efficient chargeback mechanisms in the present of a highly dynamic environment.

Hence, for solutions in the offing, a service approach needs to be given a serious consideration. Strategist need to assess the state of technology and determine whether a service approach will yield a lower lifetime cost for a project compared with the more traditional static solution stack approach. The potential benefits are

- *Less complexity.* Servicelets represent a higher level of abstraction, which in turn are more aligned with business entities than the technical activities associated with more traditional solution integration approaches. A smaller semantic gap means that IT will have less explaining to do to the business both in initially justifying a project and during progress reports.

- *Lowered long term risks.* The pay-as-you-go system will likely reduce long term capital commitments.

- *Agility.* Integrating an application from preassembled components, such as servicelets speeds up the integration process by orders of magnitude. Virtualization allows bringing a server online in minutes instead of the weeks or months that it would take to procure a physical server. Mid course corrections become easier to attain with less emphasis on infrastructure projects, for instance in house data centers whose lifetime may span decades.

- *Transparency.* Ironically, the information hiding associated with servicelets in the end makes it easier to assess the health of a project because the state of the project is measured on basis of the pre-agreed metrics codified in the SLAs from constituent servicelets.

- *Business efficiency.* Some IT scarce resources previously committed to maintaining, building, and planning computing infrastructure and for sustaining legacy applications can now be deployed to higher value tasks.

Chapter 7

Case Studies for Deploying Virtual Service Oriented Grids

The next wave is using virtualization to provide a complete simplification of how you do that—being able to build, develop, deploy, maintain and update applications, where an application can be a composite application of multiple virtual machines, and delivering that from any place over any set of hardware resources, be it on-premise or off-premise in a cloud, if you will...

— Diane Greene, VMware CEO

In this chapter we will present a number of case studies to illustrate the concepts covered to this point. The case studies come in the form of forward-looking hypothetical scenarios because many of the events described have not taken place yet.

Delivering IT Services to the Home

In this case study we bring a virtual service oriented grid perspective to the consumer space. A challenge in the consumer space is bringing the same level of service that is almost taken for granted in the corporate environment. These services may include help desk services, a hotline or Web chat service for troubleshooting, and installation and storage services for preserving data integrity. These services do exist today but they tend to be expensive, of questionable quality, and yield inconsistent results.

The most common usage model at the consumer's home for a desktop or laptop device is as a point device for work and play such as an Internet client end point. The device may have sophisticated video and audio capabilities for a realistic gaming and multimedia experience, but it still gets used as a point device. Transcending this model is potentially daunting to the consumer. One alternative to navigate a complex environment is through services. We see this pattern in other contexts such as real estate or the legal system. Unfortunately information technology services for the consumer are currently neither plentiful nor affordable. These circumstances leave potential benefits of distributed computing to the consumer unrealized. The consumer gets exposed to unnecessary levels of technical complexity representing hurdles that can be overcome only by hobbyists and the most technically savvy consumers.

In a virtual service oriented grid environment we view computers and anything that is connected to computers as part of an integrated system. Complexity gets hidden behind standardized service offerings where the visible abstractions are defined in terms appropriate to the service and not imposed by shortcomings in the underlying technology. Distributed computing is powerful. This power can be used to manage the system's internal bookkeeping, reducing the administrative and usage workload to the user, effectively hiding the complexity of the implementation.

In a virtual service oriented environment, devices not normally associated with a grid, such as a coffee pot, can be redesigned to become a node in a grid. The decision for networking a device depends on whether the device, provisioned with a processor, networking and sensors is more valuable than the standalone appliance. Networking a device should not be done only because it is technologically possible. Adding bells and whistles with collateral complexity will not bring success in the long term.

The home grid can be augmented with distributed, connected monitoring devices. These devices can monitor electricity, water, and gas consumption in real time. In particular, it becomes possible to keep track of electricity consumption on a per circuit basis or on a per device basis. Control functions are also possible: the system can activate a shutoff valve if there is a hose break in the washing machine, or activating the water heater during off-peak hours.

The challenges of delivering IT services to the home are similar to those of delivering IT services to small businesses. We see the same inside-out/outside-in SOA roadblocks but perhaps in more extreme forms. If we look at a consumer's home there is even less ability than in a small business to spread the cost of a large IT investment or to have a large portfolio of servicelets from which to build applications. Deploying a data center for the benefit of one home is not realistic either.

If we look at the aggregate total of household computational assets in a large city, they may comprise millions of laptops and PCs. However, if we look at a home as an organizational unit, the value of the assets within the organizational unit is paltry compared to the assets in use by even one single corporate departmental unit.

Furthermore, these assets are geographically dispersed. Also the budgets involved are relatively small both in per capita terms and in total terms per dwelling unit.

It is a well known fact that technical complexity, even if it's only perceived by the user, gets in the way of technology adoption. The results are unmet user needs and missed market opportunities for potential providers.

The delivery of applications and services today is highly device-centric: once an application is installed in a machine, the application is bound to that machine. This is contrary to the principle of separation of data, applications, and compute engines. The user is forced to use the particular machine to run the application. A malfunction in the device denies the user access to the application and data.

A number of high value home information management applications have not been integrated or are waiting to be implemented. Examples are energy, utility, and security management functions mentioned above. These are still opportunities waiting for prime time, which we believe will eventually become marketable with the cost efficiencies brought by virtual service oriented grids.

An example of an energy management application is the real time display of electric energy consumption by circuit, a particularly valuable application in a period of fast rising electric bills. Where applicable, the consumption of natural gas and heating oil would also be monitored.

Likewise, a display for water consumption would be useful for water conservation. Secondary sensors would provide finer grained information, similar to the information about electric circuits. In this case the information would be specific to zones in the sprinkler system, kitchen, and bath rooms. It is also possible to monitor specific appliances such as the dishwashing machine, the clothes washing machine and water heater. As in corporate systems, this information even when available in some form is not useful if it is locked in islands where it cannot be processed or integrated.

For utility monitoring systems, the breakeven point will be reached when the cost of delivering the services becomes smaller than the cost of the utilities saved, perhaps sooner if these services get combined with tax breaks or government subsidies for energy saving. The efficiencies brought by IT to businesses do not need to stop at the business level. The same principles are applicable to consumer settings.

Security functions might include cameras, motion and intrusion sensors. Processing power is needed to make the data coming from these sensors useful. A grid approach will make it easy to use a distributed computing approach to use local processing power to perform local data reduction. For instance, days or weeks of static images from cameras are not useful until some event takes place. Forcing the user to flip videotapes or other recording media on a regular basis is not a practical solution and represents another example of exposing the user to unnecessary complexity. It won't be too difficult to use local processing of the raw video data and transmit information only when there are specific incidents.

Now let's look at the challenge of delivering IT services to the home from a virtual service oriented grid perspective.

Federated Business Services

In order to understand how IT services will be delivered to the consumer end user, it might be useful to first understand how consumer services are delivered in the context of more mature industries. For this purpose, let's go through a scenario involving automobile insurance as a service delivered by a large insurance provider.

A consumer, Maria, needs to take care of a minor accident with her car. Her settlement scenario today looks something like this:

- Maria calls a toll-free number and talks to an insurance adjuster.
- She provides the customer representative details of the police precinct where the accident report was filed.
- The customer representative gives her the address of an insurance adjuster and she takes her car to have the damage assessed.
- Maria is presented a list of repair shops and selects one based on location.
- She is assigned a car rental for the duration of the repairs.
- She is presented a bill for the deductible portion of the repairs.
- She drops off the car at the body repair shop and one week later, she picks it up like new.

In this relatively simple scenario there are many more moving parts than are apparent at a first look. Here are some observations.

- The insurance company Maria deals with may not have a physical presence at all in the city where Maria lives.
- The insurance adjuster may not even belong to the insurance company. The adjuster represents a contracting service provider working with multiple companies.
- The car rental is one of the major national rental providers, not affiliated with the insurance company.
- The repair shop may subcontract portions of the repair job, for instance replacing a cracked windshield or the washing and detailing prior to returning the vehicle to the owner.
- Assume enough process maturity to the extent that the cost for repairing the vehicle is determined by the adjuster. This allows the owner to receive a single bill *prior* to the execution of the job.

The handling of the repair service represents a carefully synchronized dance choreographed by the insurance company. Most of the participants in this dance are not affiliated with the insurance company, yet they carry a number of activities on behalf of the insurance company. Also, most of the handshakes to initiate these activities take place behind the scenes without requiring explicit intervention from Maria.

Implicit in the layout and execution of these processes is a high degree of maturity and predictability. If every task during the repair has a more or less predictable cost and time to execute, essentially SLAs promised by the providers to the insurance company, the insurance company can make these tasks happen predictably as well, with low risk of deviations from the norm. The insurance company can figure out the cost and time to process a claim by virtue of having carried out this process thousands of times.

Process maturity also requires smooth exchange of metadata. Metadata includes the information put forward to issue an order, the identification and authentication of the transacting parties, the means to bill and pay for the service, and the means to handle exceptions, when they occur.

Contrast this process with the process in a less developed economy where interactions with every party need to be negotiated from ground zero and the potential for fraud is rampant. Under these conditions, the same repair job might end up taking a year or more instead of a week.

In order to minimize negative outcomes, organizations in less mature economies tend to be more vertically integrated with the insurance company owning the support desk and the adjuster service, retaining a very small and tightly controlled list of repair shops if not owning the shops outright. This environment forces insurance companies to in-source a broad range of capabilities, even in areas outside areas of the organization's core expertise. Predictably, these functions may not be handled very well with a corresponding impact on customer quality of service. Under these circumstances, there are usually very few, highly stovepiped insurance providers, seriously limiting competition and customer choice and quality of service.

A number of mainstream applications are still developed this way. This is the existing paradigm, rarely challenged. This leads to the stovepipe paradigm illustrated in Figure 2.9 back in Chapter 2. The expense of this traditional model represents a high barrier to entry for new participants. Generally, only large and well capitalized vendors can play in this market.

Niche players can participate, but need to charge very high license costs in order to recoup development costs. For instance, a large independent software vendor can offer general purpose project management software for a few hundred dollars a copy, but the vendor must sell millions of copies to break even. A small ISV offering a specialized project management package will sell far fewer copies, but must charge thousands of dollars per license.

Traditional software offerings change relatively slowly, usually paced by yearly release cycles requiring a high level of investment.

IT services become sparser and sparser as the size of the organization being served decreases from a large enterprise to a small business until they become practically nonexistent at the individual consumer level. The consumer is left to his or her own resources when it comes to equipment selection and repair or application installation and maintenance. One possible reason is that the same inside-out/outside-in dynamics we observed in Chapter 2 are at play: IT services need to be applied to an organization of a certain size to attain critical mass. Without that critical mass it is not economically viable to have these services delivered, either as a single-stack customized solution, or even as an in-sourced assembly of service components.

The notion of critical mass associated with a large organization gets restored when technology and social maturity advances to the point that service components can be aggregated across economic ecosystems. This is the tipping point reached with the pervasive adoption of virtual service oriented grids. Events with mash-ups and cloud computing may be signaling that the industry is reaching this tipping point.

A national or statewide services provider may be able to establish a business case for a viable IT help desk service. Here are some basic requirements:

1. Establishing a well-defined set of *canonical services*. Example services are: call center triage, replacing a hard drive, removing a virus, upgrading memory, network installation and configuration.

2. The delivery of these service components is done at *predictable cost*.

3. The service provider can put together a service product by *combining service components*, that is, servicelets, with a reasonable probability of making a profit. If the cost variance for the component services is high, the provider will have to enter the market at a higher price to cover the risk. Doing so reduces the number of customers willing to subscribe to the service.

4. *Continuous improvement* is necessary for sustainability. A virtuous cycle ensues as the ecosystem goes through the learning curve: the service component suppliers get more business, which in turn increases their level of experience, which allows them to offer their service components at lower cost and cost variance.

5. *Constituent services become standardized and generic* at the interface level to the point that even competing service providers see no down side from drawing from the same pool of servicelet providers.

Here are some examples of home IT services. These are top level services offered as explicit service offerings. A consumer may mix and match services from more than one provider.

- *Content service.* The consumer has the option of purchasing single content items or acquiring content through an aggregated content library. The content can be downloaded or shipped as dictated by the DRM license.

- *Storage service.* Following the virtual service oriented grid principle of decoupling, data is no longer bound to a specific physical device. Another principle is that the user must not be used as a point of integration because doing so exposes the customer to internal complexity unrelated to the task at hand. Having to do backups is a violation of this rule. A backup is imposed on the user and needs to be performed to compensate the less than perfect reliability of the storage devices in which data resides. A backup is not logically related to the intended function of the data.

  If there is only one PC in the system, the PC's hard drive is the only option. However, once there are multiple PCs and a server possibly with RAID storage, as described in the virtual infrastructure services, it becomes possible to spread out the data to minimize the risk of loss should one device fail. To minimize risk even further, data should be allowed to migrate off site. The details of data migration, replication and encryption must be managed by the system or under the provisions of the storage service. The traditional backup function becomes implicit. These functions must not be foisted on the unsuspecting user.

- *Data presence service.* This service allows data to follow the user. This service is built on top of the storage service. It provides a consistent view of the user data regardless of the user's location inside the home or while traveling. This service translates the data to form appropriate to the device used to access it: the data would look like a shared drive if the data is accessed from a laptop running the Microsoft Windows operating system. The user's content library should be accessible from remote locations without requiring the user to upload or download content to a mobile device. Otherwise the user would be called to become another integration point for the system, being called to manage data replication across multiple devices. This behavior, while historically acceptable, will eventually be fulfilled by the system.

- *Security service.* This service provides for the identification, authentication and authorization for household members, for managing the firewalls and mopping up after a virus outbreak, and for alarm monitoring services. A single sign-on, distributed identity service may also be necessary. The system comprises access to resources beyond the purview of a single operating system. Even for capabilities provided by the operating system, such as Microsoft Active Directory, their complexity is probably beyond what the average home consumer is willing to deal with. Hence these capabilities need to be integrated as part of security service offering.

- *Help desk and monitoring services.* This service provides a hotline or chat line for system usage and troubleshooting. This is the equivalent of the remotely managed services provided by managed service providers (MSPs). With advanced remote management technology, truck rolls and home visits should be relatively infrequent. Most repairs, updates, upgrades, and other management activities would be done remotely.

Application and Data Services

How does a virtual service oriented grid get instantiated in the home? Recall that a virtual service oriented grid environment is an environment where data, applications and execution vehicles are not particularly bound to each other.

It is easy to associate data with the hard drive where the data is stored. Unfortunately this association has drawbacks: if the hard drive fails, the data stored within is lost. Under this paradigm, data needs to be backed up periodically to have it restored if the medium in which it is stored fails.

Because of the historical evolution we have been conditioned to accept backups as part of inconvenient but necessary safe computing practices. This sacrifice is unnecessary. With the current state of technology, backups should be banished as part of system housekeeping that the system takes care of internally. From a service perspective, the role of the user is to select a level of quality of service (QoS) up front, and possibly establish a service level agreement with a service provider. The user is dealing with business level service abstractions and not with underlying implementation artifacts.

The service level agreement (SLA) may include the installation of a utility program that manages data migration across devices within the premises and possibly off site. The SLA would also specify privacy and security guidelines that lead to the selection of the encryption algorithms and processes to be used for offsite storage. For instance, the service provider can increase the level of privacy by striping the data across multiple subcontracted storage service providers.

The virtual service oriented grid environment at the home will depend on a number of services that are not necessarily directly user accessible, but are needed to enable applications to function. A cable provider such as Comcast can provide a number of services, among them broadband and a content (cable TV) service. Today the incoming cable into the home is fed into a signal splitter to connect to a cable modem as shown in Figure 7.1. One of the bifurcations goes to a set-top unit to feed a signal to an HDTV display. The other bifurcation feeds a cable modem which then connects to a PC via Ethernet or a USB cable.

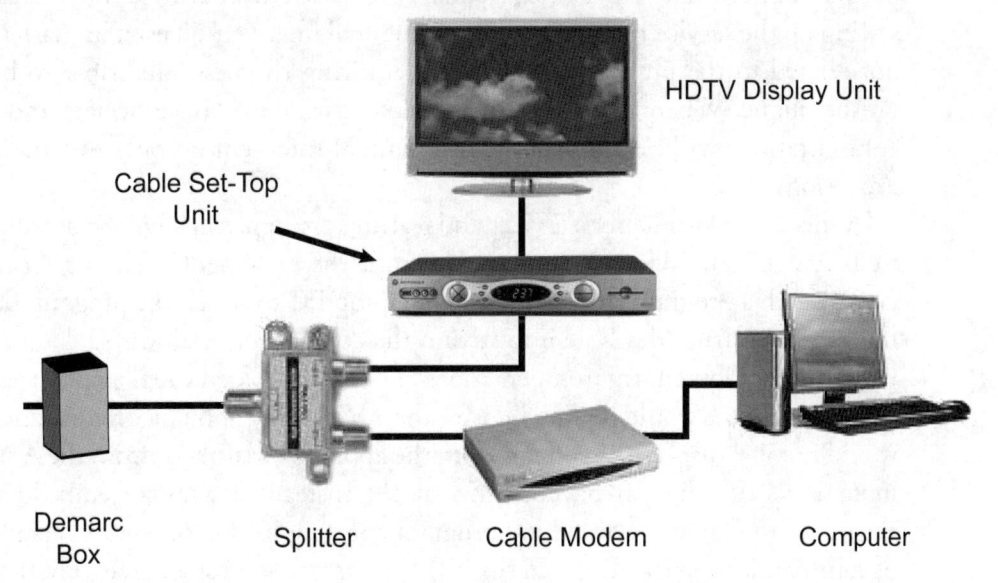

Figure 7.1   Cable Setup for Broadband and Cable TV services

Even though both systems in Figure 7.1 are digital, they are two independent unrelated point computing systems. A PC user can't watch cable TV programs. On the other hand, if a user watching TV wants to find out a review of a particular program, he or she is out of luck except for the very sparse programming information defined by the cable provider. This system is inflexible and it does not allow devices to function at their full potential.

The data and cable TV worlds are integrated in the virtual service oriented grid home environment at the network interface device (NID). The network interface device features powerful software-defined signal processors to virtualize a number of cable TV tuners, which are allocated on demand to household members watching a program. The content is then streamed to the target display device designated by the user. The NID also implements a modem and a router as software or using dedicated hardware modules.

The two services from the cable company mentioned so far, namely broadband and cable TV, can be delivered by the cable company as servicelets. This setup is much more flexible than the completely configured service delivered to ordinary subscribers. Today, even with Web browser interfaces, setting up the service requires significant manual intervention even in matters not related to the physical installation, requiring the new subscriber to be on the phone. When these procedures become available as servicelets, most configurations will be automated with manual intervention only to handle exceptions.

Once these foundation services and features are in place, it will be possible to assemble a TV viewing application from these elements. The user can launch such a program from a desktop or laptop PC to watch the program on the PC, or instruct the system to stream the content to a wall display.

This distributed environment does not preclude dedicated appliances. These appliances would be "intelligent": the TV viewing appliance for instance would not just display the content from the appliance's tuner or from the A/V input jacks. It may not have a tuner at all. Instead, it runs an embedded version of the same TV watching program running in the PC and is capable of commandeering the tuners in the NID just as the desktop does, except that the appliance is controlled with dedicated buttons instead of mouse clicks. Likewise, this device may have a capability to play radio stations and CDs from the jukebox.

Some of the foundation services need not be directly accessible by the consumer. For instance, providers for the storage service and the data presence service depend on storage aggregators and bulk storage providers mentioned in Figure 2.13.

Relationships can be bi-directional: the consumer takes on a provider role in the consumer-facilitated storage framework as described later in this chapter.

Virtual Infrastructure Services

The architecture of a virtual service oriented grid system in the home will build bridges to the present day array of point computing devices consisting of PCs, laptops, PDAs, music players, and home entertainment, plus automation and control systems that are totally separate entities.

The number of possible ways for architecting a home system is infinite. For the purposes of this discussion, let's assume three subsystems:

- Information technology subsystem
- Home automation subsystem
- Security subsystem

For brevity, we will cover only the IT subsystem in detail.

The IT subsystem comprises a network that reaches most every room in the home, starting with a patch room containing the entry point for voice, data and telecom services, a network reaching most every room in the house. We use Ethernet cabling for stationary equipment and wireless (Wi-Fi or Bluetooth) for mobile equipment.

Under the virtual service oriented grid approach, the resources within the system will be pooled whenever possible and allocated according to a specific policy. For instance, a software PBX takes care of routing voice calls. Even if the home only has a single POTS line, the system can be augmented with voice over IP to make it capable to send and receive multiple calls concurrently. Phone numbers can still be used, but it should not be necessary to remember them anymore. They are essentially hardware pointers and the system can map them to any imaginable interface preferred, whether voice activated, text, or touch based.

Likewise, for listening to broadcast programs, the system will feature a bank of tuners allocated on demand for listening to radio broadcasts. For listening to a particular station, the user may set a policy to use the content from the Internet version of the radio station instead of from the airwaves.

One of the critical elements in the home grid is the patch room or network closet depicted in Figure 7.2. The network interface device is the gateway to the outside world. Depicted is a highly integrated network interface device with highly available multi-modal connectivity. Typical arrangements will be less sophisticated, with only one or two modes installed, such as POTS (plain old telephone service) and one of cable, fiber, DSL, or fixed WiMAX.

The processor module functions as a DMZ server, acts as a firewall, and may host personal Web servers for household members. It also has an important function from a grid perspective: it replaces today's set-top boxes. A set-top box typically supports only one display device. Installing a set-top for every display device in the home is unwieldy. Worse than that, a set-top device pigeonholes the device behind it as a point device, limiting its range of possible functions. This setup limits the flexibility that a virtual service oriented environment can bring.

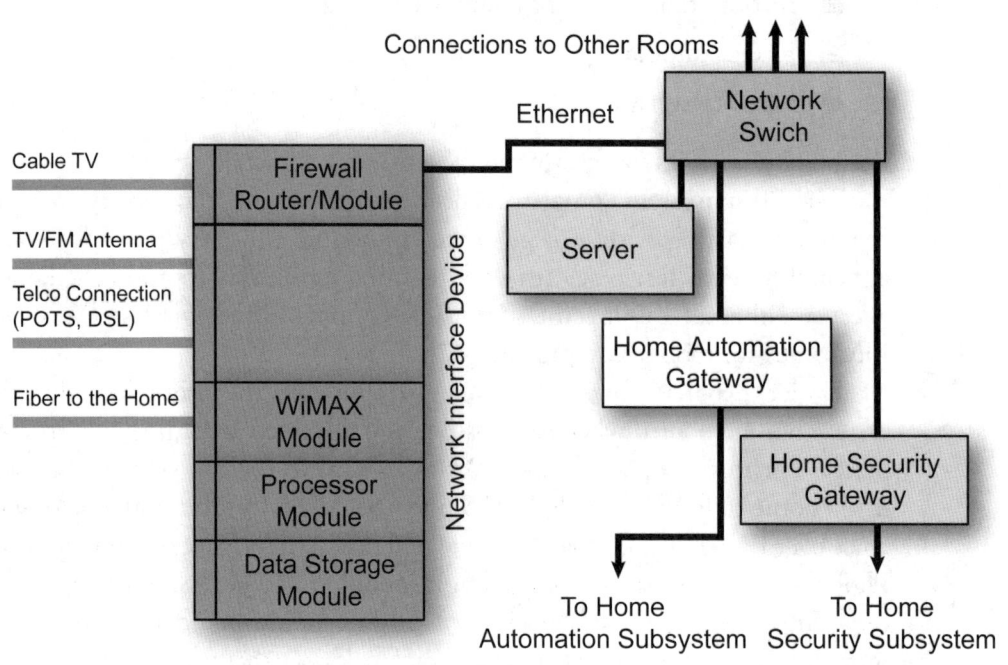

Figure 7.2   Patch Room

Assuming that the processor module in the NID is speedy, perhaps by virtue of having a large number of processor cores, the NID can implement a bank of tuners using software-defined radio technology. In a pooled resource grid fashion, these tuners are allocated on demand whenever a household member turns on a display device to watch a program, whether video on demand or a broadcast channel. The video from the program is then streamed to the target display. Note that the content can be streamed to *any* networked display

The network switch links the network interface device with other rooms in the household.

Attached to the switch is a server acting as the local file server and providing basic internet services such as DHCP and DNS. This server may also act as the data repository for the consumer-facilitated storage described in this chapter.

The home automation and home security subsystems also connect to the network switch.

From the user perspective, the most lavishly appointed room will be the entertainment or family room, shown in Figure 7.3. Other rooms will likely contain a subset or smaller versions of the equipment in the entertainment room. This room contains a networking switch to accommodate the large number of IP devices. It saves bringing that many cables from the patch room, especially when the number of devices may not be known at design time.

The most prominent feature in the room is the large display computer. This computer is designed to play back media with dedicated controls, with a physical button panel or reconfigurable pressure sensitive screen. The device is simple to use: turn the device on, insert a CD or DVD and press Play. In addition to playing single media, the large display computer functions as a slave computer to reproduce streamed content from any device in the house or the Internet.

The remote handheld controller is used mainly to control the large display computer. It has dedicated buttons, but it is not of proprietary design. It is a commodity device, such as a PDA, mobile internet device (ID), ultramobile PC (UMPC), a laptop, or even a cell phone that has a configured control panel for the large display computer.

Dedicated controls constitute an important feature. Forcing the user to boot a computer and launch a program to play a CD is not a friendly feature.

The role of the DVD jukebox is to store DRM protected media whose content cannot be moved into the cloud.

The telephone is a VOIP phone with a standard 12-button pad. It can be used as a POTS phone. The phone device can be a POTS phone connected through an Ethernet bridge or a "native" VOIP phone with an Ethernet jack. Calls made through this phone are routed to fit specific policies, for instance, using POTS for local calls and using VOIP for additional line usage or for international calls.

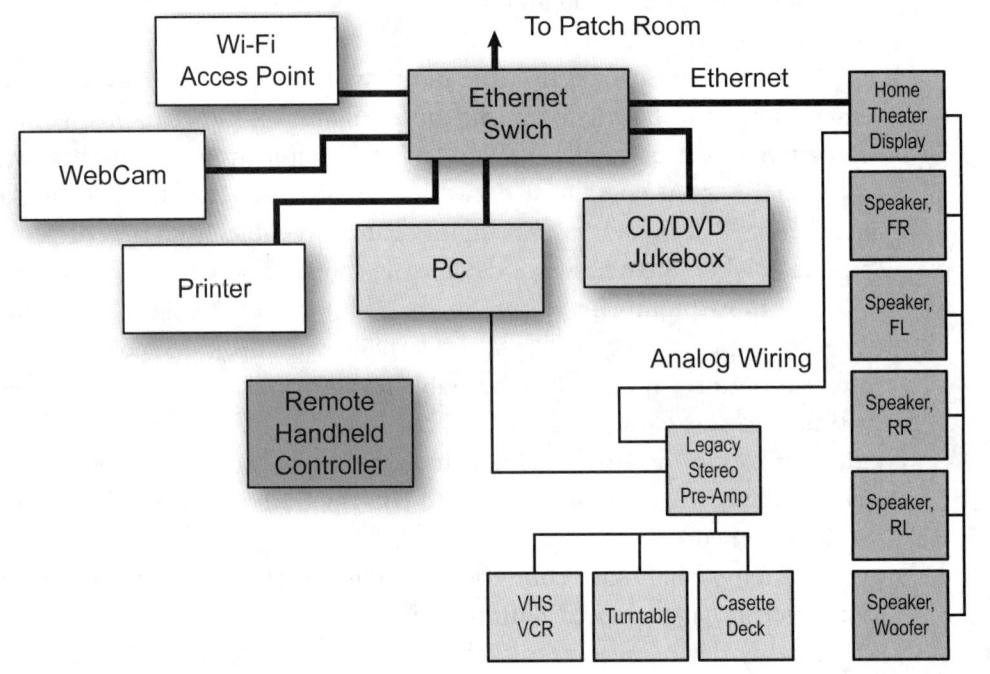

Figure 7.3   Entertainment Room

The system supports legacy devices. Figure 7.3 shows an analog stereo receiver/preamplifier with a vinyl record turntable, a cassette deck and a VCR deck. The PC functions as a gateway for digitizing legacy content or for streaming the content to other devices in the grid. This content can be rendered on the large display through analog cables or sent to the PC to be streamed to the large display or to any other networked rendering device. The analog option is for listeners who would object to an analog to digital and a digital to analog conversion for the legacy content. This option is available only for local devices.

A Wi-Fi access point is provided for supporting mobile devices. Both the PC and the display computers support Bluetooth controllers if need be. Even though the display computer does not normally have a keyboard attached to it, it can be configured through a remote terminal session.

The room PC and the large display computer are essentially stateless devices; neither is used for permanent data storage. These computers may contain locally installed applications, although not as a preferred policy. Binding an application to a specific computer would be done only due to licensing restrictions. Even though these machines are semi-stateless, they may still have fairly steep performance and storage requirements to run digital conversion and signal processing applications and for content buffering. They also must be capable of delivering high quality video and multichannel audio.

Figure 7.4 depicts a setup for a home office for a work from home worker.

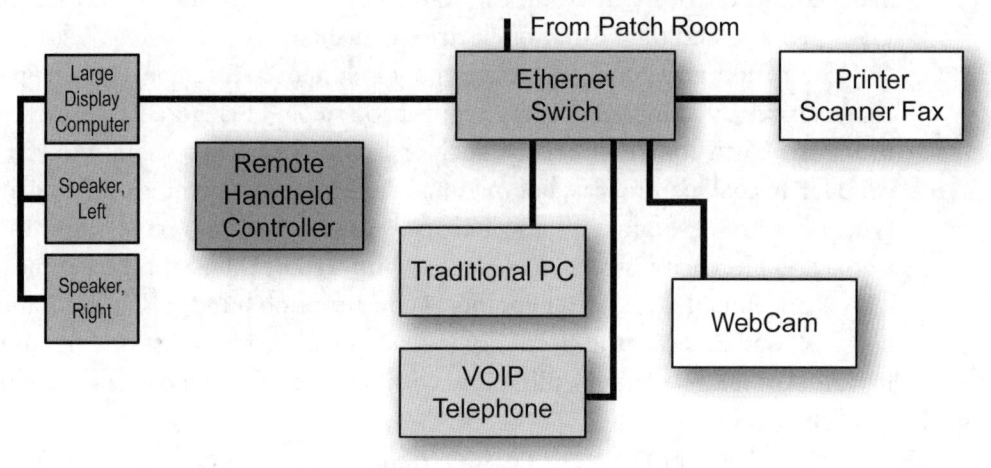

Figure 7.4   Home Office

A large display may be in use to support video conferencing or for displaying technical diagrams.

Figure 7.4 also shows a networked printer, scanner, copier and fax machine as well as a Webcam. The Webcam may be part of the security subsystem and may be combined with a microphone, smoke, temperature and other sensors.

Equipment in other rooms will be smaller versions of the equipment in the entertainment room or the home office.

Information Technology Architecture of an Electric Power System

Along with healthcare, the electric power industry is probably one of the industry whose operations and planning would greatly benefit from integrated information technology. In this case study we attempt to illustrate the broad applicability of virtual service oriented grid concepts in an industry segment that has not seen intensive use of IT commensurate to its size and economic impact. While the information technology examples might be applicable in many countries, for specificity, most examples in this section were drawn from US experience and the history of electricity in the US.

The concepts behind an electric power system are simple in principle, characterized by a number of energy conversion steps. This process is illustrated in Figure 7.5. A source of energy, such as hydro power in a dam, wind in a wind farm, coal, natural gas, hot magma in a geothermal plant is used to drive generators. In solar farms photovoltaic cells are used to convert sunlight into electricity. Electricity is generated at a few hundred or thousand volts at most. This is not enough to carry it to points of consumption hundreds or thousands of miles away. As far as the electricity is concerned, the transmission lines used to transport it look like very thin pipes with relatively limited current carrying capability.

The voltage provides a measure of pressure, whereas the current is proportional to the amount of electrons flowing through a wire. The power transmitted is proportional to the product of the voltage times the current.

A step up transformer is used at the generation substation close to the generation station to raise the voltage to 230,000 volts, 345,000 volts or even more using transformers. Since power remains constant except for conversion losses, the current becomes very small. Transmission lines can carry this current level without undue overheating.

The transmission line terminates at an electric substation near a city; transformers are used to reduce the transmission voltage to an intermediate voltage, from 4.16 to 38 kilovolts feeding the distribution network covering the last few miles. The distribution network can use underground cables or is strung in poles. A last transformer is used to down convert the distribution voltage from distribution to the voltage of eventual consumption.

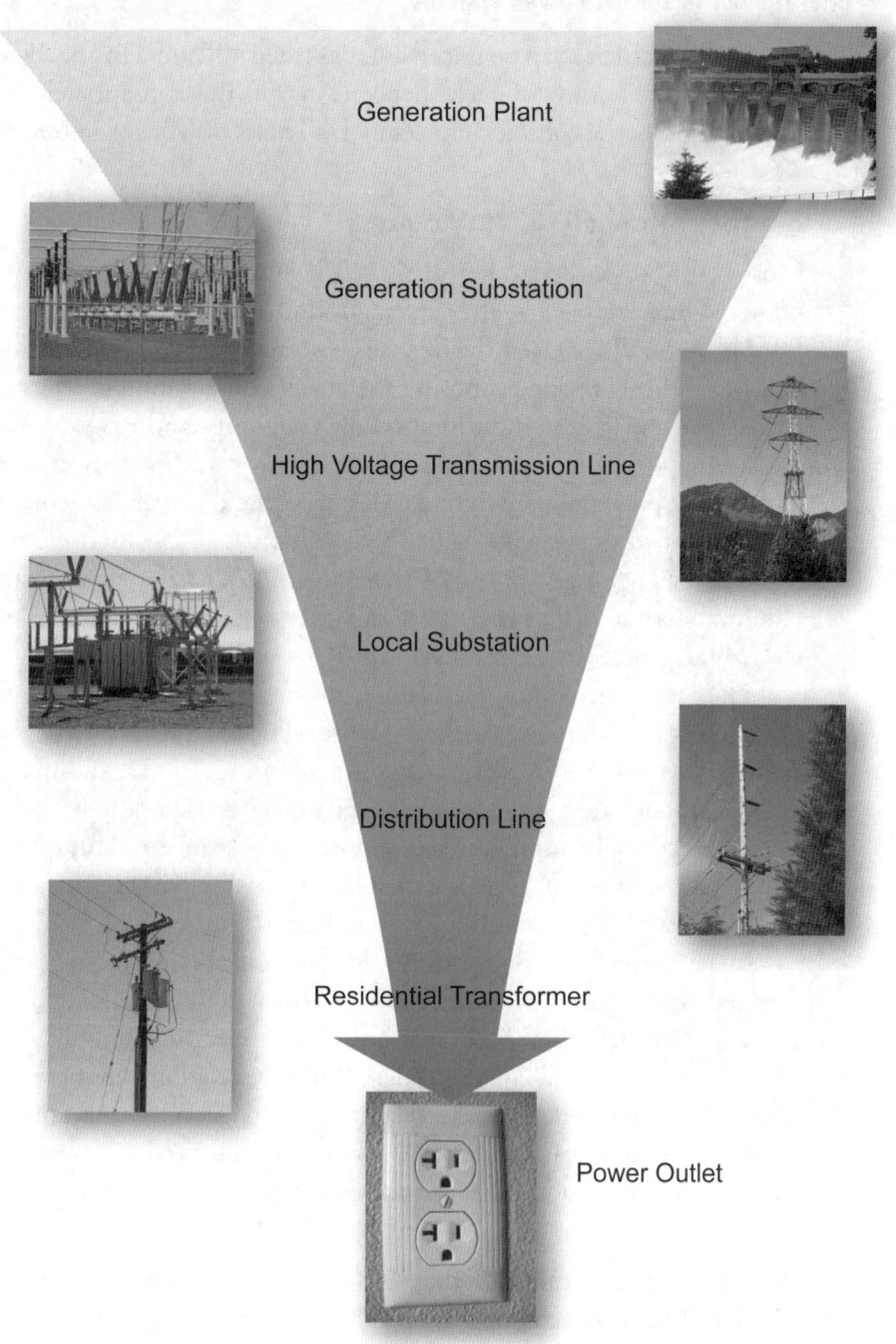

Figure 7.5   An Electric Power System

Brief History of Electric Power Systems

The history of electricity can be traced as far as three millennia by the discovery of magnetic attraction by a Greek shepherd in 900 BC appropriately named Magnus, and properties of static electricity by Thales of Miletos in 600 BC.

> ### Electricity through the 19th century
>
> Most of the discoveries up to the 18th century were of qualitative nature. Quantitative research starts around the 18th century with Isaac Newton discovering the inverse cube law of magnetic attraction and Benjamin Franklin proposing the law of conservation of charge.
>
> Also in the 18th century Joseph Louis Lagrange and Pierre Simon Laplace apply the new developed discipline of calculus to electricity and gravity phenomena. Lagrange discovers the divergence theorem, first applied to gravity and later Pierre Simon Laplace discovers the formula for Lagrange's potential theorem. In 1785 Charles Augustin Coulomb uses a torsion balance to quantify the inverse square law of electrostatic force. In 1793 Alessandro Volta invents the voltaic pile.
>
> The rate of discoveries accelerates during the 19th century with notable contributions by Simeon Dennis Poisson on the theory of potential, as well as discoveries, experiments and scientific and mathematical models developed by Michael Faraday, Karl Friedrich Gauss, Laplace, Hans Christian Oersted, Andre Marie Ampère, Humphrey Davy, Georg Simon Ohm, Joseph Henry, Gustav Kirchhoff, James Clerk Maxwell, John Poynting, Heinrich Hertz, and others.
>
> In particular, Faraday introduced the concept of electric field. Oersted advanced the knowledge on magnetism and magnetic field theory. Ohm described basic relationships in electric circuits. Maxwell discovered a set of equations describing the relationships between electric field, magnetic field, electric charge, and electric current in one of the most significant milestones of theoretical physics, essentially summarizing the findings from the preceding hundred years.

By the last two decades of the 19th century the scientific principles of electricity and electromechanical and electrochemical energy conversion were well known enough to allow the design of practical machinery and ensuing commercial applications. Entrepreneurs like Thomas Edison and George Westinghouse entered the market.

When it comes to emerging technology, the opportunities to convert scientific principles into practical applications are infinite. Often these applications are developed by different teams in fierce competition. Early power systems were no exception: the systems offered by Edison and Westinghouse were quite different and incompatible. Edison's was a direct current system, whereas Westinghouse used an alternating current system based on the inventions of Nikola Tesla.

The direct current system had an initial advantage; it was well suited for incandescent lighting; wires could be connected in parallel, and there were no practical AC motors in the beginning comparable to existing DC motors. However, alternating current proved to have a long term advantage: loads could not be further away than about two miles under the 100-volt Edison system. Voltage drops became unacceptable for longer distances. In contrast, in AC systems it was possible to raise the voltage to carry it through larger distances and to lower and regulate it. Systems could be designed to be more scalable and required less copper to function. This design led to the system still prevalent today consisting of large, centralized generation stations.

The Westinghouse system developed technical superiority and practicality through the application of the inventions of Nikola Tesla and the AC analysis methods, including the *phasor* analysis developed by Charles P. Steinmetz allowing highly scalable system designs. AC systems eventually overtook the more empirically designed Edison system. Steinmetz' methods simplified the analysis of AC circuits with an ingenious use of complex number algebra replacing previous methods requiring the much more tedious use of time-domain differential equations.

The electric industry in the US continued through a tumultuous period through the mid-1930s characterized by furious growth and countless mergers and acquisitions and standards wars, not just between direct and alternating current, but between different instances of alternating current systems. Power delivery to the consumer was eventually standardized at 110 V, 60 Hz in the United States and most of the Americas and 220 V, 50Hz in most of Europe. Half of Japan still runs at 50 Hz where as the other half runs at 60 Hz

A significant milestone took place in 1935 with the passing of the Public Utility Holding Company Act. The US Congress passed this legislation to reign in the chaos in the electric utility industry and the excesses that led to the Wall Street crash of 1929 and the subsequent Great Depression. PUHCA established electric utilities as vertically integrated, regulated monopolies, essentially instances of the silos described in Chapter 2 and depicted in Figure 2.1.

The silos established by PUHCA became very large toward the 1980s and their structure made real-time collaboration difficult. This real-time collaboration was important to maximize system stability to make blackouts less likely and for the economic operation of the system as a whole.

The US Federal Energy Regulatory Commission (FERC) mandated deregulation at the heels of the Energy Policy Act passed by the US Congress in 1992. By a controversial act of law, the vertical silos were transformed into the structure depicted in Figure 2.2, but in a more extreme form. In a perhaps naïve attempt to prevent collusion, up-and-down organizations that previously had close coordination were forbidden from talking to each other. Instead, companies called Independent System Operators or ISOs were created to coordinate horizontal resources. The previously vertically organized companies were reorganized into horizontal companies providing generation services, transmission services, distribution services, and so on. The outcome of deregulation has been mixed, with fierce defenders and detractors on both sides. This climate of deregulation allowed the now infamous market manipulations of Enron. PUHCA was eventually repealed in 2005.

Application of Virtual Service Oriented Grids to the Power Industry

The electric power industry moves relatively slowly compared with other industry because of technical and political reasons: it is capital intensive and its assets literally cover the whole country. Negotiating the rights of way for a new transmission line can take years, if not decades. Yet is has gone though radical transformations: the formation of regulated monopolies in 1935, deregulation in the 1990s leading to the repeal of PUHCA in 2005.

The current structure is a loose federation of companies and organizations dealing with generation, transmission, and distribution that must work cooperatively across the country and even across borders.

The generation subsystem must react in real time to track consumer demand, yet in this age of computers a still often used power management mechanism is real people making telephone calls.[1]

Computer models are used in planning processes through complex models for managing water flows in dams, or analyzing the behavior of new generators and transmission lines or for fault analysis. However, these models are not used for real time control of the system.

The requirement for coordination in a federated environment in the electric power industry makes it a good candidate for a virtualized service oriented grid environment. One would envision an information system infrastructure that mirrors the physical structure of a power system. In this parallel infrastructure it is possible to define composable servicelets out of specific entities within the power system. The architecture we describe in this case study is of necessity futuristic, since no deployments with any degree of completeness exist today.

The information architecture for an electric power system is depicted in Figure 7.6. At the highest level of abstraction a whole power system can be condensed into single servicelet with two interfaces, one for the utility's clients and a second one for the utility's partners and suppliers, both drawing from a common servicelet representing the whole utility.

The external exchanges with consumers, partners, and suppliers constitute, by definition, instances of federated business services.

Services to customers may range from simple informational Web sites to Web services based interfaces for bi-directional data exchange ranging from meter reading data to readout and control data related to carry out specific energy policies. These energy policies may range time of day billing to partitioning energy delivery into different quality of service (QoS) categories.

QoS may range from off-peak or best-effort to committed delivery. Power under committed delivery includes lighting and power to outlets, whereas lower quality power may get assigned to water heaters, zonal heating and cooling as well as refrigeration. The utility benefits by being able to schedule power delivery more flexibly, not just generation. The customer benefits through lower rates overall.

---

1   R. Klashner, *ICT and the Deregulation of the Electric Power Industry: A Story of an Architect's New Tool*, Journal of Digital Information, Volume 5, Issue 4, Article No 269, 2005-03-30.

This environment becomes possible under the IT-to-the-home scenarios described in the opening section of this chapter, where electricity delivery is partitioned into circuits or zones, each with a QoS index associated with it. Each circuit is instrumented to be metered individually. For zones with QoS less than committed delivery, the utility will have the option of cycling the circuits on an off according to the specific energy policy. While this environment introduces complexity, rapidly escalating energy prices from dwindling resources and environmental concerns about pollution and carbon footprint will make this information technology intensive environment increasingly more attractive.

For industrial customers load management based on QoS, including time-of-day billing and load shedding are well known. Distributed generation whereby the utility can actually purchase power from industrial customers with generating capability is an increasingly common arrangement. What will be different is that this power can be used to implement more sophisticated policies beyond making up for possible peak load shortfalls. Such policies may include using distributed generation to increase the grid's stability margins and improved voltage control.

Chapter 7: Case Studies for Deploying Virtual Service Oriented Grids ■ 237

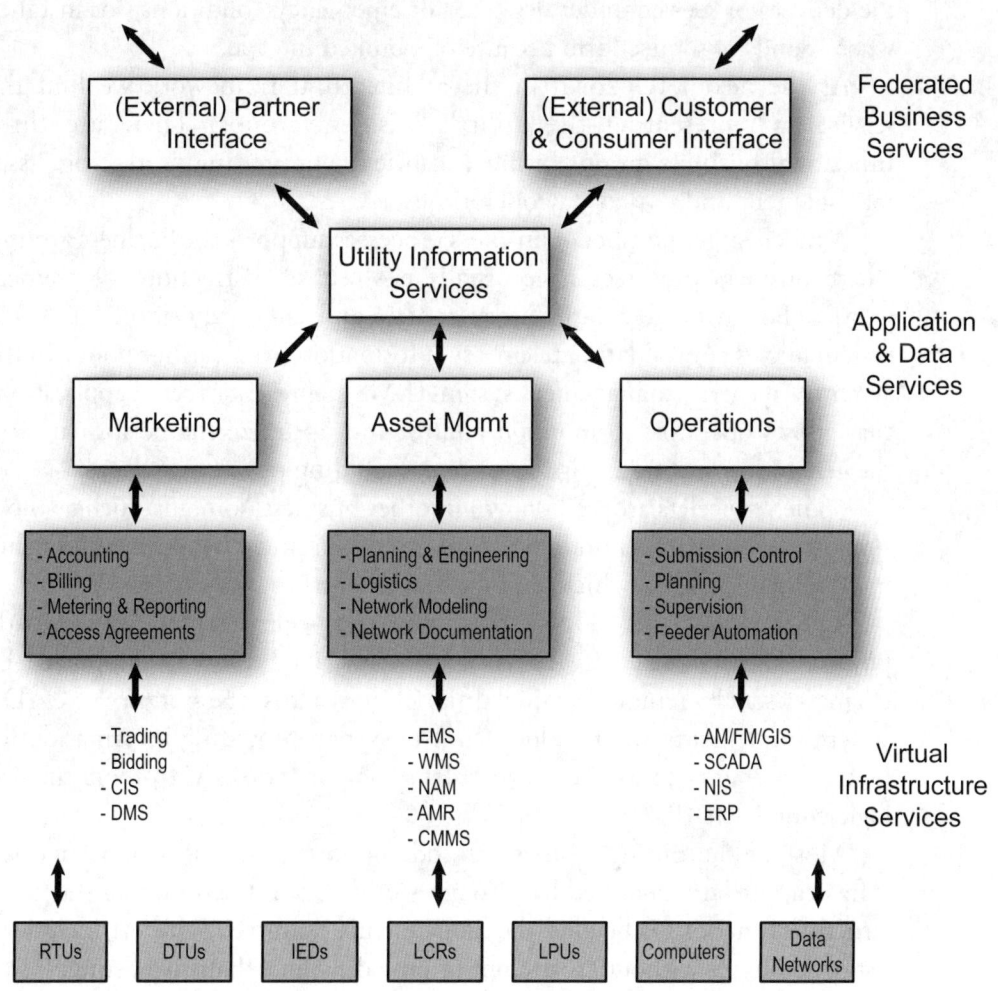

Figure 7.6 IT Enterprise Architecture of an Electric Power System from a Virtual Service Oriented Grid Perspective

The increasing availability of distributed generation, not just from hydrocarbon sources, namely diesel or bunker-c plants or natural gas powered turbines, but also from the pervasive deployment of photovoltaic and wind turbines will increase flexibility in power delivery. Tightly managed generation and workloads will make it easier to bring a system back on line or continue the delivery of service under degraded or emergency conditions, for instance when islands of service form because of a broken intertie.

At the next level down in the architectural framework we find the servicelets representing the utility's business groups. There are three functional business groups in most utilities, representing marketing, asset management and day-to-day operations.

A much larger number of business processes supports the business groups. These business processes have usually evolved as abstractions of physical entities. For instance a supervisory control and data acquisition (SCADA) system allows consolidating telemetry information from various points in the system. An energy management system (EMS) represents a set of applications that allows operators to monitor, control and optimize the performance of the generation and transmission system, including power exchanges.

Some servicelets are well known in other business domains, such as those supporting enterprise resource planning (ERP), and customer relationship management (CRM), which are found in enterprises of most any size.

The bottom layer is populated with servicelets representing mostly physical entities. The SCADA function described above is supported by telemetry sent by remote terminal units (RTUs) across the system. A SCADA system implements an open loop control system providing information for human operators to assess and perform control actions via programmable logic controllers (PLCs).

Most of the business processes and supporting physical or virtualized infrastructure are identified by acronyms. A detailed description of the infrastructure functions is beyond the scope of this example. Table 7.1 includes a list of acronyms without an attempt of providing an exhaustive listing.

The purpose of the diagram in Figure 7.6 is to provide conceptual clarity. Even though it has a vertical structure, it does not necessarily represent a siloed vertical stack, although the diagram can be applied to a utility following the traditional regulated monopoly model.

Table 7.1 List of Acronyms

Term	Description
AM/FM/GIS	Automated Mapping Facility/ Facility Management/ Geographical Information System
AMR	Automated Meter Reading
CIM	Common Information Model
CIS	Customer Information System
CMMS	Computerized Maintenance Management System
CRM	Customer Relationship Management
DMS	Distribution Management System
DPU	Display Point Unit
DTU	Distribution Terminal Unit
EMS	Energy Management System
ERP	Enterprise Resource Planning
IEC	International Electrotechnical Commission
IED	Intelligent Electronic Device
LCR	Load control receiver device
LMS	Load Management System
NAM	Network Asset Management
NIS	Network Information System
PLC	Programmable Logic Controller
RTU	Remote Terminal Unit
SCADA	Supervisory Control and Data Acquisition
WMS	Work Management System

A self-sufficient siloed stack can be the departure point, whereby, through the application of SOA technology, the initial monolithic structure is reorganized into servicelets, exactly as in the evolution model described in Chapter 2.

For instance, compute intensive simulations for network and generation planning might have been done in the past with computers owned by the utility. Today these runs can be outsourced and carried out using externally hosted grid resources. Logically this is accomplished by opening up an interface that allows data about the utility's network assets to be extracted and reassembled into models to be run using the external compute resources.

Likewise, an independent system operator, or ISO, an organization that coordinates generation, transmission and demand for electric power from a pool of participants may use relatively low-level monitoring data from the participants. Hence the architecture depicted in Figure 7.6 is actually an instance of the network of servicelets as shown on the right hand side of Figure 2.3.

Also, Figure 7.6 does not imply a completely automated, with closed loop machine-to-machine controls throughout. It encompasses processes where manual procedures still prevail. The open loop SCADA system is one such example, where humans monitoring sensor data make decisions on the mix of generation needed to meet the forecast demand.

The control actions need not be issued by machines conversing using XML Web services. Humans using telephones can accomplish the same goals, provided that the time scales allow such control.

An increasing adoption for Web services in power systems[2] is to be expected, even though, for a variety of reasons some practitioners and decision makers do not view these changes favorably. This adoption will be driven by the same goals seen in other disciplines, namely, to control costs and to increase business agility. This transition will be facilitated by a number of standards, such as IEC 61970 defining a common information model, or CIM helping the interoperability of energy management, SCADA and network planning processes. Likewise IEC 61968 describes common information models related to asset management systems (AMS), work management systems (WMS), construction management, distribution network management, geographic information systems (GIS) and outage management. Also, IEC 61850 is a standard for the design of substation automation. This list is not exhaustive by any means, and there is continuing work by a number of standards committees.[3] IEC is an acronym for the International Electrotechnical Commission.

---

2   Q. Chen, H. Genniwa, W. Shen, *Web Services Infrastructure for Information Integration in Power Systems*, IEEE Power Engineering Society General Meeting, June 2006, paper 1-4244-0493-2/06.

3   See http://en.wikipedia.org/wiki/IEC61850.

Beyond integration using Web services, a number of researchers are working on SOA implementation strategies[4]. As in the healthcare industry, the electric energy industry is still one of the major industries that have yet to adopt a pervasive strategy for IT integration and automation.

The status quo will likely change given the increasing concern in society about energy shortages and concern about the overall stability of the electric grid in the face of challenges in obtaining rights of way for transmission lines and locating space for placing new generation. The promise of the application of sophisticated information systems is radical improvement in the management of existing resources, which in turn yields improved operating margins, even in the face of limited resources and deferred investment.

Grid Computing Example: Smart Electric Meters

The origin of the venerable and pervasive induction-type electric watt-meter still in use today goes to the dawn of industrial electricity. In 1885 Galileo Ferraris, an electrical engineer from Turin discovered that two out-of-phase alternating current fields could make a solid piece of metal, the *armature*, rotate. The invention of the electric meter itself is attributed to Elihu Thomson in 1888, based on the Ferraris discovery.

In this section we will focus and expand on a small part of Figure 7.6, namely the AMR or automatic meter reading function. Today generally a labor and fuel intensive task requiring a truck roll and a meter reader armed with a scope to take actual reading at the watt meters in the customers' premises. The process carries certain risks such as angry dogs or annoyances that make carrying out the task difficult, such as locked gates and overgrown vegetation.

To reign in costs, some utilities read meters every other month, even when the service is billed monthly. Consumption is estimated for the months when an actual reading is not taken, the estimate based on historical consumption. The estimations degrade accuracy, which can lead to customer complaints representing extra time and cost to resolve, in addition to the loss of customer confidence in the service.

---

4   H. Xiaoqing, J. Hao, X. Anbang, *SOA-Based Integration of Electric Utility in Open Electric Market*, 3rd Int'l Conf. on Electric Utility Deregulation and Restructuring and Power Technologies, April 2008, paper 978-7-900714-13-8/08.

Even though manual processes can be integrated into a virtual service oriented grid infrastructure, a modicum of automation will increase efficiency and the speed of processing. Automation will also increase data accuracy through fewer data entry or re-entry and processing steps.

It is possible to think about a meter reading transformation strategy along these three lines:

1. Retrofit the existing equipment
2. Functional meter replacement
3. Grid approach involving additional applications

A retrofit strategy involves leaving the legacy meters in place and attaching an optoelectronic digital device to the meter. This device can optically read the meter or track the rotation of the armature in a Ferraris type of meter.

The second strategy replaces the electromechanical meters with digital readouts.

Readings from the device can be taken from a handheld device or from a reading device installed in a vehicle using radio frequency identification (RFID) technology. This alternative still requires an operator driving a vehicle and traveling to the customers' premises. The data collected, although no longer transcribed manually, still needs to be scrubbed and uploaded.

Both the digital retrofits and the digital meters may be networked, at this point data collection can be done without any site visits. Instead of readings every one or two months, digital technology allows taking and storing multiple readouts, as frequently as once every fifteen minutes. This capability allows time-of-day billing to implement pricing incentives to discourage the use of electricity during peak hours when it's most expensive.

The transition to digital metering brings an opportunity from a virtual service oriented grid perspective for power utilities not only to optimize their operations but also to deploy new applications with a potential for new revenue streams.

This unconventional approach to deploying new technology has been used before. For instance, in 1996 Philip Anschutz founded Qwest and began installing fiber-optic cable along the rights of way of the Southern Pacific Railroad. After a series of mergers, this idea allowed a small railroad company to become a major player in the telecommunications industry today.

A key observation is to look at electric meters not as a measuring device, but as a computer node in a grid. R.W. Beck Inc. in Seattle, Washington estimates the population of electric, gas, and water meters in the United States at around 130 million[5]. The deployment of computerized electric meters could form the basis for one of the largest grids in the country, if not the world. This system can become the focus of a vast number of applications.

The nodes in a metering grid would be more capable than the embedded processor in a digital meter with a generous allotment of memory and non volatile memory for storing programs and applications. These nodes are to be managed remotely, not just to query them for consumption data but also to configure them and load new applications and to implement a storage grid. The nodes will also have a significant autonomy and self-management and self-configuring capability to minimize the administrative burden. For instance, nodes will spontaneously form a mesh with neighboring nodes, selecting the most efficient physical medium among several alternatives that include WiMAX, Wi-Fi, perhaps through the emerging 802.11s mesh networking standard, broadband over power lines (BPL). The architecture of the system will also need careful consideration to security issues given the multi-tenant environment.

The architecture of the metering grid is shown in Figure 7.7. It essentially follows the same structure of Figure 7.5 reflecting the inherent reuse philosophy of servicelets. The metering system relies heavily on preexisting information technology supports to make it realizable within manageable cost and complexity.

Consumer-provided energy management applications attach to the consumer Web services interfaces. A consumer application can retrieve metering data from the utility on a real time basis for the benefit of customers wishing to manage their power consumption.

The binding of a consumer application to the utility's Web services interface also represents a contract. The specification of the contract is in terms of service level agreements (SLAs) and policies. The utility does not micromanage power consumption, specifying to the end user consumer when every light switch should be turned on or off. However the consumer application negotiates specific consumption targets by following certain policies. For instance, the customer may decide to purchase lower quality

---

[5] http://tdworld.com/customer_service/much_more_smart_meter/

and lower cost power and allocate this power to climate control applications. During periods of heavy load the utility has the prerogative of trimming the power allocation under the provisions of this contract.

Costs to the consumer are minimized to the extent that the actual consumption matches the targets. This process takes place today in energy markets with large customers. A servicelet environment will allow scaling down this process down to the individual consumer.

Although meters are physically in the back end, and customer data flows through the metering nodes for consumers choosing to get their Internet access through one of the metering nodes, logically they are separate, and hence are depicted separately in Figure 7.7.

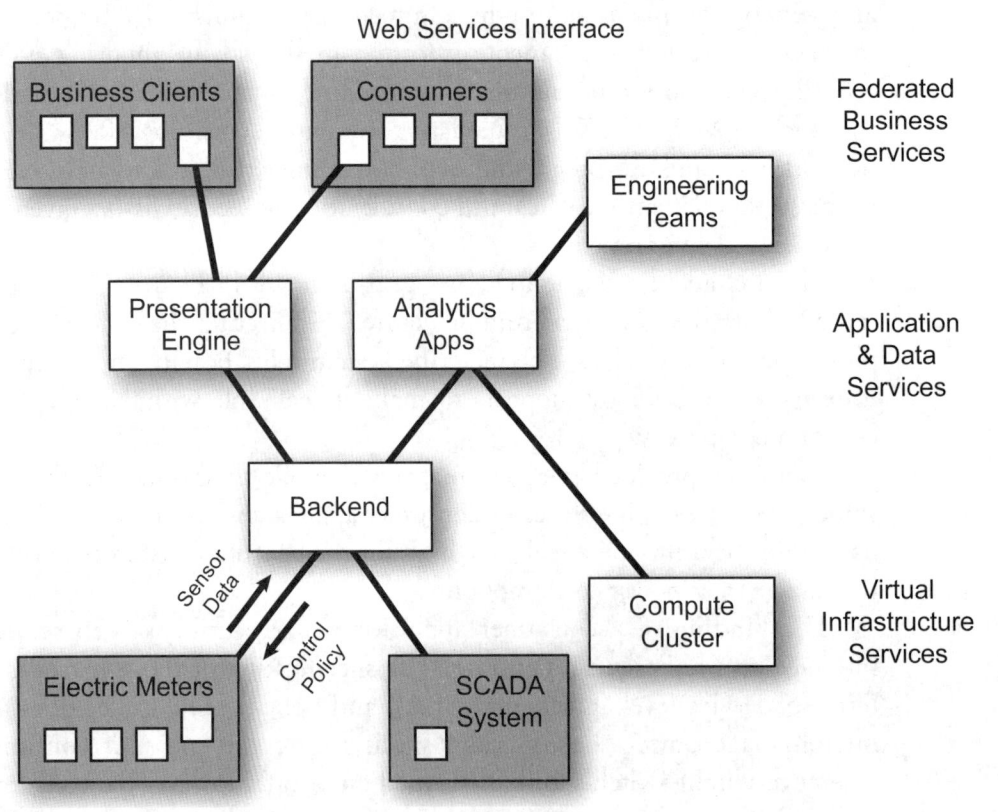

Figure 7.7   Information Technology Architecture for an Electric Power System

In Figure 7.7 we show two boxes, one housing analytics applications and a compute cluster. The analytics applications refer to applications normally run by engineers and planners such as load flow, static and dynamic stability analysis, relay coordination, and short circuit analysis. Data for the analytics runs comes from internal databases representing the system configuration as well as some real time data coming from sensors, either in the SCADA system or in sensors embedded in metering nodes.

In a virtual service oriented environment the participation of third parties would be feasible and encouraged to share the investment costs and manage economic risks.

In addition to time-of-day billing here are just a few new power-related applications:

- Monitoring of individual power circuits. Even though all the electrons look the same, they carry different costs and QoS properties. A consumer can take advantage of different QoS levels to optimize utility costs, for instance using off-peak rates for water heaters and dish washing, medium quality service for climate control and high quality, on-demand energy for lighting and entertainment.

  The implementation of these policies would be entirely optional to customers willing to invest in additional on-the-premises monitoring equipment. The utility provides Web services interfaces for the specific capabilities. The customer is free to contract out and implement functionality appropriate to the premises consistent with the principle of loose coupling for SOA. It would be perfectly logical to implement energy management policies using the home IT infrastructure described earlier in this chapter, matching electricity from different energy sources to respective loads, each one metered individually and in real time.

- The metering grid would allow two-way communication, enabling not just fine-grained monitoring as described above, but also the implementation of specific control policies. The utility can aggregate or disperse control directives to carry out a specific policy: a directive may apply to a single account, or to all the residences in a specific neighborhood.

The control policies would enable load shedding and delivering service even under degraded conditions. Continuing operations after the loss of an intertie would be possible even after the formation of islands as long as there is enough distributed generation to deliver power to the loads within.

The finer control in a metering grid would also allow prioritizing energy allocation during emergencies, ensuring for instance that hospital, emergency response organizations and airports continue to be supplied.

- The metering grid also would implement a sensor network, facilitating the application of regional monitoring and control policies. When an outage occurs, the metering nodes can yield a very fast damage assessment, acting in a coordinated fashion to quickly build a map of the system integrity. The application of control policies would also allow bringing the system online much faster than would otherwise be possible with existing technology. In general, new system management strategies will increase the system's stability margins, possibly allowing recovery from the relatively minor incidents that can cascade out of control such as 2003 Northeast blackout. This blackout started with a line sag leading to a short. The economic loss estimates from this event range between USD 6.8 billion and USD 10.3 billion.

- Supporting "boutique" power, allowing consumers to select specific energy sources, whether wind, hydro, or more conventional sources. The account setup today is cumbersome, where the customer is allowed to specify an energy source at account setup. The selection is never changed unless the terms of the account are also changed. The metering grid would allow changing the allocations in real time. It also would allow the implementation of audit records and account statistics to determine whether service SLAs have been met. The customer is given compensation if the terms are not met. A net metering agreement would be trivial to implement when the customer has a generation capability on the premises.

Because a virtual service oriented grid environment can easily support a multi-tenant environment, a metering grid represents an excellent general purpose application platform capable of hosting applications by multiple parties under the servicelet model. The multi-tenant capability of the metering grid will enable new revenue streams for utilities. Here is a sampling of potential general applications:

- Where the available bandwidth allows it, a metering node can function as an Internet gateway for wired or wireless services, telephony and television services.
- The metering node can be provisioned with a variety of sensors: a microphone and video camera for delivery of surveillance services, a variety of sniffers and chemical sensors for civil preparedness.
- Nodes can be fitted with thermometers, barometers and hygrometers to enable weather services to perform a fine-grained assessment of weather patterns across the service area.
- Nodes can become gateways for the implementation of composite consumer facilitated services where the consumer is actually the service provider such as the consumer facilitated storage system described below.

The nodes will have a capability for local data reduction to minimize network traffic. For instance, a surveillance application will only send image changes over a baseline; there is no point in sending the same static image millions of times.

The existence of the nodes will potentially multiply the economic impact of power utilities through shared investment with third parties, the additional revenues from network tolls and from the new services provided.

Building a metering grid is not without challenges. Security is one of the foremost; a system hijacking or hacking event would be catastrophic. Consumer trust will need to be won; they must not feel that the system will be built on their pockets while others benefit. Likewise, savings from improved power management will need to be distributed fairly. Regulatory clashes will be certain. Electric utilities entering the market with tens of millions of metering nodes will upset cable and telecommunications provider environment. The deregulation climate in the power industry will also add some interesting twists: for instance, what will be the terms by which independent system operators (ISOs) will relate to generation and distribution companies?

On the other hand, in an event not too unlike the Qwest railroad roots, utilities will be realizing additional economic value from one of their most precious assets, their rights of way for transmission and distribution power lines.

Implementation of the Laptop Loss Management Service

At this point we have developed enough concepts to perform an architectural analysis of the laptop loss management service we started describing in Chapter 1.

One assumption that is becoming more and more valid today is that laptops, even though they are roving devices, can be considered intermittently connected. In fact laptops can be provisioned for multi-modal connectivity utilizing a combination of technologies from wired Ethernet to a broad range of wireless technologies including Wi-Fi, WiMAX and a number of G3/G4 telecom-provided data services combined with GPS services so they stay connected almost all the time even if they are physically misplaced or stolen. These laptops are effectively part of a *grid*. This would not be only a computational grid but also an *administrative* grid; a grid established for system management purposes.

It is tempting to think that provisioning a laptop so it can "phone home" would suffice. It helps, but unfortunately it is not sufficient. As indicated above, a system that would work for misplaced laptops will be of little help in the UK government incidents that involved only data disks, no laptops. We could devise a point solution for every imaginable device and still have a system with significant security gaps. The coordination among solutions would become an administrative nightmare.

What can be done to improve the odds of data recovery? The first is to realize that in a grid environment data exists as a virtualized resource, not bound to any specific device. A laptop is treated as a cache or temporary holding device for the owner's data. Hence most of the data would exist disembodied in the system except for small portions that have not been flushed. The data in the laptop is stored in encrypted form.

If a persistently connected laptop is misplaced under these circumstances, a GPS and an administrative communication link to the lost device would be used to determine its location. If it is not safe to physically retrieve the device, a policy is applied to check for tampering and to retrieve cached data that has not been flushed. This flushing can be done fairly quickly as it usually involves a small portion of the total storage capacity. Once the data cache has been flushed, the laptop can be locked up and set to display a message with instructions for returning it. This functionality is implemented through the data presence service shown in Figure 7.8.

Chapter 7: Case Studies for Deploying Virtual Service Oriented Grids ■ 249

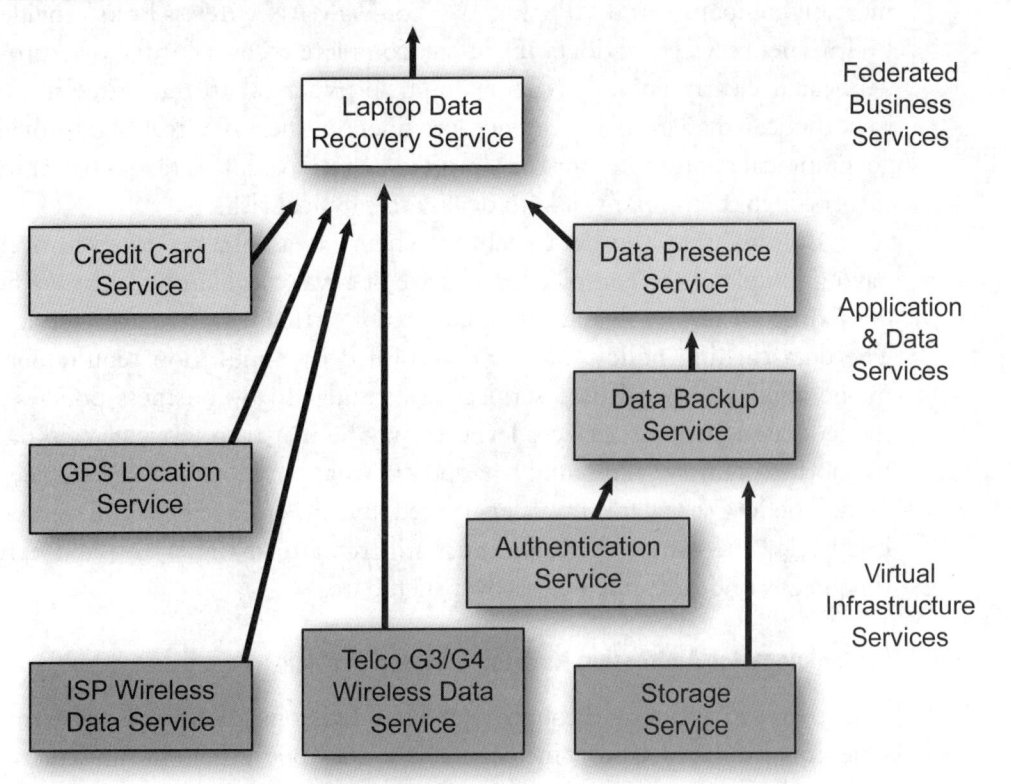

Figure 7.8   Service Composition for a Laptop Data Recovery Service

This example also illustrates the inherent robustness of grid storage through replication: if any of the data containers is lost there is enough replication in the system to restore the data in the lost containers with high likelihood.

Elaborating on the data caching system, the memory of a laptop functions as a cache for the hard drive, and the hard drive is used as a cache for network storage. Data migrates and diffuses through a chain of devices with a degree of replication statistically consistent with pre-specified SLA goals. Also, under a virtual service oriented grid environment, the data need not be entirely contained in an organization's data center or even multiple data centers. The infrastructure could be built from services from external providers.

Also, note that true to a service oriented environment, this scheme works through the composition of services that include G3/G4 data links telecommunication companies and GPS and WiFi or WiMAX wireless links provided by Internet service providers. Even the complete recovery infrastructure is delineated clearly enough that it would be practical to outsource it to a hypothetical data recovery service provider. If the GPS readings provide geographical coordinates for the laptop to be retrieved, this task is better left to a specialized company able to deal with physical risks.

Assuming that the data caching scheme is a solution to circumvent having to upload the complete hard drive of a wayward laptop, the specifics of caching are not resolvable in the context of virtual infrastructure services. The data caching policy may be determined by application requirements in the application and data services layer and also by business policies at the federated business services layer. It may be illegal to move certain data to another country. This might happen if an anonymous storage service is used. The fact that data travels encrypted and the storage host can't decode it is irrelevant. Hence this data must still remain in the laptop and extra time needs to be allocated to recover such data.

Methodology for Addressing the Stolen Laptop Problem

Now that we have gone through some considerations about recovering from stolen or misplaced laptop incidents, how does one go about constructing such a solution?

These services are already available in the marketplace. An Alcatel-Lucent venture announced in 2007 a service provided through Sprint, the Sprint-Secure Laptop Guardian based on the Evros† mobile security technology developed by Alcatel-Lucent Bell Labs. The solution consists of a card, essentially another computer with a TPM that works in tandem with the laptop. The card communicates with a special purpose appliance installed at the customer's premises. This solution is a highly integrated, single provider solution available only to Sprint subscribers with significant proprietary content (the special purpose laptop card and the specialized appliance).

As the technology for laptop recovery matures and assuming that a virtual service oriented grid environment becomes firmly entrenched in the market, we can expect this service to become available not just from a few large providers with deep pockets in selected regions. Instead, the service will be available worldwide from a network of providers transparently, much in the same way cell phone subscribers can roam away from the home area. Because of the standardized interfaces, a provider can make a business out of aggregating the services of smaller providers over a large geographic area possibly spanning several countries, or perhaps roaming standards will eventually be established.

Because there were few precedents, if any, and the models for service delivery were not fully formed, Alcatel-Lucent had to launch a significant research project requiring low level hardware and software integration and significant software development. In a mature virtual service oriented grid environment the same service can be put together by combining a few servicelets.

Figure 7.8 illustrates some of the constituent servicelets: A credit card service allows the service provider to be compensated through a recurring credit card charge. A GPS location service allows determining the location of the asset at any given time. A recovery service may use multiple physical transports to ensure that at least one can be used to call back home. A data presence service is essentially an automatic data migration service, one step up from a backup: A system scan is performed periodically, and any updated file is picked up and migrated into the system. There is no notion of recovery. If a customer logs into another computer, the data presence service displays the last uploaded file. The system warns of pending changes that have not been flushed.

It is likely that the radically reduced cost to deliver an application in a virtual service oriented environment will become an incentive for a large number of service offerings. We'll see not just service end points for consumers, but also a large number of offering modalities, such as bundling, vertical specialization, manageability features, scalability and many more. Any of the variants will offer the minimal capability in this family of services. Any of the variants will provide the minimal capability of retrieving the data in the laptop, and if necessary, provide a certified confirmation of the laptop being disabled. The confirmation needs to have the force of a legal proof accepted by the court of law.

Storage in an Virtual Service Oriented Grid Environment

In this example we present one more hypothetical example of a service made up of servicelets. Not just a few servicelets, but possibly millions. It is a storage service where the actual bits of data reside in storage space leased back from consumers. This example could represent a way to implement the storage service for the data presence service described in the previous section. There are no specific design rules requiring that the storage be actually hosted in a data center.

One group of people is at the forefront of innovation in grid technology. Unfortunately they use their skills for nefarious purposes. These are the hackers who write and disseminate *botnet* programs; a type of computer virus that once installed in a machine allows it to be commandeered by a remote user. A computer so infected is said to have become a *zombie*. Botnet technology strives for scalability. The goal of an infection bot is to create armies of zombies involving thousands of nodes. These nodes can be "managed" to work in parallel in grid fashion for disseminating other viruses, creating more zombies, for sending spam or for phishing purposes. There are even trading markets where zombies are sold by the bunch in a truly service oriented fashion. This resource management certainly does not occur in a manner anticipated by system administrators.

Here is one example for shared storage in a grid environment that we call the *white zombie* scheme. There is commandeering, but in clearly delineated ways, with the approval of the resource owners under an explicit contract. The scheme, a consumer-facilitated storage framework allows compensation to the resource owners for resource usage.

This scheme may first become practical in the semi-closed environment of a broadband services provider, where the consumer leases on the premises storage, say, 1 terabyte or more to the services provider in exchange for a remission from the subscription fees. Some entrepreneurial spirits may rent so much storage that there is a net flow of cash from the services provider to the consumer.

For the consumer-facilitated storage, a participant would join a virtual service oriented grid through downloading and installing a software kit that exposes data and manageability interfaces for an amount of storage authorized by the consumer, essentially allowing the user to provision a hard drive into a servicelet. There is nothing extraordinary in converting a physical asset into a servicelet. In other words, servicelets need not be purely software entities. Most any human activity can be recast as a servicelet. This can happen whenever the same forces that led to servicelets are at play: activities are standardized, predictable in cost, and can be invoked or triggered by other applications. In this context routines implementing a quote for a mortgage or changing the oil of a car have a lot in common.

Once the amount of storage is defined, the service provider pools and manages the storage resource through a standardized interface whether the storage device is a NAS device or a PC or laptop computer. This scheme is illustrated in Figure 7.9.

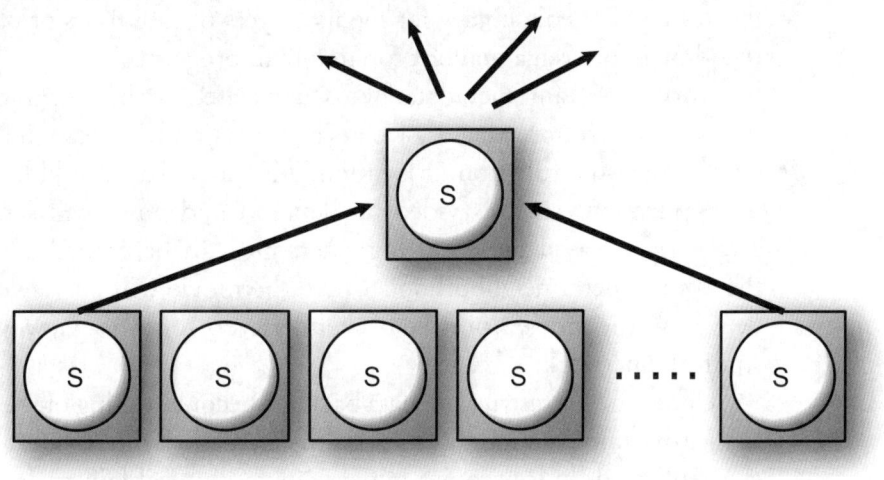

Figure 7.9   Pooling of Storage Resources under the Consumer-facilitated Storage Framework

The data in the storage resource is not accessible by the consumer; it is striped and encrypted. The consumer agrees to abide by a certain SLA for the service provider, for instance that the storage resource be online anywhere between 50 percent and 90 percent of the time, verifiable through the management interface. The service provider figures a certain amount of redundancy so it is possible to reconstruct data from the component stripes even if certain stripes are not available because the host is turned off.

We call this scheme a *white zombie* with a resource being commandeered by the service provider, but with the consent of subscribers. To provide some rough numbers, assume a subscriber base of 10 million with an attach rate of 10 percent. This represents 1 million customers. If each consumer agrees to rent out 1 terabyte, the aggregate storage is 1 million terabytes, a very large amount of space, even after some de-rating is factored in for redundancy.

The aggregated storage capacity can be used for a number of applications. One service could be a data presence service. A registered subscriber gets immersed in a data "cloud" that follows the subscriber everywhere and provides multiple access methods supporting almost any device. If it's a laptop or a PC, the store might look like an extra hard drive. The store could take the guise of a media library for media players or ring tones or phone lists for cell phones, or even a mailbox for an e-mail program.

Two important metadata items associated with consumer facilitated storage are location, that is, where it resides and latency and bandwidth, which are also a function of location. This metadata would be meaningful for applications such as video on demand and download services, where a recently released movie in high demand can be cached at the edge, in the same general neighborhood where the movie will be viewed instead of delivering the movie from the backend servers for every view, which would strain the network.

Under this infrastructure data backups become a thing of the past; at least explicit backups. As soon as data is "injected" into the cloud, it diffuses and gets replicated, so it becomes impervious to physical failure. It also becomes permanent even if a specific device is turned off. This injection takes different guises depending on the physical devices used. The initial store starts perhaps with a copy of the data in the local hard drive. However, if the device is connected to the Internet, it soon gets replicated and diffuses into the cloud according to the provider's preset policies.

Democratization of Computing with Virtual Service Oriented Grids

On the hardware side, virtual service oriented grids today represent the culmination of two major transitions. The first transition lowered the cost of computing MIPS (millions of instructions per second) through the application of networking and distributed computing technology. The second transition is broadening the appeal of these MIPS to business applications beyond the scientific and engineering applications representing only the narrowest of the slices of application space.

The evolution of hardware for high performance computing (HPC) is captured in the bottom row of blocks in Figure 0.1 shown in the preface for this book.

Since the dawn of electronic computing in the 1940s, research and development of computer hardware has been driven by the need to address the toughest computational problems in the military market segment. These projects have been generally well funded, albeit in a feast or famine, winner-take-all fashion. The most sophisticated hardware has been developed for this segment first with spinoffs into civilian applications occurring a few years later.

Because of the narrow scope and the state of the art nature of the applications hosted on these machines, HPC installations have traditionally been the most expensive at any time, catering only to a very small population of advanced researchers. Machines built by Sperry Univac, Control Data, Cray, and some mainframes by IBM and other manufacturers are examples of this era.

Beginning in the late 1980s, Intel and IBM pioneered efforts to use commodity processors to build large computing clusters built to industry standards. These efforts improved the cost efficiency of high performance computing machines by at least an order of magnitude over mainframes.

Progress toward cost efficiency accelerated considerably with the research on grids beginning in the late 1980s and early 1990s. Perhaps because of more constrained budgets in academia, early research on grids with the goal of reducing the cost of large scale computation started in universities. One of the most notable grid projects is Condor started at the University of Wisconsin.

Unlike High Performance Computing on state of the art, purpose-built and customized hardware, the grid approach strives to use commodity network components and computers including utilizing CPU time from computers already deployed. This usage model is known as *cycle harvesting* or *scavenging*.

The motivation for cycle scavenging was that nodes in a grid were made up of relatively powerful workstations sitting on researchers' or students' desks. Because these workstations were in use by individuals, the workloads varied significantly, but in most cases these resources were used only at a fraction of their capacity. The Condor system had a facility to package portions of computations for remote execution at a computer not heavily used. Monitoring and managing distributed resources takes time, effort, and additional computation. Breakeven is reached when the payoff from sending a job to run remotely exceeds the effort spent in packing the job and retrieving the results, assuming the process can be carried out on a timely basis and that the resource owner is willing to place the resource in a discoverable pool available to the community of users.

While the Condor research defined an infrastructure for sharing physical nodes, the introduction of virtualization allowed partitioning a physical resource into multiple logical resources, more or less transparently. For instance, a powerful server can be split into eight virtualized servers, each perhaps one eighth as slow. If the workloads running in each virtual partition require only one eighth of a server, running a workload in a physical server would have run it only at 12.5 percent utilization.

Coalescing eight workloads in a single physical server increases the cost efficiency for that particular server eightfold. In practice, the cost equation is even better.

In practice, workloads tend to be peaky. Figure 7.10 illustrates an actual performance trace of a server. There are four graphs represented; the graph on top records memory utilization; the middle depicts CPU utilization. There are two graphs close to the bottom depicting the utilization of the network interface controller (NIC). Even though the CPU utilization in particular averages about 10 percent, the graph exhibits a number of spikes. When similar workloads are placed in virtualized partitions, these spikes do not usually occur at the same time and the spikes are averaged out. Hence this particular machine could easily accommodate up to eight of these workloads after a memory upgrade. Because of the averaging effect across the eight virtual instances the utilization of the virtualized machine will be less than 100 percent, leaving some headroom for workload variations.

Chapter 7: Case Studies for Deploying Virtual Service Oriented Grids ■ 257

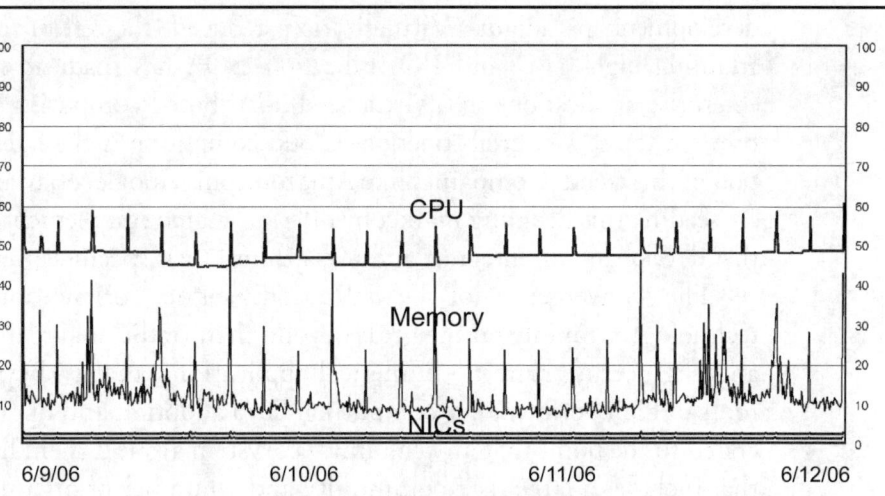

Figure 7.10 Performance Trace of a Server Workload.

While virtualization facilitated the transparent partitioning of grid resources, the introduction of the service oriented paradigm is broadening the appeal of grid beyond scientific applications and into enterprise applications: The appearance of grids represents the first of the two major transitions in computing leading to virtual service oriented grids. This transition led to almost unlimited availability of CPU cycles in a distributed setting to any application capable of harnessing these cycles.

Application capability is a critical consideration. The adoption rate of grid technology through most of the first decade of the 21st century has been slow for two reasons: applications require a redesign in order to work well in a distributed grid setting. However, perhaps a more important reason is that technology strategists, business planners, and decision makers have been slow in becoming aware and building awareness in their organizations about realizing benefits from grid technology. The floodgates will open when grids transcend their origin as a technology experiment and the business community realizes that harnessing this technology yields a competitive advantage.

This brings us to the second transition, represented by the integration of grids with virtualization technology combined with SOA as the application development paradigm. Virtualization reduced the effort associated in attaining high CPU and I/O utilization. SOA has made it easier to host enterprise applications in a virtualized, distributed computing environment through the servicelet abstraction. Cloud computing is the latest manifestation of this trend. Companies like Amazon.com, Google, eBay and Microsoft are seeding this fledgling market by offering a large complement of servicelets that developers can integrate and reshape into their specific applications.

The convergence of virtualization, service orientation, and grid technology is rapidly taking grids beyond their traditional realm of scientist and engineering running numerical applications, that is, beyond the grid roots in high performance computing. Grid adoption and uptake has accelerated to the point that an economic ecosystem around them has developed that includes a large user community and a number of organizations, well established as well as upstarts, catering to the needs of these users.

The range of applications run under a virtual service oriented environment has widened considerably over the initial scientific and engineering applications that constituted the base for HPC applications.

Today, high technology companies such as Google, eBay, and Microsoft through Microsoft Live deploy servers in the hundreds of thousands. Intel uses nearly a hundred thousand machines for circuit design and simulation applications (electronic design automation or EDA) alone. These large deployments in a sense represent a triumph of distributed computing. The deployments are not generally standalone, but part of a larger system with various degrees of interconnectedness.

Virtual Service Oriented Grids and Energy Usage

Up to the 1990s the largest total cost of ownership for computing equipment was represented by the capital outlay for the acquisition of the equipment itself. In the first decade of the 21st century, due to advances in computer technologies and in semiconductor manufacturing, the major cost fraction shifted to the energy required to operate the equipment during its expected lifetime.

Because energy consumption has nationwide consequences, the application of grid concepts today and its implications on power consumption is perhaps more fitting today than it was in the early days as an academic exercise for load sharing and leveling.

The deployment of servers per capita in countries leading in Internet adoption such as South Korea and Japan is such that their energy consumption usually ranks between 1 and 2 percent of the *total* national electrical energy system production.[6]

Most of these servers need to be available 24/7, every hour of the day and every day of the year. Unfortunately, these servers are not used efficiently, with load factors between 5 and 20 percent at most. In many cases servers are run at utilization factors in the single digits. Yet the cost of energy has been going up. The net effect is that electricity cost, which used to be a second order consideration in a data center facilities' budget now outranks the purchasing cost as a fraction of the total cost of ownership.

Data centers today are not very efficient in terms of energy usage. As Figure 7.11 indicates, in a typical data center only a fraction in the order of one percent of the power fed into a data center actually ends up associated with running an application. Because we are starting from such a small figure, the opportunities for improvement are enormous. The introduction of virtualization can improve the efficiency not just by a few percentage points but by several times the current rate, anywhere from 3 to 20 times more efficient or more.

However this transition requires some investment. It is almost certain that existing hosts will not have enough memory or CPU horsepower to support a virtualized environment. Because of the multiple guests running in a physical host, application may be constrained in memory or network bandwidth.

Budget needs to be allocated to additional operating system and application licenses in addition to the hypervisor licenses running in the physical hosts.

It is all too easy to spawn more virtualized guest instances; it is another matter to manage them. Processes need to be established to manage virtualized machines, for instance to manage libraries of virtualized machine images and to launch them. If commodity servers led to server sprawl, virtual machine sprawl can become even worse.

---

6   Information corroborated from multiple sources. See for instance J. G. Koomey, *Estimating Total Power Consumption* by Servers in the U.S. and the World, http://www.koomey.com

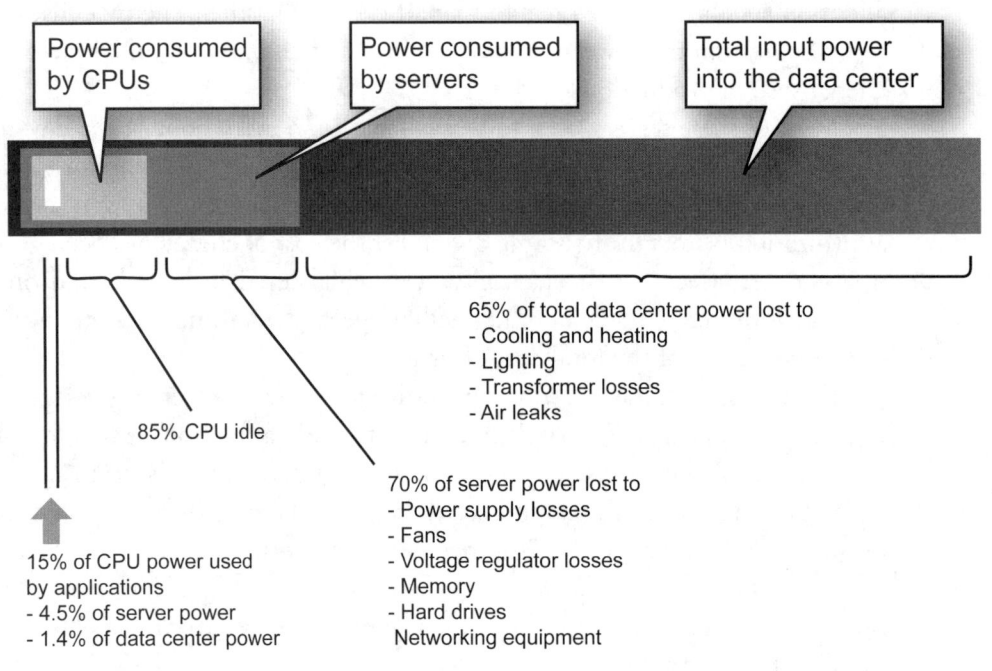

Figure 7.11 Power Allocation in a Data Center[7]

Another factor to consider in the design of data centers hosting virtual service oriented grids is power density, not just power. While the number of MIPS per watt has been steadily improving over the years, the physical size of servers has been shrinking even faster. The same amount of compute power that used to take a 3 or 4 U unit is now packaged in high density, small form factors such as 1U or 1 EIA rack unit[8], or blade form factors. Server energy densities have gone up from 1 to 2 KW per cabinet using the older pedestal form factors to over 10 KW with rack servers to over 20 KW and more with blades.

Hence, even though computing capacity is available in ever smaller form factors, an existing data center may not be designed to take advantage of them.

---

7   Ainsworth et al, *Going Green with IBM Active Energy Manager*, IBM Redbook, REDP-4361-00

8   Rack form factor servers are stacked like pancakes in a cabinet. Hence, a standard 42 U rack can hold 42 servers where 1 U equals 1.75 inches.

Data centers designed to host mainframes had a design power density of 30 to 50 watts per square foot. Today's designs require in the order of 150 to 225 watts per square foot according to DatacenterDynamics in San Francisco.

If a new data center is deployed today to these specifications, it will likely run out power within the next 5 years, as many data center operators are experiencing today. A holistic approach and a careful long term planning are essential to manage these challenges. Otherwise, hot spots start developing as new equipment is introduced. It is not uncommon today to see rows of half full cabinets, not because of reserve space being left for future expansion but because it is not feasible to load up the cabinets without hot spots developing.

Beyond the operational efficiencies brought by virtualization at the server level, virtual service oriented grids hold the promise of increasing energy efficiency globally. Virtual service oriented grids may revolutionize disaster recovery. The concept of primary and backup data centers is a concept associated with physical resources. In a service oriented environment the physical binding will become less relevant. Decommissioning a data center will become a simpler task: it will be only matter of migrating the services to an alternate provider. Disaster recovery planning will likely become less painful because the planning will be in terms of logical entities related to the application instead of unrelated, hard to map physical entities.

Because the components of a composite application need not be co-located, a developer can select the most efficient service component for a given application. This capability does not exist today, mainly because there are no consistent mechanisms to convey metadata associated with the constituent services in a composite application. This metadata can capture anything from the power needed to run the service to electricity rates that would allow the service consumer to plan usage all the way to the carbon footprint of the service.

An outstanding problem with metadata exchange across services is the problem of *semantic translation*. If anything, a common problem today in managing computer resources today is not lack of data, but too much of it. A contemporary server is instrumented with temperature sensors in a number of critical components; it can also provide figures for power consumption and a number of intrusion alarms. However, there is no commonly agreed method in aggregating this information so it's meaningful to the guest virtual machines or to the applications running inside the virtual machines.

This problem goes both ways: policies from above eventually need to be translated into specific control commands to the servers supporting an application. One typical policy request would be to reduce the power consumption of an application by X percent in exchange for a Y percent degradation in QoS. This policy request needs to be translated into commands that are understood by the server management mechanisms such as a command to slow down the processors or to reduce the amount of physical memory allocated to a virtual machine.

Business Opportunities for Virtual Service Oriented Grids

In this chapter we highlighted some of the opportunities that lay ahead with virtual service oriented grids, from expanding the reach of information technology service to the mostly untapped consumer market to building grids in unexpected places such as in swarms of electric power meters. We have barely scratched the surface of the opportunity space. The authors would be very interested in hearing new ideas based on the reader's experience.

Chapter 8

Virtual Service Oriented Grid Strategies: Steps Toward the Future

It's hard to make predictions, especially about the future.

If you don't know where you are going, you will wind up somewhere else.
—Yogi Berra, manager of the Yankees

Setting up a strategy for virtual service oriented grids is a trying exercise mainly because of its federated nature. For instance, in the following section on strategy for small and medium businesses (SMBs), players may involve an SMB proper interested in subscribing to servicelets, an SMB encapsulating internal expertise and exporting a servicelet, an enterprise IT organization prospecting SMB-provided service for hire, or an enterprise IT organization opening up partner Web services APIs.

It might be the case that the interests of one player may be at odds with another: a content and data service, such as traditional cable TV and Internet service, can be framed as a servicelet. The consumer subscribing to the service might not like the fact that as part of the metadata exchange the service provider collects information about the viewing habits in the household and subjects IP packet traffic to content-based QoS. More ominously, if the customer subscribes to the cable company's voice over IP service, the government may require the company to provide back doors for wiretapping purposes without the customer being aware of it.

Necessary conditions for successful adoption of virtual service oriented grids in an economic ecosystem are Champy's three conditions of openness, mutuality, and interoperability described in Chapter 2, as well as an environment with a modicum of enlightened self interest among ecosystem participants. This enlightened self interest is manifest when an individual actively participates in a standards organization or attends a technical conference where there is cost involved in the activity but no immediate obvious economic reward for participation. Attaining consensus and promulgating a standard represents progress toward Champy's three conditions for ecosystem participants, with the practical side effect of lowered cost of business for all ecosystem participants.

In order to simplify the discourse, we have split the strategy-making discussion in three contexts: A national-level strategy, where we also underscore opportunities for emerging markets, a strategy for large enterprises, and a strategy for SMBs. Since the potential actors are many, the discussion emphasizes activities that need to take place with specific actions by some of the actors without an attempt to provide a complete matrix covering the landscape from the perspective of every conceivable player, which would be an unnecessarily lengthy and complex discussion.

Toward a Virtual Service Oriented Grid National Strategy

Because of the pervasive use of industry standards, virtual service oriented grids constitute a great leveler across countries and for participants within a country, resulting in a playing field as level as in any industry.

Servicelets, the constituent components of service oriented grids, are networked resources that can be summoned from anywhere in the world via the Internet. Hence any country intent on developing a national strategy for virtual service oriented grids will have a rich base from which to start representing billions of dollars of investment. New players can take immediate advantage of intellectual property, discoveries, and practices that have already made it to market in a true instance of federated technology development.

The servicelets making a composite application are loosely coupled, change-tolerant, and self-describing, making integration tasks more forgiving and less complex than more traditional methods.

Because of the incremental nature of SOA, a large upfront investment is not an obligatory requisite. Service providers like Tencent in China started with hosted servers from data center providers. At some point the company's anticipated growth rate of about 50 percent per year became so large that their demand outstripped the capabilities of Tencent's downstream providers. However, at this stage the company had developed enough financial strength that it had no difficulty in tapping internal resources and capital markets to deploy fully owned data centers. Given the facility with which servicelets can cross organizational boundaries, there is nothing intrinsically unique about the relationship between an in-sourced and an out-sourced servicelet nor were there specific technical barriers in this case. It was a matter of business considerations in terms of cost and the ability to deploy data center resources fast enough.

A virtual service oriented grid environment brings agility and reduced capital costs to emerging markets. Access to capital markets has been a traditional roadblock in emerging economies. Reduced capital requirements mean it is possible to put business plans into effect that would be impossible to execute using more traditional IT approaches. Increased agility means shortened evolutionary cycles and the opportunity to try out creative business models. The slower traditional IT approaches discourage risk taking and by the same token, discourage "transplanting" processes that were successful in other contexts, making it difficult to realize benefits from reuse.

Reduced capital requirements, lower technical barriers, and lower integration cost not only benefit large players by reducing risk and increasing return on investment. These factors also make virtual service oriented grids accessible not just to large players, but to small and medium businesses as well as NGOs. It opens opportunities for government funded research centers and educational institutions to perform research on virtual service oriented grid deployment models more applicable to the local economy without the need to spend vast sums of money in building data centers or multiyear software development programs. Shorter integration cycles mean the cost of failure is relatively small, yet the potential payoff from the research is not diminished in any way.

Without the need for intensive capital investment, virtual service oriented grids put advanced and emerging economies on equal footing when it comes to technology development. All it takes is wits and brain power. Access to capital markets, usually associated with developed economies, becomes less critical. Local talent is now in the position to directly address local problems and concerns instead of needing to wait for solutions to trickle down from more advanced economies where local interests are not even a consideration.

With reduced technical barriers and reduced risk in developing new services associated with virtual service oriented grids, service and content localization and customization come to the forefront. National level strategies need to pay attention to encouraging local businesses and service providers to develop diverse services that address the needs of local customers. Localizing and customizing a technology capability represents a more incremental effort than the initial cost to develop the technology in the first place. This is another facet of the incremental nature of SOA.

Experience in integrating services with local knowledge and imported, undifferentiated servicelets will take local developers through a learning curve enabling them to become experts not just in assembling applications, but eventually building services to the extent that the region becomes a net exporter of services.

It is interesting to note that the most popular Internet service companies in China are not the big names that so dominant in the other part of the world such as Google, Microsoft Live, Amazon, Yahoo, and so on, but are rather local companies with strong cultural and content appeals to Chinese customers, such as Baidu, Tencent, Alibaba, and Sina, even though these local companies are trailing their U.S. counterparts in technology.

In fact, local thought leaders have applied and translated lessons learned from global technology leaders in developed markets, a process that is still evolving today. Nonetheless, because of the ubiquitous nature and fast proliferation of Internet technologies, the local companies can compete and win against more technically superior international companies. It is just matter of time before these players become global leaders in their own right.

To make the process more exciting, the path to global prominence will likely not involve retracing the steps of the giants in the industry. Some patterns will persist; using an analogy in speech, the process will be more like paraphrasing than repeating the same words. That is, success will certainly involve forging new paths for these dynamic players. China for instance may deemphasize the culturally-dependent aspects of servicelets offered and instead take advantage of the strength of the country's rapidly advancing infrastructure services to offer data center services, storage and compute services, application services, and application integration services.

In other words, integration experience with virtual service oriented grids will open opportunities for local companies to innovate and win on customized servicelets and content, as the underlying technology and infrastructure becomes more distributed, ubiquitous and easily adopted. For nations, especially in emerging markets, interested in growing a local information industry past the learning phase, a pivotal transition point will be developing services. This transition marks a quantum jump in value creation, and with value creation revenue should follow, boosting the local economy and bringing opportunity for market participants. This state of affairs becomes possible because virtualized resources can be summoned from anywhere in the world through the Internet for both producers and consumers of services.

A Maturity Model for the Adoption of Virtual Service Oriented Grids

The evolution from the outside-in to the inside-out paradigm introduced in Chapter 2 is quite applicable to emerging markets entering the arena without prior virtual service oriented grid activity. This process is easier explained through a maturation model that we identify as the servicelet market maturity model, summarized in Table 8.1.

Under this maturity model, without prior history, the portfolio of services available to service developers is the general portfolio available from transnational service providers. We call this initial phase the *undifferentiated* phase. The portfolio of servicelets available is the same for any market starting at that particular time. From this initial undifferentiated phase the strategy to bring the economic benefits from the adoption of virtual service oriented grids should encourage the development of locally produced servicelets to take advantage of the initial base of servicelets and bring the benefits of the initial portfolio of servicelets to the local economy.

Once local needs are met, the developers in an emerging market, having gone through the learning curve, can start looking out to other markets and start developing servicelets that have universal appeal or are targeted to specific needs in other markets, and the cycle starts anew. This process is fundamentally the same as other technology adoption processes the authors have observed in the past, including technology adoption in the PC industry. It is also a reflection of the same process that has occurred since time immemorial, where as efficiency from a certain economic activity improves, productivity increases beyond local needs, at which point excess production can be sold at a profit for the benefit of the producer and the consumer.

As mentioned above, even during the initial, undifferentiated phase, for most developers in an emerging market, a diversified base of services is already available. However, without differentiation, players cannot yet take advantage of unique factors that would allow them to build a sustainable business. Furthermore, the generic servicelets available in the open market may not be terribly useful by themselves in their original raw form.

Table 8.1 Servicelet Market Maturity Model

Phase	Name	Description
1	Undifferentiated phase	Initial phase; entering servicelet market
2	Consumer phase	Bootstrap phase; augment pre-existing servicelets with locally produced servicelets; limited number of verticals. The emerging market is a net importer of servicelets.
3	Producer phase	Producer phase; locally built servicelets are exported for consumption outside initial ecosystem. Small companies grow to fund in-sourced projects. Large companies expose internal servicelets for outside consumption.
4	Innovator phase	Providers start branching into new verticals

During the second phase the developing market becomes a net consumer of servicelets. Developers recombine the initial portfolio of servicelets into composite applications that are useful in the new market. They also start augmenting the initial portfolio of servicelets with servicelets that fulfill the needs of the local market. Typical components are servicelets supporting cash, credit, and banking transactions in local currency.

Even if a basic infrastructure of computational and storage resources is not readily available, these resources may be brought in as computational servicelets in the form of a virtualized server or servicelets representing storage resources. Small business that cannot afford a data center may use servicelets representing hosted servers in some other country.

Applications need to be engineered to be latency tolerant and to minimize the use of bandwidth. This is achieved through extensive use of asynchronous programming and parallelism as mentioned in Chapter 3. A loosely coupled, distributed application will require more CPU cycles to complete than an equivalent monolithic, self-contained implementation. Extra CPU cycles should not be a concern in an era when CPU cycles become cheaper and cheaper. In fact, if the distributed application is designed to be scalable, through the application of concurrent resources, it might actually run faster than if run on a single CPU locally.

In any case, the monolithic alternative is not really an alternative because it would be more expensive, and there may not be local expertise to carry out the project. Furthermore, in an environment where CPU utilization factors are low, the extra cycles are essentially free, where human time and expertise are not. In a developing economy the cost of labor may be lower than in an advanced economy. However, it is still a scarce resource, perhaps scarcer in relative terms compared to a developed economy.

As the players in an emerging market acquire experience in developing and marketing servicelets their productivity will rise to the point that it becomes practical to start developing servicelets for export. At some point during this evolution the consumer/producer relationship starts turning until the players in the marketplace become net producers of servicelets.

To give a hypothetical example, international entities doing business with the evolving market start using the locally produced banking modules initially intended for local consumption. As organizations acquire more experience in marketing servicelets they may decide to expose servicelets for external consumption. Exporting these services may be motivated by the need to support B2B transactions or simply by the desire to turn on additional revenue streams. This is perfectly feasible for as long as buyers for these services exist.

The last phase in the maturation process is the optimizing or innovator phase where service providers in the emerging market are not just content in delivering services within existing frameworks but also create new paradigms. Also, prior to this phase virtual service grid manifestations may have occurred in just one or at most a small number of industry verticals. The innovator phase sees the proliferation of virtual service oriented grids across a large number of vertical markets to the point that work associated with virtual service oriented grids becomes a measurable or significant component in the national GDP and a focus for economic growth.

A Prescription for Virtual Service Oriented Grid Adoption

Because the goal for virtual service oriented grid adoption is transformative, a strategy for the adoption of this technology on a national scale in a small, developing nation needs to consider a planning horizon in the order of five to ten years. In addition, these plans need to align or at least be consistent with current goals for economic development. For instance, if the country expects to graduate x thousands of specialists in software engineering, computer science, and information technology, virtualized service oriented technology will provide a consistent focus point for curriculum development and for identifying current gaps in education and determining how the nation's investment in computer education should be directed.

For organizations assessing the adoption of virtual service oriented grids there are two co-adjuvant factors: the level playing field and the incremental nature and high value of reuse of SOA. The incremental nature means that large, upfront capital investments are not necessary and should be discouraged as a matter of policy.

In principle, all that's required is a communication infrastructure and free flow of information as discussed in the section "A Dose of Reality" below that allows the integration of servicelets and the reuse of servicelets already available through the Internet. Second, the level playing field means that any time is a good time to start and that opportunities are open broad participation, from small businesses providing niche services to government organizations implementing an e-government strategy. See Table 8.2 for a few servicelet examples.

From the servicelets described in Table 8.2 it is possible to build applications from the very simple that most any small business can implement to applications of national scope.

An example of a simple application is a virtual bookstore catering to cash customers where the interface to the customer is a physical storefront. The customer walks into the storefront, orders a book from the clerk, leaves a down payment, and one or two weeks later walks in again to pick the book and pay the balance.

After the order is placed, the clerk turns around and places the order from an Internet bookseller and orders the book on the store's own credit. Once the client has an established an account with the virtual bookstore, the ordering process by the cash customer can be automated.

The customer can place an order through a mobile device or even a cell phone. The application run by the storefront invokes a Web service to access Amazon.com. The cost of the transaction is covered through a Web service provided by the credit card issuer or through a PayPal Web service.

Similar storefronts already exist in the United States allowing walk in customers to sell goods through eBay using a similar implementation.

At the other end a complex project can be a national-level electronic health record (EHR) system. In the initial state, hospitals, clinics, and physicians' offices may already have an EHR application up and running. However, more likely than not, the different implementations cannot communicate with each other. The integration process consists of adding a middleware wrapper to each implementation so it can be invoked by other servicelets. The national-level EHR application would be a composite of the regional EHR implementations.

Virtual service oriented grids can improve the public's perception of the government by making services more accessible and by promoting transparency. The actual implementation cost may be very small compared to the benefits stemming from elimination of duplication, the removal of bureaucratic barriers, and increased operational efficiency.

Table 8.2 Servicelet Examples

Vertical	Description
Generic Services	- Credit/ Debit/ Cash transactions - Personal commerce - Transaction aggregation - Credit to cash storefronts - Theft and loss mitigation for mobile devices
Education	- Class registration - Curriculum development - Course development - Dissemination of course content - Purchasing textbooks - Prepaid cards for food, communication, and other services
Agriculture	- Dissemination of information - Weather forecasts, - Planting recommendations, - Import/export paperwork - Management of harvest loans and micro-loan administration - Disaster preparedness and management
Healthcare	- Legacy integration - Integration of electronic health records - Integration of heterogeneous healthcare IT encompassing federated health systems and affiliated clinics and clinical labs.
Government services	- Paying utility bills - Filing tax returns - Sales tax/ VAT collection - Vehicle registration - Business licenses - Information systems for polling and elections
Consumer services	- Data presence service - Storage and backup - Virtual drives - Location and device independent content storage - Security services including virus/worm infection prevention, scans and repair - PC and network hardware service, including installation, maintenance and repair. - Location independent and device appropriate media delivery - Virtual communities and social networks - Information search and wikis

What should be the approach? We recommend an incremental approach rather than launching massive, high-visibility projects, taking advantage of investments already made or already approved. The need to support a servicelet infrastructure can provide guidance for communication infrastructure projects, for instance for defining broadband service bandwidth requirements and how the deployments should be deployed: should the investment emphasize the delivery of entertainment content to consumers or should it also consider providing access to small businesses?

It is also important to be able to frontload the adoption process. The incremental nature of SOA makes it practical to bring in early successes. This factor cannot be overemphasized. Early successes are essential as a benchmark for adoption. At the same time, these milestones help participants build confidence.

Emphasis on early results also establishes a very fast feedback cycle that promotes collective learning and allows ecosystem participants to go through the learning curve of virtual service oriented grid adoption very fast. It allows the discovery of methods that work and those that don't.

Most of the extant adoption experience comes from practice in advanced economies. This experience can only provide general guidance about the shape of adoption in other economies.

Every instance of adoption will have unique aspects driven by local circumstances, the policies driving the strategy, and the expected goals and results. For instance, economies whose wealth is derived from oil and extractive industries may want to take advantage of this circumstance to diversify their wealth base and formulate a plan to build local information technology and computer science skills and eventually build a knowledge-based industry.

A variant of this dynamic is playing out with economies where salary arbitrage plays a significant role or in export-oriented economies such as India and China, respectively. This situation is temporary. In India the demand for skilled labor is high and salaries are rising fast. Salary levels need not reach parity with the countries being served. They only need to rise to the point where the salaries plus the outsourcing overhead equal the salaries in the target country.

The overhead for outsourced services can be tangible, that is, can be measured in monetary terms such as extra travel, fees, and taxes, but can also be intangible, such as extra time at the executive and engineering levels assessing, managing services, meeting compliance and privacy regulations, and possible concerns about security and managing SLAs across borders.

For export based industries, the cost of goods produced is also rising fast due to the rising cost of labor, the cost of commodities to build the goods and the cost of energy to build and transport the goods. As their cost rises, these countries will be at a cost disadvantage with a new wave of emerging economies such as Vietnam. Hence it is in the national interest of these countries to also diversify their wealth base with a knowledge-based industry, not just for exporting services, but also to satisfy internal demand as their population grows more affluent.

There is an excellent opportunity for wealth creation by addressing local needs because there will always be a local, culture component, possibly dependent on local laws or regulations, or one that cannot be outsourced across borders due to security reasons. Imported services tend to be more general purpose; infrastructure services may not be in a position to fulfill these needs due to culture barriers or because these services cannot be deployed by law.

Undertaking activities related to virtual service oriented grids will also be helpful to advanced, export oriented economies such as Korea, Japan, and Taiwan to tap into new value streams and increase the value of their export offerings through services. For instance servicelet technology will make it easier for automotive manufacturers in Japan and Korea to provide roadside assistance service similar to the OnStar† service provided by General Motors in the United States. Today OnStar is a wholly owned subsidiary of GM. Demand from other automotive manufacturers can potentially create a new industry whose goal is to provide automotive servicelets worldwide to a variety of automotive manufacturers.

Likewise, computer manufacturers in Taiwan might decide to go beyond competing in terms of cost and start competing on basis of value by delivering some of the IT services to the home described in Chapter 7. This way, services and in particular repair services becomes an additional revenue stream instead of today's cost and a drag on profits.

There is no precondition for the new wave of economies like Vietnam to go through an initial outsourced manufacturing and export phase. An opportunity exists for these economies to leapfrog to the knowledge export phase.

A virtual service oriented grid economy is knowledge based and does not require large amounts of upfront capital investment. In fact, efforts aimed at increasing information technology local skills and knowledge will accelerate economic advancement, lessening the need to make a living through labor arbitrage.

The recommended strategy is to set up a number of pilots in local universities and applied research institutions. The project should be in a highly visible area where there is acute public need, selected to yield first results in a year or less. The emphasis of this project would be in technology integration to showcase the agility aspects of virtual service oriented grids and to garner momentum and public support. Project participants need to be cognizant of momentum and scalability considerations.

If the pilot is successful, principals need to be willing to bring in new participants and replicate the success in other business verticals. An example of a project can be integrating a variety of databases or information systems and bringing information to large segments of the population.

The information in these databases can be used to identify persons with criminal records to assist in the eradication of human trafficking, provide weather information, and advice to farmers or even used to manage micro-loans.

True to the grid nature, these applications would be highly distributed, pulling information from databases and information services all over the world and delivered to all kinds of mobile devices through a data presence service. The information would be delivered in a manner appropriate to the presentation device in use, whether a PC, laptop, ultramobile laptop, mobile Internet device, PDA, or cell phone. The information is also delivered as a Web service, making the service application also a servicelet available to developers to build other applications or to eventually support new devices not yet invented.

Because of the level playing field, the business climate for virtual service oriented grids will be complex. For general infrastructure services the first mover advantage will usually play out: some countries will take the lead in providing storage services, delivering virtualized services for hosting, or in delivering management services. However, there will also be niche opportunities in the sense of local opportunities waiting to be realized. Because of this and perhaps with the nudge of national policies, it should not be too difficult to attain a broad based virtual service economy with a "long tail," that is, with service developers and providers large and small. Large providers will still be there to play, but there will be room for a cottage industry consisting of a large number of small and medium size service providers.

A significant number of companies in emerging markets, Tata Industries being an example, are achieving global prominence. Information intensive companies, especially those with federated structure, can take advantage of virtual service oriented grids to accelerate their process of global projection.

A Dose of Realism

In practice, the concept of virtual service oriented grids as a great leveler may be stretching the point a bit. A good communication infrastructure helps. It would be hard, although not impossible, to build composite applications over dialup lines. On the other hand, the need for a good communication infrastructure is not specific to servicelets. It's a basic infrastructure requirement such as telecommunications, energy, and potable water.

Regarding the communication infrastructure, best in the world is not a prerequisite. A happy medium is possible between national investment and communication capability. The United States is a leader in servicelets, yet connectivity available to business and consumer is not the best in the world by far.

Legal barriers can get in the way as well: Laws that restrict the free flow of information will get in the way of building distributed applications.

If a government license is required to build compound applications, this process would negate the agility benefits of building applications on-the-fly. Licensing processes that might take months to resolve will essentially kill any market for third-party servicelets. Only internally developed and consumed, such as inside-out servicelets, would be feasible. Without third party outside-in servicelets it will be impossible to reach a critical mass for a servicelet ecosystem and the SOA component of virtual service oriented grids will remain relatively expensive.

It is actually very easy to run afoul of existing regulation in a virtual service oriented environment, mainly because the resources in a composite application are discovered, assigned, and deployed very fluidly. These resources can reside anywhere in the world.

In some countries the purchase of goods and services with foreign currency is highly regulated, which is what will happen for any application hosted outside the United States that uses Amazon.com or Google Web services.

These transnational resources represent investments already made and encapsulated intellectual property essential to bootstrapping a budding marketplace of locally produced servicelets.

In some countries the use of the Web, essentially a business to consumer (B2C) interface, is already controversial. If we add to that a business-to-business (B2B) and machine-to-machine automated interaction capabilities, the deployment of virtual service oriented grids will stir even more controversy.

From a technical perspective, latency is an ever present consideration in distributed systems, and servicelets are no different in this respect. Although servicelets are potentially accessible worldwide, it does not mean the cheapest instance half a world away is the best alternative in a composite solution.

Some services are highly latency tolerant. For instance, a backup service would require high bandwidth but not low latency. Hence if it takes a few seconds for the data to arrive at its destination the application will still work. The storage service chosen for this application would be subject more to legal and price considerations than to latency considerations. The same might not be true for an online gaming engine, requiring servicelets assigned to a participant to be geographically close.

Services that are latency sensitive need to advertise their location as part of the metadata to enable the invoking application to assess whether using a particular servicelet would lead to performance compromises.

Building a Virtual Service Oriented Grid Corporate Strategy

Large corporations share some of the considerations for governments that we described in the previous sections such as attaining efficient operations across organizational silos. The main difference is that a corporation strives to maximize return to shareholders' investment while governments' goals attempt to maximize return on taxpayers' dollars.

One of the goals will be to attain structural cost reductions as depicted in Figure 2.8. As in the government strategy, the approach to virtual service oriented grid adoption most likely to succeed is an incremental one with the same outcomes: to aim for long term transformation to attain the structural cost reductions depicted in Figure 2.8 while striving to attain early, albeit limited successes to keep the adoption momentum going. This dynamic leads to the characteristic shape of the graph, where costs keep increasing at the historical rate even after a strategic decision is made to adopt virtual service oriented grids, but gradually begins to taper off as more and more organizations adopt and internalize a virtual service oriented grid framework into their culture.

In spite of the federated nature of servicelets, a decision to embrace the strategy and its execution needs to be made top-down and managed centrally. This is because even though local operational decisions are made semi-independently in the federated environment characteristic of large organizations, the methods applied must be uniform across the entire corporation to maximize interoperability. In this environment some requested actions may require sacrifices for the greater good of the company and may be unpopular. Executive support is essential to override these concerns and to ensure that the organizations making the sacrifices are recognized for their contributions or are assigned additional resources to carry their mission successfully.

Because the methodology applies globally across the entire company, a governance board needs to be established to oversee all aspects of the methodology. By the same token, acceptance of the mandates of the board requires the consent of the governed and hence the board needs to have a fair representation across the company. The board will need to make difficult choices. In some cases the benefits accrued by a certain department come from short term costs incurred by another organization. The board ensures that in the long term costs and benefits are apportioned fairly with the support from constituents.

A concern that figures prominently among corporate concerns is the protection of intellectual property rights (IP rights). Effectively, in emerging markets weak or unenforceable IP legislation or regulation and a lack of the associated tradition for respecting intellectual property has prevented a strong local software development industry from flourishing or even forming. The software-as-a-service (SaaS) model for distribution possible in a virtual service oriented environment brings opportunity for change. The servicelet as a mechanism for abstraction and information hiding also makes it easier for the servicelet entity to become a unit for the encapsulation of IP.

A side effect of the IP encapsulation brought by servicelets will be renewed incentives for software development in emerging markets, which have been held back because existing IP protection mechanisms are so inadequate that they remove the economic incentives to bring innovations to market. This change will move the industry beyond the opportunistic business that it is today.

Because servicelets are offered through a connected service infrastructure, traditional license management and software revenue will be transformed into service revenue. Online service IP protection and license validation will bring a more reliable and effective revenue stream than the traditional shrink-wrap software distribution.

The authors hope that a more reliable revenue collection infrastructure combined with opportunities for new entrants across the globe will allow market forces to do their work and actually result in lower fees for consumer of services as well as a rationalization of the current fee structure that does not allow for the dynamic environment under virtual service oriented grids.

A business strategy need not assume mutually exclusive alternatives between the traditional licensed software and a strictly software-as-a-service model. Both models can coexist. Strategists will need to consider choices that include application components that run locally for best customer experience to server-based components that provide the greatest IP protection.

Virtual service oriented grids constitute a technology for early adopters. Stephanie Overby captured a set of tips for success in emerging technologies[1]. Paraphrasing these tips in the context of virtual service oriented grids:

- *Communicate with business leaders.* Present business leaders with a jargon-free tutorial on virtual service oriented technology emphasizing business benefits to the corporation.
- *Communicate with stakeholders in organization at large.* Share information on potential benefits and drawbacks. You need to be candid on potential impact on jobs and roles within the organization.
- *Invite more conservative members.* More conservative members in the IT team may provide technical insight to sidestep strategic blunders.

---

1 Stephanie Overby, *The Secrets of Early Adopters*, CIO Magazine, July 1 2008, pp. 30-41.

- *Test the servicelet technology.* The incremental nature of virtual service oriented makes it easy and inexpensive to conduct pilots. Some of the cloud services may be available on a free trial.
- *Create a repeatable process.* Fulfilling this item may bring the chicken and egg dilemma. A repeatable process may imply a certain level of maturity without which repeatable processes and consistent results are not possible. Proceed on a case by case basis.
- *Harness the energy of early adopters.* Make sure early successes are broadly communicated.
- *Consider segmenting the user base.* Virtual service oriented grid technology is complex, but also incremental, allowing a phased rollout.

Overby also provides a set of criteria for deciding whether to adopt a technology. Translating her recommendations to the context of virtual service oriented grids,

- Do virtual service oriented grids fit the current IT environment?
- Have clear business benefits been identified, even though data is still incomplete for a ROI assessment?
- Have risks been identified?
- Is an elevator pitch in place for executive staff members?
- Have users for the compound applications been identified?
- Is there a test and development strategy in place that minimizes disruption to the business?
- Have reliable vendors been identified for servicelets singled out to be outsourced?
- How will compound applications be scaled within the current environment?
- Has the in house expertise been assessed and outside consulting resources identified when needed?
- What will be the effect of virtual service oriented grids on customers and suppliers?

Virtual Service Oriented Grid Strategy for Small Businesses

As mentioned in Chapter 2, according to the U.S. Small Business Administration, small firms, defined as independent business having fewer than 500 employees, constitute 99.7 percent of all employer firms in the United States. Furthermore, small firms pay more than 45 percent of total U.S. private payroll and have created more than half of nonfarm private gross domestic product (GDP).[2] The number of businesses in the United States totals about 27 million, out of which only 17,000 were large firms in 2004. In other words, looking at the statistical distribution of all businesses in the United States, there is a long tail represented by SMBs. This long tail has a significant economic impact that cannot be ignored.

New businesses usually start small. Hence it is not surprising that Gartner estimates that about 90 percent of all new businesses created in the United States are in the SMB segment[3]. Servicelet-based compound applications hold the promise of bringing the benefits of a broad range of IT services to SMBs that to date has been the privilege of large companies.

Worldwide, N-Able estimates 66 million SMB companies across the globe with 900 million computer users.

A benefit of virtual service oriented grids for SMBs and emerging markets is that it allows balancing between capital and operating expenses.

Virtual service oriented grid composite applications are highly intermediated, that is, they consist of numerous functional pieces are brought in by anonymous contributions from different players. There is complexity stemming from the potentially large number of moving parts.

CRN magazine quotes Bill Gates on occasion of his departing keynote address for the Consumer Electronics Show in Las Vegas, "Microsoft platforms have evolved to allow users to build applications that run not only on PCs, but also on devices such as mobile phones and televisions. Increasingly, these applications will be complemented by cloud-based services," Gates said.[4]

"Complementariness" is an important word. A virtual service oriented grid environment allows building applications on demand and essentially on real time. Paradoxically, it also lessens demand on local infrastructure.

---

2 U.S. Small Business Administration Frequently Asked Questions

3 http://www.networkworld.com/news/2006/022706-smb-outsourcing.html

4 CRN Magazine, issue 1257, p. 12, January 14, 2008.

This property of servicelets is valuable and useful in SMBs and emerging markets. Emerging markets may not have a sophisticated and highly developed foundation IT infrastructure. SMBs might not have the critical mass to develop a broad base of infrastructure functional parts from which to build needed business applications. A cloud environment, an instance of virtual service oriented grids will allow pulling those missing infrastructural components from outside service providers, across international borders if necessary, to bootstrap the development process.

If the component becomes critical, or requires finer grained functionality, it can always be pulled in house as experience with the particular application is acquired, such as what Tencent did when it switched from leasing hosted servers to building company owned data centers. The change might also involve moving the functional block from a recurrent cost to a capital investment. Developers and integrators can focus on local needs and import foundation services from outside as needed.

In any case, a good communication infrastructure is needed for this to work. It is possible to use batch and delay-tolerant algorithms in some case given that most applications will involve machine-to-machine communications. However, doing so will significantly impair scalability and performance.

A Maturity Model for Managed Services Providers

A managed services provider, or MSP, is an entity that makes a living out of managing someone else's assets. The equipment may be customer equipment hosted on the MSP's premises, or equipment that the MSP manages for a fee, deployed at the customer's premises.

The aggregation of the MSP or MSPs and the customer equipment represents an instance of a virtualized service oriented grid. A large MSP can easily have hundreds of customers, companies from small to large, managing thousands of servers over a wide geographic area with both CPE and data center hosted equipment. The existence of MSPs as a viable business indicates that metadata, that is, information about the systems is becoming as important as the information that the systems contain.

The proportion of MSP managed servers (nodes) owned by SMBs is probably large, if only because an SMB may use one to ten servers, a small number that would not justify building a data center around these servers.

Large companies will have the wherewithal to deploy wholly owned data centers. They may use externally managed servers from the services they outsource.

Not all MSPs are created equal. As part of strategic planning it is useful to establish a maturity model to measure progress by steps toward a goal. Such a maturity model defines a number of stages along with metrics to determine whether specific stages have been reached.

The specific maturity model adopted is less important than having one in the first place along with an organizational consensus in adopting one as the basis for ongoing strategic checkpoints. It will be up to strategists or chief architects to put one together.

The specific model will be a function of the organizational goals. Starting points can be derivatives of the Software Engineering Institute's Capability Maturity Model for software development, or Gartner's Infrastructure Maturity Model. An excellent example, N-able has developed a maturity model applicable to managed service providers. This model has five stages, as described in Table 8.3.

A discussion on maturity models is relevant to MSPs and their clients alike, given that both parties have a stake in delivering and receiving services that are scalable, high quality at the lowest possible cost.

Table 8.3 The N-able MSP Maturity Model

Stage	Name	Stage Characteristics and Metrics
1	Break-fix	• Ad-hoc processes • Technicians' goal is spending 100% time fixing problems reported by customers • Service delivery, cost, outcomes unpredictable • Low morale and customer satisfaction
2	Responsive	• Some processes documented • Work style still reactive; some problems caught by monitoring equipment before customer gets exposed to the fault.
3	Proactive	• Preventive maintenance reduces number of incidents • Corrective actions still a significant part of technician's workload, but work efficiency has improved
4	Managed	• Utility approach to service delivery • Costs become quantifiable and predictable • Technician time is abstracted out. Customer pays for value of services received, not technician's time.
5	Value	• Optimizing stage, where cost tradeoffs become explicit • MSP's and client's processes become integrated

Reference: *IT Service Delivery: From Basic Automation through to Managed Services*, N-able white paper, 2008

Service granularity poses challenge to the delivery of services to SMBs. A 100-employee firm cannot afford an ERP specialist, a Chief Security Officer, and a Database Architect when the total number of people dedicated to IT may not number more than three or four. Chances are that these skills are not needed on a full-time basis, yet they may be needed on an ongoing basis, and hence bringing these skills as hired consultants is less than satisfactory when they are needed in the long term. This challenge is similar to that of scaling down IT services to the home discussed in Chapter 7, only slightly less so.

A virtual service oriented grid environment allows fine grained control of IT capabilities by virtue of carving up resources that may require a sizable investment, namely a data center and highly skilled staff and amortizing the investment over multiple service instances.

Adoption of Virtual Service Oriented Grids in SMB Space

Characterizing the types of small businesses most likely to adopt virtual service oriented grid technology or to offer servicelets is not an easy task. These firms are at the leading edge of innovation.

According to an NFIB poll[5] only 11 percent of small, employing business owners purposefully innovate or create inventions with the intention of selling them. However, 21 percent derive revenue from design work whether or not the designs can be patented or copyrighted. These companies usually have 10 or more employees. About 5 percent own at least one patent and 13 percent hold a copyright that they actively exploit as a source of revenue. About 4 percent of small businesses classify themselves as both producers and consumers of technology and about 65 percent claim they are extensive users of technology. Yet 16 percent actively avoid the use of technology for various reasons: it is seen as a depersonalizing force, changes the atmosphere in the business, or would have the business serve technology rather than the other way around.

Diana Hicks[6] points to numerous public policy studies on smaller firms regarding the promise to bring growth and new jobs. The implicit premise for these studies is that when it comes to technology, SMBs are like large firms, only smaller, and that becoming a large firm is the natural outcome of large firm survival and success. She discovered that the influence and staying power of some very successful technology firms does not correlate to size.

Some SMBs, even though small, become technology suppliers to much larger firms or to market segments, wielding a sustained influence disproportionate to their size and become well established. These SMBs are called *serial innovators* and spend substantial time and money on innovation.

The work of serial innovators tends to concentrate less on a specific product and more on core technologies and processes. This circumstance fits well with the nature of virtual service oriented grids. We can expect the SMB segment to become a significant player both as a technology supplier for virtual service oriented grids and as a consumer for servicelets. Suppliers are more likely to be represented in the 5 percent that own at least one patent in the NFIB poll, whereas the 65 percent users of technology represents a potential audience.

Hicks also claims that smaller firms place more emphasis on *tradable* technology, that is, a technology portfolio whose goal is to be placed outside the company as opposed to be used in house or not at all.

Tradable technology exhibits the following distinguishing characteristics:

---

5   National Federation of Independent Businesses, *NFIB National Small Business Poll*, Volume 5, Issue 6 (2005)

6   Diana M. Hicks, Deepak Hegde, *Highly innovative small firms in the markets for technology*, School of Public Policy, Georgia Institute of Technology, Elsevier, Science Direct, May 2005.

- *Higher impact*, as measured by how the technology is referenced by others.
- *Broader impact*. The technology is applied in multiple market segments.
- *Broader based*. The technology depends less on incremental development and immediate precedents.
- *More science linked*. Science provides a more generalized underpinning that allows a technology to be applied in multiple contexts.

In terms of higher impact, a new patent can easily get lost in the bureaucracy of a large organization, never to be used again or referenced by other researchers, internal or external. The impact of a discovery that gets shelved is minimal to naught.

The impact of a discovery is relatively narrow in a large enterprise when the discovery gets applied only to the company's own processes. Technology deployment is localized. SMBs do not have this luxury. Their survival depends on placing the discovery in a broader context to maximize revenue potential. Virtual service oriented technology is inherently horizontal, and hence there is good alignment with SMBs bringing innovation in this field and trying to execute on a broad impact strategy.

Likewise, SMBs usually do not have a large technology portfolio to draw from, and hence they have fewer opportunities to self-cite. Consequently, technologies originated by SMBs are more likely to be more original, that is, represent a significant departure from pre-existing art or methods. Such technology with fewer linkages to prior art tends to be more generic and general purpose, facilitating the division of labor across companies in technology markets, one of the objectives of a well-established servicelet ecosystem. General purpose technologies can play a role of enabling technologies, instead of being part of finished turnkey (but also black box) solutions. This is another alignment point with the servicelet architecture.

Finally, science linked knowledge is much more abstract than say, the knowledge embodied in the patent for a widget, which is essentially a one off instance. The abstraction associated with science linked knowledge allows applying this knowledge in previously unrelated areas, hence making the technology more tradable.

The first challenge is that traditional classification systems for SMBs do not work very well to explain the dynamics of technology adoption. Diana Hicks[7] reports that well known classification such as Michael Porter's from Harvard University are too coarse grained. So is the US Government's North American Industry Classification System (NAICS) where most SMBs with potential interest in service oriented grids would fall under the "other" category. Hicks developed a taxonomy based on the characterization of serial innovators. This characterization is useful to establish a framework to understand the adoption of virtual service oriented grids by SMBs, both as producers and consumers. Table 8.4 describes Hicks' taxonomy along with potential strategies associated with each type of SMB in the taxonomy.

---

7   Diana M. Hicks et al., *Identification of the Technology Commercialization Strategies of High-tech Small Firms*, U.S. Small Business Administration (2006)

Table 8.4 Taxonomy of Innovative Small Firms

Type of Firm	Description	Potential Sources of Competitive Advantage	Possible Virtual Service Oriented Strategies
R&D organization or contractor	Typically, a very small firm with a highly qualified workforce (PhD level scientists, MDs, and/or Master degree holders) that has developed a deep understanding of scientific phenomena in a limited number of research areas in which they conduct basic/applied research with a commercial orientation. Outputs are working prototypes, patents, or novel production processes and tacit know-how.	• Explicit and tacit knowledge base developed over time and often inherited from previous employers (govt. labs, universities, large corporate R&D labs) • Special formal or informal ties with previous employers/clients/institutions • Highly specialized areas for which there is often only monopolistic (e.g. DoD, DoE) or oligopolistic demand • Strong, reputable R&D team	• Package new discoveries into servicelets to be plugged into existing composite applications • Standards-making activities to improve cross industry coordination across knowledge base and lower costs • Cross agency coordination to ensure compatibility in composite applications
Science-based product/service firms	Typically, a small firm that develops applications based on findings made in basic research laboratories. Often spinouts from the science base or from large established firms. Outputs include FDA-approved drugs, medical devices or diagnostics, novel electronic devices.	• Patented library of molecules with therapeutic potential that was identified in a university lab/govt. lab or in-house • Patented medical device initially developed in a university lab/by a medical practitioner • Linkages to the science base • Strong R&D team and alliance/partnership skills	• New applications can be packaged into servicelets • Low level integration of servicelets from R&D organizations

Type of Firm	Description	Potential Sources of Competitive Advantage	Possible Virtual Service Oriented Strategies
Highly specialized component supplier (high volume production)	Typically, a small firm that develops discrete patented products that are often used in larger systemic products of medium to high complexity (e.g. car, TV set, scientific instruments, etc). Output is typically discrete components manufactured in volume.	• Internal R&D, co-design with OEM • Efficient manufacturing processes • Low-cost but skilled labor force • Reputation • Flexibility to follow large customers (OEM, ODM) overseas • Long-term contracting relationships	• This segment is a net consumer of servicelets where software accompanies the supplier products
Specialized subcontractor firm (one-offs or very low volume production)	Typically, small firms that excel in very specialized technologies for which applications need to be customized and integrated in often highly complex integrated products (aircraft carriers, mass transport system, intelligent buildings, manufacturing systems, etc.)	• Customization and external integration capabilities • Flexibility • Track record, reputation • Bidding and positioning skills, customer relationship capabilities • Product boasts many unique features	• Development of highly specialized servicelets. • Activities toward preserving interoperability in spite of a highly customized environment.

Type of Firm	Description	Potential Sources of Competitive Advantage	Possible Virtual Service Oriented Strategies
Product solutions provider	Typically, a small firm that identifies a market need that needs to be addressed holistically, and provides a turnkey solution for that problem	• Strong internal system integration skills • High degree of vertical integration • Strong customer service skills	• This category is a prototypical servicelet consumer. • Virtual service oriented technology will help this firm bring solutions to market faster. • Some firms may grow a servicelet development capabilities to fill integration gaps
Service solutions provider (technical consultants)	Typically, a firm that tailors a service to the needs of large customers (chip design services for wafer foundries, software development that addresses a particular business need).	• Close relationship with client • Strong customer service skills • Strong external system integration skills • Strong engineering and implementation skills, customer relationship capabilities • Long-term supply and maintenance contracts	• This segment is a net consumer of servicelets • Consultants need to develop expertise in servicelets available in their area of competency, for instance, servicelets supporting manufacturing automation
Consumer goods supplier	Typically, a small firm that develops and often manufactures niche consumer products, e.g. barbeque sets, sports goods, coffeemakers, etc.	• Targets niche markets with high-quality products • Strong brand reputation • Flexible, efficient manufacturing system	• This segment is a net consumer of servicelets for business process automation

On a positive note, the tradition of the small inventor, the Edison of the 19th century is still alive and healthy in SMBs. Complexity of technology has not subsumed the individual inventors into the corporate folds. A technology marketplace with specialized division of labor with SMBs as technology suppliers exists today. Virtual service oriented grid technology, under the guise of servicelets presents a good vehicle to encapsulate these relationships. However, the situation is highly dynamic. It is not uncommon for these SMB suppliers to lose their identity through acquisition.

One final note linking back SMBs with national strategy: A national development policy needs to include special considerations for SMBs, allocating investment directed toward development of servicelets aimed at SMB users. SMB users need to have a strong play in the development process as well. Established telecom carriers such British Telecom and China Telecom could partner with independent software vendors to offer SaaS servicelets to their SMB subscribers. SMB can also take advantage of services available today, such as Google Apps or MS Live Office, to cover the basic needs of their office automation needs. At the same time, Internet service providers need to be open to business opportunities fulfilling needs of the SMB market.

A healthy, pervasive ecosystem and healthy virtual service oriented dynamics for SMBs go hand in hand. An SMB alone cannot move a market. However, the aggregated needs of millions of SMBs will constitute a powerful economic force that independent software vendors and telecom carriers can only ignore at the risk of missed opportunities.

Chapter 9

Epilog

The cloud is basically a combination of grid computing, which was mostly about raw processing power, and software as a service. In effect, the cloud is network virtualization.

—Dennis Byron, Analyst, Research 2.0

John Gage, one of the founders of Sun Microsystems, is said to have coined the phrase "The Network is the Computer." Inherent in this vision is the notion of a set of networked resources available and configurable on demand. Virtual service oriented grids extend this notion to most facets of human activity.

Effectively, the world *is* the computer, not in the sense of the dystopic world of *The Matrix* imagined by the Wachowski brothers where machines have taken over humanity, but from the realization that effective business applications require seamless integration of technology, people, and processes. This realization comes from the strong Internet roots of virtual service oriented grids and depends on the collaborative work of many constituencies. As a technology, virtual service oriented grids are inherently neutral: neither good nor bad. Certainly they are not immune to manipulation by commercial or political interests. Thomas Jefferson's dictum, "the price of democracy is eternal vigilance" applies to virtual service oriented grids because of the large and multiple constituencies involved. Also there exist security issues that do not normally exist in vertical, siloed environments. However, the economics of virtual service oriented grids are hard to resist, and economics may determine whether or not a project gets carried out at all.

On the positive side, it is central to the concept of service orientation that the distance between people, technology, and business processes should be as small as possible. In fact, these three entities are seen as a continuum. This continuum presents an opportunity to bring people and cultures together into mutually beneficial relationships and provide an efficient medium to ensure that intellectual capital benefits large segments of humanity.

Virtual Service Oriented Grids Today

Strategic decision makers and architects can look at this continuum for opportunities for global optimization and to uncover new business opportunities. The untapped opportunities are enormous. It is important to note that this is not pie-in-the-sky technology; the opportunities relate to plans and decisions we make and actions we carry out today, not to a nebulous payoff in the future. The virtual service oriented paradigm allows us to look at resources available today in a new light, as high level components for building new business applications. Moreover, if we look at technology alone, without the people and process contexts, we will almost certainly miss opportunities. From a business perspective, missed opportunities translate into money left on the table.

Within the business and technology continuum there exist countless options and variations. Building a successful business implies discovering and assessing different process alternatives. Take electronic banking, for instance. The existing distributed computing infrastructure allows a funds transfer using the following methods:

1. From an ATM machine
2. From a personal computer
3. Via a telephone call with a bank's customer representative
4. In person, with the customer walking to a teller at a physical branch office of a bank.

For each of the alternatives above, if a computer is used, virtual service oriented grid components are certainly involved, but in different combinations and intensity. Even the most manual of the alternatives, alternative #4, has a bank teller keying data into a distributed enterprise resource planning application that eventually triggers a number of transactions at the database back end: regardless of the method used, each one of the alternatives above ends up with a debit in one account and a corresponding credit in another account.

A process architect or designer looks at the complete string of actions and optimizes the whole chain to the benefit of the business, for instance encouraging customers to avail themselves of the first two alternatives while discouraging the use of the last two. Providing incentives for customer to use alternative 4 only because new front end machines have been installed at tellers' stations would make no sense. While this example might seem silly, it is not too far from how technology is selected and deployed today.

Implementations today support simple bank transactions on cell phones via instant messaging. Consistent with the silo theory covered in Chapter 2, these solutions are vertical, single-vendor, purpose-built implementations. In a not-too-distant future we can expect to see banking being extended beyond proprietary, closed devices and beyond the current edge of the data network, represented today by cell phones, PDAs, and the swarm of consumer PCs and wired and wireless laptops. Proprietary or not, the aggregation of these edge devices defines a grid containing hundreds of millions of nodes whose collective power is largely untapped today. Some cloud applications such as Skype are starting to use this power to route voice packets.

This transition to a servicelet as building block will take place with the support from additional device classes just entering the market such as more capable mobile phones, mobile Internet devices (MIDs) and ultramobile PCs (UMPCs). The transition will not happen instantly. Some time will be needed to allow for adequate public discourse and for government regulations to catch up with technology. In addition to public discourse, internal discussions need to take place within potential service providers, product suppliers, and integrators to establish viable business models.

Nonetheless, this transformation is already quietly happening and its pace will accelerate in the near future. In this context, including virtual service oriented grids in the current strategic planning is a relevant and legitimate topic.

After all, the technologies that underlie virtual service oriented grids have been around for quite a while. It's their banding together that's accelerating change.

The transformation is in midflight around the world, and because it's happening at the heels of recent trends in economic globalization, new players are certain to arise. The catalyzing factor is the servicelet paradigm that elevates the level of abstraction at which business applications can be assembled. This is just like the PC revolution of the 1980s as described in Chapter 3 freed up people from having to build PCs starting with transistors, resistors, capacitors, and low-level components. The ability to build PCs from interoperable baseboards, chassis, and power supplies literally enabled millions of small businesses and consumers to build their own computers and marked the rise of large players like Dell.

Furthermore, the servicelet notion is not just about being to land a new server in minutes using virtualization technology. Servicelets also encompass software application components and business process building blocks for quickly assembling applications. Servicelets accelerate the speed at which applications can be brought to market by several orders of magnitude, especially in developing markets even without the luxury of an established information technology infrastructure.

By lowering technology barriers for building computers, the PC revolution opened opportunities to millions of small businesses and individual consumers around the world. This trend continues unabated in the virtual service oriented grid environment.

It is interesting to note that distributed computing opened up opportunities for small players, that is, players in the long tail, the 99.7 percent of small businesses in the United States as mentioned in Chapter 8: Amazon.com opened the worldwide marketplace to thousands of small booksellers. Likewise, thousands to millions of small merchants sell their wares today through eBay.

The deployment of computing resources on a global basis continues. What is different this time around is a departure from the now familiar pattern of global consolidation of resources in the hands of a few large companies. In a departure from the past, even small companies will be able to avail themselves of global resources. The emphasis here is on the opening up of opportunities for small companies, not large companies, and not just in countries with developed economies, but countries anywhere in the world.

A good communication infrastructure makes the processes easier to implement, but is not absolutely essential. Web services can be carried out over dialup, albeit slowly. In the worst case, transactions can be carried out even if postal mail or manual data entry are involved. A shining example is the case of Drishtee.com in India.[1] Drishtee.com has created a network of staffed kiosks in several states in India, including Uttar Pradesh (North India), Assam (East India), Haryana (West India), Orissa (East India), Tamil Nadu (South India), Uttaranchal (North India), Manipur, and Arunachal Pradesh (N.E. India).

One of the services Drishtee.com provides is filing government forms: to find out about market prices for crops, to obtain marriage or gun licenses, caste or domicile certificates, and retrieve land records. For villagers in rural India, transacting with the government directly could mean a two-day trip to the nearest town. Instead, the villager can go to one of the kiosks where a staffer can fill in the required electronic form on a PC. The forms are aggregated once daily to district hubs where an ombudsperson routes the requests to the appropriate government office. The aggregation process is done manually using dialup lines.

Dispositions for requests make a similar trip back to the originating kiosk, where the returned forms are printed and handed back to the requester. The aggregation of computers in kiosks and hubs forms a service oriented grid, at least conceptually. The fact that it uses batched processes and that manual steps are part of the communication structure does not invalidate the concept. Viewed as a virtualized service oriented grid, this infrastructure can be seen in a new light. This analysis would make it possible to establish a long term technology upgrade strategy that meets evolving and changing business requirements. For instance, if the manual processes for exchanging forms becomes burdensome with business growth this analysis would point to bringing in an automated messaging facility using XML Web services.

Virtual service oriented grids are for today, not for tomorrow. Their incremental nature allows attaining change without the risks associated with forklift upgrades. This trait is essential for gaining organizational support early on. At the same time, strategic plans need to be designed with an eye

---
1 T. Salvador, J. Sherry, *Taking the Internet to the People*, IEEE Spectrum, October 2005.

toward a significant future payoff to ensure long term survival. Ultimately it is results and value to customers and members of the organization that count. Without it the plans won't last no matter how skillful the positioning is.

The usefulness of virtual service oriented grids does not come from some inherent magic powers in the technology. It's because of its potential for altering relationships worldwide. It can revitalize "old" technologies as we saw with the electric power industry by allowing end users to optimize energy consumption and facilitating the management of distributed generation within the current environment. It puts developing and advanced economies alike in an equal footing. Servicelets allow harnessing global resources, such as storage, computation and applications to address local problems. This is almost another instance of the saying attributed to David Brower "Think globally, act locally," although it is actually of interest to architects. The actors, the developers assembling applications from servicelets, need only be aware that building blocks exist and are available for building business solutions.

Solving business problems in finite time and within budget implies taking a hard look at available in-house technology. Strategists and architects also need to look at external components available for hire. Outsourcing a servicelet may make economic sense from a societal perspective. Developing a servicelet in the first place may have required a high level of investment and expertise. Putting the servicelet in the marketplace and available for reuse allows amortizing the investment over multiple deployments not only within a single organization, but across several companies.

Virtual service oriented grids constitute a powerful abstraction tool to address tough problems. Economics provide an incentive to look at the problem at the highest level of abstraction possible. We see a similar pattern in other domains. It is actually difficult to read a book letter by letter, or even word by word. The brain can be trained to integrate letters into words and words into sentences in a process not unlike that of the semantic translation problem discussed in Chapter 3. Most people will "understand" a book at the conceptual level in terms of the ideas discussed and perhaps the overall structure or "architecture" of the book. Only occasionally will they dive a few conceptual layers down, for instance for a direct quotation. Likewise, an experienced pianist is only occasionally aware of single notes in the keyboard. Most of the time she will be concerned with harmonic relationships, which are structured groups of notes, themes, and the overall structure of a musical piece. Hence, as we saw in Chapter 3, the success of companies like Boeing does not come from snapping rivets into aircraft faster than anyone else, but from a systems integration expertise without peer that brings together suppliers from all over the world. It is not a surprise that in the process of carrying their business, Boeing makes extensive use of virtual service oriented technology for both aircraft design and supply chain management.

The Future of Virtual Service Oriented Grids

It will take business leaders with vision and strategic thinking to lay out the foundation of virtual service orientated grids in places where they do not exist today. It will also take forward thinking computer platform vendors, software vendors, network service providers, and systems integrators to build solid and interoperable platforms on which the various parts needed for virtual service oriented grids will run. The challenges are not trivial, but the returns for the parties involved are potentially large.

Crossing the chasm to virtualized services from distributed computing, as in past instances of technology adoption, will require the applied talents of many a visionary leader. The underlying processes for adoption were covered in Chapter 2. Virtual service oriented technology will become more common as the different components are perfected, and maturing industry standards enable synergies across components.

The transformation will not happen spontaneously. It will take business leaders with awareness of the cost dynamics between the inside-out and the outside-in models for SOA adoption to make the changes happen. As in Internet processes of the recent past, opportunities await for first movers, while laggards or organizations that hesitate will likely end up as second tier players.

If recent history is an example, new players will rise to prominence in the new virtual service oriented grid and cloud environment, while others will exit the stage.

This book is our first attempt to describe the vast expanse of virtual service oriented grids from a business strategic perspective. Leading companies in the industry and startups alike are exploring ways to create value in this new environment and in the process profit handsomely.

The intent of the authors of this book was to capture the *zeitgeist* of virtual service oriented grids, in the process highlighting opportunities of emerging Internet applications in a virtualized, distributed, and globalized service oriented infrastructure. These developments bring capabilities to assemble business applications in a fraction of the time that it would take with more traditional methods. In addition to improvements in the speed of business, new technologies and devices will extend the reach of these applications into markets that are untapped today. We anticipate a sea of change in the small and medium size business market and emerging markets, from emphasis (and obsession) on margin allocation to value creation. SMBs can become both providers and consumers of services under this new computing paradigm.

A new era of opportunity with computing services may be dawning upon the new Enterprise IT, bringing benefits to all IT stakeholders.

Glossary of Acronyms

ADS Application and data services

AM/FM/GIS Automated mapping facility/facility management/ geographical information system

AMR Automated meter reading

ANSI American National Standards Institute

ASP Application services provider

ATM Automated teller machine

ATM Asynchronous transfer mode

AWOL Absent without leave (military)

B2B Business to business

B2C Business to consumer

BI Business Intelligence

BOV Business Operational View

CERN Organisation Européenne pour la Recherche Nucléaire, formerly Conseil Européen pour la Recherche Nucléaire. In English, Organization for Nuclear Research

CFD Computational fluid dynamics

CIM Common information model

CIS Customer information system
CMMS Computerized maintenance management system
COM Component Object Model
CORBA Common Object Request Broker Architecture
CPU Central processing unit
CRM Customer relationship management
DARPA Defense Advanced Research Projects Agency
DCOM Distributed COM
DHCP Dynamic host configuration protocol
DMTF Distributed Management Task Force
DMS Distribution management system
DNS Domain name system
DPU Display point unit
DRM Distributed resource management
DRM Digital rights management
DMZ Demilitarized zone
DSL Digital subscriber line
DTU Distribution terminal unit
EA Enterprise architecture
EAI Enterprise application integration
ebXML e-Business XML
EDI Electronic data interchange
EC2 Elastic Computing Cloud [service]
EDA Electronic design automation
EGA The Enterprise Grid Alliance
EHR Electronic health record
EIA Electronic Industry Association
EISA Extended ISA
EMS Electronic manufacturing services
EMS Energy management system

ENIAC Electronic numerical integrator and computer
ERP Enterprise resource planning
FBS Federated Business Services
FCC [US] Federal Communications Commission
FERC Federal energy regulatory commission
FSV Functional Service View
FLOPS Floating point operations per second
FTD Federated technology development
GDP Gross domestic product
GGF Global Grid Forum
GPS Global positioning system
GRID Not an acronym for anything. Should be spelled grid.
HaaS Hardware as a service
HDTV High definition television
HPC High performance computing
HR Human resources
HTML Hyper Text Markup Language
HTTP Hyper Text Transport Protocol
ICT Information Communication Technology (an ITIL term)
IEC International Electrotechnical Commission
IETF The Internet Engineering Task Force
IP Internet Protocol
IP Intellectual property
IPR Intellectual property rights
IPDC Internet portal datacenter
ISA Industry standard architecture
ISA Instruction set architecture
ISO International Standards Organization
ISO [Electrical] independent systems operator
ISP Internet service provider

ISV Independent software vendor
IT Information technology
ITIL Information Technology Infrastructure Library
KTBR Keep the business running
LAN Local area network
LCR Load control receiver [device]
LMS Load management system
MAN Metropolitan area network
MCA [IBM] Micro Channel Architecture
MID Mobile internet device
MIMD Multiple instruction, multiple data
MIPS Millions of instructions per second
MSP Managed services provider
NAC Network access control
NAM Network asset management
NAS Network attached storage
NGO Nongovernmental organization
NID Network interface device
NIS Network information system
ODM Original design manufacturer
OEM Original equipment manufacturer
OASIS Organization for the Advancement of Structured Information Standards
OGF The Open Grid Forum
OGSA Open grid services architecture
OLAP Online analytical processing
OMA Open Mobile Alliance
OPM Other people's money
OPS Other people's systems
OSI Open systems interconnection

PaaS Platform as a service

PBX Private branch exchange

PC Personal computer

PCI Peripheral component interconnect

PDA Portable digital assistant

PLC Programmable logic controller

POTS Plain old telephone service

PUHCA Public utility holding company act

QoS Quality of service

RAID Redundant array of independent/inexpensive disks

ROI Return on investment

RTU Remote terminal unit

SaaS Software as a service

SAN Storage area network

SCADA Supervisory control and data acquisition

SETI Search for extraterrestrial intelligence

SGML Standard Generalized Markup Language

SIMD Single instruction, multiple data

SISD Single instruction, single data

SLA Service level agreement

SMB Small and medium size business

SNA IBM Systems Network Architecture

SOA Service oriented architecture

SOAP Simple Object Access Protocol

SOI Service oriented infrastructure

SOM System Object Model

SOP Service Orientated Provider

TCO Total cost of ownership

TCP/IP Transmission Control Protocol/Internet Protocol

TPM Trusted platform module

UDDI Universal Description Discovery and Integration
UMPC Ultramobile PC
UTP Unshielded twisted pair
XML Extended Markup Language
VAR Value added reseller
VCOR Value chain operations reference [model]
VIS Virtualized infrastructure services
VLSI Very large scale integration
VM Virtual machine
VMM Virtual machine monitor
VOIP Voice over IP
VSG Virtual service oriented grid
VT Virtualization technology
W3C The World Wide Web Consortium
WAN Wide area network
Wi-Fi Trademark from the Wi-Fi Alliance for the IEEE 802.11b standard
WiMAX Worldwide interoperability for microwave access
WMS Work management system
WS Web services
WS-I Web Services Interoperability
WS-BPEL WS business process execution language
WSDL Web services description language
WSRF WS resource framework

Index

A

abstraction
   cost and, 179
   economics of, 298
   level of, 177
   service abstractions by HaaS, 195
   with servicelets, 180, 211
AC motors, 223
account statistics, 246
acronyms, glossary of, 301–306
administration tools, 188
administrative grid, 248
ADS. *See* application and data services
advanced economy, 269
Advanced Technology bus Attachment (ATA), 113
agility
   adoption of Web services for, 240
   business agility with grids, 9
   changing business conditions and, 154
   data centers and, 156, 198
   demand fueled by agility of new technology, 51
   federated technology development and, 87
   licensing and, 276
   resource pooling and, 108
   service orientation and, 136
   with SOA, 200
   technology integration and, 175, 211
   with virtual service oriented grid, xxiii, 159, 265, 275
   virtualization and, 133
   Web servers and, 151
agriculture servicelet, 272
aircraft industry, 49
AJAX, 191
Alcatel, 250, 251
Alibaba, 266
alternating current system, 223
Amazon.com
   as business service provider, 40–41
   Elastic Computing Cloud, 41, 182
   as service provider, 52, 65–66
   transnational resources, 277
American Express travel reservation application, 24–25

American National Standards Institute (ANSI), 162
Ampère, Andre Marie, 232
amplifier, audio, 104
AMR (automated meter reading), 239, 241–247
Anschutz, Philip, 242
ANSI (American National Standards Institute), 162
APIs (application programming interfaces), 205
Apple
  computers, 92–96
  iPhone, 182
  iPod, 32
  as Web 2.0 innovator, 182
application and data services (ADS)
  data caching policy and, 250
  IT services to the home, 221–224
  in layered usage model for grids, 98
  in three-layer grid model, 29
  in virtual service oriented grid structure, 24, 25, 26–27
application capability, 257
application lifecycle, 143
application programming interfaces (APIs), 205
application service provider (ASP), xxiv
application services, 221–224
application workloads, 105–109
applications
  development of, xxi–xxiii
  development time for, 53
  disaggregation/reaggregation of, xxii
  grid computing challenges, 150
  for laptop loss management service, 23
  service orientation benefits for, 135–136
  servicelets for national strategy, 270–272
architecture
  architecturally unbalanced system, 102
  balanced, importance of, 120–121
  balanced grid architecture, 109–120
  composite usage model, 74

  of DEC PDP-11 line, 78–79
  of electric power system, 230–247
  grid usage attributes, 101–103
  of IBM system, 76–77
  ISO OSI model, 90–91
  service oriented architectural tenets, 136–140
  standards for grid architecture, 170–171, 173
  tightly coupled, 203
  virtual infrastructure example, 208–210
ASP (application service provider), xxiv
asset discovery/management, 142, 192
ATA (Advanced Technology bus Attachment), 113
ATM machine, 294
atoms, 45–46
attributes, grid usage attributes, 101–103
audience, target, 179–180
audio electronics, 104
audit record, 145, 246
audit service, 144–145
authentication
  home IT service for, 221
  laptop loss management service, 249
  metadata, 218
  security enforcement, 193
  security for virtual service oriented grids, 141, 144, 145
  shared messaging service fabric, 138
authorization
  of credit card purchase, 17
  by security service, 221
  security service for virtual service oriented grid, 144
  for virtual service oriented grid, 141
  visible grid requirement, 99
automated meter reading (AMR), 239, 241–247
automatic rifles, 33
automation
  SOI framework and, 192
  in virtualization infrastructure, 188–189

automatons, 14
automobile
   adoption of, 48–49
   engines, power of, 109–110
   OnStar service, 274
   rhetorical question about, 33
   transformation with, 157
   virtualization continuum analogy, 103–104
automotive industry
   Covisint Web-based exchange, 183
   insurance, 216–218
   logical layering for, 34
   rentals, leasing, 184
   shared stack components, 46–47
   supporting industries for, 52
A/V
   cable setup for broadband/cable TV services, 222–224
   home IT subsystem, 225–229
   impedance match, 104
   IT services to the home, 214
availability
   high availability, 189, 190
   load balancing and, 132
   replication for, 11

B

B2B (business-to-business), 172–173, 277
backup
   consumer facilitated storage and, 254
   data services for, 221–222
   latency tolerant, 276–277
   storage service for, 220
   of virtualization infrastructure, 189, 190
Baidu, 199, 266
balanced grid architecture, 109–120
bandwidth
   application engineering to minimize use of, 269
   for backup service, 277
   broadband service requirements, 273
   bulk storage providers and, 71
   clusters and, 102
   computer node and, 9
   consumer facilitated storage and, 254
   grid nodes and, 12
   Internet download speed, 3
   laptop loss management service and, 22
   metering node and, 247
   over-provisioning and, 153
   QoS in networks and, 153
   for scale-out architecture, 115–120
   for virtualized environment, 259
   visible grid requirement, 99
   of WiMAX channel, 22
bandwidth acceleration, 120
banking, electronic, 294–295
bare metal
   HaaS availability at, 194, 196
   hypervisor, 127
   provisioning, 142, 192
   provisioning for virtualization infrastructure, 186
Bartels, Andrew, 155
baseboards, 75–76
Basic Input/Output System (BIOS), 82
Beck, R. W., 243
behavior
   changes for outside-in SOA, 68–69
   dynamic behaviors, 107, 178
Bell Labs, 250
Berra, Yogi, 263
bill-back, 67
binder, 205
binding
   delayed binding, as useful paradigm, 202–204
   delayed binding for deployment flexibility, 204–207
   mechanism of services, 17
BIOS (Basic Input/Output System), 82
Bittel, Lester R., 175
Bluetooth, 225
Boeing Company, 81, 299
bookstore, virtual, 270–271

Bossidy, Lawrence A., 31
botnet, 252
bottlenecks
   latency, bandwidth and, 118, 119
   from unbalanced architecture, 116
   utilization factor and, 105
BOV (Business Operational View), 168–169
BPL (broadband over power lines), 243
brick and mortar, xv, 69
British Telecom, 291
broadband over power lines (BPL), 243
broadband service
   bandwidth requirements, 273
   DSL broadband link, 120
   for home IT infrastructure, 222, 223
   virtual service oriented grid adoption and, 273
   for white zombie scheme, 252
Brooks, Frederick, 77
Brower, David, 298
budget. *See also* costs
   economics of service orientation, 54–57
   MOOSE spending, 155
buffer, 117
building blocks. *See* virtual service oriented grids, building blocks for
bulk storage providers, 71
Burke, Edmund, 123
bus bar, 7
business agility. *See* agility
business application
   building of by SMBs, 282
   business processes that support, 170
   implementation cost of, xxii
   integration of technology, people, processes, 293
   life span of, xxiii
   MIPS, 255
   notion of service and, 17
   servicelets and, 72, 296
   sharing idle resources, 147
   SOAs as, 20
   speed of assembly of, 300
   virtual service oriented grids for, 294

business continuity
   backup, high-availability for, 190
   virtualization for, 132
business efficiency, 211
business gap, 100
business grid
   acquisitions for entities at, 102–103
   requirements for, 99
   standards for, 170
   structure of, 98
   usage attributes, 101
   usage models for, 100
   use of term, 97
business innovation, 54, 55–57
business leaders, 279
business model
   collaborative, move towards, 175
   interdependent, 40
Business Operational View (BOV), 168–169
business optimization, 85–87
business process
   for electric power industry, 238–239
   integration of technology, people, processes, 293–294
   representation by SOA services, 63
   service needed for virtual service oriented grid, 143
   standardization, validation for SOA, 68
   standards for, 168–170
   virtual service oriented grid standards, 170, 172–173
   X-engineering and, 37–41
business transformation
   from convergence of virtualization, service orientation, grids, 31
   Internet as agent of change, 35–36
   merging of silos, rise of collaboration, 43–53
   rhetorical question, 33–35
   SOA, adoption of, scalability of, 58–72
   solution stacks, need for, 41–43
   technology adoption in social/economic context, 32
   X-engineering, 36–41

business usage models, 97–101. *See also* business grid
business-to-business (B2B), 172–173, 277
Byron, Dennis, 293

C

cable modem, 222–223
cable TV, 222–224, 226
cache
    laptop loss management service, 22, 23, 248, 249
    latency and, 117, 119
    size of, 115
    speed of application and, 114
cache memory
    application performance and, 114
    in computer-storage hierarchy, 112
    connection to CPU logic, 112, 113
    scale-out architecture, 115
CAD (Computer Assisted Design), 37, 182
Canada, 3
canonical services, 66, 219
Capability Maturity Model, 283
capacity planning
    for data center, 187
    operation tool for, 189
    by SOI, 193
    for virtual service oriented grid, 142
capital investment, 265–266, 275
capital markets, 265, 266
Carrefour supermarkets, 181
case studies
    democratization of computing, 254–258
    electric power system, IT architecture of, 230–247
    energy usage and virtual service oriented grids, 258–262
    IT services to the home, 213–229
    laptop loss management service, 248–251
    storage in virtual service oriented grid environment, 252–254
cell phone
    bank transactions on, 295
    demand for, 181–182

    information delivery to, 275
    inside-out servicelets and, 27
    micropayments by, 2–3
    mobile standards, 168
central processing unit (CPU)
    balanced grid architecture for performance, 110–120
    capability, workload of, 74
    connection to memory, 113
    cores in grid structure, 8
    dual-core processors, 10–11
    extra CPU cycles for grids, 269
    multi-core CPUs, 3
    performance advancements, xii
    physical grid and, 99
    power density and, 152
    scale-out architecture, 115
    time to solution and, 29–30
    in virtual infrastructure, 208, 210
    virtualization and administration of machines, 188
    workloads, 256–257
centralized data centers, 198–201
CERN (Centre Europén pour la Recherche Nucleaire), 35
Champy, James
    openness, mutuality, interoperability principles, 180, 183, 264
    on X-engineering, 36–37, 38, 39
change, 195. *See also* business transformation
chasm, 299
Chevrolet, 46
China
    Internet service companies in, 266
    micropayments by cell phone in, 2–3
    salary levels in, 273
    services offered by, 267
    Tencent, 265
China Telecom, 291
chipset
    in Composite Usage Model, 99, 101
    in computer development process, 75–76
    layered framework and, 92, 98
CIM. *See* Common Information Model

classification, for SMBs, 287–290
cloud
    Dennis Byron on, 293
    Diane Greene on, 213
    DVD jukebox role and, 227
    testing servicelet technology, 280
    in white zombie scheme, 254
cloud computing
    decentralized virtual data centers, 200–201
    description of, 199
    development of, 258
    Elastic Computing Cloud, 41, 182
    federated business services as, 25
    inside-out servicelets and, 27
    laptop loss management service and, 23
    Skype, 295
    for SMB adoption of grids, 281, 282
    tipping point for adoption of grids, 219
    virtual service oriented grid as, 24
    virtual service oriented grids as, 24
cluster
    applications run at cluster level, 101
    computing clusters, 255
    description of, 7
    in electric power system, 244, 245
    in grid structure, 8
    in hierarchical usage model, 92
    interconnect performance of, 99
    nodes of, 12, 97, 100
    performance bottlenecks, 102
    workload and, 13
coding, custom, 177
Cohen, Robert, 50–51
collaboration
    collaborative business models, 154
    as end state of maturation process, 41
    rise of, 43–53
    shared stack components, 46–47
    on standards, 163
    in X-engineering, 37–38
COM (Component Object Model), 206
Comcast, 222–223
commodity processors, 255
commodity servers
    capabilities of, 151
    issues of, 152
    server sprawl from, 259
Common Information Model (CIM)
    for adoption of Web services by electric power industry, 240
    by DMTF, 167
    resource standards built on, 173
Common Object Request Broker Architecture (CORBA), 206
communication
    with business leaders, stakeholders, 279
    messaging standards, 172
    with metering grid, 245–246
    security of VSG for, xxiv–xxv
communication infrastructure
    for adoption of virtual service oriented grid, 276, 282
    as not essential, 297
Compaq, 82
compilers, xvi
complementariness, 281–282
Component Object Model (COM), 206
component services, xxi
component-based development, 134
componentized objects, 206, 207
composable services, 15–16
composite application. *See also* virtual service oriented grids
    communication infrastructure, 172, 276
    customer pull, 180
    Diane Greene on, 213
    energy usage and, 261
    federated business services term, 25
    interoperability of, xxi
    in outside-in SOA, 64
    servicelets of, 265, 268
composite framework, 92
composite usage model
    application to virtual service oriented grids, 96–101
    to define logical layers within grid system, 74

grid usage attributes, 101–103
historical example, 92–96
layered framework for usage models, 89–96
value of virtual service oriented grids, 87–88
compound application
built from shared service components, 50
description of, 18–19
inside-out SOA transformation, 62
outside-in SOA transformation, 62–66
self-optimizing, xxii
for Service Oriented Providers, 51
structure of virtual service oriented grids, 24–29
computation
democratization of, 254–258
distributed, 84
grid computing resources, 9
problem, grids for solving, 3, 9–10
resources, more demand for, 50–51
virtualization for, 125–126
compute engine, 74
compute grids, 149
computer
architecting for performance, 109–120
evolution of computer hardware, xviii, xix
historical federated technology development, 75–82
for home IT infrastructure, 227, 228–229
other people's systems, use of, 4–6
virtualization of, 125–126
virtualization usage models, 129–133
Computer Assisted Design (CAD), 37, 182
Computer Data Products, 82
computer industry, silos in, 42–43
computer model, 76, 235
computing. *See* cloud computing; grid computing; high performance computing; utility computing infrastructure
Condor, 5, 255, 256
configuration, 145

connecting technology
for computer link to storage, 113
for laptops, 248
consolidation
description of, 106
server, 129–132
consumer
Apple computers and, 92–96
application, 243
computer design and, 76, 77
customer pull, 38–39, 180–182
delivering IT services to the home, 213–229
gains from outside-in SOA environment, 65
goods supplier, 290
IT services for individual consumers, 48
consumer phase, 268–269
consumer services servicelet, 271
consumer-facilitated storage, 252–254
consumer-provided energy management, 243
content service, 220
continuity. *See* business continuity
Control Data Corporation, 255
convergence. *See* virtual service oriented grid convergence
CORBA (Common Object Request Broker Architecture), 206
corporate strategy, 277–280
cost settlement, 67
costs
for adoption of virtual service oriented grid, 265
of centralized data center, 198
of commodity servers, 151
cost efficiency in computing, 254–255
of distributed systems, 154
economic impact of layers, 101, 102–103
economics of service orientation, 54–57
energy consumption for computing, 258, 259

of hardware, 152
for integration of IT solutions, 177–179
outside-in SOA transformation and, 65
perception of high capital cost, 100
reduction, corporate grid strategy goal, 277–278
reduction in integration costs, 207
reductions with virtualization, 133
of silo breaking, 44
SOA for reduction in, 17, 58
Coulomb, Charles Augustin, 232
coupling
    loose coupling, 137, 203–204, 265
    tightly coupled architecture, 203
Covisint, 183
CPU. *See* central processing unit
Cray Computer, 255
credential conversion, 144
credit card service, 251
CRM (Customer Relationship Management) service, 198
CRN magazine, 281
culture
    changes for outside-in SOA, 68–69
    service oriented design culture, 196
current, 230
customer pull, 38–39, 180–182
Customer Relationship Management (CRM) service, 198
cycle scavenging
    in data center grid, 20–21
    description of, 11–12
    motivation for, 255–256
    resources mined from, 150
cycle times, 13

D

data
    laptop loss management service, 22–23, 248–251
    Managed Service Provider, 69–70
    in OGSA approach, 141
    storage in virtual service oriented grid, 252–254
    virtual data masters, 27
    in virtual infrastructure, 208–209
    virtualized grid environment and, 21–22
data business requirements, 23
data caching, 249, 250
data center
    commoditization of, 150–155
    energy usage by, 259–262
    federated technology development for, 87
    management tools for, 188–190
    transition to decentralized virtual data centers, 198–201
    virtualization for load balancing, failover, 132
    in virtualization infrastructure, 186
    virtualized, management of, 187
data center grid, 20–21
data encryption, 68
data grid, 11, 149
data presence service
    home IT service, 220–221
    for laptop loss management service, 22–23, 251
    in white zombie scheme, 254
data services
    home IT infrastructure, 221–224
    for virtual service oriented grid, 143–144
Data Type Definition (DTD), 172
DatacenterDynamics, 261
Davy, Humphrey, 232
DC motors, 223
DEC. *See* Digital Equipment Corporation
dedicated resources, 43
delay, 9
delayed binding
    for deployment flexibility, 204–207
    as useful paradigm, 202–204
Dell
    growth of, 44, 296
    Solectron and, 37
    X-engineering by, 38–39

Dell, Michael, 38–39
deployment. *See also* case studies
    delayed binding for flexibility of, 204–207
    speed of, 43
deregulation, 234
derivation, 144
design, 73
design, of virtual service oriented grids
    architectural balance, 120–121
    composite usage models, 87–103
    essential properties, 73–75
    federated technology development, 75–87
    virtualization continuum, 103–120
developers
    cloud computing and, 258
    cost of technology development, 89
    focus on local needs, 282
    local, 266
    maturity model for adoption of grids, 267, 268
    service orientation and, 135
    servicelet for building applications, 275
    solution development in isolation, 41
    virtual service oriented grids and, 298
development, application, 53
diagnostics, 142, 193
dialup, 276, 297
Digital Equipment Corporation (DEC)
    fall of, 44
    PDP 11/40 minicomputer, 207
    product development strategies of, 78–80
direct current system, 223
disaggregation, xxii
disaster recovery
    with SANs, NAS, 70
    virtual service oriented grids for, xx, 261
    virtualization for, 132
    in virtualization infrastructure, 189
discovery
    asset discovery, 142, 192
    service discovery, 138

tradable technology, 286
virtual service oriented grid standards, 171
disintermediation, xxi
distributed computing
    description of, 84
    opportunities from, 296
    transition to virtualized services, 299
distributed environment, 3
Distributed Management Task Force (DMTF)
    Common Information Model, 173
    description of, mission of, 165
    relationship with other standards organizations, 166
    standards defined by, 167
distributed resources, 75
distributed systems, 153–154
distributed teams, 83–84
distribution
    complexity with, 10
    content distribution system, 32
    of electric power system, 230, 231, 234, 247
    of software, 278–279
    time to market, 85
DMTF. *See* Distributed Management Task Force
DocBook, 172
dot-com crash, xv
Drishtee.com, 297
DTD (Data Type Definition), 172
dual-core processors, 10
Dyer, David, 44–45
dynamic behaviors, xxiii, 107, 178
dynamic loading, 135
dynamism, 53

E

EAI (Enterprise Application Integration), 28, 191
eBay
    cloud computing, 258

success of, 47–48
  as Web 2.0 innovator, 182
ebXML Registry Information Model, 172
EC (electronic commerce) hubs, 47–48
e-commerce, 38–39
economics. *See also* costs
  of abstraction, 298
  economic impact of layers, 101, 102–103
  of service orientation, 54–57
  of using other people's systems, 4–5
EDI (Electronic Document Interchange), 182
Edison, Thomas A., 223
education servicelet, 272
EGA. *See* Enterprise Grid Alliance
EHR (electronic health record) system, 271
Elastic Computing Cloud (EC2), 41, 182
electric power system, 230–247
  application of virtual service oriented grids, 234–241
  description of, 7
  history of, 232–234
  IT architecture of, 230–247
  process of, 230–231
  smart electric meters, 241–247
electrical power industry, 134
electricity
  consumption monitoring, 214
  cost of, 152
  energy usage, grids and, 258–262
  history of, 232–234
  process of electric power system, 230–231
  utility computing infrastructure and, 155–156
electronic banking, 294–295
electronic commerce (EC) hubs, 47–48
Electronic Document Interchange (EDI), 182
electronic health record (EHR) system, 271
electronic manufacturing services (EMS), 37
Electronic Numerical Integrator and Computer (ENIAC), 109, 177
embedded grids, 98
embedded IT usage model, 131, 133

embedded nodes, 12
emerging markets
  agility, reduced costs for, 265
  change in, 300
  cloud environment for, 282
  global projection of, 276
  IP rights and, 278, 279
  local information industry, 267
  national strategy and, 264
  outside-in paradigm and, 202
  servicelet market maturity model, 268, 269
  virtual service oriented grids for, 281
EMS (electronic manufacturing services), 37
EMS (energy management system), 238
encapsulation, 137
encryption, 68
end points, 29–30
end user, 150. *See also* consumer
end-of-life, 143
energy, 258–262. *See also* electric power system
energy management, 214, 215
energy management system (EMS), 238
Energy Policy Act, 234
ENIAC (Electronic Numerical Integrator and Computer), 109, 177
enlightened self interest, 264
Enron, 234
Enterprise 2.0, 24
Enterprise Application Integration (EAI), 28, 191
enterprise computing
  data centers, 150–155
  next generation of, 155–158
Enterprise Grid Alliance (EGA)
  merger to create OGF, 165
  part of OGF, 167
  relationships between standards organizations, 166
enterprise grids, 149
enterprise IT
  collaborative business model, 154
  new era of opportunity, xv, 300

principles of, 2
service orientation and, 135
virtual service oriented grid strategies, 263
Enterprise Resource Planning (ERP) SAP application, 60
entertainment room, 227–228
environment isolation usage model, 131, 132
Ethernet
for grids, 13
for home IT infrastructure, 222, 225, 226, 227, 228, 229
layered framework for usage models, 91
node connection with, 113
standardization of networking, xvii
event handling, 189
Evros, 250
execution environment provisioning, 143
execution management
in OGSA approach, 141
for virtual service oriented grid, 143
execution resource allocation, 143
expansion cards, 81–82
explicit encapsulation, 135
export based industries, 274
Extended Markup Language (XML)
data transformation into XML format, 27
for hardware interoperability, 172
SOI optimized to handle XML traffic, 192
standards for, 163, 167
Web services, 70
extra-grid, 100

F

Facebook, 181
failover, 132, 152
Faraday, Michael, 232
FBS. *See* federated business services
Federal Communications Commission (FCC), 43
Federal Energy Regulatory Commission (FERC), 234
federated application, 24
federated business services (FBS)
for electric power industry, 235
home IT infrastructure, 216–221
in layered usage model for grids, 98
in virtual service oriented grid structure, 24–27
federated environment
federated technology development today, 83–85
governance in, 85–87
history of technology development in, 75–82
service orientation design for, 139–140
Federated Technology Development (FTD)
for global companies, 121
governance in federated environment, 85–87
historical perspective of, 75–82
national strategy for virtual service oriented grids, 264
today, 83–85
federation
data services for virtual service oriented grid, 143–144
properties of grid systems, 73–74
FedEx, 35, 38
FERC (Federal Energy Regulatory Commission), 234
Ferraris, Galileo, 241
file server, 112
finite state machine, 14
First Internet, 32
flexibility, 203, 204–207
Flickr, 181
food industry analyst, xxiii–xxv
force, 103–109
Ford, Henry, 49, 123
Ford Model T, 49
forking, 84–85
Fortran subroutines, 205
Foster, Ian, xvii
France, 3
Franklin, Benjamin, 232

FSV (Functional Service View), 168–169
FTD. *See* Federated Technology Development
functional encapsulation, 137
Functional Service View (FSV), 168–169
functional testing, 68
future, of virtual service oriented grids, 299–300

G

G3/G4 telecom-provided data services, 248
Gage, John, 293
Gartner, 181, 281
Gartner Infrastructure Maturity Model, 19, 283
Gates, Bill, 281
Gauss, Karl Friedrich, 232
gearbox, 104
General Electric, 35
General Motors (GM), 274
Global Grid Forum (GGF)
　merger to create OGF, 165
　part of OGF, 167
　relationships between standards organizations, 166
Globus Alliance, 167
Globus Toolkit, 146
glossary of acronyms, 301–306
GM (General Motors), 274
Goldfarb, Charles, xix
Google
　cloud computing, 258
　free search engine, map, Gmail services, 181
　Gmail, office productivity suite, 198
　in IPDC market, 198
　mega-data centers, 201
　transnational resources, 277
　as Web 2.0 innovator, 182
Google App, 291
governance, in federated environment, 85–87

governance board, 278
government services
　benefits of, 271
　description of, 272
　national strategy for virtual service oriented grids, 264–277
GPS, 248, 250, 251
Greene, Diane, 213
grid architecture. *See* architecture
grid computing
　challenges of, 150
　description of, 146–147
　evolution of, 147–148
　as helper technology for virtualization, 133
　origins of, xvii
　smart electric meters, 241–247
　standard consortia landscape, 164–168
　standards for, 163
　types of grids, 149
grid manager, 208, 210
grids. *See also* virtual service oriented grids
　as building block, 124
　convergence of, 21–22, 31
　convergence of virtualization, service orientation, grids, 257–258
　definition of, 7
　parallelism, replication with, 9–11
　physical description of, 11–13
　research on, 255
　structure of, 7–8
　technology pedigrees for, xviii–xix
　use of term, 9
　X-engineering and, 39, 40
grid-thinking, 2
guest
　administration of VM guests, 188
　virtual machines, 128, 261
　virtualization transition and, 259
　virtualization usages, 130, 131

H

HaaS. *See* hardware as a service
hackers, 252
hard drive
    adding to computer, 110–111
    in computer-storage hierarchy, 112
    data associated with, 221
    latency at node level, 117
hardware
    costs, data centers and, 152
    evolution of, xviii, xix
    for high performance computing, 255
    physical grid, 97
    SOI roadblocks, 196
    virtual service oriented grid standards, 171–172
    virtualization support, 127
hardware as a service (HaaS)
    building platform, challenges of, 196
    characteristics of, 195–196
    definition of, 194
    emergence of, 179
hardware host, 74
harvesting, xvii, 255
HDTV, 222–223
healing, self-healing service, 145
healthcare servicelet, 272
help desk service, 219–220, 221
helper technologies, 133
Henry, Joseph, 232
Hertz, Heinrich, 232
Hicks, Diana, 285, 287–290
high availability
    load balancing, failover and, 132
    in server virtualization infrastructure, 189, 190
high performance computing (HPC)
    circle of applicability for, 50
    evolution of hardware for, 255
    evolution with emphasis on performance, 20
    grid ancestry rooted in, 147
    in grid genealogy diagram, 21
    grids for, 258

highly specialized component supplier, 289
Hillis, Danny, 36
home automation, 225, 226, 227
home IT service. *See* IT services to the home
home office, 229
host
    integration specific to, 105
    server consolidation, 130, 131, 132
    storage, data and, 250, 253
    support for virtualized environment, 259
    view of physical resources, xxv
    of virtual service oriented grid, xx, 108
    virtualization and, 20, 74, 106, 107
    virtualization by, 14–15
hot spots, 261
HPC. *See* high performance computing
Humana Inc., 35
hydro, 230, 246
Hyper Text Markup Language (HTML), xviii–xix, 167
Hyper Text Transport Protocol (HTTP), 167
hypervisor
    consolidation with, 106, 107
    deployment of, 185, 186
    free bare-metal x86 hypervisor, 127
    interoperability, standards and, 174
    management of, 188
    virtualization usage models, 129

I

IBM
    in computing history, 255
    development pipeline of, 83
    outsourcing for computers, 80–81
    savings with Internet use, 35
    7090 system, 207
    significant events in PC development history, 81–82
    Solectron and, 37
    Systems Network Architecture standard, 162
IBM System/360, 76–78, 80
IBM System/370, 76–77

ICE (internal combustion engine), 103–104
IDE (Integrated Drive Electronics), 113
identity mapping, 144
idle cycles, 147
IEC 61850, 240
IEC 61968, 240
IEC 61970, 240
IETF. *See* Internet Engineering Task Force
impedance match, 104
incremental approach, 273, 277–278
incremental nature
   of SOA, 270
   of virtual service oriented grids, 297–298
Independent System Operator (ISO), 234, 240
India
   Drishtee.com, 297
   salary levels in, 273
Industry Standard Architecture (ISA) bus, 82
InfiniBand
   to close architectural gap, 102
   to close latency gap, 118
   data transmission, 120
   for grid connection, 13
   as overlay technology for I/O, 113
   scale-out architecture, 115
information architecture, 134, 235
information modeling, 197
Information Power Grid (IPG), xvii
information technology (IT)
   architecture of electric power system, 230–247
   integration of IT solutions, 177–179
   IT services to the home, 213–229
   traditional IT infrastructure design, 179
information technology subsystem, 225–229
Infrastructure Maturity Model, Gartner, 19, 283
infrastructure services, 142
innovation
   serial innovators, 285
   by SMBs, 291
   taxonomy of small innovative firms, 287–290
innovator phase, 268, 269–270
inside-out SOA
   description of, 59
   servicelet market maturity model, 267–270
   SOA transformation, 61–62
   software "shims" addition, 27
   technology trend analysis for SOE framework, 28
insurance, 6, 216–218
Integrated Drive Electronics (IDE), 113
integration, 137. *See also* technology integration
integration cycles, 53
integration process, 176
integrators
   focus on local needs, 282
   future of virtual service oriented grids, 299
   roadblocks for SOI, 196
   transition to servicelet, 295
Intel Corporation
   in computing history, 255
   dual-core processors, 10
   recursively composable services, 15
   "white spaces" debate, 43
Intel Prescott, 10
Intel QuickPath™ Technology, 113
Intel Virtualization Technology (VT), 127
Intellectual Property Rights (IPR)
   corporate concern about, 278–279
   definition of, 163
   of industry consortia, 164
interconnect technology
   architecturally unbalanced system, 102
   in Composite Usage Model, 101
   for scale-out architecture, 115–120
interface
   service defined by, 17
   standard, for HaaS, 195

standard interfaces for service
  orientation, 137
standardized, 58, 251, 253
internal combustion engine (ICE), 103–104
International Electrotechnical Commission,
  240
International Standards Organization (ISO),
  90–91, 168–169
International Telecommunications Union,
  182
Internet
  as agent of change, 35–36
  disintermediation from, xxi
  ISO OSI model, 90–91
  logical layering, 35
  metering node as Internet gateway, 247
  Second Internet, transition to, 32
  service companies in China, 266
  standards for, 167
  X-engineering and, 37, 38–39
Internet client end point, 214
Internet download speed, 3
Internet Engineering Task Force (IETF)
  description of, mission of, 165
  relationships between standards
    organizations, 166
  standards defined by, 167
Internet gateway, 247
Internet Portal Data Center (IPDC),
  198–199
Internet service
  in China, 266
  for home IT infrastructure, 226
  mobile, 43
Internet Services Providers (ISPs), 250, 291
interoperability
  for adoption of virtual service oriented
    grid, 264
  cost benefits of, 57
  impetus for, 53
  SOI roadblock, 196
  standards for, 161–162, 163, 174
  for successful partner push, 183

target audience and, 180
  in virtual service oriented grid
    environment, xxi
  virtual service oriented grid standards,
    171
  of Web 2.0 technologies, 180–181
  X-engineering principle, 39
intertie, 238, 246
intra-grid, 100
Intuit, 198
IPDC (Internet Portal Data Center),
  198–199
IPG (Information Power Grid), xvii
IPR. *See* Intellectual Property Rights
ISA (Industry Standard Architecture) bus,
  82
Islands (of information), 216, 238, 246
ISO (Independent System Operator), 234,
  240
ISO (International Standards Organization),
  90–91, 168–169
ISO Open-EDI Reference Model, 168–169
ISO OSI model, 90–91
isolation
  enforcement by SOI, 193
  environment isolation usage model, 131,
    132
  security service for virtual service
    oriented grid, 145
ISPs (Internet Services Providers), 250, 291
IT. *See* information technology
IT departments
  decentralized virtual data centers,
    200–201
  requirements for, 175
  service orientation and, 135
  virtualization benefits for, 184–185
IT help desk service, 219–220
IT operations processes, 193
IT services, 48
IT services to the home
  application, data services, 221–224
  challenges of, 213–214

federated business services, 216–221
grid-thinking for, 2
utility monitoring, 214–216
virtual infrastructure services, 224–229

J
Japan, 2–3, 274
Jefferson, Thomas, 293

K
Kapor, Mitch, 73
keeps the business running (KTBR), 54–55
kiosk, 297
Kirchhoff, Gustav, 232
Korea, 2–3, 274
Korea Telecom, 199

L
Lagrange, Joseph Louis, 232
LAN (local area network), 113
Land's End, 44–45
Laplace, Pierre Simon de, 232
laptop
   as edge device, 295
   information delivery to, 275
   loss management service, 22–23, 248–251
late binding, 107
latency
   application engineering for latency tolerance, 269
   clusters and, 102
   computer node and, 9
   consolidation of data centers and, 157–158
   consumer facilitated storage and, 254
   grid nodes and, 12
   national grid strategy and, 277
   for scale-out architecture, 115–120
   visible grid requirement, 71
latency hiding, 117
layered framework, 89–96
layers
   of Composite Usage Model, 96–101
   logical layering, 34–35
   of standards, 168–173
   of virtual service oriented grids, 97–101
Lee, Wei-jen, xi–xiii
legacy
   adoption of SOA, 58–59
   cost of, 54
   integration with virtual service oriented grid, 123–124
   SOI and, 197
legal barriers, 276
level playing field
   for adoption of virtual service oriented grid, 270
   complex business climate for grids, 275
   with virtual service oriented grids, 264
library, 205–206, 207
licensing
   corporate grid adoption strategy and, 279
   of software, virtualization and, 178–179
   software licensing crisis, 211
   for virtual service oriented grid, 276
Life Sciences, layering in, 89
lifecycle, 143
Linden Labs, 41
LinkedIn, 181
linker, 205
load, 153. *See also* workload
load balancing
   service needed for virtual service oriented grid, 142
   by SOI, 193
   virtualization usage model, 132
load shedding, 236, 246
local area network (LAN), 113
local businesses, 266, 267
local market, 268
local needs, 274
locality of reference, 114
locally produced servicelets, 267
logging, secure, 144–145

logical isolation, 145, 193
logical layering, 34–35
Lone, Raymond, xix
long tail, 276, 281, 296
loose coupling
    pros/cons of, 203–204
    service oriented architectural tenet, 137
    servicelets of composite application, 265
Lucent, 250, 251

M

made to order, 207
Magnus, 232
main memory, 112
mainframes, 151
Malcolm Baldridge National Quality Award, 37
MAN (Metropolitan Area Network), 13
manageability
    for consumer facilitated storage, 252
    extended manageability technologies, 133
    features, 251
    latency and, 157
    PC system with features for, 103
    SOA design for, 139
    standards for, 171
Managed Service Provider (MSP), 69–72, 282–284
management
    of resources by SOI framework, 192–193
    service orientation design for manageability, 139
    of SOI, 197
    of virtualization, 187, 188–190
many-to-many relationship, 74
mapping
    identity, 144
    virtualization for, 106–109
mash-up
    for outside-in SOA transformation, 63
    of services, 58
    tipping point for adoption of grids, 219

Massachusetts Institute of Technology (MIT) Sloan Center for Information Systems Research (CISR), 19–20
Matrix, The, 293
mature industries, 53
maturity
    for business transformation, 32
    process maturity, 218
    signs of, 46
    specialization and, 70
    of technology, reuse and, 89
Maturity Model
    for adoption of virtual service oriented grids, 267–270
    Gartner Infrastructure Maturity Model, 19
    for managed services providers, 282–284
Maxwell, James Clerk, 232
MCA (Micro Channel Architecture) bus, 82
Media Exchange, 199
memory
    architecting computer for performance, 110–120
    in computer-storage hierarchy, 112
    CPU connection to, 113
    virtual memory, 126
mesh, 7
mesh networking, 243
message passing, 135
messaging
    reliability standards for, 172–173
    service orientation and, 134
    unified messaging model for service orientation, 137–138
messaging service fabric, 138
metadata
    for consumer facilitated storage, 254
    data services for virtual service oriented grid, 144
    MSPs and, 282
    for process maturity, 218
    semantic translation, 261–262
    standards for, 172

meta-model, 92
meter reading, 241–247
metering
   usage of VMs, 187
   utilization metering for virtual service oriented grid, 142
metering grid, 243–247
metering node, 244–245, 246, 247
Metropolitan Area Network (MAN), 13
Micro Channel Architecture (MCA) bus, 82
microprocessors, 75–82
microservice, xxi, 19
Microsoft Corporation
   cloud computing, 258
      IBM and, 82
      "white spaces" debate, 43
Microsoft Office Live, 198–199, 201, 258, 291
MID. *See* Mobile Internet Device
middleware, 206
Mind journal, 125
MIPS (millions of instructions per second), 254–255, 260
mission critical
   business applications, 147
   commodity servers and, 151
   enterprise grids support for, 149
   SOA transformation and, 62
mobile device
   demand for, 181–182
   standards for, 168
   transition to servicelet as building block, 295
Mobile Internet Device (MID)
   demand for, 181–182
   information delivery to, 275
   inside-out servicelets and, 27
modem, 222–223
modularity, 57
money. *See* costs; economics
money transfers, 68
monitoring
   facility monitoring, 189
   hardware devices for, 171
   home IT service, 214–216, 221
   of power circuits, 245
   by SOI, 193
   virtual service oriented grid standards, 171
monitoring device, 214
monitoring service, 142
monolithic
   application architecture, 135, 136
   CPU cycles for, 269
   reorganization of structure, 239
   services as not, 201
   solutions, 163
Monte Carlo simulations, 119
Moore's Law, xii
MOOSE spending, 155
Mosher, Edward, xix
movie analogy, 204–205
MSP (Managed Service Provider), 69–72, 282–284
Mulholland, Andy, 47
multi-core CPUs, 3
mutuality
   for adoption of virtual service oriented grid, 264
   for successful partner push, 183
   target audience and, 180
   X-engineering principle, 39
myths, of service orientation, 140

N

N-Able, 281, 283, 284
NAC (Network Access Control), 145
NAICS (North American Industry Classification), 287
NAS (network attached storage), 70, 253
National Federation of Independent Businesses (NFIB), 285
national strategy, 264–277
   in general, 264–267
   maturity model for adoption of grids, 267–270
   prescription for grid adoption, 270–276
   realism about, 276–277
   SMBs and, 291

Negroponte, Nicholas, 1
network
    for computing grid, 9
    grid, physical description of, 11–13
    IT subsystem for home, 225–229
    resources, 188
Network Access Control (NAC), 145
network attached storage (NAS), 70, 253
Network Interface Device (NID)
    data/cable TV integration with, 223, 224
    for home grid patch room, 225–226
"Network is the Computer, The", 293
network traffic
    latency of hard drive and, 117
    metering grid and, 247
    security management, 188
    SOI optimized to handle high volume, 192
    in virtualization usage model, 131
New United Motor Manufacturing Inc. (NUMMI), 275
Newton, Isaac, 232
NFIB (National Federation of Independent Businesses), 285
niche player
    demand for grid services, 101
    diversity of services, 72
    local opportunities, 275
    services for specific virtual markets, 201
    stovepipe paradigm and, 218
NID. See Network Interface Device
nodes
    in computer-storage hierarchy, 111, 112
    connecting technology for, 113
    cycle scavenging, 255–256
    electric meters as, 243, 247
    examples of, 11–13
    as generic name for bus bar, 7
    grid computation and, 9
    in grid structure, 8
    in hierarchical usage model, 92
    latency, 117
    management software, problem with, 102
    of physical grid, visible grid, 99–100
    of visible grid, 97

nonfunctional capabilities, xx–xxi
North American Industry Classification (NAICS), 287
NUMMI (New United Motor Manufacturing Inc.), 275

O
OASIS. See Organization for the Advancement of Structured Information Standards
OEM. See Original Equipment Manufacturer
Oersted, Hans Christian, 232
OGA (Open Grid Architecture), 173
OGSA. See Open Grid Services Architecture
Ohm, Georg Simon, 232
Olsen, Kenneth, xi–xii, 161
OMA. See Open Mobile Alliance
OnStar, 274
Open Grid Architecture (OGA), 173
Open Grid Forum (OGF)
    description of, mission of, 165
    Open Grid Architecture from, 173
    standards defined by, 167
Open Grid Services Architecture (OGSA)
    development of, 167
    grid computing standard, 146
    services for, 141
Open Mobile Alliance (OMA)
    description of, mission of, 165
    relationship with other standards organizations, 166
    standards defined by, 168
Open-EDI Reference Model, 168–169
openness
    for adoption of virtual service oriented grid, 264
    for successful partner push, 183
    target audience and, 180
    X-engineering principle, 39
operating cost, 17. See also costs; total cost of ownership
operating system (OS)
    historical computer design and, 76–77

virtualization usage models, 129
with/without virtualization, 127–128
operation tool, 189–190
OPM (other people's money), 4
OPS (other people's systems), 4–6
optimization
    of application, 105
    automation tools for, 189
    self-optimizing service, 145
orchestration, 192
Organization for the Advancement of Structured Information Standards (OASIS)
    description of, mission of, 165
    ebXML Registry Information Model, 172
    relationships between standards organizations, 166
    standards defined by, 167, 173
organizations. *See* standards consortia
Original Equipment Manufacturer (OEM)
    automobile manufacturers, 183
    IBM computers in OEM industry, 80
    silos in industry, 42
OS. *See* operating system
OS-neutral, 127
other people's money (OPM), 4
other people's systems (OPS), 4–6
outage, 240, 246
outside-in SOA
    decentralized virtual data center and, 200–201
    description of, 58–59
    Managed Service Provider example, 69–72
    scalability of SOA in, 202
    size of organization and, 184
    SOA transformation, 62–66
    technology trend analysis for SOE framework, 28
outside-out model, 27
outsourcing
    data centers and, 158
    effect of, 55
    federated technology development and, 87
    overhead for outsourced services, 273–274
servicelet, 298
storage, 70–71
virtual service oriented grids as ultimate form of, 202
Overby, Stephanie, 279–280
overhead
    for outsourced services, 273–274
    run time, for loosely coupled systems, 204
    of scoreboarding, 14

P

PaaS (platform as a service), 179
parallel nodes, 12
parallelism
    grid computing, 9
    for improved performance, 121
    overhead with, 10–11
partitioning, 256, 257
partner "push", 182–183
patch room, 225–226
pay-as-you-go system, 211
pay-for-performance, 88
PayPal, 68, 271
PC (personal computer). *See also* computer
    computation resources, demand for, 51
    information delivery to, 275
    node example, 11–12
    revolution, 296
PC grid
    description of, 20
    in grid genealogy diagram, 21
PDA. *See* Personal Digital Assistant
PDP-11 line, Digital Equipment Corporation, 78–80
peer-to-peer communication, 117–118
performance
    architecture balance and, 102
    balanced grid architecture for, 109–120
    grid computing challenge, 150
    outside-in SOA challenges, 67
    replication for, 10

utilization factor, 105
virtualization continuum and, 108–109
Personal Digital Assistant (PDA)
   demand for, 181
   as edge device, 295
   information delivery to, 275
   inside-out servicelets and, 27
   mobile standards for, 168
   remote handheld controller, 227
personal information, 1
phasor analysis, 223
physical environment, 141
physical grid
   economic impact of, 102–103
   in layering system for virtual service oriented grid, 98
   requirements from visible grid, 99
   standards, 171
   usage attributes, 101
   use of term, 97
physical infrastructure, 156
physical mapping, 106–107
physical requirements, 23
physical resources, 184
pilots, 275
pipeline
   distributed development pipeline, 83–85
   federated technology development for, 87
   in FTD today, 83–85
   in historical FTD, 75–78, 80–81, 82
planning, 270. *See also* capacity planning
platform as a service (PaaS), 179
point device, 214
Poisson, Simeon Dennis, 232
policies, 195, 197
Pontiac, 46
Porter, Michael, 287
power. *See also* electric power system
   power transfer of ICE engine, 103–104
   utility computing infrastructure and, 155–156
power consumption
   by servers, 152
   standards for, 171
   virtual service oriented grids and, 258–262
power density
   data centers and, 152
   virtual service oriented grids and, 260–261
power grid, 146
Poynting, John, 232
predictions, 88
Predictive Enterprise, 24, 25
privacy
   enforcement, 145, 193
   outside-in SOA challenges, 67
problem diagnosis, 142, 193
problem solving, 9
process, 31. *See also* business process
process abstraction, 105–106
process maturity, 217, 218
processors, 10–11. *See also* central processing unit
procurement
   dynamic behaviors and, 107
   online, 35
   server deployment, 151
producer phase, 268, 269
product solutions provider, 290
protocol
   for clusters, 12
   functional service view, 169
   in grid computing, 146
   for grid connectivity, 11, 13
   interoperability, 99
   for interoperability, 171
   for new services, xxi
   for outside-in SOA, 67
   for RTUs, 134
   security, 172, 204
   for service orientation, 137
   transaction standards, 173
   Web services/grid computing standard consortia, 165, 167
prototype, 288

provisioning
    automated provisioning tools, 154
    bare metal, 192
    commodity servers, 151
    computer with hard drive, 110–111
    dedicated physical servers approach, 152
    execution environment, 143
    HaaS, 196
    hardware devices for, 171
    laptop to "phone home", 248
    new server, 107
    in OGSA approach, 141
    over-provisioning, 153
    self-configuring services and, 145
    server utilization and, 147
    by SOI, 192
    speed of, 43
    for virtual service oriented grid, 142
    virtualization infrastructure and, 186, 188, 208
Public Utility Holding Company Act, 223–224
publication, of SOI service, 197
pull, customer, 38–39, 180–182
push
    partner "push", 182–183
    in X-engineering, 38–39

Q

quality of service (QoS)
    as binding mechanism, 17
    for electric power industry, 235–236
    management for virtual service oriented grid, 142
    monitoring of individual power circuits, 245
    outside-in SOA challenges, 67
    over-provisioning, 153
    resource allocation and, 147
Qwest, 242

R

R&D organization or contractor, 288
radio, 225
radio frequency identification (RFID)
    adoption by Wal-Mart, 183
    inside-out servicelets and, 27
    for meter reading, 242
reaggregation, xxii
recovery service, 251. *See also* disaster recovery
recursion, 15–16
redundancy, 11
Reengineering the Corporation (Champy), 37
Reflection on the Revolution of France (Burke), 123
registration, 138
regulations
    adoption of SOA for compliance, 58
    governance in federated environment, 85–87
    outside-in SOA challenges, 67
reintermediation, xxi
relationships
    alteration of, 298
    partner "push", 182–183
reliability
    grid computing challenge, 150
    mutuality principle and, 39
    service orientation and, 40
    silo architecture and, 43
    standards, 172–173
    of storage device, 220
remote access, 143
remote handheld controller, 227
remote terminal units (RTUs), 134, 238
repeatable process, 280
replication
    for availability, 11
    data services for virtual service oriented grid, 143
    for performance, 10
    scale-out architecture through, 115

through coordination of distributed resources, 75
resource allocation, 143, 188
resource consumption, 209
resource discovery, 171
resource management, 171
resource management services, 142
resource orchestration, 138–139
resource outsourcing, 4
resource pooling, 31, 108
resources. *See also* virtual resources
    delayed binding, 202–204
    fungibility of, 158
    in OGSA approach, 141
    service orientation design for, 138–139
    standards for, 173
    virtualization for reuse of, 184
results, early, 273
return on investment (ROI)
    dot-com crash and, xv
    grid computing and, 4, 147
reusable components, 40, 137
reuse
    as building block principle, 123
    for cost reduction, 89
    economics of service orientation, 54, 56, 57
    loose coupling with service orientation, 137
    SOA adoption in SMB space, 64
    in SOA transformation, 60
    virtualization for, 184
RF (royalty free), 163–164
RFID. *See* radio frequency identification
RISC-based hosts, 151
roadblocks, 97
ROI. *See* return on investment
Rosenblum, Mendel, 126–127
RosettaNet, 182–183
router
    in computing grid, 8
    embedded nodes, 12
    in home IT system, 223, 226
    RTUs as, 134
royalty free (RF), 163–164
RTUs (remote terminal units), 134, 238
R.W. Beck Inc., 243

S

S3 (Simple Storage Service), 41
SaaS. *See* software as a service
salary levels, 273
Salesforce.com, 198
SAML (Security Assertion Markup Language), 172
Samsung Electronics, 43
Samsung Micro-Electronics, 43
SAN. *See* storage area network
Sandia Red Storm system, 102
scalability
    data centers and, 158
    of service orientation, 58–72, 202
    standards for, 174
    tightly coupled architecture and, 203
scale-out, 115–120
scale-up, 112, 114
scavenging. *See* cycle scavenging
scavenging grids, 149
schema
    data transformation into XML format, 27
    messaging, 134
    XML Schema, 172
science linked knowledge, 286
science-based product/service firms, 288
scoreboarding, 14
SCSI (Small Computer System Interface), 113
Second Internet, 32
security
    administrative tools for, 188
    data center security, 187
    enforcement by SOI, 193
    facility monitoring/control, 189
    grid challenge, 150
    home IT infrastructure functions, 216
    infrastructure, 190

laptop loss management service, 22–23,
    248–251
  of metering grid, 247
  in OGSA approach, 141
  outside-in SOA challenges, 67
  services security standards, 172
  theft/loss of personal information, 1
  in virtual infrastructure, 208–209
  of virtual service oriented grids, xxiv–xxv
Security Assertion Markup Language
    (SAML), 172
security management, 188, 215
security policy enforcement, 145
security service
  home IT service, 221
  for virtual service oriented grid, 144–145
self interest, enlightened, 264
self-configuring service, 145
self-describing applications, 135
self-healing service, 145
self-management services, 145
self-optimizing service, 145
semantic translation, 261–262
sensor network, 246
serial innovators
  description of, 285
  SMBs and grids, 291
  taxonomy of small innovative firms,
    287–290
serialization, 83
server
  consolidation virtualization usage model,
    129–132
  in data center, 12, 150–155
  energy consumption of, 259
  for home IT infrastructure, 226
  in initial siloed state, 59–61
  MSP maturity model and, 282–283
  utilization, grid evolution and, 147
  virtual infrastructure example, 208–210
  virtual infrastructure, transition to,
    185–190
  virtualization, workload reduction from,
    256–257
  virtualization adoption and, 184–185
  virtualization continuum, 105–109
server consolidation, 129–132
server farm
  diagram of, 186
  planning virtualization infrastructure,
    187–188
  security infrastructure for, 190
server sprawl
  from commodity servers, 259
  decentralized virtual data centers instead
    of, 198
  description of, 152–153
service. *See also* Web services
  abstractions, 195
  adoption of SOA, outside-in model,
    58–59
  atoms of service, 45–46
  in inside-out SOA transformation, 61–62
  in Managed Service Provider example,
    71–72
  needed for virtual service oriented grids,
    141–145
  outside-in SOA transformation, 62–66
  service component, building, xxi–xxiii
  service oriented architectural tenets,
    136–140
service fabric, 138
service grid, 138–139
service integrators, 59
service level agreement (SLA)
  as binding mechanism, 17
  in compound applications, xxii
  for data services for consumer, 222
  service parameters codified in, 201
  virtualization and, 107, 108
service orientation
  architectural tenets, 136–140
  benefits of, 135–136, 211
  as building block for virtual service
    oriented grid, 124
  business transformation with, 157

in computing infrastructure, 191–197
convergence of, 21–22, 31
convergence of virtualization, service orientation, grids, 257–258
description of, 15–20
distance between people, technology, business processes, 294
economics of, 54–57
evolution of, 134
history of, xvi–xvii
myths, 140
other people's systems, use of, 4–6
of physical infrastructure, 156
scalability of, 202
services needs for virtual service oriented grids, 141–145
technology pedigrees for, xviii–xix
X-engineering and, 39–40
service oriented architecture (SOA)
    adoption of, xiii
    benefits of, 134–135
    collaborative business model under, 175
    compound applications, 18
    convergence of virtualization, service orientation, grids, 257–258
    definition of, 17
    description of, 17–18
    for electric power industry, 241
    flexibility, abstraction with, 191
    hardware as a service, 194–196
    incremental nature of, 270, 273
    initial siloed state, 59–61
    inside-out or conventional SOA, 61–62
    Managed Service Provider example, 69–72
    for next generation in enterprise computing, 156–158
    outside-in model of adoption of, 58–59
    outside-in SOA, 62–66
    outside-in SOA, challenges for, 67–69
    scalability of, 58–72, 202
    SOI framework, 191–194
    transformation toward, 19–20
    X-engineering and, 40
service oriented enterprise (SOE)
    FBS implementation of, 25
    SOI framework, 191–194
    technology trend analysis for, 28
    virtual service oriented grids as, 24
service oriented infrastructure (SOI)
    framework, 191–192, 194
    hardware as a service, 194–196
    tasks of, 192–193
    technical roadblocks for, 196–197
service oriented management (SOM), 193, 195
Service Oriented Providers (SOPs)
    description of, 51–52
    diagram of, 52
    observations about, 53
service providers
    gains from outside-in SOA environment, 65–66
    Managed Service Provider example, 69–72
    outside-in SOA challenges, 67–69
service registry, 68
service repository, 19
service solutions provider, 290
servicelet
    benefits of, 211
    as building unit for compound application, 19
    corporate grid adoption strategy, 277–280
    development of, xxi–xxiii
    for electric power industry, 235–240
    inside-out, 27
    integration of IT solutions, 177
    in Managed Service Provider example, 71–72
    market maturity model, 267–270
    for national grid adoption strategy, 264–265, 270–272
    realism about, 276–277
    for SMBs, 281–282

storage in virtual service oriented grid, 252–254
in structure of virtual service oriented grid, 24–25
testing, 280
use of term, xxi
virtual service oriented grids today, 295–299
Web 2.0 technologies, 180–182
SETI@home, 11
set-top unit, 222
SGML (Standard Generalized Markup Language), xviii–xix
shareable service, 138
shims, 156
signal splitter, 222
silo
    breaking of, 43–46
    of electric utility industry, 234
    in industry, 42–43
    initial siloed state, 59–61
    merging of silos, rise of collaboration, 43–53
    shared stack components, 46–47
    from silos to network of services, 48–50
siloed environments, 53, 203, 294
Simple Object Access Protocol (SOAP)
    standards for, 167
    virtual service oriented grid standards, 172
    Web services standard, 137, 168
Simple Storage Service (S3), 41
Simula language, xvi–xvii
Sina, 266
single supplier pipeline model, 80–81
single-instruction, multiple data (SIMD), xviii, xix
single-instruction, single-data (SISD), xviii, xix
Skype, 295
SLA. See service level agreement
small and medium business (SMB)
    adoption of SOA, 58–59

grid-thinking for, 2
Managed Service Provider example, 69–72
maturity model for MSPs, 282–284
opportunities from distributed computing, 296–297
outside-in SOA challenges, 67–69
outside-in SOA transformation, 62–66
as providers/consumers of services, 300
scalability of SOA, 202
strategy, 263, 281–291
Small Business Administration, 59, 281
Small Computer System Interface (SCSI), 113
Smalltalk language, xvi–xvii
smart electric meters, 241–247
SMB. See small and medium business
SNA (Systems Network Architecture), 162
SOA. See service oriented architecture
SOAP. See Simple Object Access Protocol
social component, 180–181
SOE. See service oriented enterprise
software
    corporate grid adoption strategy and, 278–279
    delayed binding, 205–207
    history of, 177
    for home IT infrastructure, 218–219
    licensing, 178–179, 211
    optimization of, 105
    package software, 177–178
    SOI roadblocks, 196
software as a service (SaaS)
    for decentralized virtual data centers, 198
    emergence of, 179
    opportunity for change with, 278
    standards for, 171
    virtual data centers and, 199–200
Software Engineering Institute, 283
software service vendor, 71
software "shims", 27
software technology attributes, 101, 102
SOI. See service oriented infrastructure

Solectron, 37, 182
solution stacks
    in Managed Service Provider example, 70
    need for, 41–43
    shared stack components, 46–47
SOM (service oriented management), 193, 195
SOM (System Object Model), 206
SOPs. *See* Service Oriented Providers
source file, 205
South Korea, 3
Southern Pacific Railroad, 242
speakers, audio, 104
specialization, 70
specialized subcontractor firm, 289
Sperry Univac, 255
Sprint-Secure Laptop Guardian, 250
stability
    of electric grid, 241
    of HaaS platform, 196
    metering grid and, 246
    of power system, 234, 236
    service design for, 137
    of virtualization, 127
stacks
    layered framework for usage models, 89–96
    shared stack components, 46–47
    silo breaking, 44
    from silos to network of services, 48–50
    solution stacks, need for, 41–43
Standard Generalized Markup Language (SGML), xviii–xix
standard interfaces, 137, 195
standardization
    of business process, 68
    for level playing field, 183
standardized interfaces
    laptop loss management service and, 251
    pooling of storage resources, 253
    SOA conversion, 58
standards
    for adoption of virtual service oriented grid, 264
    domains of standards, relationships of, 168–173
    evolution of standardization, 162–164
    for grid computing, 146
    for interoperability, 161–162
    standard consortia landscape, 164–168
    trends, challenges for development of, 174
    Web services standards, 196, 240
standards consortia
    in general, 164
    list of, 165
    relationships between, 166–168
    standardization, evolution of, 162, 163–164
    trends, challenges for development of standards, 174
standards-based network, 7
Steinmetz, Charles P., 223
storage
    architecting computer for performance, 110–120
    data services for consumer, 222
    future of, 6
    home IT service, 220
    for laptop loss management service, 248–251
    outsourcing, 70–71
    replication for availability, 11
    in virtual service oriented grid environment, 252–254
    virtualized, 185
storage aggregators, 71
storage area network (SAN)
    data availability, disaster recovery with, 70
    as overlay technology for I/O, 113
    for virtualized storage, 185
storage service
    anonymous, 250
    in computer-storage hierarchy, 112
    Elastic Computing Cloud, 182
    for home IT services, 213–214, 220, 222, 224
    latency and, 277

in virtual infrastructure, 208
in virtual service oriented grid
 environment, 252
stovepipe
 expense of, 218
 initial siloed state, 59–60
 traditional application, 61
supercomputer
 communication of nodes in, 9
 cost of, 8
 laptop and, 108–109
supervisory control and data acquisition
 (SCADA) system, 238, 240
suppliers, 80–81. *See also* vendors
system, 33–34
System Object Model (SOM), 206
systems integrator, 81
Systems Network Architecture (SNA), 162
systems thinking, 49

T
Taiwan, 274
tamper-resistant
 security mechanisms, 67
 servers, xxiv
 virtualization configuration, 133
target audience, 179–180
Tata Industries, 276
TCO. *See* total cost of ownership
TCP/IP (Transmission Control Protocol/
 Internet Protocol), 13, 167
technical community, 100
technical usage models. *See* visible grid
 technicians, 92–96
technology
 adoption in social/economic context, 32
 criteria for adoption of, 280
 effect of introducing new, 56
 emergence/utilization of, xi–xiii
 federated technology development,
  75–82
 integration of technology, people,
  processes, 293–294

standardization, evolution of, 162–164
 tradable, 285–286
technology integration
 decentralized virtual data centers,
  198–201
 delayed binding, as useful paradigm,
  202–204
 delayed binding for deployment
  flexibility, 204–207
 integration of IT solutions, 177–179
 IT departments, requirements for, 175
 patterns of, 210–211
 selection of units of, 176
 service orientation in computing
  infrastructure, 191–197
 service orientation, scalability of, 202
 virtual infrastructure example, 208–210
 in virtual service oriented grid ecosystem,
  179–183
 virtualization in utility computing
  infrastructure, 183–185
 virtualization infrastructure, 185–190
Telecom, 225, 291
telephone, 227. *See also* cell phone
Tencent, 199, 265, 266, 282
Tesla, Nikola, 223
testing
 of outside-in SOA, 68
 of service, 201
 servicelets, 280
Thales of Miletos, 232
Third Internet, 32
Thirty Years' War, 33
Thomson, Elihu, 241
three-tier, 126, 151, 184
tightly coupled architecture, 203, 206
time, 53, 66
time of day billing, 235, 236, 242
time to market, 206–207, 296
time to solution, 29–30, 108–109
tipping point, 44, 219
torque, 103–104
total cost of ownership (TCO)
 for computing equipment, 258

cost of electricity and, 105, 259
electricity cost in, 152
reductions with virtualization, 133
Tower of Babel, 162
Toyota, 34, 46
TPM (trusted platform module), 23, 250
tradable technology, 285–286
traffic. *See* network traffic
transaction standards, 173
transformation. *See* business transformation
transformer
in electric power system, 230, 231
impedance match and, 104
transmission, 104
Transmission Control Protocol/Internet Protocol (TCP/IP), 13, 167
transmission line
computer models and, 235
in electric power system, 7, 230, 231
rights of way for, 234, 241
transparency, 211, 271
trusted platform module (TPM), 23, 250
Turing, Alan M., 125
TV service, 222–224, 226

U

ubiquity, 137
UDDI (Universal Description Discovery and Integration), 19, 167
ultra mobile PCs (UMPCs), 27
undifferentiated phase, 267, 268
United States
slower adoption of newer technologies, 2–3
small businesses in, 281
United States Army, 177
Universal Description Discovery and Integration (UDDI), 19, 167
universities, 275
University of Wisconsin, 5, 255
unshielded, twisted pair (UTP) cable, 113
U.S. Department of Veterans Affairs, 1
USA Today, 3

usage attributes, 101–103
usage models, 129–133. *See also* composite usage model
USB, 222
utility computing infrastructure
benefits of, 154–155
as next generation of enterprise computing, 155–158
service orientation in, 191–197
virtualization in, 183–185
utility management, 215, 222, 243–244
utility monitoring, 214–216
utilization, 153
utilization factor, 105, 269
utilization metering, 142
UTP (unshielded, twisted pair) cable, 113

V

validation, 68
value, 87–88
Value-Chain Operation Reference (VCOR), 183
vendors
gains from outside-in SOA, 65
of packaged software, 177–179
service orientation for innovation, 135–136
SOI roadblocks, 196
standards for interoperability, 161–162, 174
vertical feeders, 91
vertically integrated
electric utilities as, 234
Ford Motor Company as, 49
information systems, 162
insurance companies, 218
servicelets and, 72
solution stacks, 70
verticals, industry, 41–42
very large scale integration (VLSI), xvi
Vietnam, 274
virtual appliances, 133
virtual computer, 146

virtual data masters, 27
virtual domains, 141
virtual environments, 138–139
virtual fabric tool, 190
Virtual Infrastructure Services (VIS)
   home IT infrastructure, 224–229
   in layered usage model for grids, 98
   in virtual service oriented grid structure, 24, 25, 26–27
virtual machine monitor (VMM)
   diagram of, 128
   environment isolation usage model, 131
   function of, 127
   server consolidation usage model, 130
virtual machine sprawl, 259
virtual machines (VMs)
   energy usage and, 259–262
   service orientation design and, 138–139
   virtual infrastructure, transition to, 185–190
   in virtualization infrastructure, 127–128
   virtualization usage models, 129–133
virtual memory, 14–15, 126
virtual organizations, 100
virtual resources
   capacity planning, 193
   definition of, 126
   management of, 142, 188
   physical resources and, xxv
   pool of, 133, 139
   release back to resource pool, 143
   service orientation and, 138
   VMM between physical resources and, 127
virtual service oriented grid convergence
   capability, process, maturity in business transformation, 32–41
   economics of service orientation, 54–57
   in general, 31
   merging of silos, rise of collaboration, 43–53
   scalability of service oriented architecture, 58–72
   solution stacks, need for, 41–43
virtual service oriented grid environment/architecture
   architectural balance, 120–121
   composite usage models, 87–103
   essential properties, 73–75
   federated technology development, 75–87
   virtualization continuum, 103–120
virtual service oriented grid strategies
   corporate strategy, 277–280
   in general, 263–264
   national strategy, 264–277
   for small businesses, 281–291
virtual service oriented grids, building blocks for
   data center, commoditization of, 150–155
   grid computing, 146–150
   next generation of enterprise computing, 155–158
   overview of, 123–124
   service orientation, 134–145
   transition toward VSGs, 159
   virtualization, 125–133
virtual service oriented grids, emergence of
   end points for, 29–30
   grid, structure of, 7–8
   grids, overview of, 8–11
   grids, physical description of, 11–13
   laptop loss management service, 22–23
   other people's systems, use of, 4–6
   PC grids, data center grids, 20–22
   principle behind, 1–4
   service orientation, 15–20
   structure of, 24–29
   virtualization, 14–15
virtual service oriented grids (VSGs). *See also* case studies; technology integration
   balanced grid architecture, 109–120
   composite usage model applied to, 96–101
   future of, 299–300
   industry example, xxiii–xxv
   integration of technology, people, processes, 293–294

nonfunctional capabilities, xx–xxi
resources deployed in, xx
service atoms of, 45–46
standard consortia landscape, 164–168
standards, domains of, 168–173
technology integration, 179–183
today, 294–299
use of, xix
virtualization continuum in, 103–120
virtualization
as building block, 124
convergence of, 21–22, 31
convergence of virtualization, service orientation, grids, 257–258
description of, 14–15
Diane Greene on, 213
evolution of, 125–128
history of, xvi
many-to-many relationship, 74
other people's systems, use of, 4–6
platform with/without, 129
by SOI, 192
technology pedigrees for, xviii–xix
transition to virtualization infrastructure, 185–190
in utility computing infrastructure, 183–185
utilization transformation, xii
virtualization usage models, 129–133
workload reduction with, 256–257
X-engineering and, 39, 40
virtualization continuum
application workloads, server performance and, 105–109
audio electronics analogy, 104
automobile analogy, 103–104
balanced grid architecture, 109–120
force and workload relationship, 103
virtualization infrastructure, 185–190, 208–210
virtualization technology
emergence of, 125
grid integration with, 257–258
Intel Virtualization Technology, 127

outside-in SOA with, 202
virtualized services, 139, 299
VIS. *See* Virtual Infrastructure Services
visible grid
in layering system for virtual service oriented grid, 98
nodes in, 100
requirements for, 99
usage attributes, 101
use of term, 97
virtual service oriented grid standards, 170–171
VLSI (very large scale integration), xvi
VMM. *See* virtual machine monitor
VMotion, 187
VMs. *See* virtual machines
VMWare
Consolidated Backup, 190
HA, 190
virtualization products, 126–127
VMotion, 187
VOIP phone, 227
volatile memory, 110
Volta, Alessandro, 232
voltage
AC systems and, 223
in audio electronics analogy, 104
measure of pressure, 230
VSGs. *See* virtual service oriented grids

W

W3C. *See* World Wide Web Consortium
Wachowski brothers, 293
Wal-Mart, 183
WAN (Wide Area Network), 13
water management, 215–216
Watson, Thomas J., xi, 49
Web 2.0
demand from, 180–182
service orientation and, 135, 191
virtual data centers and, 199
virtual service oriented grids as, 24
worldview philosophy of, 51

Web 3.0, 135
Web Service Description Language (WSDL)
    for hardware interoperability, 172
    service discovery, 19
    Web services standard, 137, 167, 168
Web Services Interoperability (WS-I)
    description of, mission of, 165
    relationships between standards organizations, 166
    standards defined by, 167
Web services (WS)
    adding front ends in SOA transformation, 60
    for electric meter reading, 243–245
    for electric power industry, 240
    for hardware interoperability, 172
    interoperability of, 207
    name for ADS, 25
    service orientation and, 134–135
    SOA adoption in SMB space, 64
    standard consortia landscape, 164–168
    standard interfaces for service orientation, 137
    standards for, 163, 196
    technology to invoke service, 19
Web-based Enterprise Management (WEBM), 167
Web-based solutions, 163
Westinghouse, George, 223
"white spaces" debate, 43
white zombie, 252–254
Wide Area Network (WAN), 13
Wi-Fi
    in hierarchical usage model, 91
    for home IT infrastructure, 225, 228
    for laptop loss management service, 248
    for metering grid, 243
WiMAX
    for home IT infrastructure, 225, 226
    for laptop loss management service, 22, 23, 248
    for metering grid, 243
wind, 155, 230, 237, 246

wired
    Internet over wired networks, 90–91
    laptop connection to wired Ethernet, 248
    laptops, 295
    metering node as gateway, 90–91
wireless
    access points, 12
    laptop connection, 22, 248, 249, 250, 295
    metering node as gateway, 247
wiretapping, 264
workflow automation, 143
working set, 114
workload
    of compute engine, 74
    force, relationship to, 103–109
    virtualization continuum, 103–109
    virtualization for load balancing, failover, 132
    virtualization to reduce, 256
workstation
    cycle scavenging, 11, 255–256
    grids allowed use of less expensive, 8
    scavenging grids, 149
    sharing of idle workstations, 5, 50
    usage model and, 99
World is the Computer, The, 293
World Wide Web
    growth of Internet after, 35
    technology pedigrees for service orientation, xviii–xix
World Wide Web Consortium (W3C)
    description of, mission of, 165
    relationships between standards organizations, 165
    standards defined by, 167
WS. See Web services
WS Business Process Execution Language (WS-BPEL), 167, 173
WS Resource Framework (WSRF), 173
WS-Atomic Transaction, 173
WS-Basic Profile, 167
WS-Coordination, 173

WSDL. *See* Web Service Description Language
WS-I. *See* Web Services Interoperability
WS-MakeConnection (WS-MC), 173
WS-Management, 167
WS-ReliableMessaging (WS-RM), 173
WS-Security, 167, 172
WS-Security Profile, 167
WS-Transaction, 173
WS-Trust, 167, 172

X

x86 microprocessor, 126–127
X-engineering
    for change, 36–37
        by Dell, 38–39
        implementation principles of, 39–41
        Solectron example, 37
X-Engineering the Corporation (Champy), 37
X-Engineering Transformation (Champy), 38
XML. *See* Extended Markup Language
XML DTD (Data Type Definitions), 172
XML Schema, 172
XML Web services, 70
XSLT (Extended Stylesheet Language), 172

Y

Yahoo, 182, 201
YouTube, 181

Z

zombie, 252–254

Continuing Education is Essential

It's a challenge we all face – keeping pace with constant change in information technology. Whether our formal training was recent or long ago, we must all find time to keep ourselves educated and up to date in spite of the daily time pressures of our profession.

Intel produces technical books to help the industry learn about the latest technologies. The focus of these publications spans the basic motivation and origin for a technology through its practical application.

Right books, right time, from the experts

These technical books are planned to synchronize with roadmaps for technology and platforms, in order to give the industry a head-start. They provide new insights, in an engineer-to-engineer voice, from named experts. Sharing proven insights and design methods is intended to make it more practical for you to embrace the latest technology with greater design freedom and reduced risks.

I encourage you to take full advantage of Intel Press books as a way to dive deeper into the latest technologies, as you plan and develop your next generation products. They are an essential tool for every practicing engineer or programmer. I hope you will make them a part of your continuing education tool box.

Sincerely,

Justin Rattner
Senior Fellow and Chief Technology Officer
Intel Corporation

Turn the page to learn about titles from Intel Press for system developers

ESSENTIAL BOOKS ABOUT IT BEST PRACTICES

Service Oriented Architecture Demystified
A pragmatic approach to SOA for the IT executives

By Girish Juneja, Blake Dournaee, Joe Natoli, and Steve Birkel
ISBN 1-934053-02-3

The authors of this definitive book on SOA debunk the myths and demonstrate through examples from different vertical industries how a "crawl, walk, run" approach to deployment of SOA in an IT environment can lead to a successful return on investment.

One popular argument states that SOA is not a technology per se, but that it stands alone and can be implemented using a wide range of technologies. The authors believe that this definition, while attractive and elegant, doesn't necessarily pass pragmatic muster.

Service Oriented Architecture Demystified describes both the technical and organizational impacts of adopting SOA and the pursuant challenges. The authors demonstrate through real life deployments why and how different industry sectors are adopting SOA, the challenges they face, the advantages they have realized, and how they have (or have not) addressed the issues emerging from their adoption of SOA. This book strikes a careful balance between describing SOA as an enabler of business processes and presenting SOA as a blueprint for the design of software systems in general. Throughout the book, the authors attempt to cater to both technical and organizational viewpoints, and show how both are very different in terms of why SOA is useful. The IT software architect sees SOA as a business process enabler and the CTO sees SOA as a technology trend with powerful paradigms for software development and software integration.

SOA can be characterized in terms of different vertical markets. For each such market, achieving SOA means something different and involves different transformational shifts. The vertical markets covered include healthcare, government, manufacturing, finance, and telecommunications. SOA considerations are quite different across these vertical markets, and in some cases, the required organizational shifts and technology shifts are highly divergent and context dependent.

Whether you are a CTO, CIO, IT manager, or IT architect, this book provides you with the means to analyze the readiness of your internal IT organization and with technologies to adopt a service oriented approach to IT.

ESSENTIAL BOOKS ABOUT IT BEST PRACTICES

Managing IT Innovation for Business Value
Practical Strategies for IT and Business Managers

By *Esther Baldwin and Martin Curley*
ISBN 1-934053-04-X

Successful companies actively cultivate new ideas, put those ideas to work quickly and efficiently, and harvest the business value benefits of successful innovations. Discussions of innovation often focus on what a company offers, that is, its products and services. In *Managing Information Technology Innovation for Business Value*, Esther Baldwin and Martin Curley show how successful IT innovations pay back handsomely as well. Innovation is not just about what a company offers, innovation is also about how a company conducts business and how IT innovation can transform an organization into a significantly more efficient company.

Drawing on their experience with innovation in Intel's engineering operations, Baldwin and Curley emphasize that IT innovation does not require whole-scale invention. An innovative IT solution reapplied in a new context can provide even greater business value because the initial investment in developing the solution has already been made.

Managing Information Technology Innovation for Business Value includes examples and case studies from IT organizations as well as from Intel Corporation. It also includes assessment techniques, skill set descriptions, and a capability maturity framework to help IT organizations understand where they stand as innovators and what steps they can take to strengthen their competencies.

❝ Innovation is not just about new products and services. It's also about how an innovative organization conducts business practices and the invaluable role of IT in those processes. For innovation to 'stick' it must become a systemic mindset like quality and safety. *Managing Information Technology Innovation for Business Value* offers invaluable and fresh stories that can be applied to any size IT organization. ❞ -
Charles Chic Thompson, Batten Fellow at the UVA Darden Business School

❝ What can a small-medium business (SMB) learn from the IT experts at Intel? Some common-sense lessons on IT innovation management. Innovation can be incremental, for example, and a proven innovation can be re-applied over and over in new and different settings. That's a key message for those of us who serve the SMB market. ❞ — Mathew Dickerson, AXXIS Technology, Australia.

ESSENTIAL BOOKS ABOUT IT BEST PRACTICES

Managing Information Technology for Business Value
Practical Strategies for IT and Business Managers

By Martin Curley
ISBN 0-9717861-7-8

Managing Information Technology for Business Value is Martin Curley's call for IT and business planners to reformulate the way they manage IT. Traditionally, IT success has been measured in terms of internal IT systems parameters, such as availability, capacity, and processing speed.

It is Curley's contention that if IT is to deliver business value, then IT should be measured in core business terms, such as customer satisfaction, revenue growth, and profitability.

At a time when some corporations are reducing IT spending and once again looking at IT as a cost center, Martin Curley's *Managing Information Technology for Business Value* provides a necessary and timely counterbalance.

The book introduces a capability maturity framework for improving the business value from information technology. The framework includes structured improvement paths and best practices from Intel and the Industry.

❝ *If you're buying one book on the subject of business value from IT, this is it. Curley shines a light on the path ahead for ambitious users of IT. If you have any impact on how IT gets used in your organization, you owe it to your shareholders to read this book. It will impact your bottom line!* ❞

—John Fleming, CEO,
Enzo Consulting

❝ *IT is moving from the back room to the board room—pushing corporations through a strategic inflection point, and presenting CIO's with new and often unforeseen challenges. In this engaging book, Curley offers practical advice and insights into how to respond to these challenges. I consider this book required reading for all IT executives.* ❞

—Prof. Paul Tallon,
Carroll School of Management,
Boston College

Measuring the Business Value of Information Technology
Practical Strategies for IT and Business Managers

By David Sward
ISBN 0-9764832-7-0

In today's fast moving competitive business environment, companies increasingly demand that IT investments demonstrate business value through measurable results. Intended for IT professionals and consultants as well as business managers, this book covers one of the most important strategies any company can establish to help manage IT in the coming years. Namely, the creation of an IT Business Value customer focused approaches to determine the business value for any IT investment an organization may make.

Based on financial concepts and drawing on his background as a Human Factors Engineer, Sward makes the case that the process of establishing and running a business value program can ultimately create a new mindset for IT professionals. While Sward recognizes this will not happen overnight, he believes it serves to instill a belief that an organization can and will create a competitive advantage and increase shareholder value not by just deploying information technology, but by deploying the *right* information technology by linking IT to corporate objectives and focusing all efforts on the requirements of the end user.

> **❝**David Sward explains the why's, what's, and how's of IT value measurement, presents an intuitively appealing vocabulary, and offers an impressive portfolio of instruments to manage IT investments to produce measured business value. Sward's Measuring the Business Value of IT should be required reading for all managers involved in innovating business processes enabled by IT. **❞**
>
> —Lars Mathiassen, Professor, Computer Information Systems, Center for Process Innovation, J. Mack Robinson College of Business, Georgia State University

> **❝**Intel's IT Business Value program deserves to be widely emulated. David Sward was one of the program's founders, and he gives the inside details on how it was developed and implemented. This book should influence IT investment and management practices for years to come. **❞**
>
> —Robert Laubacher, Research Associate, MIT Sloan School of Management

ESSENTIAL BOOKS ABOUT IT BEST PRACTICES

Applied Virtualization Technology

Usage Models for IT Professionals and Software Developers

By Sean Campbell and Michael Jeronimo
ISBN: 0-9764832-3-8

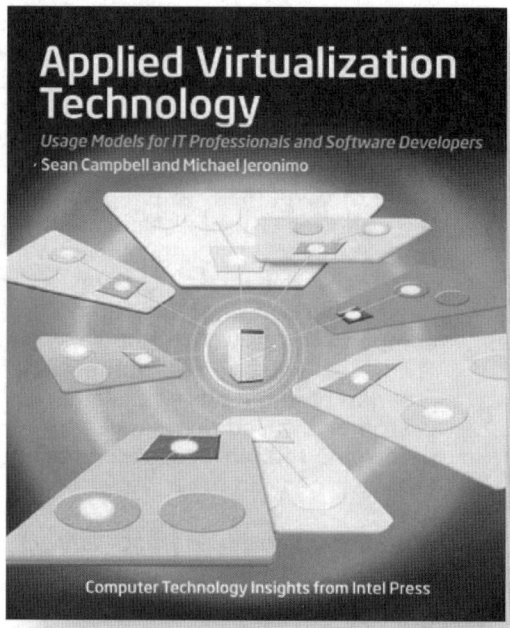

Server and desktop virtualization is one of the more significant technologies to impact computing in the last few years, promising the benefits of infrastructure consolidation, lower costs, increased security, ease of management, and greater employee productivity.

Using virtualization technology, one computer system can operate as multiple "virtual" systems. The convergence of affordable, powerful platforms and robust scalable virtualization solutions is spurring many technologists to examine the broad range of uses for virtualization. In addition, a set of processor and I/O enhancements to Intel server and client platforms, known as Intel® Virtualization Technology (Intel® VT), can further improve the performance and robustness of current software virtualization solutions.

This book takes a user-centered view and describes virtualization usage models for IT professionals, software developers, and software quality assurance staff. The book helps you plan the introduction of virtualization solutions into your environment and thereby reap the benefits of this emerging technology.

Highlights include:

- The challenges of current virtualization solutions
- In-depth examination of three software-based virtualization products
- Usage models that enable greater IT agility and cost savings
- Usage models for enhancing software development and QA environments
- Maximizing utilization and increasing flexibility of computing resources
- Reaping the security benefits of computer virtualization
- Distribution and deployment strategies for virtualization solutions

ESSENTIAL BOOKS FOR SYSTEM DEVELOPERS

Enhance security and protection against software-based attacks

The Intel Safer Computing Initiative
Building Blocks for Trusted Computing
By David Grawrock
ISBN 0-9764832-6-2

With the ever-increasing connectivity of home and business computers, it is essential that developers understand how the Intel Safer Computing Initiative can provide critical security building blocks to better protect the PC computing environment. Security capabilities need to be carefully evaluated before delivery into the marketplace. Intel is committed to delivering security capabilities in a responsible manner for end users and the ecosystem.

A highly versatile set of hardware-based security enhancements, code-named LaGrande Technology (LT), will be supported on Intel processors and chipsets to help enhance PC platforms. This book covers the fundamentals of LT and key Trusted Computing concepts such as security architecture, cryptography, trusted computer base, and trusted channels.

Highlights include:

- History of trusted computing and definitions of key concepts
- Comprehensive overview of protections that are provided by LaGrande Technology
- Case study showing how access to memory is the focal point of an attack
- Protection methods for execution, memory, storage, input, and graphics
- How the Trusted Platform Module (TPM) supports attestation

In this concise book, the lead security architect for Intel's next-generation security initiative provides critical information you need to evaluate Trusted Computing for use on today's PC systems and to prepare your designs to respond to future threats.

ESSENTIAL BOOKS FOR SOFTWARE DEVELOPERS

Multi-Core Programming
Increasing Performance through Software Multi-threading

By Shameem Akhter and Jason Roberts
ISBN 0-9764832-4-6

Software developers can no longer rely on increasing clock speeds alone to speed up single-threaded applications; instead, to gain a competitive advantage, developers must learn how to properly design their applications to run in a threaded environment. This book helps software developers write high-performance multi-threaded code for Intel's multi-core architecture while avoiding the common parallel programming issues associated with multi-threaded programs. This book is a practical, hands-on volume with immediately usable code examples that enable readers to quickly master the necessary programming techniques.

Discover programming techniques for Intel multi-core architecture and Hyper-Threading Technology

The Software Optimization Cookbook, Second Edition
High-Performance Recipes for IA-32 Platforms

By Richard Gerber, Aart J.C. Bik, Kevin B. Smith, and Xinmin Tian
ISBN 0-9764832-1-1

Four Intel experts explain the techniques and tools that you can use to improve the performance of applications for IA-32 processors. Simple explanations and code examples help you to develop software that benefits from Intel® Extended Memory 64 Technology (Intel® EM64T), multi-core processing, Hyper-Threading Technology, OpenMP†, and multimedia extensions. This book guides you through the growing collection of software tools, compiler switches, and coding optimizations, showing you efficient ways to get the best performance from software applications.

66 *A must-read text for anyone who intends to write perform-ance-critical applications for the Intel processor family.* 99

—Robert van Engelen,
Professor,
Florida State University

About Intel Press

Intel Press is the authoritative source of timely, technical books to help software and hardware developers speed up their development process. We collaborate only with leading industry experts to deliver reliable, first-to-market information about the latest technologies, processes, and strategies.

Our products are planned with the help of many people in the developer community and we encourage you to consider becoming a customer advisor. If you would like to help us and gain additional advance insight to the latest technologies, we encourage you to consider the Intel Press Customer Advisor Program. You can register here:

www.intel.com/intelpress/register.htm

For information about bulk orders or corporate sales, please send e-mail to:
bulkbooksales@intel.com

Other Developer Resources from Intel

At these Web sites you can also find valuable technical information and resources for developers:

www.intel.com/technology/rr	Recommended reading list for books of interest to developers
www.intel.com/technology/itj	Intel Technology Journal
developer.intel.com	General information for developers
www.intel.com/software	content, tools, training, and the Intel® Early Access Program for software developers
www.intel.com/software/products	Programming tools to help you develop high-performance applications
www.intel.com/netcomms	Solutions and resources for networking and communications
www.intel.com/idf	Worldwide technical conference, the Intel Developer Forum

6174-0147-2745-7793

If serial number is missing, please send an
e-mail to Intel Press at intelpress@intel.com

IMPORTANT

You can access the companion Web site for this book on the Internet at:

www.intel.com/intelpress/grid

Use the serial number located in the upper-right hand corner of this page to register your book and access additional material, including the Digital Edition of the book.